CREATING SUSTAINABLE CAREERS IN
STUDENT AFFAIRS

CREATING SUSTAINABLE CAREERS IN STUDENT AFFAIRS

What Ideal Worker Norms Get Wrong and

How to Make It Right

Edited by Margaret W. Sallee

Foreword by Kristen A. Renn

STERLING, VIRGINIA

Published by Stylus Publishing, LLC.
22883 Quicksilver Drive
Sterling, Virginia 20166-2019

Library of Congress Cataloging-in-Publication Data
Names: Sallee, Margaret, 1977- editor.
Title: Creating sustainable careers in student affairs : what ideal worker norms get wrong and how to make it right / Edited by Margaret W. Sallee.
Description: First edition. | Sterling, Virginia : Stylus Publishing, [2020] | Includes bibliographical references and index. | LCCN 2020053510 (print) | LCCN 2020053511 (ebook) | ISBN 9781620369517 (paperback) | ISBN 9781620369500 (hardback) | ISBN 9781620369524 (pdf) | ISBN 9781620369531 (ebook)
Subjects: LCSH: Student affairs services--Administration. | Student affairs administrators--Training of.
Classification: LCC LB2342.9 .C74 2020 (print) | LCC LB2342.9 (ebook) | DDC 371.4--dc23
LC record available at https://lccn.loc.gov/2020053510
LC ebook record available at https://lccn.loc.gov/2020053511

13-digit ISBN: 978-1-62036-950-0 (cloth)
13-digit ISBN: 978-1-62036-951-7 (paperback)
13-digit ISBN: 978-1-62036-952-4 (library networkable e-edition)
13-digit ISBN: 978-1-62036-953-1 (consumer e-edition)

Printed in the United States of America

All first editions printed on acid-free paper
that meets the American National Standards Institute
Z39-48 Standard.

Bulk Purchases

Quantity discounts are available for use in workshops and for staff development.

Call 1-800-232-0223

First Edition, 2021

For Phoebe and Maeve, the best thing to ever happen to me

CONTENTS

PART TWO: THE TOLL OF STUDENT AFFAIRS WORK

PART THREE: HOW VARIOUS IDENTITY GROUPS NAVIGATE STUDENT AFFAIRS WORK

FOREWORD

L ike many people who decide at some point that they want to pursue a career in student affairs, I was an involved—perhaps overly involved—undergraduate student. I went to Mount Holyoke College, which even featured in the classic book *Involving Colleges*, and I took the concept rather seriously. My senior thesis was about the impact of involvement on academic performance and goals. But like many people who enter student affairs, I had no idea that one could actually *work* in this field until I encountered a mentor who introduced me to it as a profession. Before I started my master's program I was primed as an "ideal worker" for student affairs. I knew how to prioritize multiple and competing demands, how to run a meeting, and how to work 14 hours a day. I learned to keep my "personal" life—which hit some major rough spots—from interfering with my academic work and campus involvement. I was proud of my ability to do it all and aimed for what Nannerl O. Keohane later dubbed "effortless perfection"—the state of appearing to be a peak performer without breaking a sweat to do so (Lipka, 2004, para. 5). When I entered student affairs I entered a field that was a solid match for someone with my orientation to the world of work in higher education. I didn't pause to examine any of the assumptions that are laid bare in the book you are about to read. I wish that I had.

As a scholar I look at life through an ecological lens (see Renn & Arnold, 2003). One tenet of ecological approaches is that individual organisms (like student affairs professionals) interact with their environments in adaptive ways. If one finds an ecological niche (or job) that is salubrious, one thrives; if one lands in an inhospitable niche, one adapts oneself, leaves, or perishes. Taking this perspective from early career through senior executive leadership in student affairs, it becomes clear how the field attracts talent from people who were already pretty good at thriving as busy, engaged undergraduates into positions that require them (us) to be busy, engaged new professionals. Those new professionals who thrive under the conditions described in Part One of this book may be promoted into supervisory roles, where they recreate the conditions that worked for them, perpetuating the cycle, while those who do not thrive leave the field. If a new professional is not already aligned with the often unspoken ideal worker norms, they may come to believe that they are to blame for not achieving effortless perfection. As illustrated poignantly and painfully in Part Three of this book, the experience of minoritized student affairs professionals in this professional ecosystem can be starkly unforgiving.

Ecological systems offer another option for addressing person-environment mismatches. It does not have to be the case that one adapts or leaves. It is possible for an organism to act on the environment to create change, to reframe the ecosystem. This potential is appealing as it offers agency to individuals, a way to focus on so-called work–life balance through self-care and other individually enacted attempts to respond to professional demands by reframing them as part of a larger personal ecosystem (see chapter 6 for a full discussion). But this reframing is itself part of the neoliberal project to place responsibility in individuals for addressing systems over which they, by design, have no control.

What if, instead of just individuals reframing their own ideas about work, work–life balance, and self-care, there could be actual change to the system in which we do our work? This approach to ecological systems—that we can change the system to make it healthier, more life-giving, and more sustainable for *all of us*—is the point of this book. By calling us into a conversation about how the ideal worker norm shapes the student affairs profession, these contributors invite us to consider fresh possibilities for changing local (office, unit, department, institutional) and profession-wide assumptions and expectations. Of course, given the power structures inherent in institutional life and the field as a whole, this project cannot be done by graduate students and new professionals. It must be done by people wielding power to create cultural and policy change in offices, departments, and divisions. It must be done by midlevel and senior professionals who lead on campus and in professional associations. Faculty in student affairs/higher education graduate preparation programs have our role to play as well.

As you continue into the introduction and book chapters, I hope you will carry with you these ideas about student affairs professional ecosystems and the idea that we have for too long asked ourselves and one another to display effortless perfection. Certainly the COVID-19 pandemic has created enough disruption to call the ideal worker norm into question, but there is no guarantee that 5 or 6 years from now we won't find ourselves back where we were in January 2020. This book was conceived and largely written *before* the pandemic; its lessons will be relevant after. It is the responsibility of leaders in institutions and in the field to take seriously these ideas and use our power and influence to create a more sustainable, inclusive student affairs profession. We owe that to our colleagues, to ourselves, and to the students and institutions we serve.

Kristen A. Renn,
Professor of Higher, Adult, and Lifelong Education and Associate Dean of
Undergraduate Studies for Student Success Research
Michigan State University

References

Lipka, S. (2004, May 21). Feminine critique. *The Chronicle of Higher Education, 50*(37), A35. https://www.chronicle.com/article/feminine-critique/

Renn, K. A., & Arnold, K. D. (2003). Reconceptualizing research on peer culture. *Journal of Higher Education, 74*(3), 261–291. https://doi.org/10.1080/0022154 6.2003.11780847

ACKNOWLEDGMENTS

I have felt that this book has needed to be written for a long time. For the past 15 years, I have studied the ways that ideal worker norms have shaped the lives of faculty, staff, and students. Nowhere were those effects more apparent to me than in conversations that I had with my student affairs master's degree students and professional colleagues in the field about the demands that had been placed on them. My students would often come talk to me, struggling with the expectations placed on them to balance their incredibly demanding assistantships and coursework. My student affairs colleagues often lamented that they were expected to work long days and weekends in order to meet the needs of their students. Many struggled with burnout and considered leaving the field. I looked everywhere for books that might speak directly to the student affairs field about addressing this issue but found none. So I decided to create one.

This is a unique book in that it recognizes that a number of different factors affect the work lives of student affairs professionals, including functional area, institutional type, demographic factors, and mental health issues. So, first and foremost, I want to thank the contributors who all agreed to be a part of this volume. Their collective insights help to address the variety of factors that contribute to unhealthy work habits in the field. I want to acknowledge the anonymous reviewers who offered helpful feedback on the first draft of this book. They pushed all of the contributors to introduce more critical lenses, which helped strengthen the chapters and the ultimate contribution of the book. I am particularly grateful to Kevin Ahuna, Matt Ardila-Weigand, Amy Bergerson, Jaime Lester, Raechele Pope, and Alyssa Stefanese Yates for giving me feedback on various pieces of this project; their insights helped clarify the book's purpose. I am also particularly grateful to Chris Kohler, my graduate assistant, who not only helped me with various aspects of my work but also took on the difficult task of putting together the book's index. A special thanks goes to David Brightman, my editor at Stylus Publishing, who has been a calming and constant sounding board throughout this process. Another special thanks to McKenzie Baker, the book's production editor, whose fantastic attention to detail has only made this book stronger

I wrote the proposal for this book while I was pregnant with my children, and it will be published when they are nearly 3 years old. As a friend recently quipped, books take a lot longer to birth than babies. I want to thank my children's nanny, Beth LaPrade, for providing them with such loving care and for creating space for me to focus on my scholarship without having to worry about my children's well-being. But most of all, I want to thank my children, Phoebe and Maeve, for bringing such joy to my life and reminding me what is really important in this world—and why it is more important than ever to resist the driving message in ideal worker norms. We are so much more than our work, and my children have made me even more than I ever dreamed possible. As I tell them every night as I put them to bed, "[They are] the best thing that ever happened to me."

INTRODUCTION

Problematizing the Ideal Worker in Student Affairs

Margaret W. Sallee

Careers in student affairs can be both rewarding and exhausting. Not only does the field demand long hours, but today's student affairs professionals work with students with increasingly complex needs (Long, 2012). Both demands can take a toll on staff, leading to consequences ranging from burnout to departure from the institution or even the field. As the contributors to this volume suggest, the current structure of student affairs work is not sustainable, unless institutions want to contend with continually replacing one part of its workforce while the other part is left to carry the burden. To a great extent, student affairs work depends on employees fulfilling ideal worker norms—the notion that an employee is available to work nonstop without any outside responsibilities (Acker, 1990). Such assumptions may prove too burdensome, leading employees to depart the profession.

The purpose of this book is to explore the impact of ideal worker norms on the student affairs profession. As this introduction and subsequent chapters detail, the field places inordinate burdens on staff to respond to the needs of students, often at the expense of their own families and well-being. These demands have been long established in the field and were confirmed during the COVID-19 pandemic, which began to unfold as this book went to press. Many student affairs professionals struggled to get their offices online to continue to provide support for students, all the while navigating concern about their own health and that of their families. At the beginning of the pandemic, many institutions quickly pivoted to move their faculty and students to working and taking classes virtually but continued to expect staff to report to campus, putting them at risk. Even throughout the pandemic, some institutions kept their residence halls open, expecting staff to continue to provide support to students while most other staff worked at home. The institutional message was clear: Staff exist to support the needs of the institution, even potentially at personal sacrifice. These concerns were exacerbated for student affairs professionals with multiple identities, including parents or other caregivers; people of color tasked with supporting students of color; and others from marginalized groups. Although some campuses sent messages

1

recognizing the unique burdens on certain populations, other campuses did not, leaving them to navigate additional demands on their own.

Although the chapters in this book were written before the pandemic, their message remains relevant today. The contributors use ideal worker norms in conjunction with other theories to interrogate the impact on student affairs staff across functional areas, institutional types, career stage, and identity groups. As a whole, the contributors argue that the norms of the profession need to change to make careers in the field sustainable. In the remainder of this introduction, I explore the problems of attrition from the field before providing a more in-depth overview of ideal worker norms and how they are particularly implicated in creating unreasonable work expectations for the field. I conclude by providing an overview of the chapters to come.

Losing Talent: Attrition From the Profession

The student affairs profession loses a significant percentage of its workforce each year, particularly among those newest to the field. In part, this attrition may be due to poor work conditions. New professionals in their first 5 years of work account for approximately 20% of the student affairs profession (NASPA, 2018; Renn & Jessup-Anger, 2008); yet, this group of professionals leaves the field at staggering rates. One study found that 32% of professionals leave the field within their first 5 years (Wood et al., 1985) while another found that 61% leave within 6 years (Holmes et al., 1983). In a more recent study of 153 professionals who had left the field, Marshall et al. (2016) found that 75% of participants left before the age of 35; at the time of departure, 28% identified themselves as new professionals, 57% identified themselves as middle managers, and 12% identified themselves as senior administrators. Although new professionals may leave the field in higher numbers, these findings suggest that people across experience levels leave student affairs.

Employee departure carries significant costs—both literal and figurative—for any organization. Institutions have to contend with hiring and training the new employee when a replacement can be afforded, and redistributing the workload among remaining employees when no replacement is coming. Departing employees also take with them a wealth of knowledge and experience; senior employees who leave take institutional memory, which cannot be replaced. Although there is some debate as to whether employee departure should be of concern for student affairs (Lorden, 1998), attrition leads to significant organizational costs. Understanding the reasons why student affairs professionals might be driven to leave the field is important to help reduce these departures.

Student affairs professionals might leave the field for a variety of reasons, including excessive work hours, burnout, work–life conflict, low compensation, lack of advancement opportunities, and poor supervision. Student affairs operates outside the bounds of a traditional 9:00 a.m.–5:00 p.m. workday. Although some functional areas may be more likely to keep standard hours with minimal evening or weekend commitments, others, such as residence life and student activities, expect employees to work nonstandard hours in order to meet the needs of the student population. Although this may provide needed programming to students, it may come at the cost of employees' well-being. The excessive hours required of student affairs work may drive professionals to leave the field (Frank, 2013; Marshall et al., 2016). Just over half of the participants in Marshall et al.'s (2016) study felt that they worked excessive hours, while 70% reported excessive evening and weekend work obligations. These demands that encroached on their personal lives may have contributed to their decision to leave the field.

With excessive hours worked comes risk of burnout as well as work–life conflict (Jo, 2008; Lorden, 1998; Marshall et al., 2016; Silver & Jakeman, 2014). Over two thirds of participants in one study left the field because of a lack of a balance between their personal and professional lives (Marshall et al., 2016). Similarly, some of the participants in a study of 30 administrators who left an Ivy League university reported that they did so due to an inability to negotiate flexible work schedules; women with young children were particularly affected (Jo, 2008). Although such conflicts may drive employees to leave the field, they also significantly affect the work lives of those who remain, potentially impacting their effectiveness as employees.

The long hours associated with student affairs impact departure intentions. In addition, the low pay that comes with working in the field may similarly influence attrition (Frank, 2013; Lorden, 1998; Marshall et al., 2016; Sallee, 2019; Silver & Jakeman, 2014). One study of graduate students who intended to leave the field after earning their degrees found the low earning potential and the inability to support families as well as repay student loans were all of great concern (Silver & Jakeman, 2014). These graduate students were right to be concerned, as only 28% of the participants in Marshall et al.'s (2016) study were satisfied with their salaries when they left the field. Despite working long hours, most student affairs professionals are not well compensated for their time.

Also shaping decisions to leave are limited opportunities for advancement (Jo, 2008; Lorden, 1998; Marshall et al., 2016). Student affairs, like many organizations, is bottom-heavy; there are more employees in entry-level and middle-management positions who interact with students on a regular basis. This means there are few positions at senior levels, which limits opportunities for advancement. In some instances, in order to move forward in their career, an employee has to leave an institution for another position. In one study, one third of respondents left the institution due to lack of career advancement opportunities (Jo, 2008). However, rather than seeking employment at another institution, sometimes professionals leave the field entirely after perceiving that limited advancement opportunities would affect them regardless of institution. Such was the case for 40% of participants in another study who left the field after seeing no opportunities for advancement at their institution (Marshall et al., 2016). In short, as others have found (Rosser & Javinar, 2003), institutions that attend to the quality of their employees' work lives, professional development, and advancement opportunities are more likely to retain employees.

Supervisors can also influence employees' decisions to leave (Frank, 2013; Jo, 2008; Marshall et al., 2016; Tull, 2006). Using Winston and Creamer's (1997) definition of *synergistic supervision*, which suggests that good supervisors give their employees feedback and help them work toward personal and professional goals, Tull (2006) found that synergistic supervision was related to participants' satisfaction and intent to leave. More specifically, perceived synergistic supervision was positively correlated with satisfaction and negatively correlated with intent to leave. In other words, an employee with a poor supervisor is more likely to leave their position than one with a supportive supervisor. Other studies have found the same; half of participants in another study left their institution because of problems with their immediate supervisor (Jo, 2008).

The factors that affect employee satisfaction and departure—excessive work hours, burnout, work–life conflict, low compensation, lack of advancement opportunities, and poor supervision—are all within the purview of student affairs divisions and institutions to address. Student affairs professionals can meet the needs of their students without being overworked. There are also ways to more adequately compensate employees, even if financial resources are scarce. Similarly, there are ways to coach supervisors into adopting more supportive leadership styles. The problem, however, is that ideal worker norms pervade higher education and student affairs work, thus providing little incentive for institutions to change.

The Ideal Worker

First coined by Joan Williams (1989) and elaborated on by Joan Acker (1990), the *ideal worker* is an employee who has unlimited time to give to work and no family responsibilities in the home. As Williams (1989) explained,

> The ideal worker is one who can work a minimum of 40 hours a week and has no career interruptions (such as time out for childbirth, infant care, or care for the sick)—and can do the things required for "normal" career advancement—which frequently includes the ability to work overtime and the willingness to travel. . . . Employers are taught they can expect this. (p. 833)

In short, the ideal worker is one who is expected to devote themselves to their jobs, as many hours a day as needed, with no outside distractions. As Williams pointed out, our entire system of labor is built on the assumption that employees are available to fulfill this role. Contending with familial responsibilities is not a shared obligation, but rather a burden that is to be assumed by the individual and, in reality, by women. These assumptions have only been exacerbated by the COVID-19 pandemic, as many student affairs professionals struggle to fulfill their professional obligations while simultaneously caring for their children. It is impossible to do both well, and yet employees are expected to privilege their work over their families.

Although on the surface it might appear to be gender neutral, the ideal worker is a gendered construct. As Acker (1990) explained, predominant ways of thinking suggest that

> both jobs and hierarchies are abstract categories that have no occupants, no human bodies, no gender. . . . Filling the abstract job is a disembodied worker who exists only for the work. Such a hypothetical worker cannot have other imperatives of existence that impinge upon the job. . . . The closest the disembodied worker doing the abstract job comes to a real worker is the male worker whose life centers on his full-time, life-long job, while his wife or another woman takes care of his personal needs and his children. (p. 149)

Although the ideal worker is assumed to be genderless, it is a deeply gendered construct, as it relies on typical divisions of labor both inside and outside the home. In order for a man to be able to give himself fully to work, he must have someone at home to take care of family responsibilities. Men can be ideal workers because women are raised to assume that they can either prioritize childrearing or combine their career and childrearing (Williams, 1989). In both instances, women are unable to perform as the ideal worker. Men are also penalized by ideal worker norms as men experience societal pressure to be successful in the workplace and not take an active caregiving role.

As Acker (1990) succinctly stated, "the abstract, bodiless worker, who occupies the abstract, gender-neutral job has no sexuality, no emotions, and does not procreate" (p. 151), thus underscoring that the employee exists solely for the needs of the organization. This assumption of a lack of emotions suggests that employees will only respond to work situations in logical, unbiased ways, but it also suggests that employees are not burdened by any situations occurring in their personal lives. Further, this assumption of the emotionless worker is particularly problematic for those who perform heavy emotional labor, as those working in student affairs do.

Although Acker's original scholarship focused solely on the ways in which organizations reproduced gender hierarchies between (cisgender) men and women, in later work, she explored how organizations reproduce "inequality regimes" that have consequences across race, gender, and class (Acker, 2006). In short, both gendered organizations and inequality regimes are useful to consider how organizational structures and processes reproduce privilege and withhold power from marginalized groups. In later work, she also theorized that the ideal worker might not always be the White man and, indeed, in some organizations, might be "a woman who, employers believe, is compliant, who will accept orders and low wages" (Acker, 2006, p. 450). In other instances, the ideal worker is a woman of color or an immigrant woman. In these instances, the overall purpose of the organization has not changed to acknowledge the lives or bodies of those populating organizations; rather, these employees are looked at as easier to control and profit from, for the sake of the organization. They are still expected to adhere to the norms of "the abstract, bodiless worker" while accommodating the organization.

By considering employees as "disembodied worker[s] who exist . . . only for the work" (Acker, 1990, p. 149), organizations neglect to consider how they might meet the needs of their employees. Indeed, the relationship between employees and organizations is not assumed to be mutually beneficial. The organization bears no responsibility for investing in employees or providing opportunities for growth; rather, employees are replaceable and exist simply to meet the organization's needs. Such an approach is unlikely to lead to satisfied—or well-supported—employees.

The ideal worker suggests that all employees—whether single or partnered, parents or childless—are able to devote themselves solely to their work. Yet, as research illustrates, nonstop work can lead to burnout and other personal and organizational consequences (Lorden, 1998; Marshall et al., 2016). Indeed, in a field that attends to students' holistic development, student affairs professionals often are expected to neglect their own needs.

As should be clear, the ideal worker carries significant consequences for those working in student affairs. First, the construct applies to the experiences of those in the field; as detailed earlier, employees are expected to work long hours, including nights and weekends (Marshall et al., 2016). Such obligations call for employees to place their work demands ahead of their family responsibilities or personal needs. Although in some functional areas such demands are considered a necessary part of the position, as authors in this volume discuss, there are ways to rethink and restructure student affairs work to attend to the needs of students while simultaneously attending to the needs of the professionals who work with them.

The ideal worker also has particular implications for student affairs given its status as a feminized field, both in terms of the gender composition of employees and the skills required for success. According to data from NASPA (2018), approximately two thirds of student affairs professionals are women. As Acker (2006) suggested, women might represent the new ideal worker as they are expected to be compliant and work for low wages, not challenging organizational structures and leaving hierarchies intact. Such an assumption suggests that the operating core of the profession dares not challenge the norms of the field.

Additionally, student affairs professionals are expected to engage in helping behaviors, including providing counseling to students and advising them on other issues. Such skills have been traditionally labeled as feminine. However, ideal worker norms play out uniquely in student affairs, given that many student affairs professionals spend their days providing emotional care for their students—and yet are not expected to provide the same for their families or themselves and are thus expected to be the "emotionless" ideal worker. Clearly these demands and expectations have an impact on the well-being and work–life balance of student affairs professionals. We need to rethink the expectations associated with student affairs work—or at least interrogate the impact that those demands have on the personal and professional lives of staff members.

Organization of This Book

This book focuses on the two sides of the work–life coin in student affairs by interrogating both the conditions of student affairs work and their impact on individuals' personal lives, including the ability to attend to work and family responsibilities as well as engage in self-care. The book is divided into three parts; chapters in the first part of the book examine various facets of the structure of work in student affairs, including the impact of institutional type and different functional areas on employees' work lives. Chapters in the second part examine the personal toll that working in student affairs can take, including emotional labor's impact on well-being. The final part of the book narrows the focus to explore how different identity groups, including mothers, fathers, and people of color, navigate work–life issues. Although chapters consider various aspects of the work–life puzzle in student affairs, they are linked by a shared interrogation of the ways that ideal worker norms operate. All chapters conclude by offering recommendations for practice that both individuals and institutions can use to address the challenges highlighted. Although all chapters offer recommendations for individual actors to navigate within the current system, individual action alone cannot address the concerns identified in this book. Thus, the recommendations for policy and practice and those targeted toward those in positions of power emphasize the need for organizational change.

Although ideal worker norms provide a useful lens to explain the expectations of the field, many chapters use additional frameworks in conjunction with ideal worker norms to further interrogate the conditions of the field. Chapter contributors adopt a variety of frameworks, including socialization theory (chapter 5), neoliberalism (chapter 6), critical race theory and hegemonic Whiteness (chapter 10), sense of belonging (chapter 12), and gendered organizations (chapter 13). For example, in chapter 6, Pamela Graglia, Karla Pérez-Vélez, and D-L Stewart consider how ideal worker norms are reflective of neoliberalism, which prioritizes free market solutions, often neglecting the individual for the sake of the organization. Other chapters find similar intersections between ideal worker norms and other frameworks, using them in tandem to bring different demands placed on student affairs professionals to light.

The chapters in Part One of the volume examine various facets of the nature of student affairs work. In chapter 1, Laura Isdell and Lisa Wolf-Wendel continue the work of this introduction by expanding on how ideal worker norms impact the field of student affairs. They address how a variety of features, including socialization to the field as well as supervisor interactions, can perpetuate ideal worker norms and make it challenging for employees to achieve work–life integration. Although all student affairs professionals experience ideal worker pressures, the demands differ by functional area. The next two chapters narrow the lens to consider the experiences of employees in specific departments. In chapter 2, Benjamin B. Stubbs uses theories of agency to focus on how employees in student activities, Greek life, and campus recreation navigate expectations that they frequently work outside the typical workday in positions with varying responsibilities that often include student crises. Additionally, employees in these areas reported working with supervisors who both explicitly and implicitly promoted ideal worker norms. Such expectations lead employees to express exhaustion and burnout. Residence life is the focus of chapter 3, by Amy S. Hirschy and Shannon D. Staten. In this chapter, the contributors consider how the requirements of careers in residence life perpetuate ideal worker norms while simultaneously stymieing employees' attempts to achieve any separation between their personal and professional lives. By living where they work and often dealing with student crises, hall directors simply cannot avoid being always available to the organization.

Just as functional area shapes the type of ideal worker pressures that student affairs professionals experience, so too does institutional type, which C. Casey Ozaki and Anne M. Hornak consider in chapter 4. The contributors discuss how the context of community colleges, liberal arts colleges, and research universities affects employees' work lives and, by extension, the characteristics desired of the ideal worker. They consider how each institutional type's mission and student population, preparation of professionals, organizational structure, and resources shape how student affairs professionals are socialized into and perform their work. The large number of high-need students at community colleges demands much of employees, as do the expectations at liberal arts colleges that staff be available at all hours to create a personalized experience for students, while the siloed nature of work in research universities creates its own unique demands.

In the final chapter of Part One, Rosemary J. Perez picks up on the discussion of preparation of professionals in the previous chapter to consider how graduate professional preparation programs perpetuate ideal worker norms through the socialization of new professionals into the field. In particular, she argues that the field is designed around the notion that the ideal worker in student affairs is a White woman without children. As a result, those who hold other identities—such as people of color and parents—face challenges in the field. She also critically interrogates the often-wielded but frequently undefined notion of professionalism and considers how it is often deployed against those not from the majority, creating challenges for their integration to and success in the field.

The chapters in Part Two of the book shift the focus from the demands of student affairs work to the impact of those demands on employees' well-being. In chapter 6, Pamela Graglia, Karla Pérez-Vélez, and D-L Stewart explore how a turn toward neoliberalism in the academy has shaped student affairs work. Neoliberalism's emphasis on managerialism, which prioritizes efficiency and competition, is well served by the norms of the ideal worker. However, employees cannot always work at the pace the system demands. As such, the contributors suggest that there needs to be attention to the rhythm and timing of student affairs work. Further, neoliberal values come at the expense of professionals' own care. They propose a shift in language from an emphasis on self-care to a notion of *us-care*, underscoring that care should be a communal undertaking.

The next two chapters both focus on emotional labor and burnout in student affairs. In chapter 7, Molly A. Mistretta and Alison L. DuBois consider how student affairs professionals contend with burnout and compassion fatigue in their daily practice. Given that college students are coming to college with an array of issues, including prior trauma, student affairs professionals may experience their own trauma as a result of working with students. After providing definitions of *burnout* and *compassion fatigue*, the contributors discuss how residence life paraprofessionals in one study were particularly affected by these constructs in their work with students. In chapter 8, R. Jason Lynch and Kerry L. B. Klima continue the discussion of how student affairs professionals are affected by emotional labor. Using data from two studies, the contributors suggest that student affairs professionals contend with students' own traumas as well as navigate their own mental health issues while working in the field. These burdens impact their interactions with students, coworkers, and leaders on campus.

The chapters in Part Three turn their attention to how different identity groups navigate student affairs work. Chapter 9, by Carrie A. Kortegast, explores how LGBTQ student affairs professionals experience ideal worker norms. Kortegast points out how the assumption that the ideal worker is a cisgender heterosexual male means that LGBTQ professionals' very existence defies organizational logic and challenges the disembodied worker. She explores how national and institutional policies affect the ways in which LGBTQ student affairs professionals carry out their work. In chapter 10, Ginny Jones Boss and Nicole Bravo explore how student affairs professionals of color navigate working in an environment that was not designed to meet their needs. They bring together critical race theory and hegemonic Whiteness to interrogate how organizations are not only gendered but also racist, creating challenges for student affairs professionals of color. The contributors argue that these professionals are expected to blend in to the norms of the majority while simultaneously being reminded that they can never do so. As a result, these professionals end up performing significant emotional labor, attending to their own needs as well as those of students of color.

In chapter 11, Sonja Ardoin discusses how social class shapes the experiences of student affairs professionals by shining a lens on professionals from poor and working-class backgrounds. She examines the classed nature of the ideal worker and student affairs work, including notions of professionalism, which pose a challenge for people whose primary socialization and grounding is outside the middle class. She explores how professionals from poor and working-class backgrounds engage in "class work" (Gray & Kish-Gephart, 2013), having to interact with others who already know the implicit values of the university.

In chapter 12, Melanie Lee and Megan Karbley consider how new student affairs professionals are pushed to adhere to the ideal worker norms and the consequences this may have for their persistence in the field. The contributors focus on sense of belonging, which explores how college students thrive when they feel like they matter on campus. Although the theory was originally developed to consider college students, the contributors uniquely apply it to their dataset of new professionals. As the contributors discuss, new professionals who feel supported by their supervisors and colleagues in opportunities for advancement and growth are more likely to report a desire to stay in the field for the length of their careers. The contributors point out that by treating employees as more than cogs in the machine and not simply ideal workers expected to do the organization's bidding, campus agents may stem the tide of attrition in the field.

The next two chapters focus on the ways that parents of different genders navigate work–family issues in student affairs. In chapter 13, Margaret W. Sallee, Alyssa Stefanese Yates, and Michael Venturiello introduce Acker's (1990) concept of gendered organizations to consider how fathers in student affairs contend with ideal worker norms and the penalties such norms have on fathers who wish to be engaged parents. The contributors argue that a variety of features of organizations, including divisions along lines of gender and interactions among people, reproduce gendered norms, which ultimately penalize fathers who do not fulfill the image of the ideal worker. In chapter 14, Sarah Marshall considers the unique experiences of women with children who have advanced to dean's positions or higher. She explores the strategies that these women adopt to challenge ideal worker norms and manage work–life conflict, including building support networks and letting go of perfectionist tendencies. These strategies and others stand in opposition to the ideal worker, who is expected to operate in isolation and be constantly in pursuit of perfection, no matter the cost.

In the book's conclusion, I tie together the lessons offered from the preceding chapters and underscore actions that individuals and institutions might take to create a more nurturing work environment for student affairs professionals. The conclusion also offers suggestions for needed future research addressing the intersections of student affairs work and work–life issues. The chapters in this book offer a set of tools that student affairs professionals can use to address work–life issues in their own careers as well as the careers of those whom they supervise. In so doing, the field will extend its mission of providing care for the whole student to providing care to the whole professional and, in the process, potentially stem the high attrition rate of professionals from the field.

References

Acker, J. (1990). Hierarchies, jobs, bodies: A theory of gendered organizations. *Gender & Society, 4*(2), 139–158. https://doi.org/10.1177/089124390004002002

Acker, J. (2006). Inequality regimes: Gender, class, and race in organizations. *Gender & Society, 20*(4), 441–464. https://doi.org/10.1177/0891243206289499

Frank, T. E. (2013). *Why do they leave? Departure from the student affairs profession.* [Doctoral dissertation, State University of New York, University at Buffalo]. https://search-proquest-com.gate.lib.buffalo.edu/docview/1512626829?pq-origsite=summon&accountid=14169

Gray, B., & Kish-Gephart, J. J. (2013). Encountering social class differences at work: How "class work" perpetuates inequality. *Academy of Management Review, 38*(4), 670–699. https://psycnet.apa.org/doi/10.5465/amr.2012.0143

Holmes, D. R., Verrier, D., & Chisholm, P. (1983). Persistence in student affairs work: Attitudes and job shifts among master's program graduates. *Journal of College Student Personnel, 24,* 438–443.

Jo, V. H. (2008). Voluntary turnover and women administrators in higher education. *Higher Education, 56*(5), 565–582. https://www.jstor.org/stable/40269088

Long, D. (2012). The foundations of student affairs: A guide to the profession. In L. J. Hinchliffe & M. A. Wong (Eds.), *Environments for student growth and development: Librarians and student affairs on collaboration* (pp. 1–39). Association of College & Research Libraries.

Lorden, L. P. (1998). Attrition in the student affairs profession. *NASPA Journal, 35*(3), 207–216. https://doi.org/10.2202/1949-6605.1049

Marshall, S. M., Gardner, M. M., Hughes, C., & Lowery, U. (2016). Attrition from student affairs: Perspectives from those who exited the profession. *Journal of Student Affairs Research and Practice, 53*(2), 146–159. http://dx.doi.org/10.1080/19496591.2016.1147359

NASPA. (2018). *Data on NASPA members, disaggregated by gender and professional level.* Author.

Renn, K. A., & Jessup-Anger, E. R. (2008). Preparing new professionals: Lessons for graduate preparation programs from the national study of new professionals in student affairs. *Journal of College Student Development, 49*(4), 319–335. https://doi.org/10.1353/csd.0.0022

Rosser, V. J., & Javinar, J. M. (2003). Midlevel student affairs leaders' intentions to leave: Examining the quality of their professional and institutional work life. *Journal of College Student Development, 44*(6), 813–830. https://doi.org/10.1353/csd.2003.0076.

Sallee, M. W. (2019). Complicating gender norms: Straight versus gay and queer fathers in student affairs. *The Review of Higher Education, 42*(3), 1233–1256. https://doi.org/10.1353/rhe.2019.0035

Silver, B. R., & Jakeman, R. C. (2014). Understanding intent to leave the field: A study of student affairs master's students' career plans. *Journal of Student Affairs Research and Practice, 51*(2), 170–182. https://doi.org/10.1515/jsarp-2014-0017

Tull, A. (2006). Synergistic supervision, job satisfaction, and intention to turnover of new professionals in student affairs. *Journal of College Student Development, 47*(4), 465–480. https://doi.org/10.1353/csd.2006.0053

Williams, J. C. (1989). Deconstructing gender. *Michigan Law Review, 87*(4), 797–845.

Winston, R. B., & Creamer, D. G. (1997). *Improving staffing practices in student affairs.* Jossey-Bass.

Wood, L., Winston, R. B., & Polkosnik, M. C. (1985). Career orientations and professional development of young student affairs professionals. *Journal of College Student Personnel, 26,* 532–539.

PART ONE

THE STRUCTURE OF STUDENT AFFAIRS WORK

I

HOW THE STRUCTURE AND DEMANDS OF STUDENT AFFAIRS REFLECT IDEAL WORKER NORMS AND INFLUENCE WORK–LIFE INTEGRATION

Laura Isdell and Lisa Wolf-Wendel

T he work of student affairs professionals is critical to student learning and development in higher education, as it focuses on all aspects of student life that involve personal and interpersonal development and helps support academic learning. The scope of work for student affairs professionals is differentiated by functional area, specialization, expertise, and training and can include areas such as housing, student activities, judicial affairs, orientation programs, sorority/fraternity life, admissions, registration, financial aid, counseling, advising, and other aspects of student life. In these roles, professionals help college students navigate their new environment; provide academic, social, and career support services; engage in student conduct processes; and facilitate participation in student organizations and campus activities (Rosser, 2000; Young, 1990). As Kuh et al., (2007) described, student affairs professionals are responsible for the other 80% of student learning that occurs on campus—all the learning that takes place outside the boundaries of the classroom, which also extends beyond a traditional 8:00 a.m.–5:00 p.m. workday. In fact, student affairs professionals are often the first responders for students in moments of crisis, including suicide attempts, sexual assault, and other health and psychological emergencies (Kuk, 2012).

Student affairs has historically favored those who can prioritize job duties over personal responsibilities, particularly regarding the need for availability during the traditional workday and after-hours response. As the workforce changes to include more professionals who may prioritize personal commitments over work, or at least give them equal billing (Gilley et al., 2015; Jenkins, 2018), the need to critically examine workplace demands becomes more acute.

When the nature of a job requires an employee to be able to put work first during scheduled work hours as well as after hours, ideal worker norms are perpetuated (Bailyn, 1993; Davies & Frink, 2014; Kelly et al., 2008). Families in the early to mid-20th century were typically constructed around the idea of a head of the household who was the primary breadwinner for the family (historically a cisgender man) while the other member of the couple (historically a cisgender woman) took care of home and family responsibilities (Davies & Frink, 2014; Jones, 2012; Williams, 2000). As late as 1960, only 10% of mothers were employed outside the home (Jones, 2012). As described in this book's introduction, ideal worker norms were constructed around these traditional gender roles, where the only, or primary, responsibility of the man was paid work. This meant that the employee was available and ready to work at the will of the employer and either had no family obligations or had a spouse to assume those responsibilities (Bailyn, 1993; Davies & Frink, 2014; Hochschild, 1995; Kelly et al., 2008; Sallee, 2016; Wilk, 2013; Williams, 2000).

In many ways, the student affairs profession favors someone who can put work before all other responsibilities, which can be challenging for student affairs professionals who have both work and personal commitments (Cameron, 2011; Fochtman, 2010; Rosser, 2000; Spangler, 2011; Wilk, 2013). As a result, some professionals leave the field or forego advancement opportunities to avoid sacrificing their personal responsibilities for the sake of work (Bailey, 2011; Collins, 2009; Fochtman, 2010; Jo, 2008; Marshall et al., 2016; Nobbe & Manning, 1997; Spangler, 2011; Ting & Watt, 1999). Other student affairs professionals choose to give up personal aspirations due to their perception that it is not possible to successfully navigate both the demands of home and work (Stimpson, 2009). The perceptions of incompatibility with having a life and a career in student affairs may also affect who enters the field in the first place. Undergraduates, for example, may opt out of pursuing a career in student affairs if they witness members of the profession engaging in what seems like unending work. Such a decision can have negative effects on the future quality of student affairs and ripple effects on the ability of the field to fully serve students.

This chapter explores the demands of the student affairs profession, how the culture of the profession is shaped and perpetuated by ideal worker norms, and how ideal worker norms create conflict for work–life integration goals. This topic is of increasing importance as our workforce evolves to include more individuals who prioritize personal needs that they are unwilling to sacrifice for the sake of work (Jenkins, 2018). The chapter begins with a description of the culture of student affairs in relationship to work–life management. Next, the notion of the ideal student affairs worker is examined, including the influences of socialization as well as the role that institutional leadership and supervisors play in perpetuating these cultural norms. This chapter concludes by looking at ways to consider changing the culture of student affairs and subsequent recommendations for practice for various constituency groups. We argue that student affairs work, and the context in which it occurs, needs to evolve away from ideal worker norms toward a more "life-friendly" orientation to best accomplish the goals of facilitating student success. Such an evolution will require cultural shifts that begin with how we treat student paraprofessionals, graduate students, new professionals, those in midcareer, as well as those at the highest levels of the profession.

Before proceeding farther in this discussion, a note about terminology seems in order. *Work–life integration* is a term that refers to the ability to effectively manage interactions between, and overlap of, personal and work responsibilities. We purposefully use the terms *management* or *integration* and avoid the term *balance* because few professionals with outside-of-work commitments would describe themselves as feeling balanced. Further, we use the term *work–life* or *life-friendly* rather than *work–family* or *family-friendly* because we fundamentally believe that everyone deserves a life outside of work, even people who do not have traditional family responsibilities. Much of the work–life management literature focuses on a narrow demographic, specifically young women with young children (Bailey, 2011; Spangler, 2011; Williams, 2000). This focus is too narrow. Work–life management is important for individuals of all identities, with all types of family and life commitments. Work–life management is not just the province of new parents in the early career. Rather, it is an essential consideration for those across the career trajectory, from those in entry-level positions to those who hold senior-level positions and everyone in between. We also caution the idea that work should compete with life—because, as Friedman (2014) suggested, life is the intersection of work, home, community, and self. To frame the two as wholly separate spheres is potentially problematic. In addition, we suggest that work–life integration is not merely a personal responsibility of the individual professional, but instead it is incumbent upon institutions of higher education to create policies, structures, and cultures that allow their employees to have fulfilling lives outside of work. Such work–life friendly environments are essential to facilitate recruitment and retention of high-quality individuals into the field, as well as to facilitate positive morale and greater work productivity (Beauregard & Henry, 2009; Casey & Grzywacz, 2008; Dickson, 2008; Kelly et al., 2008; Siegwarth-Meyer et al., 2001; Williams, 2000). As noted earlier, it is also a key ingredient in being able to properly serve students and facilitate their growth and development, ultimately supporting their academic learning.

It is also important to note that the literature on work–life integration upon which this chapter is based, including the phenomenon of the ideal worker norm, frames the experiences of workers through binary gender-based, heteronormative, and Eurocentric norms. For example, the literature uses terminology of *man and woman, mother and father,* and even *husband and wife.* It is important to approach this work critically, as it can easily be viewed as exclusionary of those who do not identify themselves within the traditional confines of gender and sexuality. It is also important to recognize that much of the work–family literature centers the experiences of White women. In this chapter, our intent is to be inclusive of individuals of color, those who do not identify on the gender binary, and those who identify as LGBTQIA+. As noted previously, we intend to be inclusive of all those who engage in work–life integration, regardless of family type or specific role. That said, as this chapter is largely framed by the existing literature, we acknowledge that many experiences are left out of the narrative. We recognize that the language used in this literature presumes, for example, a gender binary. These are the realities of this literature, and it is incumbent upon those of us who do this work to call out these problematic norms and to work on being more inclusive in our research and in our language moving forward.

The Culture of Student Affairs Work

Student affairs work requires expert knowledge of how the experiences of college students shape their development so that the services and programs provided address the needs of the whole student (Keeling, 2004). The historical emphasis on developing the whole student as a core value of the profession acknowledges that students exist beyond their classroom responsibilities as they also navigate work, family, or other personal obligations. Administrators in student affairs are not always afforded that same level of awareness in their workplaces, as the nature of their work is uniquely well-suited to perpetuate ideal worker norms, which assume work is the employee's primary, if not the sole, responsibility.

Recently, there has been a growing interest in how the culture of the student affairs profession contributes to ideal worker norms and therefore challenges work–life management for administrators (Bailey, 2011; Cameron, 2011; Collins, 2009; DeMinck, 2017; Fochtman, 2010; Isdell, 2016; Nobbe & Manning, 1997; Spangler, 2011; Ting & Watt, 1999; Wilk, 2013; Yakaboski & Donahoo, 2011). In a recent study by Wilk (2013), for example, while college administrators in all areas felt obligated to be on campus during normal business hours, 12 of the 14 student affairs professionals regularly worked evenings and weekends as well. This is a common experience described by student affairs professionals, often feeling there is an expectation that they are available and responsive to student needs 24 hours a day and 7 days a week (Bailey, 2011; Cameron, 2011; Collins, 2009; DeMinck, 2017; Fochtman, 2010; Howard-Hamilton et al., 1998; Isdell, 2016; Jo, 2008; Marshall et al., 2016; Nobbe & Manning, 1997; Spangler, 2011; Ting & Watt, 1999; Wilk, 2013).

It is not uncommon within the student affairs profession for employees to be required to work scheduled events after hours or to serve in a prearranged on-call rotation. These types of planned work commitments outside of the traditional 8:00 a.m.–5:00 p.m. workday afford administrators the ability to plan their personal priorities around work commitments or allow known personal commitments to influence which after-hour work commitments they take on. There are also work situations that require responses outside those planned times, which can contribute to conflict between work and personal roles. For example, a campus crisis that requires on-site response in the middle of the night or requires an unexpected late departure from work can create a challenge for someone with caregiving responsibilities or other out-of-work commitments. Personal commitments can also spill over into work, such as when a course required for a graduate degree is only available during scheduled work time or when children are out of school for events like parent–teacher conferences.

Cultural norms are embedded in the fabric of the profession and influence what it takes to be hired, to be promoted, and to be recognized as a "pillar" of the profession. The culture of a profession like student affairs becomes entrenched from the beginning of the career pathway when undergraduates are hired to serve in paraprofessional roles, like resident advisers and orientation assistants, and are told what it takes to be successful in the field—that is, dedication to the whole student they serve even if it means working beyond prescribed hours. Those who then self-select into the profession to pursue careers in the field learn the cultural norms of dedication and hard work, which are then reinforced in graduate school through practica, internships, and field experiences (Sallee, 2016). In the early career, the profession socializes its new hires to recommit themselves totally to their jobs, often asking them (directly or indirectly) to sacrifice personal time in order to demonstrate their dedication to their work as a means of eventual upward advancement.

The trend of self-sacrifice continues at midcareer, a time when student affairs professionals often begin raising families but are also pursuing advanced degrees so that they can propel themselves even further up the administrative ladder. The midcareer phrase is extended—and may take many forms—but this is typically a period in which student affairs professionals are overextended in terms of personal and professional time commitments (Bailey, 2011; Cameron, 2011; Collins, 2009; Fochtman, 2010; Nobbe & Manning, 1997; Spangler, 2011; Ting & Watt, 1999). Finally, at the senior student affairs level, the ideal worker norm is reified and reinforced as the institution places increasing expectations on those in upper leadership roles to endlessly and selflessly give of themselves to their institutions and profession. Individuals can buck this trend—opting out of the cultural norms or out of the profession altogether—but they may do so at a professional or personal cost (Collins, 2009; Fochtman, 2010; Nobbe & Manning, 1997; Spangler, 2011; Ting & Watt, 1999).

The expectations of what it means to be a successful student affairs professional are rooted in the culture of the profession and of the institutions in which these professionals work. The culture of any profession or workplace is influenced by formal structural supports and informal practices. Formal structural supports include written policies, defined procedures, and communicated departmental expectations. Informal practices include unwritten expectations and encompass how formal policies are implemented and supported by campus leadership, supervisors, and colleagues. For example, an employee may have flexibility to work from home written into their contract or they may be allowed to do this through an informal agreement with their supervisor (Beauregard & Henry, 2009; Koppes, 2008; McNamara et al., 2012). Time off for wellness, education, or other personal priorities may be granted in a policy manual or through a flexible schedule created between supervisor and employee. There is typically not a written policy that says that student affairs workers should adhere to ideal worker norms. Rather, professional and institutional norms and practices reinforce the perpetuation of these ideals.

Individual as well as institutional costs come with expecting that student affairs professionals (and all employees, for that matter) engage in all-consuming work patterns. When individuals perceive that there are not enough hours in the day to accomplish both work- and home-related obligations, they may experience negative effects in terms of their ability to do their work, career satisfaction, and/or personal well-being (Cameron, 2011; Chessman, 2018). Institutionally, the costs that are incurred from failing to pay attention to the needs of workers include turnover of employees, which can lead to an overload on remaining staff members and time and resources needed to recruit and train new employees (Lorden, 1998). Given the role that student affairs professionals play in the development of students, unending workloads can send negative signals to students about their own futures as workers. In fact, to the extent that student affairs professionals serve as role models to their students, there is added importance for them to show students how to "have a life" *and* be in a professional role after college. Further, when student affairs professionals are not operating at high levels of capacity, which comes from having high levels of personal and professional well-being, they likely are not able to positively impact their students as well as they should (Chessman, 2018). High-quality workplaces can yield employees who are more present and better able to do their jobs; in the case of student affairs professionals, this translates into better facilitating the success of students.

Socialization Into Ideal Student Affairs Worker Norms

Ideal worker norms, within the culture of the student affairs profession, are reinforced through informal and formal practices that begin as early as undergraduate student leadership positions on campus and continue into graduate training programs (Cameron, 2011; Collins, 2009; Fochtman, 2010; Howard-Hamilton et al., 1998; Nobbe & Manning, 1997; Sallee, 2016; Spangler, 2011; Stimpson, 2009; Ting & Watt, 1999; Wilk, 2013). Student affairs professionals routinely recognize their own role in shaping the culture of their undergraduate and graduate student leaders around work–life integration or how leadership at their own undergraduate institution shaped their perception of what it means to be a "good worker" in the profession of student affairs (Isdell, 2016). Sallee (2016) found that informal supports, such as faculty, peers in student affairs graduate programs, and the graduate student supervisor, all contributed to the perceived cultural norms of the student affairs position. Graduate faculty members in higher education and student affairs programs influenced role expectations for graduate students through factors such as their level of support in accommodating work- or family-related emergencies or considering evening and weekend commitments of parents when constructing course assignments. Conversely, the absence of these accommodations suggests a culture that is unsupportive of graduate students' lives outside of the classroom (Sallee, 2016).

Peers also perpetuate ideal worker norms for graduate students in their approach to scheduling group events within student affairs programs. For example, when social events are scheduled in the evening, on weekends, or are not family-inclusive, it can exclude participation from students who are managing outside personal priorities (Sallee, 2016). When lunch times are regularly used for workplace peer-level meetings, it turns that otherwise scheduled personal time into work time, which could conflict for employees who intended to use that time for personal needs. These examples of informal social workplace norms that are constructed through interactions with faculty, peers, and supervisors for those in student affairs graduate programs can either promote or hinder support of responsibilities outside the workplace (Kossek et al., 2010). When there is a lack of consideration for responsibilities beyond the campus, ideal worker norms are perpetuated for graduate students studying to become student affairs professionals.

Role of the Supervisor and Senior Student Affairs Professionals in Perpetuating Ideal Worker Cultural Norms

Supervisors and senior student affairs professionals also convey the extent to which success in the profession requires total dedication and therefore perpetuate ideal worker norms. There is no doubt that graduate students, new professionals, and even those in midcareer learn tacit lessons about the degree to which having a life outside of work is valued by watching how their more senior colleagues manage their professional and personal responsibilities. Powerful messages about how successful student affairs professionals are always on the clock or should be available on demand are conveyed by senior colleagues or supervisors who send emails at all hours of the day, call employees during their personal time, or send text messages during off hours. The unending demands of the profession are perpetuated by leaders who fail to demonstrate and model self-care, such as consistently neglecting their own fitness time or missing medical appointments and personal priorities to get work done. The ways in which senior leadership talk about their own lives outside of the profession also shape the perception of what a successful career in student affairs entails. Indeed, when mid- and senior-level professionals consistently demonstrate the inability to navigate personal relationships outside of work or share their decisions not to pursue personal interests or family goals as a result of the demands of their job, messages are sent to student affairs professionals who have personal priorities outside of work to pursue other career options—or to hide their outside interests in favor of perceived devotion to the field.

Although campus leaders and formalized policies and campus leadership influence the institutional culture supporting work–life management, supervisors can more greatly impact how the student affairs professionals navigate day-to-day work and family responsibilities. Direct supervisors at any level can perpetuate ideal worker norms and the cultural expectations of the student affairs role in multiple ways. Supervisors serve as role models and influence the perception of what it means to be a "good" student affairs professional. When graduate students and new professionals see their supervisors sacrificing personal goals such as marriage, children, or friendships, it contributes to a perception that effective student affairs professionals cannot also be successful in personal roles (Silver & Jakeman, 2014). In addition to modeling behavior, supervisors influence workplace culture through their acknowledgement and support of nonwork priorities of their staff members. It is not uncommon for two employees who report to two different supervisors to have similar evening responsibilities that keep them at work until 10:00 p.m., but who then are given different expectations regarding their presence at work the following day. Supervisors who expect their employees to be at work the following day at their normal 9:00 a.m. start perpetuate ideal worker norms. Supervisors who encourage their employees to use flextime to attend to a personal commitment during scheduled work time, rather than submit leave time, demonstrate a commitment to work–life integration rather than perpetuating ideal worker norms.

As emphasized by this example, supervisors also play a key role in conveying cultural norms through providing (or not) access to formal and informal supports for their employees. Many supervisors have discretion over how work–life policies and practices are implemented (Bailey, 2011; Jo, 2008; Koppes, 2008; Maxwell, 2005; Perry-Jenkins et al., 2000; Stone, 2007; Wilk, 2013; Williams & Dolkas, 2012). For example, several professionals at one institution in Isdell's (2016) study perceived conflict between the espoused values of the institution and reality of practice even when their personal experience was positive. While campus leadership was blamed for discrepancies between policy and practice, direct supervisors were seen as the primary influencers. Supervisors can perpetuate ideal worker norms at an institution that has established work–life policies through their lack of support related to use of the policies. Conversely, supervisors can create a positive culture around work–life management at an institution that lacks formalized policy through informal practices (Cameron, 2011; Collins, 2009; Fochtman, 2010; Howard-Hamilton et al., 1998; Isdell, 2016; Nobbe & Manning, 1997; Spangler, 2011; Stimpson, 2009; Ting & Watt, 1999; Wilk, 2013).

Changing the Culture of Student Affairs

Ideal worker norms in the student affairs profession have been created through the utility of the 24/7 role and further perpetuated by academic programs, campus leadership, peers, and supervisors. Several studies have demonstrated early career departure because of perceived, or actual, conflict in managing personal responsibilities and student affairs work (Marshall et al., 2016; Silver & Jakeman, 2014; Ting & Watt, 1999). For example, for the 153 administrators in Marshall et al.'s study, two of the top contributors to departure from student affairs were stress and burnout (53%) and work–life conflicts with night and weekend responsibilities (34%). Other professionals have remained in the field but have opted to change roles or institutions in order to have a more flexible work schedule, even though this transition resulted in a decrease in their overall pay (Jo, 2008). Still others have opted out of pursuing higher level positions due to the perceived inflexibility of these positions with greater responsibility such as deans, vice provosts, and other chief student affairs positions (Collins, 2009; Hebreard, 2010). As a result of prioritizing availability to work over ability to produce good output, the field is likely not retaining the best and brightest and likely perpetuating inequities throughout the ranks of the profession (Eddy & Ward, 2015).

One of the means to combating ideal worker norms has been the creation and support for work–life policies and practices. Isdell (2016), for example, studied institutions with strong work–life supports and found that when administrators were empowered by their supervisors to accomplish work and personal commitments through flexibility within their scheduled work time and physical location, the employees felt that they were successfully navigating work–life integration despite working beyond a 40-hour week. For these professionals with master's and doctoral degrees, the flexibility to choose how and when they accomplished their work, rather than that being dictated to them, was a key factor in their motivation to remain at their current institution and to stay in the field (Isdell, 2016).

In order to shift organizational culture from an ideal worker construct to one that is supportive of work–life integration, policies and culture must be in alignment (Sallee, 2016). Most research on administrative staff in higher education has not focused on how existing structural supports affect work–life integration (Isdell, 2016; Lester, 2013; Wilk, 2013). The importance of policy and practice alignment was demonstrated in Lester's (2013) study of two institutions that had undergone intentional changes "to establish more practices, policies, and cultural change for work–life balance" (p. 485). For example, there was great variance in how and when flexible work schedules were granted, because they were implemented through guidelines and supervisor discretion rather than formalized policy. When the women in Isdell's (2016) study of work–life friendly campuses noted discrepancy in access to workplace supports, they had a more negative view of the culture surrounding work–life management at their institution even if their own experience managing work and family was positive.

Institutions can positively influence cultural norms by creating policies or practices that enable employees' personal responsibilities to not always be secondary to work commitments, but these "work–life friendly" institutions are mostly still anomalies and do not represent the norm (Isdell, 2016; Wilk, 2013). Further, even within these progressive institutions, there is great variance on how these policies and practices are manifested to employees. In other words, the effectiveness of these work–family policies and practices is dependent on who the supervisor is and whether and to what degree they allow their employees to opt in to these practices. Institutional leadership can also encourage or discourage utilization of work–life supports and reinforce or refute ideal worker norms through their actions.

Recommendations for Practice

Work–life management is a consideration of the modern workforce of student affairs as an antidote to pervasive ideal worker norms. It is possible for student affairs professionals to successfully navigate both work and personal commitments when they have workplaces and/or supervisors that are open to creative approaches to managing both roles. This requires a shift away from ideal worker norms into a model that supports fluidity in and out of roles and allows for overlap between work and personal commitments (DeMinck, 2017; Isdell, 2016). As employees embrace commitments outside of their work responsibilities, identifying careers and workplaces that support work–life integration will be increasingly important. The next section includes advice for graduate students and new professionals, midcareer professionals, supervisors, and campus leaders as well as considerations for policy and practice.

Graduate Students and New Professionals

As we discussed earlier, graduate students and new professionals quickly learn the professional norms of the field by watching what is rewarded, valued, and modeled by their more senior colleagues. Professionals in the first few years of their career are less likely to have been at multiple institutions to see the range of ways that departments, various positions in student affairs, or institutions may provide "life-friendly" environments or perpetuate ideal worker norms.

There is likely greater struggle related to work–life integration for those who find the expectations on how they navigated competing responsibilities as an undergraduate (i.e., in their role as student/staff/athlete/worker/family member/etc.) to be incongruent with the expectations on how they navigate competing personal and work responsibilities as a graduate student or new professional. For example, if it was the cultural norm to spend 50% of their waking hours focused on student leadership roles (e.g., event planning and implementation, peer counseling, executive board duties) as an undergraduate student, then continuing to spend half of their time on weekends after also working a 5-day work week may be perceived as acceptable. However, if that was not the norm, then taking on a first position that is perpetuating ideal worker norms may be a more difficult transition. It is important to know what a person is "getting into" in any new position.

New professionals should ask good questions at interviews and try to find a fit between workplace culture and life outside of work. It is acceptable for those in the job market to ask questions about work–life management and to find out what resources are available at the institution and in the community to live the kind of life they desire. It is wise to ask questions of paraprofessionals, future peers, and supervisors about how they integrate work and life outside of work. Questions could include: (a) Can you share with me how you navigate work–life management in this department? (b) What are the typical working hours of this role? (c) How does this department support employees who work evenings or on weekends as a regular part of their responsibilities and/or when emergency situations arise? (d) What institutional policies or departmental practices are in place to support work–life management? An employer's openness to questions about work–life supports can help convey the reality of utilizing formal and informal supports as well as the underlying cultural expectations and norms around work–life integration of that department. Job candidates can also gain some insight into the workplace culture by listening to how employees discuss their own experiences navigating work–life integration and by observing artifacts in the workplace that reflect personal roles outside of the office such as pictures of family, vacations, or photos of someone running in a 5K or triathlon. Of course, the job market may encourage a candidate to take a position—any position—regardless of fit. Nonetheless, it is important to know the expectations and norms of any workplace situation as soon as possible.

It is important to recognize that new professionals often have greater face-time with student employees and leaders than their more senior colleagues and can help influence appropriate work–life integration by creating a culture that recognizes the multifaceted nature of students' roles and advocates for supports that allow them to be successful within the workplace and classroom. This includes paying student leaders an equitable wage for the time they commit to their work and creating paraprofessional leadership roles that are not all-consuming of students' time. It can also include being a good role model for students, acknowledging good work, providing professional development for student staff, and setting clear goals and boundaries for what the work entails.

For new professionals who find themselves at an institution that does not align with their work—life needs, it is important to know that not all institutional cultures are the same. A desire to be more than just a worker is valid and a reason to gradually advocate for change or potentially to leave the institution. This incongruence is not necessarily a call to leave the profession, though such a possibility is clearly an option as well.

Midcareer Professionals

Just as it is important for graduate students and new professionals to ask potential supervisors and colleagues about work—life supports during the interview process, it is equally important for midcareer professionals to do so. Midcareer professionals also play a role in fostering a positive work—life culture for their employees and challenging their colleagues and supervisors when their actions are not supportive of life demands. Additionally, midcareer professionals are able to advocate for institutional and professional change. This is a group of professionals who likely need support and continued mentoring as they often have a lot of responsibilities, including mentoring junior colleagues. Midcareer professionals also likely have more intense family responsibilities than colleagues at other career stages. This group of professionals needs to be empowered to make change and provided support to be successful.

Supervisors

It is imperative for institutions to create structural supports, policies, and cultures that enable administrators to live beyond the boundaries of their work. Where institutional supports are lacking, however, supervisors can mitigate work—life challenges by providing opportunities for flexible work schedules, job sharing, work from home, or condensed work weeks. Additionally, when supervisors empower their staff to manage their own schedules by granting them flexibility in how their work and personal responsibilities overlap or coexist, it can mitigate stressors and ideal worker norms for the employee.

Other suggestions for optimizing work—life management and reducing ideal worker norms include setting clear and reasonable goals for what needs to be accomplished on the job, so that employees know when they have achieved them and can focus on other tasks both inside and outside of work. Further, there is great value in providing feedback to employees to tell them what they are doing well and what they can continue to work on. Acknowledging the good work of employees both publicly and privately is an important means to facilitate employee personal and professional well-being. Employees can thrive when they know that they are doing their job well.

Senior Student Affairs Officers

Many of the pieces of advice that we would give supervisors is echoed in our advice for senior student affairs officers (SSAOs). However, these individuals have some additional responsibilities, given their leadership roles at the institution and within the profession. Above all, SSAOs, as leaders, play an important role in creating workplace cultures that either enforce or disrupt ideal worker norms. As role models, they send important messages through their own actions—including when they answer emails, how they demonstrate self-care, and what questions they ask of their employees. For example, there is value in having the SSAO take an interest in employees' lives outside of work by asking questions and encouraging such activities. The SSAO is also in a unique position to influence the climate in the unit through who they hire, who they promote, and how they reward behavior. If the SSAO rewards employees for taking care of themselves and having lives outside of work, then other employees will see that working all the time is not essential. SSAOs also are able to create formal policies and encourage informal practices that support life outside of work. Through their leadership positions, they are uniquely suited to advocate within the institution and the field for both policy and cultural change. It is essential that SSAOs recognize that their own experiences and socialization toward ideal worker norms are not "the way it has to be" and that they can disrupt these cultures by demanding that the culture change. This is in contrast with the notion that because they had to endure one set of norms, so should the next generation of workers. Because culture is so embedded and can sometimes be invisible, sometimes the first step is just recognizing that the norms exist and can be countered.

Policy and Practice

While this advice is focused on what individuals should do as they navigate the various levels of their career, true change in making higher education a space that supports work–life integration rests at the level of policy and practice. It should not be up to individuals to navigate the hurdles of work–life management alone—structural supports need to be put into place. Indeed, it behooves institutions of higher education to consider ways to foster formal and informal policies and practices that facilitate the ability for all their employees to manage work–life demands. Regardless of whether work–life support structures are formalized, the goal of work–life supports is the enhancement of work performance and organizational effectiveness through the reduction of conflict between competing demands (Beauregard & Henry, 2009).

The institution plays an important role in changing ideal worker norms, which starts with recognizing and encouraging healthy living among its employees. Isdell (2016) found that student affairs professionals valued having access to campus recreational facilities and appreciated workplace cultures that encouraged employees to utilize wellness time within their work hours. This is a low-cost way to maintain healthy living among employees and to role model to students the importance of wellness. Other work–life supports institutions might provide include access to on-site childcare, tuition reimbursement, and professional development opportunities.

Institutional approaches could also include policies focused on how and when time is used, including compressed work weeks; time off for education, professional development, or physical wellness; and the ability to take unpaid vacation days, sabbaticals, or a career break (Koppes, 2008; McNamara et al., 2012). These types of programs can provide great value to employees if their utilization is encouraged and supported. For example, granting flextime to employees who have scheduled obligations after hours (i.e., on-campus events) can lead to greater employee satisfaction and improved commitment to the workplace (Dickson, 2008; Ferguson et al., 2012; Kelly et al., 2008; Kossek & Lee, 2008).

Flexible work schedules are a key contributor to work–life management for student affairs administrators, and it is important, where possible, to provide it to employees (DeMinck, 2017; Isdell, 2016; Lester, 2013; Wilk, 2013). Workplaces that support employees by giving them the ability to schedule work and personal activities to avoid conflicts are incorporating a strategy to separate work and personal domains as a mechanism to support work–life integration and to oppose ideal worker norms. Alternatively, having supports in place (e.g., technology) that allow work to be more fluid in regard to how and when it is completed is another strategy to help support effective management of both personal and professional domains and could lead to an intentional overlap of the competing areas. For example, being able to participate in a meeting via teleconference allows one to be actively engaged in work activities while also being physically present should a personal commitment require an employee to remain at home for the day. Either way, creating formalized policies around flexibility in where and when work is completed can positively affect institutional culture around work–life management. However, if implementation of flexible work schedules is entirely at the discretion of the supervisor, these types of formalized policies are just words, not practice.

Conclusion

The student affairs profession has been committed to the ideal of developing "the whole student" since *The Student Personnel Point of View* was published in 1937 (American Council on Education, 1937). That same value, of seeing an individual as more than one-dimensional, has not always been prioritized for the student affairs professional. Leaders within the profession would be well served to reflect on this incongruence between the espoused student affairs values and the reality of the practitioner's experience, just as institutions that celebrate their work–life supports can benefit from an examination of the actual lived experience of their staff, administrators, and faculty. We should ask and answer some key questions. What is role modeled by those we recognize as a pillar of the profession? Can someone serve in a leadership role within a professional organization or their institution while also having a life outside of work? Can up-and-coming professionals see student affairs leaders in their wholeness? Or are we only witness to what appears to be great personal self-sacrifice? It is essential for the leadership in professional associations (e.g., NASPA and ACPA) as well as leaders on campuses to reexamine the culture of the profession, the role expectations, and the structural supports for work–life integration to see if we are sending the right message about caring for the "whole professional." If there is not a cultural shift to expand the nature of the position beyond the construct of ideal worker norms, professionals who find themselves dedicated to a more holistic approach to their own life, who care about being actively engaged in their own wellness, community, family, and friendships outside of the workplace will leave the field or never enter a profession that requires them to be committed to the development of others' wellness at the expense of their own.

References

American Council on Education. (1937). *The student personnel point of view.* http://www.naspa.org/pubs/files/ StudAff_1937

Bailey, K. J. (2011). *Women in student affairs: Navigating the roles of mother and administrator* (ProQuest no. 3500089) [Doctoral dissertation, Texas A&M University]. Proquest Dissertations and Theses Global.

Bailyn, L. (1993). *Breaking the mold: Women, men, and time in the new corporate world.* The Free Press.

Beauregard, T. A., & Henry, L. C. (2009). Making the link between work-life balance practices and organizational performance. *Human Resource Management Review, 19*(1), 9–22. https://doi.org/10.1016/j.hrmr.2008.09.001

Cameron, T. L. (2011). *The professional & the personal: Work–life balance and mid-level student affairs administrators* (ProQuest no. DP19717) [Doctoral dissertation, Virginia Tech]. VTech Works.

Casey, P. R., & Grzywacz, J. G. (2008). Employee health and well-being: The role of flexibility and work-family balance. *The Psychologist-Manager Journal, 11*(1), 31–47. https://doi.org/10.1080/10887150801963885

Chessman, H. M. (2018). *Student affairs professionals and the concept of well-being* [Paper presentation]. Annual Meeting of the Association for the Study of Higher Education, Tampa, FL, United States

Collins, K. M. (2009). *Those who just said "NO!": Career-life decisions of middle management women in student affairs administration* (ProQuest No. 3367659) [Doctoral dissertation, Bowling Green State University]. ProQuest.

Davies, A. R., & Frink, B. D. (2014). The origins of the ideal worker: The separation of work and home in the United States from the market revolution to 1950. *Work and Occupations, 41*(1), 18–39. https://doi.org/10.1177/0730888413515893

DeMinck, D. K. (2017). Female student affairs professionals and work–life balance. In *Culminating Projects in Higher Education Administration (No. 16)*. Saint Cloud State University Repository. https://repository.stcloudstate.edu/hied_etds/16/

Dickson, C. E. (2008). Antecedents and consequences of perceived family responsibilities discrimination in the workplace. *The Psychologist-Manager Journal, 11*(1), 113–140. https://doi.org/10.1080/10887150801967399

Eddy, P. L., & Ward, K. (2015). Lean in or opt out: Career pathways of academic women. *Change: The Magazine of Higher Learning, 47*(2), 6–13. https://doi.org/10.1080/00091383.2015.1018082

Ferguson, M., Carlson, D., Zivnuska, S., & Whitten, D. (2012). Support at work and home: The path to satisfaction through balance. *Journal of Vocational Behavior, 80*(2), 299–307. https://doi.org/10.1016/j.jvb.2012.01.001

Fochtman, M. M. (2010). *Midcareer women student affairs administrators with young children: Negotiating life, like clockwork* (ProQuest No. 3435229) [Doctoral dissertation, Michigan State University]. ProQuest.

Friedman, S. (2014). What successful work and life integration looks like. *Harvard Business Review*. https://hbr.org/2014/10/what-successful-work-and-life-integration-looks-like

Gilley, A., Waddell, K., Hall, A., Jackson, S. A., & Gilley, J. W. (2015). Manager behaviour, generation, and influence on work-life balance: An empirical investigation. *Journal of Applied Management and Entrepreneurship, 20*(1), 3–23. https://doi.org/10.9774/GLEAF.3709.2015.ja.00003

Hebreard, D. (2010). *Opt out: Women with children leaving mid-level student affairs positions* [Doctoral dissertation]. Western Michigan University: Scholar Works. https://scholarworks.wmich.edu/dissertations/566/

Hochschild, A. R. (1995). The culture of politics: Traditional, postmodern, cold-modern, and warm-modern ideals of care. *Social Politics, 2*(3), 331–346. https://doi.org/10.1093/sp/2.3.331

Howard-Hamilton, M. F., Palmer, C., Johnson, S., & Kicklighter, M. (1998). Burnout and related factors: Differences between women and men in student affairs. *College Student Affairs Journal, 17*(2), 80–91.

Isdell, L. (2016). *Work-family balance among mothers who are midcareer student affairs administrators at institutions recognized for work–life policies* [Doctoral

dissertation, University of Kansas]. KU ScholarWorks. https://kuscholarworks
.ku.edu/handle/1808/22015

Jenkins, R. (2018). This is why millennials care so much about work–life balance. *Inc
.com*. https://www.inc.com/ryan-jenkins/this-is-what-millennials-value-most-in-a-job
-why.html

Jo, V. H. (2008). Voluntary turnover and women administrators in higher education.
Higher Education, 56(5), 565–582. https://doi.org/10.1007/s10734-008-9111-y

Jones, B. D. (2012). "Opting out": Women, work, and motherhood in American
history. In B. D. Jones (Ed.), *Women who opt out: The debate over working mothers
and work-family balance* (pp. 3–32). New York University Press.

Keeling, R. P. (Ed.). (2004). *Learning reconsidered: A campus-wide focus on the student
experience*. National Association of Student Personnel Administrators.

Kelly, E. L., Kossek, E. E., Hammer, L. B., Durham, M., Bray, J., Chermack, K., Murphy,
L. A., & Kaskubar, D. (2008). Getting there from here: Research on the effects of
work–family conflict and business outcomes. *The Academy of Management Annals,
2*(1), 305–349. https://doi.org/10.5465/19416520802211610

Koppes, L. L. (2008). Facilitating an organization to embrace a work-life effectiveness
culture: A practical approach. *The Psychologist-Manager Journal, 11*(1), 163–184.
https://doi.org/10.1080/10887150801967712

Kossek, E. E., & Lee, M. D. (2008). Implementing a reduced-workload arrangement to
retain high talent: A case study. *The Psychologist-Manager Journal, 11*(1), 49–64. https://
doi.org/10.1080/10887150801966995

Kossek, E. E., Lewis, S., & Hammer, L. B. (2010). Work–life initiatives and
organizational change: Overcoming mixed messages to move from the margin
to the mainstream. *Human Relations, 63*(1), 3–19. https://doi.org/10.1177/
0018726709352385

Kuh, G. D., Buckley, J. A., Bridges, B. K., & Hayek, J. C. (2007). Piecing together
the student success puzzle: Research, propositions, and recommendations. *ASHE
Higher Education Report, 32*(5). https://doi.org/10.1002/aehe.3205

Kuk, L. (2012). The changing nature of student affairs. In L. Kuk & J. Tull (Eds.),
New realities in the nature of student affairs (pp. 3–12). Stylus.

Lester, J. (2013). Work–life balance and cultural change: A narrative of eligibility.
Review of Higher Education, 36(4), 463–488. https://doi.org/10.1353/rhe.2013
.0037

Lorden, L. P. (1998). Attrition in the student affairs profession. *NASPA Journal,
35*(3), 207–216. https://doi.org/10.2202/1949-6605.1049

Marshall, S. M., Gardner, M. M., Hughes, C., & Lowery, U. (2016). Attrition from
student affairs: Perspectives from those who exited the profession. *Journal of Student
Affairs Research and Practice, 53*(2), 146–159. https://doi.org/10.1080/19496591
.2016.1147359

Maxwell, G. A. (2005). Checks and balances: The role of managers in work–life
balance policies and practices. *Journal of Retailing and Consumer Services, 12*(3),
179–189. https://doi.org/10.1016/j.jretconser.2004.06.002

McNamara, T. K., Pitt-Catsouphes, M., Brown, M., & Matz-Costa, C. (2012). Access to and utilization of flexible work options. *Industrial Relations, 51*(4), 936–965. https://doi.org/10.1111/j.1468-232X.2012.00703.x

Nobbe, J., & Manning, S. (1997). Issues for women in student affairs with children. *NASPA Journal, 34*(2), 101–111. https://doi.org/10.2202/0027-6014.1014

Perry-Jenkins, M., Repetti, R. L., & Crouter, A. C. (2000). Work and family in the 1990s. *Journal of Marriage and Family, 62*(4), 981–998. https://doi.org/10.1111/j.1741-3737.2000.00981.x

Rosser, V. J. (2000). Midlevel administrators: What we know. *New Directions for Higher Education, 2000*(111), 5–13. https://doi.org/10.1002/he.11101

Sallee, M. W. (2016). Ideal for whom? A cultural analysis of ideal worker norms in higher education and student affairs graduate programs. *New Directions for Higher Education, 2016*(176), 53–67. https://doi.org/10.1002/he.20209

Siegwarth-Meyer, C., Mukerjee, S., & Sestero, A. (2001). Work–family benefits: Which ones maximize profits? *Journal of Managerial Issues, 13*(1), 28–44. https://doi.org/10.2307/40604332

Silver, B. R., & Jakeman, R. C. (2014). Understanding intent to leave the field: A study of student affairs master's students' career plans. *Journal of Student Affairs Research and Practice, 51*(2), 170–182. https://doi.org/10.1515/jsarp-2014-0017

Spangler, S. B. (2011). *Three shifts, one life: Personal and professional experiences of female student affairs administrators* (ProQuest. No. 3460640) [Doctoral dissertation, Capella University]. ProQuest Dissertations and Theses Global

Stimpson, R. L. (2009). *An exploration of senior student affairs officers' career and life paths* (Proquest Document ID 1021198374) [Doctoral dissertation, Virginia Tech University]. ProQuest Dissertations and Theses Global

Stone, P. (2007). *Opting out? Why women really quit careers and head home.* University of California Press.

Ting, S. R., & Watt, S. K. (1999). Career development of women in student affairs. *College Student Affairs Journal, 18*(2), 92–101.

Wilk, K. E. (2013). *Work–life balance for administrators in the academy: Under ideal worker pressure* [Doctoral dissertation]. Seton Hall University eRepository @ Seton Hall.

Williams, J. (2000). *Unbending gender: Why family and work conflict and what to do about it.* Oxford University Press.

Williams, J. C., & Dolkas, J. (2012). The opt-out revolution revisited. In B. D. Jones (Ed.), *Women who opt out: The debate over working mothers and work-family balance* (pp. 151–176). New York University Press.

Yakaboski, T., & Donahoo, S. (2011). In re(search) of women in student affairs administration. In P. A. Pasque & S. E. Nicholson (Eds.), *Empowering women in higher education and student affairs: Theory, research, narratives, and practice from feminist perspectives* (pp. 270–286). Stylus.

Young, R. B. (1990). *Invisible leaders: Student affairs mid-managers.* National Association of Student Personnel Administrators.

2

"THAT'S THE JOB"

Agency and Control in Greek Life, Student Activities, and Campus Recreation

Benjamin B. Stubbs

I deal worker norms shape and influence the experience of many student affairs professionals, compelling them to work long hours for little pay and with few opportunities to advance their careers (Marshall et al., 2016). These conditions increase attrition rates and other negative outcomes that impact not only the employee but also the institution and its students. Ideal worker norms are deeply ingrained in new professionals' socialization experiences and reinforced in student affairs employment structures. Furthermore, they often go unchallenged by employees, who may fear reprisals or career penalties (Acker, 1990; Kelly's et al., 2010; Williams, 2000), and ignored by supervisors and institutions that benefit from the employees' willingness to prioritize their work above personal responsibilities and needs (Williams, 2000). These socialization experiences, employment structures, and personal and institutional incentives comprise what Lawrence (2008) termed *institutional control*: the means by which institutions influence and control the perspectives and behaviors of members of an organization, in this case, student affairs. An *institution*, according to Lawrence, is "a set of practices for which compliance is enforced through social and cultural mechanisms" (p. 172). In this instance, ideal worker norms serve as the institution.

Lawrence's (2008) theory of institutional politics describes the ways institutions shape, and are shaped by, individuals' beliefs and actions. Whereas institutional control produces the systematic power to influence individuals, the individual's means of shaping the institution are institutional resistance and institutional agency. *Institutional agency* refers to "the work of actors to create, transform, or disrupt institutions" (p. 181) in order to achieve their own interests. Organizations as well as individuals can exert this form of power, also termed *episodic* due to its typically discrete and strategic nature. *Institutional resistance* describes actors' efforts to impose limits on institutional control or institutional agency. For instance, employees who compromise between personal needs and ideal worker norms may respond to emails on weeknights, but not on the weekends. Actors can also resist institutional agency by refusing to take part in change efforts or sabotaging others' attempts to create change. Institutional politics theory offers a valuable framework for understanding the conditions that perpetuate and institutionalize ideal worker norms as well as the means by which individuals and organizations can confront them.

The purpose of this chapter is to illustrate examples of institutional control and institutional agency related to ideal worker norms in student affairs. Specifically, I sought to understand the experiences of professionals working in the areas of Greek life, student activities, and campus recreation, here referred to collectively as *campus life*. Campus life programs share a variety of features that shape the experience of staff members in these units. For instance, students—often volunteers—play a major role in program design and delivery, and events and programs in these areas regularly occur outside of traditional business hours. The chapter draws on interviews with 15 staff members representing a variety of positions and institution types in the functional areas of Greek life (four), student activities (five), and campus recreation (six). Participants were between the ages of 25 and 45 years old. Eight participants were parents, and nine were married. Of the participants, nine were women, six were men, and 11 identified as White, while two identified as Black, one identified as Hispanic, and one identified as biracial.

I conducted semistructured phone interviews with each participant. Interviews focused on understanding the experience of campus life professionals, the ways that work demands and personal responsibilities intersect, and challenges unique to these functional areas. Interviews typically lasted between 45 minutes and 1 hour and were recorded and later transcribed. My notes recorded during the interviews and the transcripts were analyzed for themes within and between cases. These themes, as well as my own experiences working in each of these functional areas, inform the content and organization of the chapter, which includes a brief review of the demands of working in campus life through the lens of ideal worker norms (Williams, 2000), exploration of the institutional control promoting these demands, and examples of institutional agency as a means of confronting ideal worker norms. I conclude by offering recommendations for promoting institutional agency and improving the work experience of campus life professionals.

It should be noted that this chapter does not comprehensively or exhaustively describe the experience of campus life professionals, but rather focuses on their experiences related to the demands of their work. Indeed, despite the outsized attention paid here to challenges and demands, participants were generally satisfied as campus life professionals. Only one participant expressed sincere dissatisfaction with her work, and while I was writing this chapter, she gained a similar position at a new institution. The general satisfaction expressed by these participants, and others (e.g., Stier et al., 2010), in the context of the demands I will describe, illustrates the dedication, commitment, and passion common among student affairs professionals. Ideal worker norms create the conditions that drive attrition (Marshall et al., 2016) and dampen the spirit and productivity of campus life professionals (Steiner, 2017). I argue in this chapter that student affairs practitioners and organizations, higher education institutions, and policymakers can leverage institutional agency to push back against ideal worker norms to create a more fulfilling and sustainable work experience for campus life professionals.

Demands in Campus Life

Professionals in campus recreation, Greek life, and student activities endure demands both typical to and distinct from other functional areas, including long and irregular hours, crisis response, and scope-of-work issues.

Long and Irregular Hours

While participants in this study offered accounts of many of the demands well established in the literature (Marshall et al., 2016; Steiner, 2017), the burden of long and irregular hours dominated the ways in which they described their work. For campus life professionals, after-hours meetings and programs and high-demand periods dictate what one director described as "the lifestyle." Most of the participants reported attending at least one after-hours meeting each week, some of which began as late as 9:00 p.m. Standing meetings comprise only part of campus life professionals' after-hours responsibilities. Student activities advisers may attend dozens of after-hours events during a single semester. At many colleges and universities, campus recreation programs like intramural contests and group fitness activities occur 7 days per week and end as late as 1:00 a.m., while sport club travel and outdoor adventure trips take place out of town and over the course of multiple days.

Campus life professionals must also navigate the challenges of peak, or high-demand, times of the year. August through October, the time period in which welcome week, homecoming, and most student training programs occur, is the peak season for many campus life professionals, but these vary from position to position and campus to campus. One Greek life professional noted that she has important work responsibilities during every weekend in January. For department heads and staff members responsible for multiple functions, the peak times become longer and more frequent. A unit head relatively new to his role remarked, "I have to be careful that the peak times for all of my areas don't end up meaning that my peak time spans the entire year." An associate director in campus recreation described juggling overlapping busy periods related to off-campus facility users, student training needs, and major events that demand her attendance, often after-hours: "There have been so many times when I've had to work 20-plus days without a day off."

Crisis Response

For campus recreation and Greek life professionals in particular, crisis response emerged as a prominent and problematic type of on-demand work for campus life professionals. "I can schedule my entire week and know that I have staff meetings to go to, and meetings with my direct reports, and meetings with campus partners, but what I can't control is the crisis side of things," remarked one associate director. Critical incidents serve as a major disruption not only in the immediate response but also as communication and reporting necessities unfold. One Greek life professional noted that, as a result of the increased scrutiny following a string of high-profile incidents nationwide, "advisers and the media and many people want to know about the situation. I'm talking to student conduct, to our health and safety people, to the communications team, and to the national organization," not to mention the students themselves. Student activities professionals also described the challenges associated with meeting the needs of multiple stakeholders in addressing bias incidents and protests, including administrators' political interest in resolving tensions quickly, legal advisers' invocation of freedom of expression policy and case law, and students' expectations that their concerns be heard and validated. A campus recreation professional described the many tasks that follow injuries, fights, or other incidents:

> Not only do I have to make sure that everyone is okay, that the staff members [involved] are okay, and that all appropriate parties have been notified, but I also have to spend time reviewing video to make sure that what I've been told is what actually happened, possibly file reports or worker's comp claims, and that puts my schedule for the entire day behind.

The size and scope of many Greek life and campus recreation programs make critical incident response routine: the University of Alabama's Greek life program recognizes 67 chapters totaling 11,000 members (Division of Student Life, Fraternity and Sorority Life, 2018), and Penn State's Campus Recreation department offers 57 club sports, 36,000 square feet of fitness equipment space, and 33 intramural leagues and events per year (Campus Recreation, 2018). One Greek Life participant serves as the direct point of contact for 10 chapters and oversees graduate assistants who are the point of contact for 30 additional chapters. In all, she is responsible for approximately 4,000 members. "You know [an incident] is going to happen eventually, but you have no idea how bad it will be, or to what extent you'll need to have all hands on deck." Just like housing departments and the dean of students' office, many Greek life units have their own on-call schedule. Despite the priority placed on critical incident response and their relative frequency, participants primarily described their efforts as reactive. As crisis response occupies an increasingly disruptive role in the experience of campus life professionals, the ideal worker construct demands that workers make the sacrifices necessary to fulfill the role.

Scope of Work

The scope and scale of their responsibilities were described by 12 of the 15 participants as overwhelming and oppressive. "A big demand for me is the sheer amount of work that needs to get done," said an associate director. Individuals in all three areas provided facts and figures to quantify the scale of their work. For instance, a recreation professional noted that her program tracked 700,000 points of participation at their major recreation center, two pools, satellite fitness facilities, climbing wall, and 40-acre outdoor sports complex staffed by more than 300 student employees. One professional noted that his institution espouses a commitment to quality over quantity, "but the quality programs that are impactful and that we all want to keep—those programs alone still require a huge amount of work."

Vacancies and reorganization often further complicate the demanding scale of campus life responsibilities. For staff members promoted to the next level in their current department, vacancies compound the challenge of transitioning to a new role and honing new skills:

> I had the opportunity to become the director of the student involvement unit, but that meant my previous position was vacant, and so I was still doing that job and also serving in the new role, where I had a lot to learn about leading a unit and supervising full-time staff members.

For this individual, the challenges posed by covering vacancies remained even after he hired someone to fill his former position: "Within a few months we lost two [other] employees, so I had to supervise the programming board and one of the fraternity and sorority councils in addition to fulfilling the duties of my job." In 2-and-a-half years as the director, his unit has only been fully staffed for a total of 4 months. An associate director in Greek life described vacancies as routine: "I've been here for 2 years, and we've had a vacancy in our area every 6 months."

Scope-of-work issues compound as campus life professionals develop a reputation as all-purpose utility players. These professionals' expertise in event planning often earns them a seat on campus-wide special event committees, and their association with the students makes them a valuable resource in responding to campus crises. They may also be perceived as fun and energetic team members, as several participants stated. Similarly, campus recreation staff members may be perceived as hands-on workers accustomed to manual labor useful in setting up and breaking down complex events. Absent clearly defined roles, campus life professionals' skill set, rapport with students, and perception as being fun and hard-working may lead others to more quickly attach these professionals to special events and last-minute projects than they would for staff members in other units. Ironically, campus life professionals seem to be valued and marginalized by these perceived characteristics. One staff member described this dynamic: "They know you have the competence and that you're willing to work the hours. They're not going to go to ask a person in the health center."

Participants demonstrated both unhappiness with and acceptance of the long and irregular hours associated with their work. Multiple participants made resigned comments, such as, "That's the job," or "I knew what I was getting into," even while describing their circumstances as exhausting, stressful, and incompatible with many of their personal responsibilities. Campus life professionals recognize the problematic nature of the ideal worker norms that pervade student affairs, but most feel compelled to adhere to them.

Institutional Control in Campus Life

Why do ideal worker norms persist in student affairs work? The negative consequences for individuals (including reduced time for personal responsibilities and needs, anxiety, and so forth) and for organizations (attrition) should generate sufficient will to address these conditions. According to Lawrence (2008), institutions leverage institutional control to shape the perspectives and actions of members of the organization. Institutional politics theory describes the power behind institutional control as systemic, "the result of social and cultural systems, rather than . . . individual actors" (p. 176). Peer shaming regarding commitment and dedication, employee recognition programs, and memes and norms related to long hours and employee burnout not only encourage compliance with ideal worker norms but also convince workers that the resulting conditions are necessary and unavoidable.

Institutional control operates on not only workers (as illustrated in the previous section) but also their supervisors, senior student affairs officers (SSAOs), and other stakeholders. Several participants' characterization of their supervisors' and senior officials' expectations illustrate the ideal worker construct of the disembodied worker (Acker, 1990) whose personal responsibilities and needs are irrelevant (Williams, 2000). One participant reflected, "When someone asks you to do something after hours, they don't necessarily know what [other conflicts you might have] because they don't know you as a person." This view of the campus life professional extends beyond the chain of supervision to students and other stakeholders. Reflecting on the way others perceive her work, a Greek life staff member said,

> You don't get praise from the volunteers [advisers] you're working with or the students . . . for the hard work that you're doing on the weekends or at night, or for all of the extra hours or the quick response to an email at night or for responding to an on-call situation, because they are just seeing you as doing your job. It's just seen as the typical job of a Greek life coordinator. It's expected of you.

This section describes three means of institutional control that foster ideal worker norm beliefs and behaviors: socialization in campus life, career imperatives, and supervisor attitudes.

Early Socialization in Campus Life

When asked why they work long hours, allow phone calls and crises to impede on personal time, or consent to any of the various demands articulated during our interview, several staff members referenced a personal work ethic or drive that made subordination to those demands seem natural and even noble. One referred to the demands of her work as "self-inflicted." It is certainly possible, and even likely, that individuals who find success in this field have an intrinsic capacity and desire for challenging, demanding work. However, in addition to an ingrained sense of duty, campus life professionals' socialization into the field may also shape their attitudes toward ideal worker norms. Socialization is "an interactive act that involves interpretation by the new professional" of their functional areas' "distinctive cultures" (Collins,

2009, p. 3). In contrast to work in career services, academic advising, and other student affairs or student services areas, campus life professionals had likely been student participants, employees, and leaders in the very programs that they now oversee, effectively beginning their socialization into the field as undergraduate students. They attended meetings at night and hosted programs on the weekends, managed crises and conflicts at all hours of the night, and admired the dedication of their advisers. It is perhaps unsurprising that they accept and even value the demands of their work given these early socialization experiences. One recreation staff member, who noted that he worked "probably too much" in his first years as a program coordinator, described his experience as a student employee:

> When I was an undergraduate student, the pro staff stayed late. They came in on weekends. The pro staff did any and everything they could for us as students. . . . That resonated with me and made me so invested in the program and the building and the patrons and my coworkers, and so I reflected that behavior as a student employee. I stayed late. I came in when I didn't have to. If they care this much about me, and my development, the least I can do is care about what they are asking us to do—to meet or exceed their expectations.

A Greek life staff member explained her views about being "always on call" in similar terms: "I know what it's like to be a sorority president and have something really scary happen and not know what you're supposed to do." These powerful experiences serve as the foundation for campus life staff members' understanding of their role, their duty to and relationship with their students, and the value of their work, and represent an often unnoticed form of institutional control. (For more about socialization into student affairs work, see chapters 4 and 5.)

Career Imperatives

Extreme work hours, inadequate compensation, and limited opportunities for advancement are consistently named in research regarding attrition in student affairs (Frank, 2013; Marshall et al., 2016). These factors create a highly competitive environment for those seeking to increase their influence, to better provide for their family, or to work at different campuses or locales. Campus life professionals feel the need to demonstrate their fitness for the next position even if they do not have specific or immediate plans to seek that position. A recreation professional relatively new to her role and satisfied with it said that, when asked to take on extra tasks or roles, she often thinks,

"How will this [opportunity] help me in the future if I want to go after a bigger job?" Another individual stated, "Putting yourself in a position for the next job requires more than going above and beyond." This associate director served for a time as her department's interim director:

> It was the most stressed I've ever been in my life. I wasn't trained to be a director and I had to learn very quickly. . . . I had my sights on getting appointed to the job permanently. How do I make sure that I continue to create great experiences for our students so that I can demonstrate that I can be successful in this job, so that I earn a higher wage and provide for my family better and move up in the field? . . . During that time we [experienced a tragic incident in the program], and I really struggled with work–life balance as a result. I was trying to understand how I could do full-time work, be a mom, be a student. It was a lot. I persevered, I got through it, but I wouldn't do that again.

This experience was a traumatic, problematic, and necessary attempt to create an opportunity for career advancement. When presented with the opportunity or request to take on more, to do more, and to work harder, participants felt that the opportunity must be taken, no matter the cost. All the department heads attributed their success at least in part to their willingness to take on problematic roles, to do extra work, and to sacrifice for their department and university.

Like the associate director quoted previously, many campus life professionals feel pressure to demonstrate their willingness and ability to contribute as called upon (Reid, 2015), regardless of the circumstances. Said one Greek life staff member,

> If I [took a vacation] on a big weekend and something bad happened, my fear is that someone up above would look at me and say, "You made a poor choice going out of town," . . . even though my presence wouldn't have stopped it. There are times when something happens and there is a call for people to help. Showing up, even if it's just to be supportive, is valued, and those are the people who get noticed.

Career imperatives, and the subtle means by which they are communicated, enforce compliance with the institution of ideal worker norms, including the expectation to be available and willing to serve (Acker, 1990). Several participants agonized over the tension between their roles as parents and spouses and this expectation. A staff member in her eighth year said:

I really care about what I do, and even though I'm immersed in a project and I want to keep working on it and knocking it out, I have to stop working, because I need to take care of my son and commit to my family. The majority of my colleagues may not have the same family demands that I have, but the expectation is that I still perform like those peers. At the same time, I'm feeling pressure at home to be present more—to be a mom and a wife more often—and to not put my job first all of the time.

Personal and home obligations were described as a challenge related to not only advancing one's career but also simply maintaining participants' current positions. Said one student activities director, "I don't know how I would do this job if I had a relationship or children."

Supervisor Attitudes

Supervisors play a major role in student affairs professionals' job satisfaction (Tull, 2006) and attrition (Marshall et al., 2016). Some of the supervisors described by participants directly communicated ideal worker expectations. These messages compelled total commitment and discouraged complaints or requests, particularly those related to personal commitments. For instance, an associate director who is a parent said, "What's expected of me is 100%, all of the time. [I'm told,] 'You're an employee of the institution and this is what you have to do.'" This approach indicates a complete endorsement of ideal worker norms. Other supervisors passively condoned ideal worker norms, allowing the systemic power of institutional control to shape their employees' behaviors. For instance, a campus recreation staff member who is also a parent reported feeling pressure to work longer hours, even though no concerns had been raised about her performance. "I don't think my supervisor is ever going to tell me to my face that he doesn't like that I leave at 5:00 p.m.," she said, "even though I know he doesn't like it." Another participant's supervisor arrived at work at 8:00 a.m. every day, even after long nights or weekend events, and others in the department felt pressure to follow his example. This supervisor never directly asked his employees to keep an 8:00 a.m.-to-5:00 p.m. schedule in addition to night and weekend work, but neither did he offer an alternative.

Several staff members described their supervisors as supportive and sympathetic to their concerns about the demands of their work, but this seemed to be a purely personal and emotional form of support. One unit head spoke with his supervisor about the way work responsibilities were negatively influencing his personal responsibilities and said, "He was very supportive." However, very little changed: "We actually looked over my schedule to see what meetings or duties could be taken off of my plate. . . . There weren't really any, except my attendance at some late night programs."

Institutional control shapes supervisors' and workers' attitudes and actions alike. In this example, neither party was able to envision a different reality. As I have described, career advancement is associated with adhering to ideal worker norms. Likely, supervisors have been rewarded, and promoted, for maintaining the status quo rather than for disrupting it. As one director explained, "I've got to this point because I do what I need to do." This dynamic is consistent with Kelly et al.'s (2010) conclusion that supervisors and employees might perceive that confronting ideal worker norms could result in "career penalties" (p. 298). Institutional control operates both on and through supervisors to perpetuate ideal worker norms and undermine the potential for institutional agency.

Institutional Agency in Campus Life

Campus life professionals may seek to challenge ideal worker norms rather than to adhere to them. Just as the institution shapes individuals through institutional control, individual actors shape the institution through institutional agency (Lawrence, 2008). Through institutional agency, either individual or organizational actors draw on episodic power to challenge the institution or, in this case, ideal worker norms. For instance, while ideal worker norms compel many campus life professionals to work irregular hours in addition to a traditional workday, three directors in this study proudly described their efforts to provide flexible schedules and reasonable hours, including actively encouraging employees to take days off after a busy weekend and expecting employees to work less than the traditional 8-hour workday during less-demanding months. Some of these practices seemed to be officially sanctioned, while others demonstrated the supervisor's willingness to bend or operate outside of official policies regarding comp time and flexible scheduling. If enough supervisors adopt similar perspectives, the institutional agency they demonstrate will eventually shape and change the norms dictating workers' behaviors and beliefs. This section describes three examples of institutional agency in which a campus life professional, a university, and policymakers confronted the institution of ideal worker norms.

Eliminating After-Hours Meetings

Most of the participants indicated that after-hours meetings created significant demands on their work and personal responsibilities but also described these meetings as necessary and unavoidable. The practical view is that students' class schedules are such that it is impossible to find a time to meet during business hours. Others noted that tradition, more so than schedules, dictated meeting times. Viewed through a critical lens, to accept the inevitability of after-hours meetings is to prioritize students' needs over those of the employee. As one coordinator stated, "We have to do what accommodates [the students]." Institutional control compels us to believe that prioritizing students' needs, and often convenience, at the worker's expense is necessary, correct, and even honorable.

However, the choice between the students' and workers' needs is often a false one. After years of program proliferation at a large public university, a student activities staff of 3 full-time professionals and 2 graduate assistants attended 35 student meetings each week with the various programming committees and officers, nearly all of them held outside of business hours. The director decided to take advantage of a scheduled 5-year program review by bringing in 3 respected and creative colleagues from other institutions and involving the students throughout the process. The staff, students, and reviewers carefully considered priorities, missions, and opportunities related to the department's work. Following the recommendations of the review team, the students and staff reduced the number of committees and broke tradition to schedule meetings during normal business hours. "Now, not a single one of our meetings starts after 5 o'clock," the director reported, "And it works!" This director demonstrated institutional agency to reject the idea that after-hours meetings are necessary and unavoidable and leveraged influence to create buy-in for a new approach.

Managing Crisis Response

As noted previously, crisis response roles disrupt staff members' other work responsibilities, such as program development and supervisory responsibilities, as well as the ability to attend to personal needs and responsibilities, such as leaving work on time, going to the gym, or enjoying weekends and holidays. Furthermore, few expressed confidence that their relationship to crisis response would, or could, improve.

Disruptive and demanding crisis response roles are not, however, necessary conditions of work in campus life. One participant described his transition to a new institution and to a new role related to Greek life crisis response:

> At my last institution, I was expected to be the point person when an incident occurred. That meant communicating with headquarters, with students, with the student conduct team, with parents, with campus partners, putting out statements, and hosting meetings. It's a very different

place here. I was prepared to do any and all of those things [if an incident occurred], but I was a little surprised and slightly relieved that I didn't need to do those things.

This director was not only not expected to take responsibility for or play a major role in the response efforts following an incident but also actively discouraged from doing so. It was explained that the communications office would talk to the media if that was needed and that the conduct staff members would "do their thing." Senior officials also questioned the value of tasks that many campus life professionals would deem standard, such as communicating with chapter headquarters in Greek life or hosting meetings with students to discuss the situation. This participant's university created conditions that prevent crises from occupying an outsized amount of the employee's work and personal time. While the participant admitted that his new role took some time to adjust to, it also allows him to focus on preventing critical incidents and committing to his family responsibilities and personal needs. No other participants indicated that their university or college employed a similar approach to crisis response, and nearly all described having significant and disruptive roles related to critical incidents and crises. This particular case may or may not have occured due to a desire to disrupt the institution of the ideal worker norm. Speaking to the motivation for this approach, the director noted, "It wasn't because people were interested in my health and sanity, it was just sort of like, 'Well we just don't do that here.'" Senior officials may have been seeking to disrupt the toll that crisis response was having on campus life personnel or merely advancing an organizational norm related to functional silos or public relations management. Nonetheless, this case offers a valuable example of the ways new practices can disrupt the current ideal worker beliefs and behaviors.

Limiting Hours

Participants described long hours and demanding peak times of year as both acceptable and problematic conditions of their work. One director said: "There are times when I totally sacrifice my personal relationship. Unless I'm very intentional about mapping out [my schedule], I would never see my spouse." The same participant worked with his supervisor to address the impact that his schedule was having on his personal life, but to little effect. As noted earlier, student affairs rewards workers and supervisors who adhere to ideal worker demands, and senior officials benefit from the dedication and long hours that these demands require. Sometimes external actors can provide an example for organizational actors willing to confront the status quo. For instance, a rule change to the Department of Labor's Fair Labor Standards Act (FLSA) proposed during Barack Obama's presidency would have increased the salary limit determining employees' eligibility for overtime pay (Hayes, 2019). The rule would have linked many new and midcareer professionals' compensation to the number of hours they worked but was blocked by a federal District Court in November 2016. An overtime pay policy went into effect January 1, 2020, but the threshold ($35,568 annually) is much lower than the threshold proposed in 2016 ($47,476).

For one participant in this study, the looming changes proposed in 2016 initiated "deep discussions" between employees and senior officials in the division of student affairs and human resources officers about hours and expectations: "We started to have conversations about flex-schedules and leave time and now there's an expectation that we think about our well-being, even for those of us who meet the salary threshold." At many institutions, those who already met the salary threshold, or who could be paid slightly more to overcome this standard, would likely experience the same ideal worker norms that the policy was meant to address. In the example provided, even though meeting the salary threshold meant that the university could legally continue to demand long and irregular hours from its employees, the spirit of the policy inspired campus leaders to create expectations that employees limit their hours and prioritize their well-being. Over time, these new expectations will shape the norms that govern employees' behaviors and actions.

These examples illustrate the use of institutional agency to disrupt and confront the institution of ideal worker norms in campus life. While the institution is deeply ingrained in many socialization experiences, supervisory relationships, and career imperatives, individual and organizational actors can work to create new conditions that better meet the needs of campus life professionals. Given enough institutional agency, ideal worker norms can be revised to be ideal for both the employer and the employee, and institutional control mechanisms will leverage social and cultural systems to limit the extra work taken on by employees, take into consideration the personal needs and responsibilities of staff members when scheduling meetings and programs, and provide increased organization and personnel support for emerging roles such as crisis response. In the final section I offer recommendations for individuals and organizations in service of this vision.

Recommendations for Practice

Early student affairs socialization experiences, career imperatives, and supervisor attitudes create intense pressures for campus life professionals to live up to the ideal worker norm by working long hours and taking on extra work regardless of their personal needs or responsibilities. These conditions reflect the findings related to attrition in student affairs, including burnout, role ambiguity, work overload, limited opportunities for advancement, and stress (Conley, 2001; Marshall et al., 2016). For those who do not leave the field, burnout and professional impairment can have detrimental effects for employees and the students they serve (Steiner, 2017). Interviews with campus life professionals illustrate the institutional control through which ideal worker norms in student affairs shape workers' behaviors and perspectives, as well as the potential for institutional agency to advance employees' needs and goals related to a more satisfying and sustainable work experience.

In this chapter, I described campus life employees' anxiety, exasperation, and uncertainty regarding their work, specifically the ways in which that work impedes on their personal responsibilities and needs. At the same time, many espoused a deep commitment to the field, their jobs, and their students, and most continue to be gratified by their work despite the demands. The purpose of this final section, then, is to promote personal needs and responsibilities as a goal worthy of pursuit and to identify ways supervisors, senior student affairs officers, and other stakeholders can mitigate the demands faced by campus life professionals for the good of all parties. According to institutional politics theory, institutional agency shapes the institution and, in turn, augments the power of institutional control to advance the new norms informed by that agency (Lawrence, 2008). By contrast, simply resisting institutional control may allow individuals to reduce the impact on their experience but will not confront or disrupt ideal worker norms. For instance, in the section that follows I recommend that graduate students and new professionals set boundaries that protect their time and well-being. Simply avoiding and ignoring requests for assistance may be a form of resistance, whereas responding to explain why one cannot volunteer or recommending the requestor reach out to colleagues in less demanding roles has the potential to change the requestor's beliefs and actions related to soliciting extra work. By following these recommendations, individuals and organizations have the potential to not only improve the experience of specific campus life professionals in their organization but also alter the field as a whole.

Graduate Students and New Professionals

Graduate students and new professionals are perhaps most vulnerable to ideal worker norms as a result of their limited influence, their desire to establish themselves as valuable team members, and others' expectations regarding their flexibility and willingness to work. Emerging professionals are also in the early stages of their socialization to the field. Graduate students and new professionals should begin to establish boundaries related to their irregular schedules and clarify supervisors' expectations.

Whether personal responsibilities comprise children, elderly family members, and spouses or self-care, hobbies, and personal goals, campus life staff members should value these responsibilities and set boundaries accordingly. Boundaries may include limiting attendance at after-hours programs and meetings, committing to exercise or other wellness activities during the workday, maintaining a consistent departure time, or minimizing work-related communication when out of the office.

Graduate students and new professionals should also become comfortable denying requests for assistance. Many requests for assistance bring real opportunity in terms of career advancement and skills development. However, graduate students and new professionals should carefully and accurately weigh their personal responsibilities and self-care against these opportunities. Individuals who are uncomfortable refusing requests should prepare strategies that reduce this anxiety, such as recommending other staff members who are not asked to assist as often or asking about ways to contribute that do not impede on personal responsibilities and self-care. Emerging professionals who take on extra work and volunteer for programs and events establish habits and reputations that are hard to change when personal responsibilities become more demanding. In contrast, setting boundaries early may prevent burnout (Steiner, 2017) and provides a foundation for managing the work that can be built upon as responsibilities change and grow.

To confront the effects of socialization to student affairs work, graduate students and new professionals should be proactive in clarifying expectations from their supervisors regarding workload, irregular schedules, and scope of work. Staff members should seek clarity regarding arrival and departure times, their role in critical incidents, and participation in events and meetings outside of their specific duties. When tasked with new projects or responsibilities, graduate students and new professionals should inquire about the priority of the request in reference to ongoing projects and whether deadlines and deliverables are flexible. Seeking clarity invites supervisors to take responsibility for departmental culture and work conditions. At minimum, requesting clear expectations establishes an opportunity for staff members to advocate for their needs, articulate their boundaries, and request assistance related to role ambiguity.

Midcareer Professionals

Midcareer professionals may have earned more autonomy regarding their schedule or responsibilities but may also be under more pressure to advance professionally and may be navigating new personal responsibilities related to their family or personal needs. Midcareer professionals should strategically engage in their career development and adopt responsive schedule-management techniques.

Just as new professionals may feel compelled to take on extra work to establish their value to the organization, midcareer professionals may feel pressure to take advantage of any and all opportunities that might result in opportunities to gain a position with more influence and better pay. These professionals should devise career development plans that do not pose outsized demands on their ability to fulfill, and be fulfilled by, their personal and professional roles. For instance, a Greek life professional might contribute an article to a newsletter or blog instead of facilitating 3-day leadership retreats. Campus recreation staff members might develop a program to train student employees in ways that reduce the number of events requiring professional staff attendance. While ideal worker norms encourage campus life professionals to associate career development with on-demand availability, in-person networking, and self-sacrifice, midcareer professionals should identify other ways to demonstrate competence and value.

Midcareer professionals' roles and responsibilities often place significant pressure on the individual to work long and irregular hours. In order to manage these responsibilities, staff members should aggressively and strategically manage their calendar. Those who experience disruptions should build response time into their weekly schedules. The allotted time will likely not correspond to any specific event, but the amount of time reserved should, allowing the tasks and meetings displaced by the disruption to be rescheduled during work hours. Blocking time for administrative work on a shared calendar can also prevent staff members from being invited to events or programs that are not critical.

Supervisors

Supervisors' attitudes and behaviors play a major role in the experience of campus life employees. Based on the findings of this study as well as my own experience, relatively few supervisors are fully invested in ideal worker norms. However, supervisors whose vague expectations give tacit assent to ideal worker norms seem quite common. Clearly articulating expectations not only helps employees to anticipate and prepare for the demands of their role but may also allow the supervisor to prevent employees from taking on extra work that is not necessary. This suggestion is consistent with Tull's (2006) finding that synergistic supervision—which emphasizes clear expectations—is positively correlated with new student affairs employees' job satisfaction. Supervisors should communicate clear expectations to not only their employees but also their colleagues and their own supervisors. Campus life professionals' broad skill sets, their reputation as nights-and-weekend workers, and their rapport with students often result in request for assistance from other stakeholders. Supervisors should strategically filter and manage these requests to protect employees' ability to fulfill their work and personal responsibilities.

Supervisors should also seek to provide as much flexibility as possible to employees with irregular schedules and intense pressures. Examples include flexible arrival times, encouragement to adjust work schedules to accommodate self-care and family responsibilities, reduced hours during the summer and between semesters, and being flexible when employees need to leave work or adjust their hours to accommodate personal responsibilities. Supervisors should clearly articulate support for all staff members' personal needs and responsibilities to avoid competition and confusion among employees with different personal demands, such as different relationship and parental roles. These approaches may not always be explicitly supported by senior officers, but this type of institutional agency has the potential to change stakeholders' attitudes about the kind of work expected from campus life professionals.

SSAOs

SSAOs have significant influence and authority to confront the ideal worker norms influencing the experience of campus life professionals. Divisional leaders should recognize the role that early professional socialization plays in making campus life professionals vulnerable to ideal worker norms and create an environment in which employees can successfully fulfill their duties and be gratified by their work. First, SSAOs should identify opportunities to help staff members manage the scope and scale of their work. Many participants resigned themselves to attending after-hours meetings and programs out of deference to students' class and work schedules. Departmental and divisional leaders should empower staff members to schedule and design their programs, keeping in mind not only the students but also the demands that those programs place on the involved staff members. For instance, SSAOs might encourage employers to restrict student employment and leadership positions to those students who can attend meetings scheduled at a reasonable time. They might also meet with staff members to weigh the personal toll of current operating hours for recreation professionals or assist Greek life personnel to set and enforce limits to the number of chapters recognized by the university. Many participants recoiled when I offered these and other suggestions during their interviews. However, encouragement and support for such efforts from the SSAO may produce innovative and practical solutions that benefit students and professionals alike, as in the example provided by a student activities director earlier in the chapter.

Recommendations for Practice

Two policy recommendations serve to confront and mitigate the ideal worker demands that inform campus life. First, policymakers at the campus, professional association, and government levels should consider measures to protect campus life professionals from extreme working conditions. Though it is possible to adhere to such policies without sufficiently disrupting the status quo, the Fair Labor Standards Act has the potential to directly influence the experience of student affairs workers and also shed light on existing conditions that may not be known to senior officials and other stakeholders. Policies that codify and encourage the use of flexible scheduling options or limit the degree to which campus programs rely on so-called volunteer assistance would protect individual employees and address the systemic power perpetuating ideal worker norms. For instance, consider a university or divisional policy designed to reduce the degree to which campus programs relied on the volunteer efforts of staff members in other departments, perhaps by employing a team of special-event students and supervisors or requiring a senior officer's approval. Such a policy would have major implications for campus life professionals who, as described earlier, bear a heavy burden related to campus event support. The policy would reduce not only the number of extra hours many campus life professionals spend at campus events but also, likely, the association between extra work and career advancement.

Second, campus leaders and human resources professionals should protect employees from bearing undue demands resulting from vacancies and restructuring. Additional duties and responsibilities temporarily assigned to staff members should be tied to additional compensation or reduced responsibilities in other capacities, and some level of divisional or institutional oversight should accompany department-level decisions to assign new or additional responsibilities to employees without additional compensation. These protections would incentivize institutions to fill vacancies as quickly as possible and develop strategies to accommodate vacancies that least intrude on the work and personal responsibilities of other staff members.

Conclusion

Campus life professionals navigate pressures and demands associated with ideal worker norms (Williams, 2000). Long hours, irregular schedules, and subordination to the role are driven by early socialization to student affairs work, career advancement imperatives, and supervisor attitudes. However, employees, supervisors, SSAOs, and policymakers willing to challenge the status quo and value the needs of campus life professionals can, and should, enact institutional agency to mitigate these demands for the benefit of employees, students, and other higher education stakeholders.

References

Acker, J. (1990). Hierarchies, jobs, bodies: A theory of gendered organizations. *Gender & Society, 4*(2), 139–158. https://doi.org/10.1177/089124390004002002

Campus Recreation. (2018). *Welcome to campus recreation.* Penn State Student Affairs. https://studentaffairs.psu.edu/campusrec

Collins, D. (2009). The socialization process for new professionals. In A. Tull, J. B. Hirt, & S. A. Saunders (Eds.), *Becoming socialized in student affairs administration: A guide for new professionals and their supervisors* (pp. 3–27). Stylus.

Conley, V. M. (2001). Separation: An internal aspect of the staffing process. *College Student Affairs Journal, 21*(1), 57–63.

Division of Student Life, Fraternity and Sorority Life. (2018). *Greek community grade report spring 2018.* University of Alabama. https://ofsl.sa.ua.edu/wp-content/uploads/sites/ 9/2018/07/UA-Spring-2018-Greek-Grade-Report-Final.pdf

Frank, T. E. (2013). *Why do they leave? Departure from the student affairs profession* [Unpublished dissertation]. Virginia Polytechnic Institute and State University.

Hayes, D. (2019). New overtime rules go into effect January 1, 2020. *The National Law Review, X*(297). https://www.natlawreview.com/article/new-overtime-rules-go-effect-january-1-2020

Kelly, E. L., Ammons, S. K., Chermack, K., & Moen, P. (2010). Gendered challenge, gendered response: Confronting the ideal worker norm in a white-collar organization. *Gender & Society: Official Publication of Sociologists for Women in Society, 24*(3), 281–303. https://doi.org/10.1177/0891243210372073

Lawrence, T. B. (2008). Power, institutions, and organizations. In R. Greenwood, C. Oliver, K. Sahlin, & R. Suddaby (Eds.), *SAGE handbook of organizational institutionalism* (pp. 170–197). SAGE.

Marshall, S. M., Gardner, M. M., Hughes, C., & Lowery, U. (2016). Attrition from student affairs: Perspectives from those who exited the profession. *Journal of Student Affairs Research and Practice, 53*(2), 146–159. https://doi.org/10.1080/19496591.2016.1147359

Reid, E. (2015). Embracing, passing, revealing, and the ideal worker image: How people navigate expected and experienced professional identities. *Organization Science, 26*(4), 997–1017. https://doi.org/10.1287/orsc.2015.0975

Steiner, K. (2017). Addressing the burn. *Essentials, F*(05), 1–4. https://www.afa1976.org/page/Essentials

Stier, W. F., Schneider, R. C., Kampf, S., & Gaskins, B. P. (2010). Job satisfaction for campus recreation professionals within NIRSA institutions. *Recreational Sports Journal, 34*(2), 78–94. https://doi.org/10.1123/rsj.34.2.78

Tull, A. (2006). Synergistic supervision, job satisfaction, and intention to turnover of new professionals in student affairs. *Journal of College Student Development, 47*(4), 465–480. https://doi.org/10.1353/csd.2006.0053

Williams, J. C. (2000). *Unbending gender: Why family and work conflict and what to do about it.* Oxford University Press.

3

WORK–LIFE INTEGRATION IN STUDENT AFFAIRS

A Closer Look at Housing and Residence Life

Amy S. Hirschy and Shannon D. Staten

Long-standing and pervasive issues of work–life challenges in student affairs (Marshall et al., 2016; Rosser & Javinar, 2003) signal a clarion call to examine and transform work environment norms to better align with an espoused value of the profession: creating conditions that support the whole person (American Council on Education Studies, 1937). The commitment to holistic development serves as a bedrock of student affairs professional values, and we extend this core belief to the work environment. Just as student affairs professionals focus on the development of the whole student, so too should the field consider student affairs staff members holistically, beyond just their job responsibilities.

The pulls of multiple obligations at home and work intensify if the work environment ignores the complex relationships among employees' personal commitments. Demands from one's personal life change over time; sometimes they are predictable, sometimes not. Such demands affect all employees: partnered or single, parents or childless, new or seasoned professionals. Joan Acker (1990) illuminated the problematic separation of job responsibilities from the realities of the person who performs the role. Focusing solely on the work tasks "disembodies" (p. 151) the humanity of the individual employee and assumes that what remains is an abstract worker with no commitments outside the job. Such a division reveals a gendered assumption that an "ideal" employee's life is centered on work, undistracted by personal or family needs. Ideal worker norms are predicated on the assumption that emotional or physical needs might inhibit work performance (Sallee & Lester, 2017).

Building on earlier chapters that provide an overview of the roles and responsibilities of student affairs positions, the purpose of this chapter is threefold. Focusing on work–life integration, we first examine the housing and residence life area as a case study for work expectations and conditions of staff who live and work on campus. Using boundary theory as a conceptual frame, we examine the specific challenges facing live-in staff. Second, given the characteristics and structure of live-in positions, we argue that embedded ideal worker norms adversely affect a staff member's ability to navigate healthy work–life obligations and jeopardize organizational efforts to recruit and retain staff. We conclude with recommendations for individuals and organizations to better support work–life integration, aiming to improve recruitment and retention of residence life professionals who live on campus.

Boundary Theory

Daniel and Sonnentag (2016) noted, "Boundary theory offers a framework for comparing the interplay between work and nonwork domains such as between work and family" (p. 408). Employees manage the interface of their work and nonwork life roles on a daily basis. Christena Nippert-Eng (1996b) defined *boundary work* as the "process through which boundaries are negotiated, placed, maintained, and transformed by individuals over time" (p. xiii). She offered a continuum to categorize how individuals situate themselves across the realms of work and home: The poles of the continuum are integration and segmentation. Individuals who highly integrate their professional and personal lives hold no distinction between work and home, whereas those who separate the work and nonwork arenas use a highly segmented approach to manage boundaries.

Boundary theory defines *flexibility* as the ability to negotiate the integration or segmentation of boundaries such as establishing work hours and space (Ashforth et al., 2000; Nippert-Eng, 1996a). High integration of domains signals the presence of *permeable boundaries*, defined as those that "allow one to be physically located in the role's domain but psychologically and/or behaviorally involved in another role" (Ashforth et al., 2000, p. 474). In contrast, high segmentation maintains distinct and separate roles for work and nonwork. Boundary types include physical, temporal, psychological, and behavioral (Kossek et al., 2005; Nippert-Eng, 1996a; Olson-Buchanan & Boswell, 2006).

Daniel and Sonnentag (2016) found that boundary management is a predictor of work-to-family enrichment. One method of boundary management is the ability for employees and organizations to address the changing role perceptions by negotiating the flexibility and permeability of job responsibilities, which increases the perceived support for balance by employees. Organizational leaders have realized that as employees feel more supported, their motivation to stay on the job increases. However, this flexibility may also contribute to ideal worker norms that expect an employee's accessibility to work obligations over other commitments regardless of time and place.

Work–Life Integration

Work–life integration refers to managing commitments across the work and home realms, and individuals navigate the two terrains differently based on their priorities and needs. For example, professionals and graduate students with family obligations experience quandaries of attending to work and academic responsibilities while children, partners, or other family members require their immediate attention (Brus, 2006; Renn & Jessup-Anger, 2008). However, for some, the choice is not difficult. In one study, graduate students "privileged their roles as parents" (Sallee, 2015, p. 407) when faced with a dilemma of demands from work and school. Such a choice may trigger career consequences, as it counters the ideal worker norm that stresses the primacy of job responsibilities over other obligations. Thus, family commitments and circumstances can adversely affect career mobility (Hirt & Creamer, 1998). In a study of midlevel student affairs administrators, 68% of participants agreed or strongly agreed that their desire to live close to family affected career decisions (Wilson et al., 2016).

Connections that tether employees to a particular community can challenge ideal worker norms in higher education: Career advancement is highly valued, and to move up one often has to move out regardless of their preference. For example, some institutional policies mandate a term limit for resident director positions; after a certain number of years, the resident director must leave the position regardless of performance level (Davidson, 2012). While some staff members may be ready to leave, others may prefer to stay for reasons related to work–life preferences. In such cases, individuals may prioritize personal commitments over career advancement. Rhoades et al. (2008) identified some of the culture-bound assumptions embedded in the expectations of career mobility that "run contrary to rural, working class, and various ethnic cultures, which value connection to place, family, and community" (p. 218).

Ideal worker norms pressure employees to privilege work obligations above personal responsibilities; those who resist such norms risk professional consequences. According to boundary theory (Ashforth et al., 2000; Nippert-Eng, 1996a), employees and organizational leaders alike vary in their preferences of levels of integration between work and life domains. Some employees may prefer to keep all work-related activity in the workplace during the hours they are scheduled to work, being free to not think of work while away from the work environment. Others may prefer the flexibility to address nonwork obligations such as participating in children's activities and needs during the standard workday, accepting the need to work outside the assigned work hours or workspace. The organizational climate may support a flexible and permeable work routine or require a strict work time and space environment (Daniel & Sonnentag, 2016). Regardless of how willing supervisors may be to work with employees to determine the flexibility and permeability of their position's responsibilities and expectations, it is possible that leaders will continue to define ideal worker norms for their enterprise based on the traditional expectations of their employees for work obligations over personal commitments.

Positions such as the live-in residence life role limit the ability of the staff member to fully segment their work and life domains. The physical environment of the living space located within the residence hall makes it easily accessible by residents and staff. The responsibility of the position to respond to emergency situations as well as the daily operations of the hall create unpredictable work moments that can interrupt the life domain and activity. These interruptions limit a live-in staff member's ability to manage the boundaries of their work–life domains. The level of integration between the two domains is best determined by clarifying expectations for on-duty and off-duty response to the 24/7 environment of the hall.

Scholarship examining the recruitment and retention of student affairs administrators highlights the challenges of integrating a demanding career with other aspects of life. For example, the complexity and severity of student issues and the quality of life associated with living on campus presents challenges to institutional leaders' efforts to attract residence life staff (Belch et al., 2008). Once hired, high-stress working conditions of new professionals whose responsibilities include intensive student contact as well as long and unpredictable hours can adversely affect personal life and staff retention (Barr, 1990; Belch et al., 2008; Scheuermann & Ellett, 2007). Congruent with the findings about challenging working conditions, interviews with former student affairs staff revealed that they experienced stress, work–family conflict, and burnout before they exited the field (Marshall et al., 2016). Institutional leaders who lack understanding of employees' complexities and how the job demands may affect employee well-being may face staff disengagement or attrition.

Housing and Residence Life

Riker (1965) set the stage for housing professionals by indicating the "two primary functions of college housing are first, to provide a satisfactory place for students to live, and second, to help students to learn and to grow, since this housing is part of an educational institution" (p. v). The common goal of campus housing programs centers on providing a living environment that supports student success (Fotis, 2013), with an emphasis on promoting student learning (Association of College and University Housing Officers–International, 2015a). In the following section, we examine the expectations for live-in staff in roles which provide direct service to residential students. Housing and residence life graduate and professional staff who live on campus face unique challenges to healthy work–life integration and segmentation. The challenges and possible methods for having a healthy work–life environment can be understood through boundary theory (Daniel & Sonnentag, 2016).

Live-In Residence Life Staff

Housing and residence life professionals support the academic mission by creating environments that promote development and learning among campus residents. A survey of 417 senior housing officers in the United States revealed that 95% of their entry-level residence life positions required the staff members to live in the residence halls (Wilson, 2008), exemplifying ideal worker norms where one is present in the workplace "during regular work hours and beyond" (Wilk, 2016, p. 39). Boundary theory offers that flexibility is the degree to which the spatial and temporal boundaries are pliable (Ashforth et al., 2000). Requiring staff members to live where they work challenges the level to which the employee can choose to separate the work and life domains.

Housing and residence life staff members who live in the residence halls manage the overall care of the residents and perform a multitude of duties including handling student crisis and behavior, supervising student and service staff in the hall, overseeing programming and activities, and developing student leaders (Davidson, 2012; Wilson, 2008). Beyond the community development goals residence life staff address, they also work with individual students regarding interpersonal relationships, personal health, and well-being (Werring et al., 1993). To develop residential communities, live-in staff members support students through daily events both mundane and traumatic (Schuh & Shipton, 1985). Complicating the residence life staff members' wide range of roles and responsibilities, students and their families expect timely and effective staff response and resolution of concerns that may not always be feasible (Blackney, 2015).

According to sociologist Eviator Zerubavel (1985), the segregation of the "private self" and the "public self" is most evident in the work domain (p. 148); however, work conditions for the live-in staff member create significant overlap of professional and home domains (Belch & Mueller, 2003). The physical proximity of home and work, ongoing pressures from students and staff, and overt and tacit supervisory expectations create a highly integrative environment, making the establishment of boundaries difficult. As Rankin and Gully (2018) argued, "The integrative environment pushes such employees' work and personal lives in ways that are not always healthy or fulfilling and that frequently lead to burnout" (p. 64). Those who hold live-in positions can exhibit stress and tension associated with living where they work because the integrated environment tests their ability to create boundaries between their personal and professional identities (Belch & Mueller, 2003). The flexibility and permeability of domains within the organizational expectations can help a live-in staff member manage their work–life environments. Residence life staff who live in can manage their exposure and response to work-related activities through the levels of segregation they select between work–life domains.

Challenges of Integrative Work Environments: Physical Space Boundaries

One of the tenets of boundary theory is the ability to choose the level of segmentation or integration of work and life space. Individuals who live in the same environment as where they work can create blurred boundaries between the personal and workspace that are difficult to navigate or separate (Rankin & Gully, 2018). *Space boundaries* refer to the interface between workplaces and the nonwork-related, personal areas. Preferences for segmenting or integrating boundaries for the live-in staff member may be influenced by the individual preferences and the job expectations of the position (Fonner & Stache, 2012). The nature and location of the work in residence life creates a more integrative environment than other work settings where more separation between personal and professional spaces exists. Integrative environments challenge the clarity of space boundaries; for example, when a person lives where they work, they continuously cross thresholds between work and personal spaces, making it more difficult to define and maintain separation. Live-in staff members frequently experience a lack of privacy, particularly while they are off-duty and conducting their personal lives (Rankin & Gully, 2018).

The permeable boundaries limit the ability of live-in staff to segment their work and personal domains if they choose. Students often see the staff as always accessible for their needs, which challenges an employee's ability to have private space (Rankin & Gully, 2018). For example, many staff members cannot perform personal tasks such as doing laundry or emptying their trash without running into students who may stop to talk or report a problem. Even if there is no direct contact, students see the staff member, whoever lives with them, and their guests as they come in and out of the private living area. The inability to get away from the workplace when not on duty can hinder live-in staff from taking the break they need to refresh and take care of their own needs and commitments. When working in the personal living areas of young adults, residence life staff must negotiate their personal needs for privacy while being sensitive to students' expectations of support, privacy, and safety. Many housing and residence life staff are concerned with managing a work lifestyle that allows for personal time and privacy away from the work area, without which the incidence of burnout increases (Rankin & Gully, 2018).

Additionally, the live-in staff are not only expected to live on campus but also assigned their living quarters. They do not have a choice in the building location or apartment in which they will live. Since staff apartments are not identical in design, in the amenities provided, or the location within the hall, staff may feel a disparity of value in their assigned space compared to other staff. Many residence hall facilities have cement block walls and durable surfaces and furnishings that can withstand the heavy use of multiple residents, which creates an institutionalized feeling in the living space for full-time staff (Belch & Kimble, 2006). This inability to select a living space that is personal and feels like a home can create frustration and stress with the living environment.

Challenges of Integrative Work Environments: Temporal Boundaries

Time management boundaries signify the control, and sometimes lack of control, of scheduling work and personal time in a blended environment (Belch & Mueller, 2003; Davidson, 2012; Rankin & Gully, 2018; Williams, 2000). One consequence of living in an integrative environment is experiencing a constant flow of stressors that push against any home boundaries and, in the process, shrink or destroy them. There can be conflict between the desire for flexibility and the need for structure or separation of the work-life domains (Fonner & Stache, 2012). Creating and maintaining boundaries becomes that much harder to do but may be necessary to create harmony between work and life. Some staff find it simpler to work within the organization and determine acceptable levels and actions that create integration between the domains. For instance, staff regularly check and answer work emails, phone calls, and text messages when at home to ensure responsiveness (Rankin & Gully, 2018). Even when away from the living environment, technological advances keep live-in staff bound to their work responsibilities (Wilk, 2016). Additionally, for housing and residence life staff, work situations often interfere with personal plans. Living where they work means that they are perceived to be always available, even if they are in their own apartment. Because of their proximity to residents, housing and residence life staff often respond to requests and assist students regardless of their formal work schedules (Rankin & Gully, 2018). While integration of permeable boundaries may seem unavoidable, the staff member should set the limits of that integration to protect the life domain.

Another concern of temporal boundaries is the common process of having staff serve in an "on-call" status sometimes for several days at a time. The uncertainty of when a text or call may come and what situation may present itself during the on-call time may contribute to mental- and physical-health-related consequences due to lack of sleep, anxiety, stress, and inability to plan work or personal time. In this situation, ideal worker norms devalue an individual staff member's well-being by prioritizing the caretaking roles of others.

Challenges of Integrative Work Environments: Psychological Boundaries

Housing and residence life staff living on campus typically serve in an on-call capacity to respond to student and facility emergency concerns, such as flood, fire, or power outage (Scheuermann & Ellett, 2007). Ideal worker norms for live-in staff on college campuses include the expectation to respond to and follow through with student issues and concerns in a timely and efficient manner. Live-in staff respond to incidents involving a wide array of student concerns and crises including accidents, health emergencies, deaths, drug use, Title IX incidents, suicide and self-harm attempts, and other disruptive behaviors. In addition to responding to and following up with students who are in distress, often there is a ripple effect in the community in which other residents and the student staff need support. The range and intensity of such incidents are part of the routine job responsibilities for the live-in position and significantly add to the stress of staff members concerned about their students (Davidson, 2012).

An upward trend in the number of college students who present mental health issues indicates more challenges for live-in residence life staff to manage. In a study of 275 college counseling center directors, 94% of respondents noted a greater number of students with severe psychological problems. Over half reported increases in the number of students with anxiety disorders, crises needing immediate response, psychiatric medication issues, and clinical depression (Gallagher, 2014). Similarly, a recent national college student health survey found that, within the past 12 months, of nearly 74,000 respondents, 88% felt overwhelmed, 55% felt things were hopeless, and 13% seriously considered suicide (American College Health Association, 2018). Dealing with students' strong emotions, hearing their painful stories, and setting appropriate boundaries can emotionally drain staff (Canto et al., 2017; Reynolds, 2017).

The aspects of one domain are more likely to enter another life domain when work relationships become personal (Daniel & Sonnentag, 2016). In contrast to Acker's (1990) abstract, detached ideal worker, residence life live-in staff are emotionally affected because of the connections they develop with staff and residents with whom they share a community. Living proximate to students fosters interactions both formal and informal; while helpful for relationship building, at times the contact can overwhelm.

Staff may find flexibility of time and place to have some benefits for managing the demands of work and life (Daniel & Sonnentag, 2016). Permeability supplies of a workplace such as work-provided telephone, access to the organizational network, and the expectation of employee response to management or organizational requests add to the flexibility but also add the stress of feeling continuously in work mode (Daniel & Sonnentag, 2016; Fonner & Stache, 2012) and thus promote ideal worker norms. Environmental challenges for staff include having too many demands and not enough time or resources to deal with them, all of which can exacerbate the individual sources of stress for staff such as self-doubt, perfectionism, and emotional exhaustion (Reynolds, 2017). Not surprisingly, a significant challenge of staff who help students through crises is avoiding burnout (Burke et al., 2017; Reynolds, 2017).

Challenges of Integrative Work Environments: Behavioral Boundaries

Interpersonal boundaries refer to the way housing and residence life staff manage their interactions with others based on their work or nonwork mode. New professionals sometimes struggle with how to communicate guidelines about when their student staff should contact them outside work hours without seeming uncaring or unavailable (Rankin & Gully, 2018).

Role transition is important to help communicate a clear separation of work and life (Fonner & Stache, 2012). Live-in staff face challenges to develop appropriate relationships and activities with staff and peers that allow for social and group development but also maintain distance from work contacts for time away to invest in personal relationships and pursue outside interests (Blackney, 2015; Davidson, 2012). Similarly, discussing expectations with those in the nonwork sphere (friends and family) may be difficult but is necessary. Understanding the work–life boundary will build an environment in which all can feel comfortable maneuvering (Fonner & Stache, 2012). No universal, perfect balance between work and life roles exists, so live-in staff may need to communicate to family, friends, others, and even themselves when they will be done with work and available for nonwork interactions.

Work Expectations and an Integrative Environment

Incongruence exists between work expectations for housing and residence life staff and a holistic approach to staff development and support (Acker, 1990; Barr, 1990; Belch et al., 2008; Scheuermann & Ellett, 2007). Current expectations for live-in staff and the integrated environments in which they live and work challenge holistic wellness, conditions that can negatively affect staff performance and retention. Live-in housing and residence life staff members are concerned with managing a work lifestyle that allows for personal time and privacy away from the work area (Rankin & Gully, 2018), while senior staff worry about recruiting and retaining staff in the live-in entry-level positions (Wilson, 2008). Meanwhile, graduate staff and newer professionals are not as likely to accept the rigors of the schedule, the intensity of work, and the lack of clarity between work and personal time as seasoned professionals may (Davidson, 2012).

Recommendations for Practice

To encourage healthy work–life integration among housing and residence life live-in staff, we offer recommendations for graduate students and new professionals, midcareer staff, and senior housing officers. We conclude with recommendations for policies and practices for institutions and professional associations.

Graduate Students and New Professionals

Developing healthy patterns for work–life integration early in a career is optimal, as demands from both realms will likely change and increase over time. Graduate and new professionals can discuss with their supervisors how to best design a work situation that allows time for personal commitments such as family, academics, and personal health while ensuring that the job responsibilities are met. Agreeing on the level of flexibility and permeability of the work environment will help the employee understand job expectations and job performance standards for the position. Creating a development plan that incorporates a variety of opportunities to learn and grow in the position offers new professionals a way to strategize about how to balance personal and professional realms (Allen, 2016; Belch et al., 2008). The plan can include wellness goals and strategies to manage space, time, and interpersonal boundaries related to living and working on campus. For example, one could develop opportunities away from the staff member's living unit to connect with others through professional or personal interests. Collaborative projects with other campus professionals may offer relief from the intense, often intrusive demands of living with students. The development plan may also identify ways to connect with people beyond the campus community and to either learn new skills or volunteer in areas that reflect personal values.

Live-in staff may have more control over their work and personal space than they sometimes exert. Staff members can adopt practices that strengthen the segmentation between work and personal space by clarifying work expectations with the students and staff they manage and establishing patterns that separate the space as much as possible. Staff can create and utilize a workspace separate from their living space, avoid inviting students and staff into their living area for work-related activity, and commit to not working during off-duty time or in their personal living space. Staff should identify those work tasks that can be held specifically during appointed work hours and those that cannot.

It is important for graduate and professional live-in staff to clarify and communicate the relationship they will have with the student staff and leaders when they are not on duty. Staff can set boundaries regarding when they will be available to the student staff after hours and for what purposes; discussing the expectations from the beginning will help the student staff understand the intent and still feel supported by their supervisor, especially if they know what resources are available when the supervisor is away. The live-in staff can also schedule the programs and events that they will attend, reserving some evenings and weekend times to be with the others who are not associated with the job or to pursue other interests. The staff can negotiate for time off or flexible workdays to balance times when late-hour work occurs.

Midcareer Professionals and Supervisors

Key elements to recruitment and retention of full-time live-in residence life staff include strategies to support healthy work–life integration. Personal job control is the most effective strategy to lower work–life conflict and encourage retention (Kossek et al., 2009). Supervisors can assist residence life live-in staff as they strive to integrate their complex lives (perhaps with family life, academic pursuits, and other opportunities that they value) by supporting how the employee wants to integrate or segment work–life matters. Clear expectations on role performance as it relates to availability and work will provide the base for the employee to determine their best level of integration of work–life boundaries. Strategies for support may include adjusting work schedules, identifying projects that may have the flexibility needed for the staff member, and creating an environment where staff feel valued and comfortable in requesting adjustments. Discussing professional development plans, motivations, passions, and future goals supports staff to consider ways that they can dovetail their development with the expectations of their positions. To foster staff development, supervisors can offer budgetary support to reinforce the value of healthy work–life integration (Winston & Creamer, 1997).

Midlevel professionals can advocate for the amenities and living environment that will support staff in their efforts to create homelike personal spaces in the residence halls. The live-in staff will appreciate updated, well-furnished apartments that do not resemble the areas assigned to students (Belch & Kimble, 2006). The midlevel staff can work with the facility staff to ensure the apartments are not only in good functioning order but also have high-quality finishes and appliances that create a residential environment. This includes providing updated kitchens with modern appliances, countertops, and cabinetry, as well as finishes such as flooring, wall coverings, and doors that are a higher grade than the rest of the building. Offering staff the ability to select their own furniture, paint colors, and window coverings may add to the control staff feel over their living environment. To allow staff to complete personal tasks with more privacy, provide dedicated exterior entrances to the staff apartments, laundry facilities within the apartment, and trash disposal areas separate from common areas.

Examining existing traditions through a healthy work–life perspective may illuminate patterns that hinder a holistic approach for staff. For example, housing and residence life staff receive intensive training before the fall semester that includes managing student care and crisis, conflict and mediation, policy enforcement, programming techniques, and diversity and inclusion of the community. Supervisors can design the training schedule so that the teams are not exhausted before the residents arrive. They can prioritize topics that staff must have before students move in and then offer the other topics in a variety of modes and times afterward (e.g., online modules, in-service training sessions early in the semester). Similarly, staff at all levels benefit from some unscheduled time each day to manage various commitments. Another example relates to term limits of staff in positions, requiring them to vacate the position after a specified period (Davidson, 2012). Utilizing performance-based decisions instead of arbitrary time limits acknowledges the diverse personal and professional commitments that staff hold. Supervisors can also work with facilities administrators to eliminate the practice of requiring staff to vacate their apartments over the summer. At times it may be necessary for renovations, but the move should be the exception, not the standard practice.

Senior Housing and Residence Life Officers

While the individual staff member is responsible in part for developing and maintaining work–life integration, the senior housing officer should accept responsibility for creating an environment that supports the unique needs of the live-in professional staff. First, leaders can involve the housing and residence life staff in discussions about supporting healthy work–life integration and consider employee expectations and suggestions. Clear expectations on how employees can excel in their role within the framework of setting boundaries will help all staff determine their plans. Second, given the critical roles the live-in staff play in supporting students and the residential community in crisis situations, senior officers can advocate for staff by promoting healthy work–life integration. Flexible work schedules and compensation time considerations for staff acknowledge the demanding nature of living and working with students and may not align with personnel policies in other administrative units. Senior housing officers should model healthy work–life integration for their staff and students and advocate for appropriate policies that support holistic work–life integration that may serve as a model for other units. Influencing institutional culture takes time and effort, and senior housing and residence life administrators could advocate for support of a flexible work schedule campus wide.

Policies and Practices

Knowing that housing and residence life work often does not conform to standard work times of other college and university administrators, institutional leaders can communicate clear expectations for work and a commitment to healthy work–life integration. Senior housing officers can review strategic initiatives, policies, and procedures to determine if the expectations for staff and role responsibilities reflect a supportive work environment (Belch & Kimble, 2006). From recruitment through employment and training to evaluation, policies and practices should reflect the espoused value of work–life integration. For example, senior housing leaders can review policies on work hours and locations, developing procedures that allow staff to adjust their workdays, hours, and locations within the parameters of the work required. In evaluations, merit can recognize staff who work efficiently and integrate their work expectations and caring for self.

Leaders can commit to reviewing and updating written materials such as position descriptions, recruitment material, and publications to reflect a culture that supports a holistic approach to staff role expectations and development. Asking staff to review the on-call schedule and protocols may create suggestions for improving work–life integration. Potential ideas for change include designing a weighted system for on-call which shortens the on-call time required when it covers major weekends and times of high activity due to sporting events, traditional events on campus, and other times. Another idea is to include more staff on the on-call rotation, particularly those who do not live among students. Allowing staff to adjust their office workload and times when they serve on-call and may need to respond throughout the night would acknowledge and attend to some of the boundary issues staff often experience.

Given that housing and residence life staff members often manage stressful and sometimes traumatic situations, we recommend developing a protocol for following up with affected staff to ensure they get adequate emotional support afterward. Particularly when staff are personally tasked as agents of the institution (e.g., conduct officers or those who respond to critical incidents), such emotional labor can affect their lives both in and outside work. Acknowledging the work performed in extreme situations and accommodating subsequent personal demands allows staff to recover and recalibrate their complex lives.

Beyond the scope of a single institution, leaders of professional associations can define and share best practices for work–life integration strategies with members. Professional documents guide housing and residence life leaders in staff development, program development, and evaluation. Inserting guidelines and standards for healthy work–life integration among student affairs professional documents symbolizes an important commitment to the staff members' well-being, just as they are asked to invest in the welfare of their students (ACPA & NASPA, 2015). To further develop such standards, Association of College and University Housing Officers–International (ACUHO-I) association leaders can examine professional standards from different helping professions such as social work and counseling for additional strategies to promote healthy work–life integration.

Conclusion

Student affairs professionals share expertise in supporting college students, yet challenges remain for creating healthy work conditions for employees. Institutional and professional association leaders can better support student affairs professionals as they contribute to college student success. Professional guidelines specify the knowledge, skills, and dispositions required to attend to student and institutional needs, yet espoused expectations for self-care or promoting healthy work environments for housing and residence professionals are uneven. Some of the documents note the dual needs of the individual and the institution (e.g., ACPA & NASPA, 2016; Council for the Advancement of Standards in Higher Education, 2015), but few offer specific guidelines of how professionals navigate situations when the two conflict.

Boundary theory offers a scheme to examine the tensions of navigating professional and personal roles. It provides a framework for discussion between employees and the organization about the flexibility and permeability of the work environment as early as in the interview process, which allows an employee to determine if the position will allow for their own values and needs. The concepts inherent in boundary theory point to one method for maintaining a healthy organizational environment and support for work–life integration among live-in professionals, an important strategy since senior housing leaders anticipate continuing challenges in recruiting and retaining professionals (ACUHO-I, 2015b).

Addressing conditions of work–life integration offers multiple benefits: It aligns with the espoused values of acknowledging the whole person and addresses long-standing problems with recruiting and retaining staff. Understanding ways in which the roles, responsibilities, and expectations of student affairs positions dovetail or conflict with healthy work–life integration allows individual professionals to examine their dilemmas and decisions regarding their career choices. Reexamining policies and practices related to work–life integration may help recruit and retain staff who are prepared to be career long-term contributors to the profession versus staff who burn out and leave the profession early in career. A workforce that is well equipped to meet the needs of students as well as their own changing needs (with health and wellness, family care, and other commitments) offers students and the institution a caring community, invested in holistic development for all.

References

Acker, J. (1990). Hierarchies, jobs, bodies: A theory of gendered organizations. *Gender & Society, 4*(2), 139–158. https://doi.org/10.1177/089124390004002002

ACPA: College Student Educators International & NASPA: Student Affairs Administrators in Higher Education. (2015). *Professional competency areas for student affairs educators.* https://www.naspa.org/images/uploads/main/ACPA_NASPA_Professional_Competencies_FINAL.pdf

ACPA: College Student Educators International & NASPA: Student Affairs Administrators in Higher Education. (2016). *ACPA/NASPA professional competencies rubrics.* http://www.myacpa.org/sites/default/files/ACPA%20NASPA%20Professional%20Competency%20Rubrics%20Full.pdf

Allen, E. (2016). *Tips for transitioning from graduate student to new professional.* NASPA. https://www.naspa.org/constituent-groups/posts/tips-for-transitioning-from-graduate-student-to-new-professional

American College Health Association. (2018). *American College Health Association / National College Health Assessment II: Undergraduate student reference group: Executive summary.* American College Health.

American Council on Education Studies. (1937). *The student personnel point of view: A report of a conference on the philosophy and development of student personnel work in college and university (series 1, no. 3).* Author.

Ashforth, B. E., Kreiner, G. E., & Fugate, M. (2000). All in a day's work: Boundaries and micro role transitions. *Academy of Management Review, 25*(3), 472–491. https://doi.org/10.5465/amr.2000.3363315

Association of College and University Housing Officers–International. (2015a). *ACUHO-I standards & ethical principles for college & university housing professionals.* https://www.acuho-i.org/Portals/0/doc/res/acuhoi-standards-ethical-principles-2015-final.pdf

Association of College and University Housing Officers–International. (2015b). *ACUHO-I strategic plan.* Author.

Barr, M. J. (1990). Growing staff diversity and changing career paths. In M. J. Barr, M. L. Upcraft, & Associates (Eds.), *New futures for student affairs* (pp. 160–177). Jossey-Bass.

Belch, H. A., & Kimble, G. (2006). Human resources. In B. M. McCuskey & N. W. Dunkel (Eds.), *Foundations: Strategies for the future of the housing profession* (pp. 69–95). Association of College and University Housing Officers-International.

Belch, H. A., & Mueller, J. A. (2003). Candidate pools or puddles: Challenges and trends in the recruitment and hiring of resident directors. *Journal of College Student Development, 44*(1), 29–46. https://doi.org/10.1353/csd.2003.0001

Belch, H. A., Wilson, M. E., & Dunkel, N. (2008). Best practices in the recruitment and retention of entry-level, live-in staff. In T. E. Ellett, H. A. Belch, J. Christopher, S. R. St. Onge, M. E. Wilson, N. W. Dunkel, S. Klein, E. Nestor, S. S. Robinette, & T. D. Scheuermann (Eds.), *Recruitment and retention of entry-level staff in housing and residence life* (pp. 8–9). Association of College and University Housing Officers.

Blackney, E. D. (2015). *To be or not to be satisfied: Examining job satisfaction of entry-level residence life professionals at historically Black colleges and universities* [Doctoral dissertation, The University of Southern Mississippi]. Aquila Digital Community. http://aquila.usm.edu/dissertations/177

Brus, C. P. (2006). Seeking balance in graduate school: A realistic expectation or a dangerous dilemma? In M. J. Guentzel & B. Elkins Nesheim (Eds.), *Supporting graduate and professional students: The role of student affairs* (New Directions for Student Services No. 115, pp. 31–45). Jossey-Bass. https://doi.org/10.1002/ss.214

Burke, M. G., Sauerheber, J. D., Hughey, A. W., & Laves, K. (2017). *Helping skills for working with college students: Applying counseling theory to student affairs practice.* Routledge.

Canto, A. I., Cox, B. E., Osborn, D., Becker, M. S., & Hayden, S. (2017). College students in crisis: Prevention, identification, and response options for campus housing professionals. *Journal of College & University Student Housing, 43*(2), 44–57. https://www.nxtbook.com/nxtbooks/acuho/journal_vol43no2/index.php#/p/44

Council for the Advancement of Standards in Higher Education. (2015). *CAS professional standards for higher education* (9th ed.). Author.

Daniel, S., & Sonnentag, S. (2016). Crossing the borders: The relationship between boundary management, work–family enrichment and job satisfaction. *The International Journal of Human Resource Management, 27*(4), 407–426. https://doi.org/10.1080/09585192.2015.1020826

Davidson, D. L. (2012). Job satisfaction, recruitment, and retention of entry-level residence life and housing staff. *Journal of College & University Student Housing, 38*(2), 78–93. https://www.nxtbook.com/nxtbooks/acuho/journal_vol39no1/index.php#/p/78

Fonner, K. L., & Stache, L. C. (2012). All in a day's work, at home: Teleworkers' management of micro role transitions and the work–home boundary. *New Technology, Work and Employment, 27*(3), 242–257. https://doi.org/10.1111/j.1468-005X.2012.00290.x

Fotis, F. (2013). Organizational structures. In N. W. Dunkel & J. A. Baumann (Eds.), *Campus housing management* (pp. 33–48). Association of College and University Housing Officers–International.

Gallagher, R. P. (2014). *National survey of college counseling centers.* International Association of Counseling Services.

Hirt, J. B., & Creamer, D. G. (1998). Issues facing student affairs professionals: The four realms of professional life. In N. J. Evans & C. E. Phelps Tobin (Eds.),

The state of the art of preparation and practice in student affairs: Another look (pp. 47–60). University Press of America.

Kossek, E. E., Lautsch, B. A., & Eaton, S. C. (2005). Flexibility enactment theory: Implications of flexibility type, control, and boundary management for work–family effectiveness. In E. E. Kossek & S. J. Lambert (Eds.), *Work and life integration: Organizational, cultural, and individual perspectives* (pp. 243–261). Lawrence Erlbaum.

Kossek, E. E., Lautsch, B. A., & Eaton, S. C. (2009). Good teleworking: Under what conditions does teleworking enhance employees' well-being? In Y. Amichae-Hamburger (Ed.), *Technology and psychological well-being* (pp. 148–173). Cambridge University Press.

Marshall, S. M., Gardner, M. M., Hughes, C., & Lowery, U. (2016). Attrition from student affairs: Perspectives from those who exited the profession. *Journal of Student Affairs Research and Practice, 53*(2), 146–159. https://doi.org/10.1080/19496591.2016.1147359

Nippert-Eng, C. (1996a, 9). Calendars and keys: The classification of "home" and "work." *Sociological Forum, 11*(3), 563–582. https://doi.org/10.1007/BF02408393

Nippert-Eng, C. (1996b). *Home and work.* University of Chicago Press.

Olson-Buchanan, J. B., & Boswell, W. R. (2006). Blurring boundaries: Correlates of integration and segmentation between work and nonwork. *Journal of Vocational Behavior, 68*(3), 432–445. https://doi.org/10.1016/j.jvb.2005.10.006

Rankin, P. R., IV., & Gully, N. Y. (2018). Boundary integration and work–life balance when you live where you work: A study of residence life professionals. *Journal of College & University Student Housing, 44*(2), 64–81.

Renn, K. A., & Jessup-Anger, E. R. (2008). Preparing new professionals: Lessons for graduate preparation programs from the National Study of New Professionals in Student Affairs. *Journal of College Student Development, 49*(4), 319–335. https://doi.org/10.1353/csd.0.0022

Reynolds, A. L. (2017). Counseling and helping skills. In J. H. Schuh, S. R. Jones, & V. Torres (Eds.), *Student services: A handbook for the profession* (pp. 452–465). Jossey-Bass.

Rhoades, G., Kiyama, J. M., McCormick, R., & Quiroz, M. (2008). Local cosmopolitans and cosmopolitan locals: New models of professionals in the academy. *Review of Higher Education, 31*(2), 209–235. https://doi.org/10.1353/rhe.2007.0079

Riker, H. C. (1965). *College housing as learning centers.* American College Personnel Association. http://story.myacpa.org/img/carousel/COLLEGE%20HOUSING%20AS%20LEARNING%20CENTERS.pdf

Rosser, V. J., & Javinar, J. M. (2003). Midlevel student affairs leaders' intentions to leave: Examining the quality of their professional and institutional work life. *Journal of College Student Development, 44*(6), 813–830. https://doi.org/10.1353/csd.2003.0076

Sallee, M., & Lester, J. (2017). Expanding conceptualizations of work–life in higher education: Looking outside the academy to develop a better understanding within. In M. B. Paulsen (Ed.), *Higher education: Handbook of theory and research* (pp. 355–417). Springer.

Sallee, M. W. (2015). Adding academics to the work/family puzzle: Graduate student parents in higher education and student affairs. *Journal of Student Affairs Research and Practice, 52*(4), 401–413. https://doi.org/10.1080/19496591.2015 .1083438

Scheuermann, T., & Ellett, T. (2007). A 3-D view of recruitment and retention of entry-level housing staff: Déjà vu, deliberation, decisive action. *Journal of College & University Student Housing, 34*(2), 12–19. http://prestohost88.inmagic.com/ inmagicgenie/catfiles/2008/02/Journalv34n22007.pdf

Schuh, J. H., & Shipton, W. C. (1985). The residence hall resource team: Collaboration in counseling activities. *Journal of Counseling & Development, 63*(6), 380–381. https://doi.org/10.1002/j.1556-6676.1985.tb02726.x

Werring, C. J., Robertson, D. L., & Coon, C. V. (1993). Fostering interpersonal relationships and reducing conflicts. In R. B. Winston Jr., S. Anchors, & Associates (Eds.), *Student housing and residential life: A handbook for professionals committed to student development goals* (pp. 481–500). Jossey-Bass.

Wilk, K. E. (2016). Work-life balance and ideal worker expectations for administrators. *New Directions for Higher Education, 2016*(176), 37–51. https:// doi.org/10.1002/he.20208

Williams, J. (2000). *Unbending gender: Why family and work conflict and what to do about it.* Oxford University Press.

Wilson, M. E. (2008). *Recruitment and retention of entry-level staff in housing and residence life: A report on activities supported by the ACUHO-I commissioned research program.* Association of College and University Housing Officers–International.

Wilson, M. E., Liddell, D. L., Hirschy, A. S., & Pasquesi, K. (2016). Professional identity, career commitment, and career entrenchment of midlevel student affairs professionals. *Journal of College Student Development, 57*(5), 557–572. https://doi .org/10.1353/csd.2016.0059

Winston, R. B., Jr., & Creamer, D. G. (1997). *Improving staffing practices in student affairs.* Jossey-Bass.

Zerubavel, E. (1985). *Hidden rhythms: Schedules and calendars in social life.* University of California Press.

4

THE INFLUENCE OF INSTITUTIONAL TYPE AND SOCIALIZATION PROCESSES ON THE IDEAL WORKER NORMS OF STUDENT AFFAIRS PROFESSIONALS

C. Casey Ozaki and Anne M. Hornak

Most colleges and universities in the United States have student affairs and services units whose overarching purpose is to support the growth, development, and learning of college students; yet, the varied goals of students and institutional purposes across different institutional types have a reciprocal impact on the more nuanced roles of student affairs professionals on these campuses (Tull et al., 2009). Students who work full time and are seeking a part-time, lower-cost academic experience that may not include a 4-year degree will likely select a different institution than those that could include a residential component and have undergraduate research opportunities; their needs will also vary and require different preparation and engagement in higher education. Student affairs professionals are often responsible for being the architects of engagement and tailor cocurricular experiences and thus their work to that institutional type and its students (Sandeen & Barr, 2006). Shared throughout the profession is the deeply embedded valuing of unbounded time to the exclusion of life beyond work, throughout the chapter referred to as *ideal worker norms* or *concept* (Acker, 1990; Sallee, 2016; Ward & Wolf-Wendel, 2016; Wilk, 2016), although how this dynamic manifests across institutional type varies.

In this chapter, we focus on community colleges, baccalaureate liberal arts, and doctoral research institutions in lieu of addressing the full gamut of institutional types; these examples allow us to compare differing levels, missions, organizational structures, and cultural norms that reflect how ideal worker norms are similar across types but function differently because of institutional differences. We also draw on Van Maanen and Schein's (1979) theory of organizational socialization to further clarify and critique how the ideal worker construct has manifested across institution types. This theory suggests a framework for the processes organizations use to socialize newcomers into specific organizational and, more broadly, professional values, operational and interpersonal norms, necessary skills, and organizational loyalty and identity. A socialization lens is useful in clarifying how different institutional types familiarize and habituate workers into ideal worker norms using processes unique to their mission, students, and structure, but concurrently reinforce and reproduce those norms.

Ideal Worker Construct and Socialization

If the purpose of socialization is to produce workers who are fully committed to accomplishing the goals of the institution and profession, then molding a worker who is enculturated into an ideal embodiment of skills, behaviors, and norms the institution or profession believes is necessary to achieve these goals (Perez, 2016; Van Maanen & Schein, 1979; Weidman et al., 2001). We propose that the engagement and utilization of specific socialization strategies allow institutions to tailor student affairs professional socialization to the unique goals of different institutional types and their ideal worker norms; they are also a vehicle through which these norms are reinforced and reproduced or have the capacity to be interrupted (Van Maanen & Schein, 1979).

Van Maanen and Schein's (1979) theory of organizational socialization proposes six dimensions that capture the ways, means, and processes with which an organization frames and approaches socializing new employees. Within each dimension are dichotomous tactics that reflect the range of approaches to socialization within an organization. The six dimensions are (a) collective versus individual, (b) formal versus informal, (c) sequential versus random, (d) fixed versus variable, (e) serial versus disjunctive, and (f) investiture versus divestiture. We use a socialization lens to help interrogate ideal worker norms in individual experiences and organizational functions across institutional types.

Collective Versus Individual

A collective socialization process refers to an induction process that is group oriented. New professionals are taken through a common set of experiences as they begin the socialization process, often an orientation or common training experience. Individual strategies tend to be more one-on-one and associated with complex roles where the collective identity is not as important (Van Maanen & Schein, 1979).

Formal Versus Informal

Formal socialization is the set of experiences that are tailored specifically to new professionals' roles. This is common for positions in which there are high levels of compliance. In higher education, this includes financial aid professionals who have unique roles explicit to their work. Alternately, informal socialization does not specifically distinguish a new professional's role and typically involves on-the-job training and trial and error.

Sequential Versus Random

Van Maanen and Schein (1979) discussed two distinct steps in the socialization process—sequential and random. Sequential socialization refers to formal and identifiable steps that individuals must pass through to achieve their targeted role. For example, becoming a doctor is a sequential process with a specific structure. Random socialization can be ambiguous, undefined, or constantly changing. In student affairs this is often the case where individuals can move up the hierarchy through undefined and informal ways.

Fixed Versus Variable

The fixed and variable aspects of this theory relate to the boundary passages individuals pass through to transition to other roles around and within the organization. Within the variable process there are few clues when to expect a given boundary passage. Variable socialization creates an environment where professionals are constantly kept off balance and anxious about clues to move around within the organization, whereas in a fixed socialization process, hierarchical boundary passages are clearly defined and expected (Van Maanen & Schein, 1979).

Serial Versus Disjunctive

Serial socialization processes are associated with inclusionary boundary passages. In higher education, serial processes are designed to establish legacy and groom newcomers to take over for someone currently in the position. Disjunctive socialization occurs when individuals come into roles where no one currently does that work. This often happens in roles where the individual holding the position leaves prior to a new person being hired. Disjunctive socialization can create a space for a new professional to be innovative and not tied to notions of the "ways things have always been done."

Investiture Versus Divestiture

Socialization processes that include investiture and divestiture practices are more likely found in corporate settings and the military. Investiture socialization is the viewpoint that "we like you just the way you are," and we will work with that (Van Maanen & Schein, 1979, p. 251). Alternatively, divestiture is stripping away personal characteristics to rebuild the individual's image within the institution's image.

Impact of Institutional Type

In this section we analyze ideal worker norms in student affairs across three institutional types—community colleges, baccalaureate/liberal arts undergraduate institutions, and research/doctoral institutions—and consider socialization as a vehicle for reproducing or interrupting these norms. Across each institutional type we focus on mission and student population, preparation of professionals, institutional organization and relationships, and institutional resources, allowing us to interrogate and compare how the ideal worker construct influences and differs across varied campus contexts. We note that while we explore different institutional types, many of the examples we use and elements we highlight can be found across multiple campus types. One of the biggest differences for student affairs educators on campuses with residence halls or a highly developed student activities unit is the fact that their students live on campus and have needs outside "normal" working hours.

The Ideal Worker Concept in Student Affairs at Community Colleges

Community colleges in the United States are generally 2-year institutions, though some are expanding to offering 3- and 4-year degrees, historically focused on providing general education and preparatory coursework for transfer, awarding associate degrees and certificates, and providing lifelong learning courses. Broadly, they are diverse institutions that serve their local communities. Because of their local population, most community colleges have no or limited campus housing or other traditional student affairs functional areas (e.g., campus activities, student government, judicial affairs), focusing instead on academic student services, such as advising, academic support, academic testing, financial aid, and registration and records (Cohen et al., 2014). Mission, students, and the nature of work at community colleges shape patterns in how community colleges use socialization of student affairs professionals to define and reproduce ideal worker norms for this institution type.

Mission and Student Population

As mentioned in the overview, the mission of community colleges has almost always been tripartite—transfer, degree, and lifelong learning—in nature (Cohen et al., 2014), designed to serve many diverse purposes and student goals for the local community. In 2015–2016, community colleges served nearly 40% of U.S. undergraduate students (Ginder et al., 2017) and, during the same year, among all students who completed a 4-year degree, 49% had previously enrolled at a 2-year college (National Student Clearinghouse Research Center, 2017), yet these institutions are also more likely to serve students at higher risk of not completing and an overall higher proportion of traditionally underserved student populations (Ma & Baum, 2016; National Center for Public Policy and Higher Education, 2011; National Student Clearinghouse Research Center, 2017; Shapiro et al., 2017). Their diverse population and open admissions have led to community colleges being framed as America's democratic institutions with a mission of equitable educational opportunity (Bailey & Morest, 2006). The diverse student population translates to a wide range of student demographics that necessitates that student affairs professionals at community colleges be able to work across a multitude of student identities, life situations, and needs. As such, a professional may be required to operate as an academic adviser, a personal counselor, a tutor, a financial aid counselor, a friend, and a social worker in the same week.

The mission and student population demographics that community colleges serve suggest that the work of student affairs professionals at community colleges requires the ability to work individually with students to meet their diverse needs and, to do so, often requires collaborative work that draws on generalist knowledge. Their work is generally student focused and, given that students have individual needs and goals, student affairs professionals must be flexible, have a broad understanding of the institution, and be prepared to work on the students' behalf in a highly bureaucratic setting (Hirt, 2006; Kuk, 2016; McFadden & Mazeika, 2014). As institutions with high enrollment, significant diversity, and minimal resources reliant on state and local funding, community colleges are generally structured to be efficient and have systematic processes. Hirt (2006) labeled student affairs professionals at community colleges as "The Producers" (p. 145), which acknowledges how serving the local community and other external agencies results in more frenzied decision-making and a more frantic pace of work, compared to other institutional types (Hirt, 2006; Kuk, 2016). In this context, ideal worker norms create less flexibility in work within the institution and, therefore, in the relationship between the professional's work and home life.

The more extreme conception of the ideal worker requires that student affairs professionals be all things to all people, and that they be able to do it quickly. This expectation assumes that the worker has sufficient resources, preparation, and institutional socialization. The individualized and student-centered nature of this work can be highly personal and often requires that the worker be comfortable working with sensitive and difficult subjects. To manage high needs of students individually and to address this work and the broader work of the institution creates a setting where ideal worker norms, in theory, result in a lack of bandwidth to multitask and allow any attention or focus beyond the workplace.

Preparation of Professionals

Student affairs entry-level professional preparation and socialization into the profession varies, but most common and preferred is through a graduate (master's) degree in student affairs or higher education, a formal and sequential process. Preparation programs are heavily focused on training for 4-year institutional contexts and lack purposeful preparation of professionals to work in community colleges (Dalpes et al., 2015; Hornak et al., 2016; Latz et al., 2017). As such, community college professionals have been historically minimally represented at student affairs conferences (Hornak et al., 2016). Additionally, a survey of preparation program faculty found that community college preparation was either included in one course, usually an elective, or integrated across the curriculum (Royer & Latz, 2016). Therefore, a reasonable conclusion is that the typical graduate and entry-level student affairs professional is socialized into conceptions of the ideal worker that align primarily with a 4-year institutional context and may be minimally exposed to the expectations of what community college student affairs work looks like.

However, many student affairs professionals in community colleges rise from student and classified positions to midlevel and administrative positions in student affairs (Hornak et al., 2016). These individuals are socialized into their institution through internal positions, and rarely do they receive that formal, sequential education about the student affairs profession that is so common in other institutional types. Therefore, the concept of the ideal worker at community colleges is often institutionally based and conceptually vague for those entering community college settings from a preparation program.

The serial versus disjunctive dimension of socialization may provide additional insight (Van Maanen & Schein, 1979). The serial process refers to the presence of experienced members who groom newcomers and can serve as role models, while a disjunctive process reflects situations where there are no footsteps to follow or gaps in history may exist due to change. Although community colleges have to be adaptive due to their often limited resources and sensitivity to the community and local economy (Cohen et al., 2014), as discussed, this also contributes to singular roles in a unit and employees who are serving in multiple role capacities. These characteristics combined with a relatively flat hierarchy often result in positions that are staffed by one person for a long period of time and, concurrently, roles and positions that may change quickly to meet community needs but have little precedent or history. As such, the lack of movement through positions, roles that are unique to one position and not conducted by many, and change to positions that can occur relatively often contribute to socialization that is often disjunctive in nature. When a culture is grounded in long-term and singular-role professionals and simultaneously experiences disjunctive change, socialization may toggle between disjunctive and serial. Therefore, ideal worker norms are often deeply embedded in an institutional culture and reinforced through the long-term residency of student affairs professionals who are socialized through informal, individual, and serial approaches, but the adaptability and quick-changing nature of community colleges also makes room for disjunctive forms of socialization that could provide opportunities for an interruption, challenge, and change to ideal worker norms, opportunities that may not often be taken.

The deep diversity of community colleges is demonstrated both in the form of the students served and the educational goals that students have. Therefore, the ideal worker construct at this institution type expects a person to individualize their work with students, fulfill multiple roles, and work collegially and collaboratively across units. To be successful, the professional must embody these skills and abilities in order to do their job with its many demands, resulting in significant cross-training (Dalpes et al., 2015; Hornak et al., 2016). Cross-training and collaboration are key disjunctive socialization processes. Working across multiple roles and in conjunction with others in different units means that there will rarely be individuals who have done the same work long term. The prior discussion of disjunctive socialization as a way to interrupt ideal worker norms gives way to the identification of collaboration and cross-training as specific processes that have the potential to facilitate that interruption. Serial socialization coupled with multiple and growing roles results in high levels of responsibility and is accompanied by high stress and expectations that work will be addressed in the same time and quality without considering the potential impact on worker's lives beyond work. Disjunctive socialization and cross and collaborative work may allow for more innovative approaches to work that potentially diffuse the piling-on of work responsibilities.

Institutional Resources

The concept of the ideal worker assumes that the professional has the opportunity and space to focus almost exclusively on their job. Such a task is challenging in most divisions of student affairs, where the work is not singular in scope or focus (Hirt, 2006, 2009). This is particularly true at community colleges, as they have historically served a wide range of students. Students select 2-year institutions for a variety of reasons, including earning associate degrees and certificates, improving basic skills, completing general education requirements before transferring, financing education at a reduced cost, living in close proximity to home, refining skills, and engaging in learning to enhance their lives (Cohen et al., 2014). This range of purposes and the diversity of students require professionals to work across multiple functional areas and have a deep bank of skills.

To function within ideal worker norms embedded in the cross-training and multiple roles that are common among community college student affairs professionals, full support, resources, and ongoing training are necessary (DeMinck, 2017). Despite the need, community colleges have historically been and continue to be underresourced (Cohen et al., 2014), contributing to a demanding work environment that pits work against nonwork lives. The local and commuting nature of students has meant that there are minimal student affairs units on campus but significant need for student services to support academic institutional goals. As such, student affairs has not historically been a priority in community colleges (Cohen et al., 2014), but as institutions have had to become more compliance driven, competitive for enrollment, and consumer driven, student affairs professionals have become more critical and the ideal worker construct more demanding. Yet, these units remain small and underresourced relative to the size of the institution.

In comparison to the community college, student affairs work at baccalaureate/liberal arts institutions share similar characteristics (e.g., often smaller institutions, staff who have multiple roles, student-focused) that produce some parallel ideal worker norms. Yet, the mission and culture of baccalaureate/liberal arts institutions represent a more traditional student affairs division. Additionally, the presence of residential students complicates the work more, as students live in campus.

The Ideal Worker Concept in Student Affairs at Baccalaureate/ Liberal Arts Institutions

Baccalaureate colleges are defined as institutions that award at least 50% of their degrees at the bachelor's level (Indiana University Center for Postsecondary Research, 2015). These institutions are both public and private and are often called *liberal arts colleges*, as many were founded with the mission of educating in a holistic way with a strong focus on the liberal arts (e.g., languages, history, math, anthropology). Liberal arts colleges heavily skew private in funding and small in size. Their focus on holistic education results in many liberal arts institutions being religiously affiliated or identifying with particular values (Cronin, 1999).

Student affairs work at liberal arts colleges is heavily organized around students, their development, and the values of the institution. The focus on the holistic development and growth of students places students at the center of their work, yet, given the small size and private nature of these institutions, often individuals or a small number of people are responsible for an area and, therefore, their work can be autonomous. Conversely, because of their shared values and small size, campus relationships are generally collegial and thus, out of necessity, student affairs professionals are collaborative and creatively draw on their relationships to accomplish their work (Hirt, 2006; Hirt et al., 2005).

Professionals at liberal arts institutions may not differ in terms of the tenets that undergird their focus on learning and development. However, institutional size and a strong effort toward collaborative leadership development (Nunez, 2013) does change the definition of the ideal worker at a liberal arts institution and the ways they are socialized. First, smaller institutions create opportunities for closer relationships with students; this complicates the ability to separate work from home, for students do not "schedule" their crises, as can be commonly seen at residential campuses. Second, the effort toward collaborative leadership may require switching between and across student and academic affairs. The lines between the two are often more blurred (Nunez, 2013). Finally, students who choose liberal arts institutions are looking for a holistic educational experience that includes cocurricular opportunities and a more intimate campus. The perception is often that student affairs includes a more personalized and higher quality experience (Hirt, 2006; Nunez, 2013). The overall emphasis on work that is heavily relationship-oriented and personalized with colleagues and students instills an expectation and sense of responsibility that results in the promulgation of ideal worker norms, where work is often prioritized over individuals and their lives outside of work.

Mission and Student Population
The mission of liberal arts institutions varies, depending on whether the institution identifies with particular religious or other values, but in general they share a commitment to the holistic growth and education of the student. Critical thinking, personal growth, and development as a productive citizen are often shared goals (Hirt, 2006). Hirt refers to student affairs professionals at liberal arts colleges as the "Standard Bearers" (p. 26), because in many ways they represent the standard of the profession. Yet, this "standard" may also lead to conflict. The concept of the ideal worker at liberal arts institutions may create tensions between what is expected and the ability to have a career and life beyond work. The focus and obligation to the personal lives and growth of students, coupled with the intimate nature of campus and close relationships with students and colleagues, leads to the belief and expectation that long hours and weekends are a necessary part of the job (Hirt, 2006; Hirt et al., 2005). In practice, time to nourish relationships and personal investment in others is expected and prioritized, often without recognition that it can infringe on life external to work. This manifests as being at work later or on the weekends, but it may also include the expectation and practice of opening one's home and family to students.

The collegial nature of small liberal arts institutions is both borne of and reinforces the close relationships that are built between student affairs professionals and their students and colleagues. Flat hierarchical structure and shared values contribute to ideal worker expectations that supporting those relationships, particularly with students, is critical to solving problems, meeting student needs, and taking responsibility for their growth (Hirt, 2006). The emphasis on being responsible for student growth and accountable to the relationships that develop in a highly responsive manner is core to the ideal worker at a liberal arts institution, but it implies the prioritization of this work and the way it is both expected and realistically accomplished to the exclusion of nonwork responsibilities and matters.

Preparation of Professionals

As "standard bearers," most student affairs professionals at liberal arts colleges are prepared through a master's program in higher education or student affairs, what Van Maanen and Schein (1979) would identify as a formal socialization process. As noted in the discussion about community colleges, most preparation programs focus on the traditional student affairs professional at a 4-year institution. As such, in many ways the liberal arts college professional is prepared and socialized through their graduate program with little conflict with the job they will enter.

At the same time, the socialization process into specific liberal arts insittutions is primarily individualized, as the number of professional staff hired each year is much lower than at larger institutions. Individual socialization may lead to more climbing through positional levels and a faster pace of upward mobility; however, it can also be limiting, as the number of higher-level positions is restricted by institutional size (Van Maanen & Schein, 1979).

Liberal arts institutions and their forms of socialization are designed to acculturate professionals into historical student affairs worker expectations, often embedded in ideal worker norms. As new professionals are socialized through their formal graduate programs into the values of the profession and individualized institutional socialization processes are tailored and specific to the institutional mission and cultures, they are designed to reinforce and reproduce conceptions of student affairs work life and ideal worker norms. To disrupt and challenge these norms requires a change to both the norms and the ways they are inducted.

Institutional Resources

In contrast to the lack of institutional resources and support for student affairs among community colleges, which impacts how ideal worker norms play out, liberal arts institutions centralize the cocurricular work of student affairs professionals. While many liberal arts institutions struggle financially, the value of student affairs work and its alignment with the overall mission of liberal arts institutions contribute to the prioritization of cocurricular work and the funneling of resources toward it (Hirt, 2006). Yet the cost of liberal arts institutions often promotes a consumerist attitude among students and parents that reinforces the expectation that student affairs professionals react as ideal workers, being responsive and creating change quickly (Bunce et al., 2017). This financial context is a factor that promotes the ideal worker in liberal arts institutions as one where this work, which is intrinsically and otherwise rewarding, is also expected to be a priority in the individual's life.

The message that the institution values this work and believes student affairs is central to the growth and development of students reinforces the expectation that one's work prioritizes and nurtures the relationships with students. While often sufficiently resourced compared to other institutional types, the sense of responsibility for the work and the fact that there is often only one or a few people responsible for that work also adds pressure to accept the ideal worker concept as normal.

The mission and culture of baccalaureate/liberal arts institutions frame the ways in which professionals are socialized, as well as how the concept of the idealized worker is defined. As we transition to the discussion of the research/doctoral institutions, the work is not necessarily different; however, the size and research orientations of the institution drive a more decentralized organizational structure, which changes socialization practices.

The Ideal Worker Concept in Student Affairs at Research/Doctoral Institutions

Doctoral universities typically include large and midsized research institutions within each state. Professionals' work tends to reside within a specific functional area (Hirt, 2006, 2009), allowing them to become experts in their focus area. The work ebbs and flows and is dependent on the professional's functional area. At these institutions, change within units can occur faster, although it tends to be slow at the institutional level; student affairs professionals are expected to adapt quickly and daily, but the decentralization of large doctoral institutions also requires them to be strategic and political (Hirt, 2006). Often, at doctoral universities, there are multiple professionals working within each functional area, offering support and opportunities to collaborate. In addition, there tend to be more hierarchical levels through which to advance.

Mission and Student Population

Although the doctoral research university's purpose has historically been viewed as a public good, there has been a shift to understanding the driving mission of these institutions as the production and dissemination of research and creative activity (MacGregor, 2017). Although waning state funding is challenging the perception of the research university's tie to public service, for public and land-grant institutions it remains a significant part of their history and identities (American Academy of Arts and Sciences, 2016). These institutions are identified as top-tier, high-achieving, and competitive by both the faculty and students they attract. While research and grant writing are the primary tasks of the faculty and in the preparation of doctoral students, this mission and the large size of these institutions influence work norms and how work is organized across the institution, including the student affairs units (Hirt, 2009).

Compared to other institutional types, the work of student affairs professionals at doctoral/research institutions is culturally and distinctly different. Although the functional areas reflect the broad areas that are common within the profession, professionals identify with the research mission and see their work as integral to that goal. Furthermore, the disciplinary expertise that dominates the membership of faculty and students on campuses is reflected in student affairs professionals' identification as specialists in their functional areas, such as advising, admissions, residential life, judicial affairs, and so on (Hirt, 2006).

Similar to the research and teaching professionals, a predominant attitude among student affairs professionals at doctoral/research universities is that the work requires whatever is needed to get the job done. As such the ideal worker is expected to commit undefined amounts of time and do so without regard to their external life (Hirt, 2006, 2009). Although this work–life imbalance is common and embedded in expected and ideal worker norms, in Hirt's (2006) studies on this topic, student affairs professionals at this institutional type acknowledged this imbalance and problematized it as an element of the work that should be recognized and addressed.

Preparation of Professionals

Similar to student affairs professionals at liberal arts colleges, most professionals at doctoral research universities have a master's degree in the field, often from a research institution; are entry-level; and are socialized and prepared to work generally in student affairs at a 4-year baccalaureate institution, including research institutions (Renn & Hodges, 2007). The emphasis on specialization and expertise in these institutions contributes to and reinforces the professionals' identification with the field of student affairs and their functional area.

Given that a majority of preparation programs are at research institutions, it is common for student affairs professionals to supervise and mentor graduate students in internships and graduate assistantships (Schuh et al., 2017). It is often through these graduate assistantship and internship experiences that professional expectations and ideal worker norms are communicated and reinforced. (For more on the transmission of ideal worker norms in graduate programs, see chapter 5.) Given the association that professionals often have with the functional area at research institutions, they are primed to socialize the future professional into the work in the functional area specifically (Schuh et al., 2017; Tull et al., 2009). To be socialized into a functional area implies a narrow education into the expectations and picture of what student affairs work looks like. Therefore, the conception of the ideal worker is more narrowly defined as well. A more general socialization, which arguably is what should occur in a master's preparation program for student affairs or higher education, provides an overview of the student affairs profession, expectations, and competencies, allowing for a more varied conception of the expectations tied to the ideal worker (Renn & Jessup-Anger, 2008; Tull et al., 2009). It is also these professionals who socialize future and new professionals into the expectations that work should be organized and prioritized above their home and family lives—they are the individuals who teach and reinforce this work as often unbounded. The irony is that they are in prime positions to interrupt the socialization into ideal worker norms that promote a sense of work–life imbalance.

Socialization at a doctoral university includes both individual and collective processes and is dependent on the unit that professionals work in. For example, in residence life individuals are collectively socialized and trained. They arrive on campus prior to students and spend considerable time "learning the ropes" (Van Maanen & Schein, 1979, p. 19). However, there are also professionals at doctoral universities who work in functional areas where the work is not shared across multiple professionals, and their socialization may be individual and informal (Van Maanen & Schein, 1979). Both processes may lead to socialization of ideal worker norms, although if the goal is to introduce and reinforce evenly and similarly, a collective and formal process is more likely to accomplish this. In contrast, individual and informal socialization allows for greater diversion from broadly accepted norms.

Institutional Organization

Doctoral/research institutions are siloed in nature. The focus on research and, therefore, identification with specific disciplines and fields has led to the organization of colleges and schools within the university as internal organizing units (Keeling et al., 2007). Therefore, there are complex and multiple parallel hierarchies across academic and other areas of the university, including student affairs. The functional areas are also relatively autonomous units, with full staff and supervisors who identify with a deep expertise and specialization in their area (Hirt, 2006; Hornak et al., 2016).

Therefore, in contrast to the liberal arts and community college institutions, where organizational structure and needs prompt significant cross-campus collaboration and training within student affairs, student affairs professionals at doctoral institutions are less likely to work across unit lines or outside student affairs (Hirt, 2006). This also is evident in the historical academic–student affairs divide that has contributed to the lack of under-standing of roles across institutions. The independent nature of this work is embedded in the ideal worker through the gendered expectation of inde-pendence in the workplace and the need to demonstrate one's unquestioned confidence and commitment to the work to be considered "ideal," irrespec-tive of home and family.

The more developed and defined levels of student affairs organization reflected in larger and more siloed functional areas means that there are also more opportunities for unit-level subcultures into which professionals are also socialized. Therefore, professionals may experience contrasting and con-tradictory cultural messages with regard to ideal worker norms dependent on their unit's leadership and subculture. For example, one way to interrupt or challenge ideal worker norms could be through creating change, and a resis-tance to change and critique may reinforce ideal worker norms. Employees in two different units in the same institution may advance similar proposals related to paternity leave, and the units' supervisors may react differently. One supervisor could be more resistant to critique of the current system and the proposal of potential changes, while the other supervisor embraces the proposal and champions the advancement of paternity leave policy. As a result, in doctoral institutions, challenge and change to ideal worker norms can be uneven and inequitable across functional areas. Conversely, a change in one area may demonstrate to and serve to "bring along" other units as they witness change and outcomes.

Student affairs' professional norms emphasize and value the diversity, inclu-sion, and individualism that people bring to the profession. This often translates into an investiture socialization orientation in hiring choices and socialization processes (e.g., professional development, mentoring, relocation assistance, and so forth) where a "we like you just the way you are" (Van Maanen & Schein, 1979, p. 250) approach allows for variability in the acculturation of individuals into differing student affairs functional areas. Therefore, organizationally creat-ing space for differential socialization experiences in how ideal worker norms are recognized, accepted, or changed is critical, as well as creating opportunities to challenge the norms associated with the ideal worker.

Institutional Resources

A consistent presence in research institutions, student affairs has been recog-nized as an important contribution to the student experience and important in their success (Hirt, 2006, 2009). However, significant recent and pro-jected trends in higher education enrollment is influencing the ideal worker construct in student affairs.

As already mentioned, the financial stability and health of colleges and universities is of serious concern now and in the projected future. The past decade has seen a precipitous divestment of states in higher education and a shift of the financial burden for college to the individual/family (Celestin, 2019). As such, colleges and universities, especially 4-year research institutions, have experienced budget model changes that shift away from state support to being based on tuition, grants, and donations (Barr & McClellan, 2018). While not limited to student affairs, student-focused cocurricular programs and the professionals who run them are often cut first, leaving fewer employees to maintain expected levels of service and resulting in a greater pressure on the time and ability to do their work in ways that do not conflict or impinge on their home lives.

Doctoral/research institutions are increasingly feeling pressure to fundraise through grants and donors. While most institutions have historically engaged in fund-raising and grant activity to some extent, the rise of student affairs units required to raise their own funds through donors, business partnerships, and capital campaigns is becoming increasingly common (Seltzer, 2017). The introduction of this type of work activity in student affairs adds a new dimension to the ideal worker expectation in these institutions, bringing with it the need for fund-raising skills, more travel, and less time in touch with students, all of which can significantly change the nature of student affairs senior administrators and leaders. In a profession with nontraditional and long work hours and expectations, this type of shift in ideal worker expectations will increasingly stress the tension between the student affairs professionals' work and home lives.

The identification of different institution types and the recognition that, while similarities exist, organizational structure, mission, students, and nature of work vary across type are not revelations. However, these differences do influence how the ideal worker concept manifests in different institutional types. In exploring the inner workings of how ideal worker norms are adopted, socialization theory illuminates the processes and adaptation of norms to different institutional types and individual organizations. Socialization processes are tailored to institutions and their work contexts, which makes them a key vehicle for enculturating newcomers into ideal worker norms and reproducing them for the institution, while also being uniquely positioned to interrupt these norms.

Recommendations for Practice

The ideal worker concept, while varied by institutional type, creates a work environment that pits work life and home life against one another, often placing the professional in a position of having to choose one over the other. This forced choice is problematic, as it has been linked to high professional attrition (Buchanan & Shupp, 2015) and prompts the questioning of student affairs' commitment, as a profession, to the holistic health, development, and inclusion of diverse employees, particularly given the profession's advocacy for similar conditions and outcomes for students. Through the examination and interrogation of the ideal worker in student affairs and across institutional types, we provide recommendations across varied temporal and positional roles in a student affairs career.

Graduate Students and New Professionals

The socialization and preparation of student affairs professionals begins in graduate programs. Institutional type impacts the ideal worker construct from the very beginning of a graduate program. Doctoral-granting institutions generally have larger divisions of student affairs, which creates more opportunities for experiential education via practicums, internships, and assistantships. However, it is important that supervisors and faculty present opportunities outside the institutional type they are working in. Many times, a 4-year residential program is the only institutional type that is studied, part of faculty experiences, or presented as an option.

It is also important for students to explore opportunities at community colleges, nonresidential colleges and universities, special focus institutions, and other institutions outside the traditional 4-year residential program. The introduction and exploration of different institutional types is not solely the focus of an adult learning or diversity class (Hornak et al., 2016; Latz et al., 2017). By being exposed earlier, the student is more likely to be familiar with and open to experiencing a range of work norms and expectations across institutional types, which can contribute to clearer career decisions and potential alignment between personal and career goals and values. It is through this exposure that faculty and administrators in graduate programs have the opportunity, from the outset of a student affairs career, to assist graduate students in recognizing ideal worker norms, examining how they present across institutional type and functional area, and questioning what perspectives and assumptions these work norms are rooted in. Finally, through these academic and applied intellectual exercises, faculty and mentors can encourage students to challenge ideal worker norms and actively consider what work–life balance might look for them and how they could reasonably achieve it.

As new professionals enter campuses, they need supervision and mentoring that introduces them to that institutional type, functional area, and associated expectations. Each institution has varying cultures and subcultures that new and early-career professionals need to learn and manage; these subcultures are tied to ideal worker expectations unique to that institutional type. It is critical that institutions create orientation programs for new professionals that extend beyond their immediate office and are inclusive of more parts of the institution. For both community colleges and liberal arts institutions, the ideal worker concept suggests a worker be able to work across institutional and functional-area boundaries. Although historically siloed across functional areas, student affairs in doctoral/research institutions is becoming increasingly collaborative and moving toward integrated units because of the funding and budgeting context in higher education. Socializing student affairs workers to operate in a collaborative and cross-functional work environment is critical. It is also critical to prepare graduate students and new professionals with the ability to construct and define work–life balance for themselves as they navigate their professional selves. In addition, connecting new professionals with a mentor who can provide more specific and tailored socialization could also be a useful longer-term approach for retention. We cannot underscore enough the critical importance of these introductory paths to the profession and key times for socializing people into its values and norms. To interrupt the content and potential processes used in early socialization phases is opportune and key to changing ideal worker norms.

Midcareer Professionals and Supervisors

On most campuses, supervisors are in a position to shape culture and practice. Additionally, they often have more political capital to navigate campus in ways that emerging professionals do not. As direct supervisors and mentors who have decision-making power on campus, they make decisions related to training, partnerships with other units—formal and informal—and the structure of work hours, all of which directly influence ideal worker norms and expectations. Supervisors have the ability to use this influence to mentor emerging professionals as well as shape the work that they are entering into. These decisions influence the success, satisfaction, and longevity of employees (Buchanan & Shupp, 2015).

Similarly, supervisors at 4-year institutions, especially at doctoral and master's degree institutions, will need to broaden their portfolios. The ideal worker construct for these institutions is based on the preparation and expectation of specialization in a functional area. As institutions face impacted and changing budget models and funding, consolidation of units that have historically operated separately will require professionals to supervise, support, and hire individuals from functional areas and offices that they may not have personal or extensive experience with in their own career trajectory.

Although supervisors and mentors are in positions to socialize professionals into institution-specific and ideal worker norms, they are also in a position to interrupt the norms that are inequitable and work against making employees choose between work and nonwork life. Rather than working from the status quo in creating work expectations and hours in student affairs broadly and functional areas specifically, supervisors should be open to and creative when developing alternative work structures and approaches, including the purposeful inclusion of employees in defining and constructing these boundaries.

Conceptualizing the work community as a family that needs to be nurtured and where professionals take care of each other can mean supporting one another's nonwork lives and the willingness and flexibility to cover each other's work when needed. This culture and practice is also supported when colleagues and supervisors get to know one another's lives in and out of work. That caring ethic and invitation to share nonwork lives begins to blur work and nonwork lives, resulting in a conception of the worker that does not deny home lives. This may be especially relevant to student affairs professionals at smaller institutions or those that adhere to distinct shared values, such as liberal arts, religious, some community college institutions, and functional units in larger institutions. These institutions and smaller units often rely heavily on relationships and cross-unit work structures where home and work lives are already likely to be intertwined. Conversely, larger and commuter institutions arguably have a greater challenge to develop community, requiring supervisors to address the recognition of the nonwork life more purposefully.

Senior Student Affairs Officers

As they lead, guide, and set the tone for the division, senior student affairs officers (SSAOs) play a critical role in cultivating ideal worker expectations and creating a work culture that promotes or challenges them. They are also in primary decision-making and policy-setting positions. As such, the SSAO must interrogate how the institution's student affairs culture, practices, and policy reinforce ideal worker expectations and the impact that has on worker satisfaction and retention. Yet, to do this effectively they need to have a grasp on how that institution type operates and is unique in the relationship between work and home lives.

The ideal worker expectations for the SSAO role are also likely to vary across institutional type. As generalists at community colleges, like their workers, they will be expected to oversee and have knowledge about divergent student services units, many of which are likely to require a significant learning curve and time spent with units. This effort is likely to come with an ideal worker expectation of unbounded time—whatever time is needed to learn the role; but this is also an opportunity for the SSAO to consider management and leadership styles that are more time-efficient and allow for greater respect of the worker's life outside of work.

In addition, SSAOs at community colleges and liberal arts institutions, especially at smaller and more rural institutions, are likely to have the lines between their home and work blurred. The local nature of community colleges and the relational and collaborative nature of liberal arts colleges often result in highly visible leadership, where the expectation is that employees wear their "SSAO hat" outside the institution or are expected to invite their work home. To disentangle this relationship is challenging and political, but the SSAO who decides to respect and protect their home life and time must determine boundaries that are consistent and may be uncomfortable and unnatural for the seasoned student affairs professional socialized into an ideal worker norm long ago.

Finally, the SSAO position at a doctoral/research institution is shifting to include greater fund-raising and more responsibilities external to the direct supervision of their units. In some ways this promotes the ideal worker concept even more, as greater travel and evening and nontraditional work time can accompany these changes. To resist shifts that increase the expectation that all time is work time, the SSAO will need to be willing to create a leadership structure and division of labor in their units that places more of the supervision, day-to-day management, and on-the-ground decision-making with their employees, requiring SSAOs to spend less time on campus and attempting to protect time at home.

Recommendations for Practice

At institutions with student affairs preparation programs, the division should work collaboratively to interrogate and diversify the ideal worker construct and the practices or policies that transmit and reinforce it. For example, administrators and faculty must have ongoing discussions where they work toward coconstructing and redefining what work life means and the ways in which it may be defined on campus within all aspects of student affairs professionals, from graduate assistants to full-time senior-level professionals. They should concurrently have these discussions in the classroom with preprofessional graduate students, setting a strong foundation as individuals traverse the nuances of student affairs at different institutions during their careers and begin to understand that the notion of the ideal worker is an artificial construct.

References

Acker, J. (1990). Hierarchies, jobs, bodies: A theory of gendered organizations. *Gender and Society, 4*(2), 139–158. https://doi.org/10.1177/089124390004002002

American Academy of Arts and Sciences. (2016). *Public research universities recommitting to Lincoln's vision: An educational compact for the 21st century.* The Lincoln Project: Excellence and Access in Public Higher Education. https://www.amacad.org/multimedia/pdfs/publications/researchpapersmonographs/PublicResearchUniv_Recommendations.pdf

Bailey, T., & Morest, V. S. (Eds.). (2006). *Defending the community college equity agenda.* Johns Hopkins University Press.

Barr, M. J., & McClellan, G. S. (2018). *Budgets & financial management in higher education* (3rd ed.). Jossey-Bass.

Buchanan, J., & Shupp, M. (2015). Factors that influence the attrition of entry-level student affairs professionals. *Journal of Student Affairs, 25,* 107. https://dx.doi.org/10.25675/10217/172176

Bunce, L., Baird, A., & Jones, S. E. (2017). The student-as-consumer approach in higher education and its effects on academic performance. *Studies in Higher Education, 42*(11), 1958–1978. https://doi.org/10.1080/03075079.2015.1127908

Celestin, S. (2019, August 8). *Less state funding to public colleges = fewer students with a degree.* National College Access Network. https://collegeaccess.org/news/464929/Less-State-Funding-to-Public-Colleges--Fewer-Students-with-a-Degree.htm

Cohen, A. C., Brawer, F. B., & Kisker, C. B. (2014). *The American community college* (6th ed.). Jossey-Bass.

Cronin, W. (1999). "Only connect": The goals of a liberal education. *Liberal Education, 85*(1), 6–13. https://www.grinnell.edu/sites/default/files/documents/Cronon_Only_Connect.pdf.

Dalpes, P., Baston, M. A., & Sanchez, F. D. (2015). Community college student affairs professionals at entry and mid-level. In A. Tull, L. Kuk, & P. Dalpes (Eds.), *Handbook for student affairs in community colleges* (pp. 281–297). Stylus.

DeMinck, D. K. (2017). *Female student affairs professionals and work–life balance* [Unpublished doctoral dissertation]. St. Cloud State University.

Ginder, S. A., Kelly-Reid, J. E., & Mann, F. B. (2017). *Enrollment and employees in postsecondary institutions, fall 2016; and financial statistics and academic libraries, fiscal year 2016. First look (provisional data, NCES 2018-002).* National Center for Education Statistics.

Hirt, J. B. (2006). *Where you work matters: Student affairs administration at different types of institutions.* University Press of America.

Hirt, J. B. (2009). The influence of institutional type on socialization. In A. Tull, J. B. Hirt, & S. A. Saunders (Eds.), *Becoming socialized in student affairs administration* (pp. 45–66). Stylus.

Hirt, J. B., Schneiter, S. R., & Amelink, C. T. (2005). The nature of relationships and rewards for student affairs professionals at liberal arts institutions. *College Student Affairs Journal, 25*(1), 6–19.

Hornak, A. M., Ozaki, C. C., & Lunceford, C. (2016). Socialization for new and mid-level community college student affairs professionals. *Journal of Student Affairs Research and Practice, 53*(2), 118–130. https://doi.org/10.1080/19496591 .2016.1143833

Indiana University Center for Postsecondary Research. (2015). *The Carnegie classification of institutions of higher education.* Author.

Keeling, R. P., Underhile, R., & Wall, A. F. (2007). Horizontal and vertical structures: The dynamics of organization in higher education. *Liberal Education, 93*(4), 22–31.

Kuk, L. (2016). Organizational and administrative models within student affairs. In G. McClellan & J. Stringer (Eds.), *The handbook of student affairs administration* (pp. 367–387). Jossey-Bass.

Latz, A. O., Ozaki, C. C., Royer, D. W., & Hornak, A. M. (2017). Student affairs professionals in the community college: Critically examining preparation programs from a social justice lens. *Community College Journal of Research and Practice, 41*(11), 733–746. https://doi.org/10.1080/10668926.2016.1222507

Ma, J., & Baum, S. (2016). *Research brief: Trends in community colleges: Enrollment, prices, student debt, & completion.* College Board. https://trends.collegeboard.org/ sites/default/files/trends-in-community-colleges-research-brief.pdf

MacGregor, K. (2017). Advocating the public mission of research universities. *University World News.* http://www.universityworldnews.com/article.php?story= 20171114091327738

McFadden, C. W., & Mazeika, M. (2014). Academic and student affairs collaboration: A value for student success in the community college environment. In L. S. Kelsay & E. M. Zamani-Gallaher (Eds.), *Working with students in community colleges: Contemporary strategies for bridging theory, research, and practice* (pp. 67–80). Stylus.

National Center for Public Policy and Higher Education. (2011). *Policy alert: Affordability and transfer: Critical to increasing baccalaureate degree and completion.* http://www.highereducation.org/reports/pa_at/index.shtml

National Student Clearinghouse Research Center. (2017). *Contribution of two-year public institutions to bachelor's completions at four-year institutions.* https:// nscresearchcenter.org/wp-content/uploads/SnapshotReport26.pdf

Nunez, E. M. (2013). Collaborative leadership on a liberal arts campus: Supporting student engagement. *Peer Review, 15*(1).

Perez, R. J. (2016). A conceptual model of professional socialization within student affairs graduate preparation programs. *Journal for the Study of Postsecondary and Tertiary Education, 1,* 35–52. https://doi.org/10.28945/2344

Renn, K. A., & Hodges, J. P. (2007). The first year on the job: Experiences of new professionals in student affairs. *NASPA Journal, 44*(2), 367–391. https://doi.org/ 10.2202/0027-6014.1800

Renn, K. A., & Jessup-Anger, E. R. (2008). Preparing new professionals: Lessons for graduate preparation programs from the national study of new professionals in student affairs. *Journal of College Student Development, 49*(4), 319–335. https://doi.org/10.1353/csd.0.0022

Royer, D. W., & Latz, A. O. (2016). Community college leadership transition through the framework of appreciative inquiry. *Community College Journal of Research and Practice, 40*(8), 695–705. https://doi.org/10.1080/10668926.2015.1072594

Sallee, M. W. (2016). Ideal for whom? A cultural analysis of ideal worker norms in higher education and student affairs graduate programs. *New Directions for Higher Education, 2016*(176), 53–67. https://doi.org/10.1002/he.20209

Sandeen, A., & Barr, M. J. (2006). *Critical issues in student affairs: Challenges and opportunities.* Jossey-Bass.

Schuh, J. H., Jones, S. R., & Torres, V. (2017). *Student services: A handbook for the profession* (6th ed.). Jossey-Bass.

Seltzer, R. (2017, October 17). Aiming for billions: an increased focus on fundraising meets a surging stock market to create ideal conditions for campaigns. *Inside Higher Ed.* https://www.insidehighered.com/news/2017/10/17/colleges-and-universities-set-high-targets-latest-fund-raising-campaigns

Shapiro, D., Dundar, A., Huie, F., Wakhungu, P., Yuan, X., Nathan, A., & Hwang, Y. A. (2017). *Completing college: A national view of student attainment rates by race & ethnicity—Fall 2010 Cohort* (Signature Report No. 12b). National Student Clearinghouse Research Center. https://nscresearchcenter.org/signaturereport12-supplement-2/

Tull, A., Hirt, J. B., & Saunders, S. A. (Eds.). (2009). *Becoming socialized in student affairs administration.* Stylus.

Van Maanen, J., & Schein, E. H. (1979). Toward a theory of organizational socialization. *Research in Organizational Behavior, 1,* 209–264.

Ward, K., & Wolf-Wendel, L. (2016). Academic motherhood: Mid-career perspectives and the ideal worker norm. *New Directions for Higher Education, 2016*(176), 11–23. https://doi.org/10.1002/he.20206

Weidman, J. C., Twale, D. J., & Stein, E. L. (2001). *Socialization of graduate and professional students in higher education: A perilous passage? ASHE-ERIC Higher Education Report, 28.* Jossey-Bass.

Wilk, K. E. (2016). Work–life balance and ideal worker expectations for administrators. *New Directions for Higher Education, 2016*(176), 37–51. https://doi.org/10.1002/he.20208

5

PROBLEMATIZING SOCIALIZATION IN STUDENT AFFAIRS GRADUATE TRAINING

Rosemary J. Perez

E ach year, I find myself sitting in advising meetings with student affairs master's students who look utterly exhausted. When I ask them how they are doing, they often reply, "Busy, but good" and proceed to talk about their assistantship and courses before sharing a lengthy list of things they are doing to "get more experiences" in the field. In response, I usually ask why they are doing so much, and it's not uncommon for students to say, "That's what student affairs people do. It seems like everyone else is doing as much or more." This pressure to "do more" is often compounded for minoritized graduate students, who regularly talk to me about the obligation they have to support and advocate for undergraduates who hold similar identities.

Although I have not told my advisees they need to do as much as humanly possible during their master's degree training, they have received subtle messages that they should participate in as many professional development opportunities as possible if they are to be marketable and prepared to enter the field. As an adviser, I regularly challenge the notion that master's degree students need to do extra work while they are pursuing their degree. I talk to students about the importance of managing their time and energy if they are to continue working in the field long term, because the goal of student affairs preparation programs is not to burn students out before they begin their post-master's degree careers. And yet, I know that telling students they should not overwork is unlikely to change their behaviors, because my comments run counter to more prevalent messages they receive about what it means to be a good student affairs educator. Furthermore, minoritized student affairs educators are often taxed with providing additional support to students and engaging in service to the university to advance inclusion at the cost of their well-being.

With this in mind, I draw upon my previous research and other literature to explore the nature of student affairs graduate training and problematize the dominant model of practitioner socialization in this chapter. Specifically, I consider the ways in which the content and structure of many student affairs graduate training programs socialize newer professionals to construct understandings of professionalism and good practice that perpetuate the notion of the ideal worker (Acker, 1990), or someone who is willing to overwork and sacrifice their well-being to serve students. I also argue that the ideal worker construct in student affairs is not identity- or power-neutral. Rather, the image of the ideal worker in the field reflects those who are White, male, cisgender, heterosexual, and/or middle-class people without disabilities or familial caregiving responsibilities (Bondi, 2012; Rios, 2015; Sallee, 2015). With this definition of the ideal worker in mind, I explore those groups student affairs graduate training serves well and examine how preparation programs contribute to the marginalization of groups with minoritized identities. I conclude the chapter with recommendations for practice that are designed to foster greater self-awareness and to create more holistic educational experiences for newer professionals.

Graduate Education and Professional Socialization

Across disciplines and fields, graduate education is designed to cultivate experts with the knowledge, skills, and habits of mind that will advance research and practice (Bok, 2013; Conrad et al., 1993; Gardner & Mendoza, 2010). While the primary purpose of master's degree and doctoral education is to foster expertise within a particular area of study, some scholars have argued that graduate training should contribute to the democratic aims of higher education by also preparing individuals to address societal challenges (Cassuto, 2015; Gardner & Mendoza, 2010; Wendler et al., 2010). In service of both aims, graduate education is structured to socialize graduate students to the norms and standards of their respective disciplinary and professional communities (Gardner & Mendoza, 2010; Golde, 2006; Perez, 2016).

Socialization Theory

Socialization refers to how newcomers learn and come to understand the cultural norms, values, standards, and practices that are part of a group or community (Grusec & Hastings, 2007). Although socialization occurs in a variety of contexts, Moore (1970) was particularly interested in how newcomers enter professions. He coined the term *professional socialization*, which he defined as "acquiring the requisite knowledge and skills and also the sense of occupational identity and internalization of occupational norms typical of the fully qualified practitioner" (p. 71). Subsequent models of professional socialization have focused on how groups structure newcomers' organizational entry (e.g., Van Maanen, 1978; Van Maanen & Schein, 1979) or the stages individuals experience as they enter a group or community (e.g., Wanous, 1992; Weidman et al., 2001). Notably, models that focus on the structure of professional socialization (i.e., organizational perspectives) frequently describe socialization as a unidirectional process where organizations engage in "people processing" (Van Maanen, 1978, p. 19). In contrast, models that attend to individual perspectives better account for newcomers' agency in the socialization process as they make meaning of their experiences and potentially influence the culture and practice of their organizations (Feldman, 1994; Weidman et al., 2001).

Regardless of approach, professional socialization is designed to foster values acquisition, commitment to the field, organizational loyalty, the development of a professional identity, and the expansion of skills for the workplace (Ashforth et al., 2007; Perez, 2016; Van Maanen & Schein, 1979; Weidman et al., 2001). Thus, professional socialization is designed to perpetuate ideal worker norms and to cultivate individuals who are devoted, committed, and equipped to meet an organization's needs and to help it achieve its goals. Moreover, ideal worker norms require individuals to put the interests of the organization above their own needs and goals. When situated in the context of student affairs graduate education, the goal is to produce an individual who possesses the field-level expertise to advance research and practice in the field and who will help their organization (e.g., college/university, department) meet its objectives (e.g., promoting student learning and development, increasing retention). In effect, socialization theories focus on the process of social reproduction within groups such as professions and, to a lesser degree, highlight individual agency as people navigate the constraints and systems that exist within the groups they are entering.

Socialization in Student Affairs Graduate Preparation Programs

Although there are many pathways into the field, student affairs graduate preparation programs are the primary means of socializing newcomers to student affairs practice. Because it is an applied field of practice, most student affairs graduate preparation programs use a dual training system of coursework and concurrent fieldwork (i.e., assistantships, practica, full-time positions) to provide individuals with the knowledge and skills that are associated with being an effective student affairs educator (Perez, 2016). Across these components, graduate students are exposed to values, beliefs, and standards that guide the field. In concept, coursework and fieldwork should be aligned, in that they are supposed to provide consistent messages about what it means to engage in good practice as a student affairs educator. Ultimately, creating continuity in messaging about the norms, beliefs, and values of the field and how they should be enacted increases the likelihood that new practitioners leave their graduate training programs as individuals who are committed to the field and its approach to supporting the learning and development of college students (Perez, 2016, 2017).

Socialization is a helpful framework for understanding how student affairs educators learn the norms and standards of the field and for illuminating how the field perpetuates constructions of the ideal worker (Acker, 1990). Here, I explore how socialization in student affairs graduate preparation programs can contribute to the marginalization of master's degree students who are racially minoritized, who work full-time, who are older than their peers, and who are parents.

Socialization to Student Affairs Values in Preparation Programs

Given the aims of student affairs preparation programs, much of what is taught reflects the highest aspirations and goals of the field. For example, many faculty use historical documents such as the *Student Personnel Point of View* (American Council on Education, 1983a, 1983b) and *Learning Reconsidered* (Keeling, 2004) to introduce graduate students to the over-arching mission of student affairs and to the values and beliefs that should guide practice in the field. Furthermore, faculty may review the American College Personnel Association (ACPA) and National Association of Student Personnel Administrators (NASPA) competencies (2015) and the Council for the Advancement of Standards in Higher Education (CAS) standards (Council for the Advancement of Standards in Higher Education, 2015) to convey field-level beliefs about the nature of effective and ethical student affairs practice. However, lessons in classes about the nature of good practice in student affairs may or may not be reflected in a student's fieldwork experiences. For example, in my qualitative longitudinal study of student affairs master's degree students, some participants described being taught the importance of holistic development and social justice in their courses but were rewarded in their assistantship for working efficiently, even if that meant not fully attending to students' learning and development and being inclusive in their practice. In this regard, some participants' efforts to be the ideal worker as defined by their assistantship provider required them to move away from enacting the student affairs values they had learned in classes and their own values (Perez, 2014, 2017). However, the gaps between coursework and fieldwork may have unexpected benefits for some students. In particular, graduate students may learn additional lessons about the nature of effective student affairs practice that are not always taught or that may be more difficult to convey via coursework, such as how to navigate political environments.

The inconsistencies I observed across students' coursework and fieldwork experiences highlighted the potential for gaps in content and pedagogy within student affairs preparation programs (Perez, 2014, 2017). Young and Elfrink (1991) found that student affairs preparation program faculty widely agreed on the essential values of the field. Specifically, faculty members indicated that values such as altruism, equality, freedom, human dignity, justice, truth, and community should guide student affairs practice. The faculty members surveyed indicated that they taught these values formally in classes and informally via role modeling (Young & Elfrink, 1991). Although diversity, social justice, and inclusion (ACPA & NASPA, 2015; American Council on Education, 1983a, 1983b; Young & Elfrink, 1991) are consistently espoused as core commitments within student affairs, these values are not always enacted within graduate preparation programs. For example, student affairs graduate programs have not regularly offered coursework to develop students' cross-cultural knowledge and skills nor have they always examined how power, privilege, and oppression relate to student affairs practice (Flowers, 2003; Gaston Gayles & Kelly, 2007; Talbot, 1996). Currently, diversity and social justice courses are more regularly offered in student affairs preparation programs to create alignment with ACPA and NASPA (2015) and the CAS (2015) standards; however, students can have inequitable experiences and feel marginalized as they navigate their programs and take courses designed to teach them about social justice and inclusion.

For instance, Flowers and Howard-Hamilton (2002) found that racially minoritized student affairs master's degree candidates often reported feeling alienated and marginalized because they did not see themselves reflected among their peers and their faculty members. Moreover, their participants described feeling dismissed by some White faculty members and recounted experiencing racial microaggressions in their classes, such as being asked to speak for their race. More than 10 years later, Linder et al.'s (2015) national study of racially minoritized master's degree candidates in student affairs graduate preparation programs yielded similar insights. While many racially minoritized participants were drawn to student affairs and their particular programs given their stated commitments to social justice and inclusion, many found that their faculty members had varying abilities to engage in meaningful conversations related to race and racism, which in turn placed more of a burden upon them to educate their White peers (Linder et al., 2015). Thus, many student affairs preparation programs attend to the learning and comfort of White students at the cost of the learning and well-being of racially minoritized students (Bondi, 2012; Linder et al., 2015; Robbins, 2016). In doing so, many student affairs graduate preparation programs centralize Whiteness in the teaching and learning process as individuals learn what it means to be a "good professional." Ultimately, centralizing Whiteness in graduate training programs conveys that the ideal worker in student affairs is White or is someone who conforms to and upholds Whiteness as the cultural norm.

Furthermore, student affairs graduate preparation programs can create challenges for master's degree candidates who are parents or who are older than their peers (Sallee, 2015; Witkowsky et al., 2018). For example, Sallee (2015) found "the demands of graduate study to be at odds with the demands of parenthood" (p. 410). Although many of Sallee's participants were adept at managing their time, they often needed to make choices about how to best fulfill their academic, familial, and professional responsibilities that required making compromises and limiting engagement. Similarly, the nontraditional women in Witkowsky et al.'s (2018) study described "re(negotiating) and (re)prioritizing" (p. 173) their roles in order to navigate the demands of work, family, and graduate school. For nontraditional student affairs students, such as those who are parents, older, and/or working full time, flexibility and support at work and within preparation programs was invaluable as they navigated multiple roles and demands. However, some participants were not consistently given the support needed, which made it more difficult to fulfill their multiple and at times conflicting responsibilities as they engaged in work–life negotiation (Sallee, 2015; Witkowsky et al., 2018).

Despite the field's espoused commitments to holistic development and inclusion (ACPA & NASPA, 2015; American Council on Education, 1983a, 1983b), nontraditional graduate students are not consistently afforded the opportunity to be whole, and, as such, they must compartmentalize their identities and experiences in order to meet the demands of the field. In effect, the structure and culture of many student affairs preparation programs are designed to best support the success of students who do not have familial responsibilities and who are not working full time. Though not stated explicitly, some graduate preparation programs send the message that the ideal early career student affairs educator is young and should not have familial commitments that would detract from their abilities to serve students.

Ultimately, a growing body of research suggests that student affairs preparation programs best serve those who are White, who are not parents, and who do not work full time (Bondi, 2012; Flowers & Howard-Hamilton, 2002; Linder et al., 2015; Sallee, 2015; Witkowsky et al., 2018). In addition to transmitting to newer practitioners the norms, values, beliefs, and standards that guide the field, student affairs graduate preparation programs also perpetuate and reproduce the systems of oppression they are embedded within by centralizing Whiteness and the experiences of those who do not have competing familial or professional responsibilities. The tensions of contributing to social reproduction and social change are constant within student affairs graduate education. However, it is unclear how often the field acknowledges these tensions, given the struggle of many preparation programs to fully honor and include those with minoritized identities.

Socialization to Constructions of Professionalism in Preparation Programs

Although research has explored how new practitioners learn about student affairs values (Bureau, 2011; Perez, 2017) and the extent to which they acquire the skills needed to work in the field full time (Burkard et al., 2005; Cooper et al., 2016; Herdlein, 2004; Renn & Jessup-Anger, 2008), there is limited research about how the field socializes individuals to notions of professionalism. Often, graduate preparation programs use the ACPA and NASPA competencies, the CAS standards, and historical documents (American Council on Education, 1983a, 1983b; Keeling, 2004) to situate the nature of good practice in the field. These documents highlight the bodies of knowledge, skills, and habits of mind that student affairs educators should possess if they are to serve students well. However, they do not clearly articulate what constitutes professionalism in the field, because this concept can be more difficult to define.

The concept of professionalism is purposefully ambiguous because it is "both an ideology of control and a mechanism for promoting adaptation and change at the macro level as well as a disciplinary mechanism at the level of individual 'professionalized' practitioners and employees" (Evetts, 2003, p. 24). This ambiguity allows groups to use the concept of professionalism to both create change across the field and to constrain individuals who do not conform to the dominant ideology of the profession. For example, graduate students and new professionals who do not adhere to the norms of the field or who actively challenge them may be told things like, "You won't get hired if you act like that." Alternatively, individuals receive unsolicited advice on how they should change their dress, behavior, and/or "attitude" to be viewed as more professional (i.e., aligned with dominant culture and, in turn, more desirable to employers). Graduate students and newer practitioners are also repeatedly told, "The field is small." Although this comment ostensibly reflects the potential benefits of and opportunities for building relationships with peers and colleagues, it is also a tool for reinforcing hegemonic views of professionalism. Essentially, individuals get the message that if they do not conform to the norms of the field and constructions of the ideal worker, their reputation and their employability will be damaged, because colleagues will speak negatively about them to others (Rios, 2015). In effect, fields such as student affairs assume shared understandings and commitments to professionalism without specifying what constitutes professionalism, which benefits some individuals to the detriment of others. Those who conform to ideal worker norms or who hold identities aligned with images of the ideal worker (Acker, 1990) in student affairs benefit from hegemonic constructions of professionalism, while those who resist these norms or who hold minoritized identities are constrained by them.

Carpenter and Stimpson's (2007) metasynthesis of student affairs literature on professionalism exemplifies the ambiguity of this concept in the field. Although they explored the nature of professionalism across multiple studies and reports, they did not define the concept for the reader. Rather, Carpenter and Stimpson focused on the process of professionalization and on the need for professional development in student affairs. Accordingly, student affairs educators may assume that professional development opportunities, including graduate preparation programs, teach individuals how to be a professional and how to approach work in a professional manner, even though these professional development opportunities fail to articulate what professionalism is and what it is not. In this regard, completing a student affairs preparation program may be viewed as certifying one's commitment to and abilities to enact definitions of professionalism that are ambiguous and are assumed to be constant across the field.

Within student affairs graduate preparation programs, the lack of clarity about what constitutes professionalism manifests itself in myriad ways and has numerous implications for newcomers. For example, some individuals may use the ACPA and NASPA (2015) competencies and their associated rubrics as a checklist to determine if they are qualified student affairs educators. However, possessing competency does not always mean that individuals are viewed as enacting professionalism. Rather than focusing on what people are able to do (i.e., competency), professionalism often attends to how people should engage in their work and demonstrate competency given the norms of the field. There is no rubric for gauging student affairs educators' professionalism, because that concept is thought to be broadly agreed upon and is (re)defined in institutional, functional area, and departmental contexts. If individuals rely too heavily on the ACPA and NASPA rubrics, they may be viewed as lacking desirable traits such as creativity or the ability to think independently despite possessing the competencies that guide the field. Furthermore, graduate students may develop an understanding of professionalism based on the idealized images of practice they discuss in classes and may find that these notions are not consistently enacted within and across their coursework and fieldwork (Perez, 2014, 2017). Discrepancies in how professionalism is defined and in turn demonstrated across graduate preparation experiences has the potential to lead newcomers to feel disappointed in and disillusioned with student affairs, which ultimately may lead them to revisit whether student affairs is the right field for them (Perez, 2014, 2017).

Although student affairs graduate preparation programs may not explicitly define professionalism, they can convey powerful messages about its nature. For example, a participant in my study of student affairs master's degree candidates described professionalism as a process of "perception management" (Perez, 2017, p. 841) in which they had to consistently work to meet the program's expectations of how to be a good student affairs educator. In this program, students received both explicit and tacit messages about how to dress, how to communicate, and how to pursue professional development if they were to be viewed as good professionals. Within this preparation program, professionalism was both embodied through constructions of acceptable dress and enacted through appropriate means of communication and pursing professional learning opportunities. Several participants in this program felt immense pressure to meet their graduate preparation program's expectations, which at times led them to feel as though they had to sacrifice their own values and ways of being in favor of performing their program's construction of professionalism. These individuals felt tension as they moved toward being the ideal worker in student affairs whose image and way of being was aligned with a single prescribed definition of professionalism. In effect, some participants wondered aloud if being a good student affairs educator required them to not be their full, authentic selves (Perez, 2017).

Although participants in my dissertation study did not name them as such, constructions of appropriateness in graduate preparation programs related to dress, communicating, and achievement were often rooted in White, male, middle-class standards. Notions of professionalism in student affairs have the potential to "reinforce social hierarchies that value White maleness above all" (Rios, 2015, para. 3) and require individuals who do not hold those identities to conform to dominant norms in order to be respected and taken seriously. In service of preparing educators who can engage in good practice, student affairs preparation programs often perpetuate images of professionalism that are rooted in racism, cissexism, classism, heterosexism, and ableism. Thus, ambiguous constructions of professionalism are also intended to perpetuate systems of oppression in addition to advancing claims of legitimacy in the field. While the notion of professionalism may support the validity of student affairs work in the academy, these claims come at the cost of silencing, marginalizing, and discounting the voices, values, and cultures of minoritized individuals.

Problematizing Professionalism in Student Affairs Preparation Programs

Student affairs graduate preparation programs are vital for training newer practitioners for work in the field. However, there is a need to scrutinize both the content and structure of graduate training, because preparation programs often struggle to enact the values that guide the field, to the detriment of minoritized students. After robust discussion, the field developed competencies and standards that guide both graduate preparation programs and full-time student affairs practice (ACPA & NASPA, 2015; CAS, 2015). In contrast, notions of professionalism often remain ambiguous in preparation programs, despite discussion about the concept in coursework and fieldwork. Professionalism may be undefined in preparation programs because faculty members may have a desire for students to develop their own definition of what it means to be a professional. However, newer practitioners are often not afforded the time to develop their personal definition of professionalism because they are regularly expected to enact unarticulated constructions of professionalism that are thought to be widely understood. In this regard, graduate students are particularly vulnerable to the paradox of professionalism because they occupy liminal space while enrolled in preparation programs. They are positioned as students and emerging professionals in some academic and work settings, yet they are expected to perform in a similar manner to full-time practitioners in other venues.

While faculty members and those who supervise graduate students often say they want new student affairs educators to create their own understandings of good practice and professionalism, the demands placed upon graduate students to enact the stated and unstated standards of the field are constant. Moreover, the field and, in turn, its preparation programs tend to frame notions of good practice, ideal worker norms (Acker, 1990), and professionalism as identity- and power-neutral because they are intended to encompass the perspectives of a diverse workforce of educators who are committed to serving all students well. Notions of neutrality may be intended to signal inclusiveness; however, the constructions of good practice and professionalism that guide student affairs are not identity- and power-neutral. As previously noted, these standards tend to reflect dominant ideologies and centralize the experiences of those who are White, male, cisgender, heterosexual, and/or middle-class, and those who do not have a disability and/or familial caregiving responsibilities (Bondi, 2012; Rios, 2015; Sallee, 2015). In the process of training and supporting the learning of student affairs educators, preparation programs' focus on cultivating professionalism may also reinforce the systems of oppression that the field espouses commitment to dismantling (ACPA & NASPA, 2015).

Furthermore, the student affairs field consistently talks about the need for work–life balance in order to retain new practitioners (e.g., Lorden, 1998; Marshall et al., 2016). However, constructions of what it means to be a good educator are often in opposition to the espoused commitment to holistic development (ACPA & NASPA, 2015; American Council on Education, 1983a, 1983American Council on Education, 1983b). In service of being a good professional who is competent and competitive for positions after graduation, graduate students often learn unhealthy and unsustainable ways of engaging in work as they observe those around them (Perez, 2014, 2017). Specifically, graduate students may gather that being a good student affairs educator involves demonstrating care and concern for students in ways that require overworking and self-sacrificing well-being. They may also learn that being a practitioner who is committed to continuous professional development requires overcommitting to service opportunities (e.g., committees, conferences, leadership roles). These demands are consistently intensified for minoritized graduate students and practitioners who contribute additional emotional labor to support those with similar identities and to educate and challenge those with dominant socially constructed identities (Bondi, 2012; Linder et al., 2015; Robbins, 2016). In this regard, efforts to meet ideal worker norms have additional costs for those who are minoritized.

Many graduate preparation programs reflect the unhealthy standards of the field because they are not designed to consistently contribute to practitioners' well-being and to honor their multiple life roles and responsibilities (Sallee, 2015; Witkowsky et al., 2018). Efforts to reinforce notions of good practice and professionalism during graduate preparation concurrently contribute to the marginalization of minoritized student affairs educators and can detract from individuals' physical, mental, emotional, and spiritual well-being. However, student affairs preparation programs have the potential to be emancipatory. It is possible for preparation programs to provide graduate students with opportunities to learn the knowledge, skills, and competencies that ground student affairs practice and to be a tool for changing the culture of the field. However, transforming student affairs requires more consistent and critical examination of how the field defines professionalism and how this affects the ways in which graduate preparation programs socialize individuals to constructions of the ideal worker.

Recommendations for Practice

To create greater alignment between the field's espoused and enacted values, student affairs educators need to interrogate their thinking about good practice and professionalism and the messages they send to graduate students. Furthermore, the field needs to more openly discuss how constructions of professionalism constrain and/or benefit individuals, depending on their socially constructed identities, their position within their organization's hierarchy, their institution's climate and culture, and their individual roles and responsibilities. Student affairs educators should also regularly wrestle with the discrepancies between what they espouse and enact as individuals as they work toward being good professionals. In doing so, it is imperative that individuals consider how the gaps between their aspirations and their actions (or lack thereof) affect others.

Student affairs uses professionalism to both increase its legitimacy in the academy and promote conformity to norms and standards of the field, even if these norms and standards are problematic at times. Rather than creating fear and penalizing individuals who do not conform, the field has the potential to trouble notions of professionalism in student affairs without compromising shared commitments to cultivating educators' competencies and to promoting students' learning and development. Interrogating individual and collective understandings of professionalism has the potential to create expansive views of good practice and better support the field's efforts to promote social justice and inclusion. This process can be particularly powerful within graduate preparation programs because these spaces are designed to socialize newcomers to the field in ways that can constrain and support their agency.

Recommendations for Graduate Students and New Professionals

With these critiques in mind, graduate students and new professionals should engage in regular reflection and discussions with colleagues about constructions of professionalism. It may be beneficial to explore these questions on a regular basis:

- How do I currently define *professionalism* and how did I come to this definition?
- How do I feel when I hear the word professionalism? Where do these feelings come from?
- How does my current definition of *professionalism* align with the dominant views in the field? The dominant views of graduate preparation programs? The dominant views of my institution?
- What messages have I been given about what will happen if I don't uphold the standards of professionalism in my program? In my assistantship? In the field?
- How am I navigating any differences between my views of professionalism and those of my professional communities?

By reflecting upon and articulating how they define professionalism in student affairs, graduate students and newer practitioners can develop a better understanding of themselves and of tensions that may surface as they navigate the field.

In addition to considering the nature of professionalism, it would be beneficial for graduate students and newer practitioners to regularly reflect on their experiences in the field and visions for the future. For example, it may be helpful to revisit questions such as the following:

- What brought me to student affairs practice?
- What leads me to stay in the field?
- What would lead me to leave the field?
- What do I need to be whole as I do this work? Are these factors present in my current workplace? In this field?

These questions may be useful to newcomers as they make sense of any mixed messages that they receive about the nature of good practice and professionalism in student affairs. Moreover, these reflection questions are intended to remind individuals that they have agency during the (re)socialization process despite the constraints they experience during graduate school.

With this said, graduate students should name and identify the contradictory messages they receive about professionalism and good practice. Perhaps more importantly, graduate students should challenge their faculty, supervisors, and colleagues when their espoused and enacted values do not align and when their actions perpetuate the exclusion and subordination of minoritized peoples. Although challenging others with positional authority may come with costs, it may be even more damaging to graduate students in the long run if they do not resist the pressure to conform to shifting definitions of professionalism and enact ideal worker norms that require sacrificing their well-being to meet the goals of their employer and of the field.

Recommendations for Graduate Preparation Programs

As I have previously noted, graduate programs are imperative to preparing student affairs educators to work in the field. Although preparation programs provide practitioners with valuable knowledge and skills for student affairs practice, they may also send harmful messages that contribute to a culture that promotes overworking and continually marginalizes those with minoritized identities. Faculty members and assistantship providers need to more openly acknowledge these tensions within programs and discuss them with graduate students if the field of student affairs is to create more continuity between its espoused and enacted values.

Moreover, preparation program faculty members need to more regularly engage in the kind of reflection they ask graduate students to do in service of becoming more reflexive practitioners. Both faculty and assistantship providers can individually reflect upon and subsequently discuss questions such as the following:

- How do I currently define *professionalism* and how did I come to this definition?
- How would I characterize the ideal worker in student affairs? What has influenced my views?
- What messages am I sending graduate students about the nature of professionalism? How am I conveying these messages?
- How does my department teach graduate students about professionalism and constructions of the ideal worker in student affairs?
- How do I respond when a graduate student behaves in ways that I perceive to be unprofessional? What informs my response? How do I respond when a colleague engages in what I define as unprofessional behavior? What informs my response?

- How can I contest notions of professionalism and of ideal worker norms in student affairs that contribute to the marginalization and subordination of minoritized students and colleagues?

By engaging in reflection and discussion with colleagues, faculty members and assistantship providers can make their underlying assumptions and beliefs more explicit. In doing so, they may better understand mixed messages that are sent to graduate students about how to be a good professional. More importantly, faculty members and assistantship providers should use reflection to explore how constructions of professionalism contribute to the marginalization of minoritized student affairs educators. In turn, they can work to honor an array of approaches to good practice in the field and in preparation programs by creating more inclusive policies and using more inclusive teaching, advising, and supervision practices.

Faculty need to regularly trouble the concept of professionalism with graduate students by more openly discussing its ambiguity and the implications this has for the field. Acknowledging the tensions of professionalism and how it is used to both advance and constrain behavior is beneficial for graduate students who are trying to understand values of the field and how they are or are not enacted. Specifically, faculty can normalize the contradictions that exist in the field and think through how to collectively work to create alignment between espoused and enacted values. Discussions such as these may also help faculty members and assistantship providers recognize how their actions reinforce and/or challenge dominant views of professionalism in student affairs and the effects these actions have on graduate students.

Recommendations for Midlevel Professionals, Supervisors, and Senior Student Affairs Officers

Although this chapter focuses on student affairs preparation programs, the topics explored have relevance for midlevel, divisional, and institutional leaders in the field. For example, those with positional authority in the field should also engage in regular reflection and discussion about their definitions of good practice and professionalism in student affairs. By participating in sustained reflection, departmental, divisional, and institutional leaders are in a better position to make their underlying assumptions explicit. Subsequently, these leaders can consider and examine how these underlying assumptions about good practice and professionalism influence their decision-making during hiring processes, setting expectations in the workplace (e.g., dress, communication), creating policies (e.g., use of leave), and evaluating employee performance. These leaders can also work to make departmental, divisional, and institutional policies and practices more inclusive so they serve more than a narrow range of students and educators who hold dominant identities. Additionally, these leaders should examine who is rewarded for enacting ideal worker norms and who is penalized for not sacrificing their well-being for the organization. Acknowledging and rewarding individuals for their efforts to create work–life balance has the potential to create better, more inclusive work environments that may foster greater satisfaction with and retention in the field.

Conclusion

Student affairs graduate preparation programs reflect the tensions of many social institutions in that they are forums for both perpetuating and challenging hegemonic views and social inequalities. More consistent and critical examinations of how student affairs educators talk (or do not talk) about professionalism, how they enact their values, and how they reward and penalize individuals based on definitions of professionalism are vital for improving graduate preparation programs. Complicating understandings of professionalism in student affairs has the potential to move the field to being more equitable and inclusive in practice while concurrently allowing student affairs educators to serve students well.

References

Acker, J. (1990). Hierarchies, jobs, bodies: A theory of gendered organizations. *Gender & Society, 4*(2), 139–158. https://doi.org/10.1177/089124390004002002

American College Personnel Association & National Association of Student Personnel Administrators. (2015). *ACPA/ NASPA professional competency areas for student affairs practitioners* (2nd ed.). Author.

American Council on Education. (1983a). The student personnel point of view: A report of a conference on the philosophy and development of student personnel work in colleges and universities. In G. L. Saddlemire & A. L. Rentz (Eds.), *Student affairs—A profession's heritage: Significant articles, authors, issues, and documents* (pp. 74–87). Southern Illinois University Press. (Original work published 1937).

American Council on Education. (1983b). The student personnel point of view. In G. L. Saddlemire & A. L. Rentz (Eds.), *Student affairs—A profession's heritage: Significant articles, authors, issues, and documents* (pp. 122–140). Southern Illinois University Press. (Original work published 1949).

Ashforth, B. E., Sluss, D. M., & Harrison, S. H. (2007). Socialization in organizational contexts. In G. P. Hodgkinson & J. K. Ford (Eds.), *International review of industrial and organizational psychology* (pp. 221–270). Wiley.

Bok, D. (2013). *Higher education in America*. Princeton University Press.

Bondi, S. (2012). Students and institutions protecting whiteness as property: A critical race theory analysis of student affairs preparation. *Journal of Student Affairs Research and Practice*, *49*(4), 397–414. https://doi.org/10.1515/jsarp-2012-6381

Bureau, D. A. (2011). *"Making them my own": Student affairs master's students' socialization to professional values* (Publication No. 3456444) [Doctoral dissertation, Indiana University]. ProQuest Dissertations and Theses Global.

Burkard, A. W., Cole, D. C., Ott, M., & Stoflet, T. (2005). Entry-level competencies of new student affairs professionals: A Delphi study. *NASPA Journal*, *42*(3), 283–308. https://doi.org/10.2202/1949-6605.1509

Carpenter, S., & Stimpson, M. T. (2007). Professionalism, scholarly practice, and professional development in student affairs. *NASPA Journal*, *44*(2), 265–284. https://doi.org/10.2202/1949-6605.1795

Cassuto, L. (2015). *The graduate school mess: What caused it and how we can fix it*. Harvard University Press.

Conrad, C., Haworth, J. H., & Millar, S. (1993). Historic and contemporary perspectives on education. In C. Conrad, J. H. Haworth, & S. Millar (Eds.), *A silent success: Master's education in the United States* (pp. 3–27). Johns Hopkins University Press.

Cooper, J., Mitchell, D., Eckerle, K., & Martin, K. (2016). Addressing perceived skill deficiencies in student affairs graduate preparation programs. *Journal of Student Affairs Research and Practice*, *53*(2), 107–117. https://doi.org/10.1080/19496591.2016.1121146

Council for the Advancement of Standards in Higher Education. (2015). *CAS professional standards for higher education* (9th ed.). Author.

Evetts, J. (2003). The construction of professionalism in new and existing occupational contexts: Promoting and facilitating occupational change. *International Journal of Sociology and Social Policy*, *23*(4/5), 22–35. https://doi.org/10.1108/01443330310790499

Feldman, D. C. (1994). Who's socializing whom? The impact of socializing newcomers on insiders, workgroups, and organizations. *Human Resource Management Review*, *4*(3), 213–233. https://doi.org/10.1016/1053-4822(94)90013-2

Flowers, L. A. (2003). National study of diversity requirements in student affairs graduate programs. *NASPA Journal*, *40*(4), 72–81. https://doi.org/10.2202/1949-6605.1281

Flowers, L. A., & Howard-Hamilton, M. F. (2002). A qualitative study of graduate students' perceptions of diversity issues in student affairs preparation programs. *Journal of College Student Development*, *43*(1), 119–123.

Gardner, S. K., & Mendoza, P. (Eds.). (2010). *On becoming a scholar: Socialization and development in doctoral education*. Stylus.

Gaston Gayles, J., & Kelly, B. T. (2007). Experiences with diversity in the curriculum: Implications for graduate programs and student affairs practice. *NASPA Journal*, *44*(1), 193–208. https://doi.org/10.2202/1949-6605.1761

Golde, C. M. (2006). Preparing stewards of the discipline. In C. M. Golde & G. E. Walker (Eds.), *Envisioning the future of doctoral education* (pp. 3–20). Jossey-Bass.

Grusec, J. E., & Hastings, P. D. (2007). Introduction. In J. E. Grusec & P. D. Hastings (Eds.), *Handbook of socialization: Theory and research* (pp. 1–9). The Guilford Press.

Herdlein, R. J. (2004). Survey of chief student affairs officers regarding relevance of graduate preparation of new professionals. *NASPA Journal, 42*(1), 51–71. https://doi.org/10.2202/1949-6605.1414

Keeling, R. P. (Ed.). (2004). *Learning reconsidered: A campus-wide focus on the student experience.* NASPA and ACPA.

Linder, C., Harris, J. C., Allen, E. L., & Hubain, B. (2015). Building inclusive pedagogy: Recommendations from a national study of students of color in higher education and student affairs graduate programs. *Equity & Excellence in Education, 48*(2), 178–194. https://doi.org/10.1080/10665684.2014.959270

Lorden, L. P. (1998). Attrition in the student affairs profession. *NASPA Journal, 35*(3), 207–216. https://doi.org/10.2202/1949-6605.1049

Marshall, S. M., Gardner, M. M., Hughes, C., & Lowery, U. (2016). Attrition from student affairs: Perspectives from those who exited the profession. *Journal of Student Affairs Research and Practice, 53*(2), 146–159. https://doi.org/10.1080/19496591.2016.1147359

Moore, W. E. (1970). *The professions: Roles and rules.* Russell Sage.

Perez, R. J. (2014). *Exploring the cognitive dimensions of professional socialization in student affairs* [Doctoral dissertation, University of Michigan]. Deep Blue. https://deepblue.lib.umich.edu/handle/2027.42/108829

Perez, R. J. (2016). A conceptual model of professional socialization within student affairs graduate preparation programs. *Journal for the Study of Postsecondary and Tertiary Education, 1,* 35–52. https://doi.org/10.28945/2344

Perez, R. J. (2017). Enhancing, inhibiting, and maintaining voice: An examination of student affairs graduate students' self-authorship journeys. *Journal of College Student Development, 58*(6), 833–852. https://doi.org/10.1353/csd.2017.0067

Renn, K. A., & Jessup-Anger, E. R. (2008). Preparing new professionals: Lessons for graduate preparation programs from the National Study of New Professionals in Student Affairs. *Journal of College Student Development, 49*(4), 319–335. https://doi.org/10.1353/csd.0.0022

Rios, C. (2015). *You call it professionalism; I call it oppression in a three-piece suit.* Everyday Feminism. https://everydayfeminism.com/2015/02/professionalism-and-oppression/

Robbins, C. K. (2016). White women, racial identity, and learning about racism in graduate preparation programs. *Journal of Student Affairs Research and Practice, 53*(3), 256–268. https://doi.org/10.1080/19496591.2016.1143834

Sallee, M. W. (2015). Adding academics to the work/family puzzle: Graduate student parents in higher education and student affairs. *Journal of Student Affairs Research and Practice, 52*(4), 401–413. https://doi.org/10.1080/19496591.2015.1083438

Talbot, D. M. (1996). Master's students' perspectives on their graduate education regarding issues of diversity. *NASPA Journal, 33*(3), 163–178. https://naspa .tandfonline.com/doi/abs/10.1080/00220973.1996.11072406

Van Maanen, J. (1978). People processing: Strategies of organizational socialization. *Organizational Dynamics, 7*(1), 19–36. https://doi.org/10.1016/0090-2616(78) 90032-3

Van Maanen, J., & Schein, E. H. (1979). Towards a theory of organizational socialization. *Research in Organizational Behavior, 1,* 209–264.

Wanous, J. P. (1992). *Organizational entry: Recruitment, selection, orientation, and socialization of newcomers.* Addison-Wesley.

Weidman, J. C., Twale, D. J., & Stein, E. L. (2001). *Socialization of graduate and professional students in higher education: A perilous passage? (ASHE-ERIC Higher Education Report No. 28).* Jossey-Bass.

Wendler, C., Bridgeman, B., Cline, F., Millett, C., Rock, J., Bell, N., & McAllister, P. (2010). *The path forward: The future of graduate education in the United States.* Educational Testing Service.

Witkowsky, P., Dinise-Halter, A., Yakaboski, T., & Long, S. (2018). Creating supportive educational communities for nontraditional women in student affairs preparation programs. *Journal of Student Affairs Research and Practice, 55*(2), 167–180. https://doi.org/10.1080/19496591.2018.1417131

Young, R. B., & Elfrink, V. L. (1991). Values education in student affairs graduate programs. *Journal of College Student Development, 32,* 109–115.

PART TWO

THE TOLL OF STUDENT AFFAIRS WORK

6

WHOSE IDEAL WORKER?

Student Affairs and Self-Care in the Neoliberal Academy

Pamela Graglia, Karla Pérez-Vélez, and D-L Stewart

F ollowing the 2016 presidential election, hate and bias incidents increased at State University. Cheyenne, a graduate hall director identifying as a Black cisgender queer woman, was a first responder to numerous such incidents in her hall, affecting both undergraduate residents and resident assistants. Personally, Cheyenne was attempting to manage her own emotions of fear, anger, and concern. When she went to her hall director for advice, David, a cisgender heterosexual White man, advised his graduate assistant to check her feelings and just "do the job." Now distraught at the lack of affirmation and support she received, Cheyenne turned to the Black faculty in her graduate program for advice, affirmation, and support.

Paul, Cheyenne's supervisor, was unsure how to respond to her obvious distress and confusion. He, too, felt rocked by the outcome of the election but did not understand what he thought were the extremely emotional responses of his coworkers and graduate students. He was taught that work was no place for emotions and that support for personal issues should be sought in places other than work. He wasn't unsympathetic, but he just was not prepared to deal with such issues in his supervisory role.

Doreen is an assistant director in fraternity and sorority life with responsibility for six of the institution's National Pan-Hellenic Council chapters and the three graduate assistants in the office. Doreen's mother, who lived far away from her, was recently diagnosed with Alzheimer's. As the oldest daughter, it was understood that Doreen, a single woman, would take care of her mother, despite the closer proximity of other siblings and extended family. Waiting until the summer when her work responsibilities decreased, Doreen moved her mother into her home and began to establish a new routine and schedule. Her supervisor, Marsha, an older woman with active parents living nearby, offered to support Doreen with flextime, comp time, and reduction of responsibilities. When the academic year began, Marsha lived up to her word, and Doreen continued to receive strongly positive performance evaluations. However, when the associate director position became available, Marsha discouraged Doreen from applying, rationalizing that Doreen's elder care responsibilities would interfere with her capacity to "do the job."

These three scenarios, drawn from actual experiences of student affairs professionals, demonstrate the challenges encountered when life and work are perceived to be in conflict. The ideal worker norm in student affairs puts work first at the expense of any personal concerns (Acker, 1990). Rewards are given for those who always show up, who do extra, and who leave their personal lives at the door. Yet, student affairs is a profession founded on the holistic development of students (American Council on Education, 1937, 1949). In contrast, the holistic lives and development of professionals are too often ignored and disregarded in favor of the mandate to "do the job." Managerialism, the product of neoliberal demands for production and efficiency in a free-market economic and political social context, has become a dominant force in student affairs administration (Gildersleeve et al., 2010). This organizational press toward the mechanization of life and work presents a conundrum for the student affairs professional. Gildersleeve et al. (2010) echoed earlier work by Joan Acker (1990), who theorized organizations as hierarchical entities with jobs performed by employees who are emotionless, abstract, bodiless, gendered as masculine, and do not take on family responsibilities in the home. However, Acker also suggested that organizations might consider how the rhythm and timing of work can be adapted to the rhythm and timing of life beyond work. For professionals in college and universities, this can be thought of as the ebb and flow of work across the academic year.

In this chapter, we deconstruct the concept of the ideal worker and the role of neoliberalism in its encroachment in student affairs work. We argue that the common approach of framing self-care in terms of work–life balance is a damaging practice in current U.S. campus climates, amplifying rather than interrupting ideal worker norms. In pursuit of self-care, we encourage student affairs professionals to reconsider how rhythm and timing can be applied to student affairs work. We also introduce the concept of *us-care* using two allegories—the long spoon and the sunflower—to disrupt the neoliberal individualism encompassed in work–life balance. Finally, we provide suggestions for working toward a work–life rhythm and offer possibilities to transform work through a communal, us-care framework.

Personal Narratives of Working in the Academy

We (Pamela, Karla, and D-L) have worked in higher education and student affairs in different capacities and over different spans of time, space, and place in the academy. We share our personal narratives of working in the academy to situate how we enter this discussion.

Pamela (she/her/hers) was born in the Midwest and raised with unwavering Protestant values, attending parochial school for the first 10 years of her education. Here she learned foundational messages about work, such as the idea that personal talents were gifts that should be given freely and without complaint in service to others. Although church doctrine claimed *sola fide* (by faith alone), a "strong work ethic" in the form of service was a central part of life in the church. Service was also an evaluative social measure, particularly for the women of the congregation. Men were individuals "called" to roles in the church and adjoining school, so additional responsibilities meant additional compensation. Women, however, were a collective organized into an unpaid women's service "league" that coordinated many of the daily logistics and performed most of the caring outreach. She did not enter the paid workforce until reaching the legal working age of 16, but service work—contributing and not being idle—was the foundation of worthiness for Pamela, internally and externally.

As of this writing, Pamela is approaching a quarter of a century in higher education at a wide range of institutions and nonprofits and in a variety of roles, both academic and administrative. In many ways, her early socialization made her the ideal worker in student affairs, often taking on additional unpaid responsibilities; consistently staying late or coming in early; regularly working to mental, physical, and emotional exhaustion without complaint; and never rejecting student or colleague requests for time or attention to process through their own experiences while remaining silent about her own. Saying "yes" to these requests often reinforced her own need to be seen as worthy, as they were framed by supervisors as "taking one for the team." As a single, childless, White woman assumed to have few commitments outside work, expectations around being available and willing to take on extra work varied greatly compared to colleagues with families. It took years to unlearn much of that early socialization and begin saying "no" to unpaid additional responsibilities as well as to learn to name office dynamics around the gendered, heteronormative, classist, and White supremacist norms of how work is supposed to be done and who is expected to do it.

Karla (she/her/hers) entered the workforce at the age of 16 eager to help herself and her family as well as gain skills and resources to move through the world. She quickly learned in her role as a shift manager that what mattered most was to get the work done and to work more to prove her worth—it was an unspoken requirement to move within the organization. Karla worked with this expectation, as an ideal worker, without regard for self through physical pain and endured performance evaluations based on little recognition of skill and a focus on her need to be more feminine and smile more. Karla quit these roles and entered higher education as a pathway to better spaces.

Karla recently entered her 14th year as a full-time student affairs professional as an assistant director, having previously served in advising, coordinating, teaching, and training roles in academic and student affairs units at public research universities. Through these spaces, Karla faced a culture of "get it done" and encountered spaces where her body and life were not recognized as a woman of color. Getting it done meant she had to work within a dominant framework of how work and life were expected to flow. Work was always to come first, to the point that she was terminated for pursuing a personal passion of teaching students music over a summer. She was rehired only when the vice president stepped in on her behalf; however, she had to compromise and leave her students before their final performance.

The demands placed on her as an employee did not support work and life with its ebb and flow but rather demanded she do the job and place institutional needs first. She has endured the examining of her medical life to prove she can be an ideal worker as well as environments of sexism and racism with passive support of supervisors. Karla has since pushed back on ideal worker norms, advocating for different ways of working through technology and modified work days, but she is still challenged with existing in spaces where she is seen as an exception rather than accepted as a professional with a different rhythm of work.

D-L's (he/him/his and they/them/their) formal work life began at the age of 17, having been told by their mother throughout his childhood that "school is your job." That first job, held the summer before D-L began college, was for a company that sold dictionary and encyclopedia sets to businesses door-to-door. A young, inexperienced, Black person with feminine embodiment was assigned to a supervisor who was an older, cisgender, heterosexual, Black man. For 2 weeks, D-L endured sexual harassment, afraid to report it to their supervisor's supervisor because they were told that no one would believe them. At the end of the second week, afraid to remain in such close quarters with this man, D-L quit that job and spent the rest of the summer unemployed.

D-L is nearing 2 decades as a full-time faculty member teaching in higher education and student affairs graduate preparation programs and

25 total years in higher education. He has taught graduate students in four institutions, all large state universities with either high or very high research missions. D-L has faced unwanted sexual advances from other faculty, hostile sexual environments in which faculty made sexual comments about students' bodies, as well as racism, cisssexism, and unyielding expectations to "do the job" despite pain and trauma in his personal life. Support and interventions sometimes came from supervisors but were not always embraced by fellow colleagues. More often, D-L has kept hidden his personal pain and challenges—just as he did as a new worker 30 years ago. Working hard, keeping emotions hidden, and always going above what was expected has made D-L an "ideal worker" in others' eyes because they performed the role of Mammy among predominantly White departmental cultures. Mammy is a stereotype that emerged during slavery when Black women took care of White families, often while forced to neglect their own. Recognizing and rejecting Mammy roles has become part of D-L's critique of ideal worker norms.

Gendered Bodies, Gendered Work

As discussed in the introduction, Acker (1990) described the ideal worker in organizations as one who is emotionless, abstract, bodiless, masculine, and who does not take on family responsibilities in the home. These sexist environments are compounded by "patriarchal ways" (Tierney & Bensimon, 2000, p. 314) of the past where manhood is all that is needed to gain promotion and career advancement. Organizations perpetuate masculine-stereotyped patterns of on-the-job behavior, rewarding those who are completely dedicated to the work with limited, if any, personal responsibilities (Acker, 2006). Studies of academic culture have illustrated these characteristics; participants described working in sexist environments that made those who were not men feel unwelcome and inferior to their masculine counterparts (Ford, 2011 Ng, 1993; Philipsen, 2008; Tierney & Bensimon, 2000). The participants in these studies were demeaned because of their academic discipline, received less support in difficult situations with students, arrived to unprepared offices, and experienced sexual harassment (Ford, 2011;Ng, 1993; Philipsen, 2008; Tierney & Bensimon, 2000). This masculine-centered and gender-neutral view of organizations has become normal and optimal (Acker, 1990, Acker, 2006), making the goal of work–life balance difficult within student affairs and higher education. This in turn affects the narrative of what and who the ideal worker is within the neoliberal academy.

The Neoliberal Academy

Neoliberalism has dominated Western thought nationally and globally from the late 20th century to the present day (Cannella & Koro-Ljungberg, 2017). Both an economic and a political philosophy, neoliberalism is grounded in an unwavering belief in the benefits of free markets and unregulated capitalism (Gill & Donaghue, 2016; Giroux, 2002; Olsen & Peters, 2005). Free markets dictate that individual and institutional transactions take place based not on the propagation of public good but instead on the production of wealth (Fish, 2009). Neoliberalism situates citizens as consumers, worships competition and profits beyond the production of goods or services, and measures the worth of individuals by their productivity and consumption (Cannella & Koro-Ljungberg, 2017; Fish, 2009; Giroux, 2002).

The neoliberal academy elevates profitability over more historically rooted values such as a broadly democratic education (Cannella & Koro-Ljungberg, 2017; Giroux, 2002). As higher education has been corporatized and commodified, the role of the university as a driver of the public good is diminished in favor of a more transactional environment (Giroux, 2002). The neoliberal academy centers students as consumers and frames faculty and staff as human capital whose value comes not from the production of knowledge or the quality of service but in their ability to generate profit (Cannella & Koro-Ljungberg, 2017; Giroux, 2002).

The Neoliberal Academy and the Ideal Worker

The neoliberal academy reinforces and benefits from masculine-centered ideal worker norms such as effectiveness, competition, ambition, and individuality (Aisenberg & Harrington, 1988; Armenti, 2004; Hughes, 1989; Philipsen, 2008; Wolf-Wendel & Ward, 2006). However, as Philipsen (2008) discussed, some faculty fail to live up to ideal worker norms and experience departmental tensions as a consequence. These workers are challenged by unclear academic expectations; they do not not initially know how much to commit to service, students, or writing and then face the challenge of balancing work and life, contributing to their guilt about their ability to complete their work. At the same time, they attempt to balance professional and personal lives along with securing their positions and rising expectations as they move into mid- and late-career stages. Each of us experienced challenges in balancing personal and professional lives with rising expectations around productivity: Karla leaving a passion while facing termination based on rising expectations not initially communicated to her, Pamela often taking additional unpaid responsibilities, and D-L often facing hostile environments to do the job at personal and painful expense—all to the benefit of the institution. Further, those who fail to conform to expectations of neoliberal, masculine-centered institutions may find their careers at risk because their departments may penalize those who do not display the correct role behavior (Cooper, 2002) of being emotionless, gender neutral, and sufficiently productive and profitable (Gill & Donaghue, 2016).

Faculty of color are likely to be further marginalized in the neoliberal academy through the intersection of racism and sexism/patriarchy (Ford, 2011; Ng, 1997). Faculty of color are assumed to have racially motivated political agendas and are limited to teaching subjects solely related to people of color (Ford, 2011). Sule (2011) found that faint forms of racism, such as tone in language or "insulting surprise" (p. 153) at the achievements of faculty of color, have cumulative effects and can be stressful for racially minoritized groups given that the academy is a gendered institution, favoring White masculinity in ways of knowing and learning (Wolgemuth & Harbour, 2008). On top of this, academics are more likely than any other occupational group to perform unpaid overtime (Gill, 2009).

Not unlike faculty, both gender and racially minoritized administrators in higher education experience pay disparities, glass ceilings, sticky floors, lack of institutional support, and continued underrepresentation at upper levels of institutions (Allan, 2011; Marshall, 2009; Martinez-Aleman & Renn, 2002). These administrators may decline or accept positions based on the needs of their family while sacrificing personal time and their health and wellness (Marshall, 2009) to meet productivity norms in the corporatized university (Gill & Donaghue, 2016). These sacrifices often unintentionally reinforce neoliberalism and uphold masculine-centered norms of neoliberal higher education—to be the ideal worker.

Further, the student affairs profession is often associated with feminine traits, including an emphasis on nonhierarchical structures as well as characteristics of caring, providing service, and supporting and nurturing students (Hughes, 1989). Pfeffer and Davis-Blacke (as cited in Bellas, 1994) found that when the gender of workers in a field becomes more diversified and reaches a tipping point of 30% women, the work of that field becomes devalued. In our observation, as student affairs work has pursued greater professionalization, it has adopted the masculine-centered and managerial character of the neoliberal academy generally. There has been an

> importing of corporate models of management into University life; the reformulation of the very nature of education in instrumental terms connected to business and the economy; the transformation of students into "consumers"; and the degradation of pay and working conditions for

academics, as well as the increasing casualization of employment, yet with little organized resistance from trade unions or other bodies . . . . speaks of the "corporate University" and of "academic capitalism," and considers the takeover of higher education by a logic of the market. (Gill, 2009, para. 12)

Seen in this way, student affairs has adopted corporate management models as a defense against its feminization and resultant devaluing in the academy. As Acker (1990) would contend, student affairs is a gendered organization with gendered bodies that are expected to conform to masculine worker traits.

Self-Care and the Ideal Worker in the Neoliberal Academy

The dominance of patriarchy in higher education (Fried, 2002), the optimization of the ideal worker as emotionless and abstract, and neoliberal productivity norms (Cannella & Koro-Ljungberg, 2017) are often at odds with the idea of self-care in the field of student affairs. Student affairs work is often considered caring work, and the field is characterized by its focus on the growth and development of students on a university campus beyond the classroom (Walker, 2008), residentially and online. This focus has developed over decades from *in loco parentis* to the education of the whole student via the use of learning outcomes and an integrated use of resources (Dungy & Gordon, 2011). Through this evolution, student affairs professionals often feel that they must be available at all times for students, aggrandizing the role of the ideal worker for the benefit of students. This tendency has been exacerbated in the digital age. With access to technology, and sometimes laptops and cell phones provided by departments, there is an ever-present pull to be always "on." Work within universities is now one without walls (Gill, 2009). With the rise of technology and online and hybrid programs, faculty and administrators find themselves working at all hours and "mobile technologies intermesh seamlessly with the psychic habitus and dispositions of the neoliberal academic subject: checking, monitoring, downloading whether from . . . beach or bed, trying desperately to keep up and stay on top" (Gill, 2009, para. 27).

The role of an ideal worker in student affairs is further compounded by the emotional labor performed by those in the field. As Guy (2013) explained, emotional labor "is the part that requires the worker to sense the emotional state of a [student] and then respond" (para. 5), although it is rarely ever written as a job duty or recognized as a critical component of work that is in the service of others, such as student affairs. Emotional labor is the work of advocating for students and the support of students who experience marginalization and alienation (Shayne, 2017). It is the pain, distress, hardship, wear, and tear of caring for others while also making others comfortable by not showing emotion (Feldman, 2015). The unaccounted toll of emotional labor in the work and the workday has led to a rise in the discussion of self-care in student affairs.

Self-care includes the activities one engages in regularly to reduce stress and maintain short- and long-term health (University at Buffalo, n.d.). The concept of self-care is not a new one; it arose in the 1960s out of the medical profession. It has recently hit the mainstream as more people realize that one cannot take care of others if they have not taken the time to take care of themselves (Harris, 2017). The mainstreaming of self-care has also emerged within student affairs under the #SAFit hashtag used on Twitter by student affairs professionals along with others such as #SAhealth and #SAwellness (Cabellon, 2015).

The incorporation of self-care in student affairs work is an effort to refocus on the self, given increased work demands, campus violence, and increasingly politicized campus climates. Yet self-care is framed as a matter of work–life balance, assuming equal attention between the two and even signaling that work should come first. Self-care is meant to occur amidst the ongoing demands of a workplace culture based on the ideal worker construct of someone who either needs no self-care or can prioritize work over self-care. A better approach would be to deconstruct the notion of both self-care and balance, instead embracing the concepts of us-care and the rhythm and timing of work and life.

Deconstructing Balance

Although work–life balance is often used within student affairs as a synonym for self-care, Fleetwood (2007a) underscores the problematic assumptions in how we think about and enact a work–life balance approach, particularly within the neoliberal academy. Work–life balance is offered as a balm for burnout and emotional fatigue (Barnes & Van Dyne, 2009; Howard-Hamilton et al., 1998,), resulting from a caring profession where boundaries are often difficult to maintain (Guthrie et al., 2005). However, the very pursuit of such artificial boundaries and dichotomous distinctions between "work" and "life" (Fleetwood, 2007b) may only reinforce the ideal worker narrative (Acker, 1990) and undermine the very self-care and meaningful lives we seek (Caproni, 2004). Embedded in work–life balance are often-unexamined ideas; for example, that work and life are separate and opposing activities, in contrast to work being part of life (Fleetwood, 2007b).

As has been discussed elsewhere in this volume, work–life conflict is a major cause of professional attrition for student affairs professionals (Marshall et al., 2016; Silver & Jakeman, 2014). Work–life balance has become the organizational solution to calls for both increased productivity and job satisfaction by the profession (Bender, 2009; Caproni, 2004; Perrakis & Martinez, 2012). Neoliberal strategies for work–life balance tend to be individual endeavors, calling on us to take personal responsibility for improving our efficiency and learning to do our work more effectively (Clouston, 2014). Even institutional responses to calls for work–life balance tend to focus on the individual rather than broader organizational policies, instead offering resiliency seminars or mindfulness workshops in hopes of personal improvement (Gill & Donaghue, 2016). However, despite work–life balance initiatives, there is little discussion in the field as to what exactly constitutes work, life, or balance. Fleetwood (2007a) suggested that evoking work–life balance as a concept is fraught and

> that work is somehow bad and life is good, so we need less of the former and more of the latter; that work and life share a common unit such that they can be compared, to ascertain if they are, or are not, in balance; that balance is synonymous with equity . . . that a balance has been achieved by some, and could be achieved by many more, perhaps all; and that [work–life balance] might be attainable if . . . employers and employees could only change their (possibly old-fashioned) inflexible ways of behaving. (p. 352)

When examined, elevating work–life balance to be a primary instrument of self-care is counterintuitive, asking professionals to parse the wholeness of their lives into categorizable parts in order to distinguish and then prioritize the important/essential from the unimportant/nonessential (Covey, 2013). We are all too apt to "overplan our lives at the expense of living our lives" (Caproni, 2004, p. 213). Work–life balance demands constant engagement and strategizing in unsustainable ways, adding to, rather than shortening, our to-do lists and failing to acknowledge the importance of honoring space for normal human cycles of ambivalence, engagement, and disengagement (Boyatzis & McKee, 2005; Caproni, 2004). In fact, the constant busyness required to work toward balance can increase physical and psychological pressures and reduce personal and family well-being (Brannen, 2005), calling into question the idea that balance is even an achievable goal.

Despite its unachievable nature (or perhaps because of it), work–life balance frameworks serve the neoliberal academy in multiple ways. First, neoliberalism and its insistence on individual responsibility demands that we as academics and administrators default to embodying ideal worker norms

(Acker, 1990) as the primary way to cope with an ever-fluctuating market to become "an enterprising, self managed and 'responsibilized' subject who can 'manage time,' 'manage change,' 'manage stress,' demonstrate resilience, practice mindfulness, etc." (Gill & Donaghue, 2016, p. 92) in order to survive. Conveniently, this approach leaves larger systemic power dynamics and oppressive organizational cultures intact and unchallenged (Caproni, 2004; Clouston, 2014; Gill & Donaghue, 2016; Giroux, 2002). Caproni (2004) goes further, questioning the range of solutions accessible to us when we are taught that seeking balance is an individual endeavor, noting, for instance, that work–life balance literature does not encourage us to be concerned with the care and support of children and families beyond our own.

Second, the dichotomous nature of work–life balance within a neoliberal system means that paid work is prioritized, demanding the majority of our time and energy (Clouston, 2014), particularly in tenuous markets where our measurable productivity is the primary indicator of our worth and continued employment (Gill & Donaghue, 2016). Striving for work–life balance in this environment benefits the system and not the worker (Giroux, 2002), where the enticement of flexible work encourages us to work more, unfettered by a standard workday (Fleetwood, 2007b). Neoliberal solutions to work–life balance are more likely to feed the workaholic nature of student affairs work (Manning, 2001) than temper it. As noted earlier, work responsibilities often seep into what is meant to be personal or family time: being on call, watching evening television with the work laptop open in hopes of "getting ahead," reading and answering emails while on vacation or waiting for medical appointments, and so forth. The high-tech, high-touch nature of modern student affairs work erases any meaningful distinctions between work life and personal/family life. Within the ideal worker narrative, work is invited to be an invisible family member.

Third, because neoliberalism abdicates organizational responsibility for balance and places it squarely on the individual (Fleetwood, 2007b), professionals are set up for frustration and failure as they attempt to achieve an unachievable goal (Caproni, 2004). Failing to achieve balance becomes a deficit of personal resiliency, a lack of efficiency, and a professional inability to reach a goal rather than a crisis of organizational culture (Gill & Donaghue, 2016). Neoliberal individualism in the pursuit of balance also assumes an even playing field, failing to take into account the additional impact of emotional labor on professionals with marginalized identities. Emotional labor and care work are not only undervalued but also result in additional stressors that make balance more difficult and impede on time and energy for work that the dominant culture deems more productive and valuable. Rather than questioning the system, socialization and internalized oppression may lead those with marginalized identities to further question their own worth and worthiness in the workplace.

We suggest that distinguishing self-care from work–life balance is more than semantic, particularly when resisting ideal worker norms. When seeking more fulfilling lives, a focus on work–life balance can elevate strategy and efficiency at the cost of our wholeness and humanity. Instead, focusing on self-care, not as an individual endeavor but in the context of community, creates possibility for us to find meaning in the rhythm of life and work.

Finding the Rhythm of Life and Work

Finding the rhythm of life and work is not an idea that can work in the same way for everyone. Finding rhythm rather than balance challenges the normative view of neoliberalism in administrative work in higher education. Although universities and departments seek to support employee work–life balance through discounted workshops, such interventions do not disrupt the dominant norms of the ideal worker. To participate in a mindfulness workshop or massage session through a campus vendor may require an employee to negotiate time away from work to engage in self-care. This may require the employee to take annual leave or to adjust their schedule to recover the work time lost to engage in self-care during the workday. Alternative options could include virtual work, as well as flextime and comp time, to better support workers whose lives beyond work make the traditional 9:00 a.m.-to-5:00 p.m., in-the-office, 40-hour work week challenging, if not untenable. Given our argument in this chapter, how might the initial illustrations that began this chapter be handled differently by the supervisors involved?

The first scenario involved a graduate student, Cheyenne, rocked by the toll of the emotional labor required of her to support students who were struggling to understand and deal with the aftermath of the last election. Her supervisor, David, could have chosen a three-fold response. First, he could have affirmed the reality of what his graduate student was feeling. Second, he could relate from the vantage point of his own social identities and how they overlapped with the political and social context. Third, he could have engaged the student in exploration of ways to manage her own needs for identity-centered support while meeting the needs of her students and the ongoing demands of her job. In this way, David would have demonstrated his investment in Cheyenne's holistic development as a person and an emerging student affairs professional.

Concerning David, it is important to recognize that those who fulfill the neoliberal ideal worker type also need to be liberated. From a critical theoretical perspective, oppressive constructs fail everyone, not just those who are the targets of marginalization. Liberation is a community goal, not an individual one. David needs mentors connected to their hearts and their minds who share his dominant identities. Within these mentoring relationships, David could build his multicultural competence, developing awareness, knowledge, skills, and actions that would support his overall professional competence (Pope et al., 2019) and equip him to be a better supervisor and worker himself.

The final scenario with Doreen and Marsha reflects a growing reality for Baby Boomer and Generation X employees—needing to provide elder care to aging parents. Marsha assumed that Doreen's need to provide dependent care for her parent would impinge upon her ability to be dedicated to her career and denied her an opportunity for career advancement. Besides the possible illegality of making such a determination, Marsha's decision reinforces Acker's (1990) conceptualization of the ideal worker as one who does not take on family responsibilities and can devote themselves wholly to their career. Alternatively, Marsha could have recognized that Doreen's dedication to her parent's care reflects the same dedication and commitment that she had been giving to her job. Her dependent care responsibilities made her a stronger employee and leader, not a weaker one.

Recommendations for Practice

Our reframing of the opening vignettes incorporates the following recommendations that we offer to turn from neoliberal, individualistic narratives of self-care to transformational, communal narratives of what we are calling *us-care*. We do not offer these as a checklist of activities, but rather as invitations to dialogue within departments and across student affairs organizations. Given the different roles and responsibilities of supervisors, graduate students and new professionals, midcareer professionals, and senior student affairs officers (SSAOs), we have provided specific recommendations for each group. We also include recommendations for institutional policy and practice.

Supervisors

First, we recommend that supervisors use staff meetings or retreats to talk through what it would mean and look like to reframe work as a shared obligation instead of as a multitude of individual ones. The allegory of the long spoons provides a useful illustration of the paradigm shift we are recommending. In this allegory, there are a group of people gathered around a large bowl of soup so wide and deep that no one can reach the other side. Each person has been given a long spoon to reach into the soup, but alas, they cannot feed themselves because the spoon is too long and tied firmly to their hand. Some of the people die from starvation after trying unsuccessfully to feed themselves with their own long spoon. Others recognize that the length of the spoon allows them to feed the person on the other side of the bowl and live. The length of the spoon is now an asset to the community. To attempt to feed only oneself is a work–life balance approach. To recognize the need to be fed and one's capacity to feed others, a communal care framework—us-care—replaces the neoliberal self-care perspective.

Second, supervisors can use mapping techniques to determine the rhythm—ebb and flow—of the work and how to apply an us-care approach to accomplish it. For example, within an office, one person's duties may peak before the semester begins and in its first 3 weeks. Another person's may peak during midsemester, while yet another's heaviest time occurs during the last month of the semester. There may be others whose workload remains steady across the term. Neoliberal approaches leave each person to fend for themselves and figure out an individual approach to "get the job done." A communal, us-care approach acknowledges shared obligations and then considers what shareable skills, or long spoons, exist within the unit and how to use them to support each other. Those shareable skills can then be used to consider how to meet each other's needs during the work cycle that was mapped. Often shareable skills are strengths or talents that come naturally or effortlessly to the individual while providing great benefit to the team or project. In addition to contributing to us-care, this approach can increase workplace community and worker wholeness by creating space for connection, meaning making, and gratitude.

Graduate Students and New Professionals

We recognize that status and power differentials constrain graduate students and new professionals from making claims on work norms. Nevertheless, we affirm graduate students' and new professionals' capacity to reframe their approach to their own work. With the multiple and competing demands of coursework and assistantship or other employment responsibilities, we have heard from our own graduate students that they feel untethered and dragged into unhealthy work norms outside of which they feel they cannot operate, due to either organizational culture or skillset. Considering the ebb and flow of those demands across the semester can provide a strategy for effective management. At the beginning of each semester, we recommend that graduate students use their syllabi as tools to initiate a dialogue with their supervisors focused on the ebb and flow of individual and shared work over the course of the academic term. Plotting when major assignments are due against when work responsibilities are at their highest opens up a conversation between the student and supervisor to begin exploring questions such as: What needs can we anticipate during these times? How can we support one another? How can we be open to one another as we learn to work together? What do we owe to each other in this relationship and in our relationship to the work? Where can we create space for rest, renewal, and celebration before and after times of peak engagement? Focusing questions around the ebb and flow of work on "we" disrupts the neoliberal narrative of self-care as an individual endeavor and creates the opportunity for the student to initiate us-care in the context of their assistantship responsibilities.

Additionally, graduate students can actively cultivate opportunities for us-care in the classroom by envisioning their cohort as the group holding long spoons who are gathered around the bowl of soup. Using the allegory as a starting place, the cohort can explore broad concepts like what it means to be a part of a learning community as well as specific support strategies such as collective notetaking or shared workloads when feasible.

For new professionals, the first 3 years of a new position comprise a transition arc described by Schlossberg and her colleagues (Anderson et al., 2012). During this time period, as professionals move in, move through, and finally move out of transition, they are reevaluating their structures and systems of support, their assessment of the situation, their understanding of themselves, and their strategies for managing significant changes in roles and responsibilities (Anderson et al., 2012). Previous coping mechanisms used in undergraduate student-leader roles and graduate student-employee roles may continue a cycle of patriarchal and corporate worker norms resulting in inconsistent episodes of self-care.

In light of this, we have a recommendation for new professionals to practice us-care and define the ebb and flow of their work and life. Crucially, we encourage new professionals to connect to communities of care. These networks, whether physical or virtual, can help support new professionals who may feel isolated in their new jobs. Unlike graduate school, when they began that new experience with a cohort of a dozen or more others who were similarly situated, new professionals may find themselves as the only "newbie" in their work unit. This isolation can feed workaholic behaviors as new professionals seek to fit into the existing work culture and attempt to prove their worth through working above and beyond. By connecting to one or more communities of care, new professionals can engage with others who are working through the same transition. Within these communities, new professionals can create long-spoon structures that sustain and maintain healthy attitudes and approaches toward the ebb and flow of work and life.

Midcareer Professionals

We encourage midcareer professionals to reflect on their work histories similarly to how we did at the beginning of this chapter. Where are there points of disconnect between how you approached your work and your attitudes toward your work? How have you allowed ideal worker norms to constrain your capacity for communal care? In what ways can you reclaim your own narrative? After this reflection, we encourage midcareer professionals to take a different approach to their work and use this approach to transform notions of self-care within their own circles of influence. The sunflower is an allegory for such a paradigm shift. Sunflowers—not unlike other plants—grow by turning toward the sun to receive the necessary nourishment provided through photosynthesis. They sense what the need is and then turn to meet that need. Likewise, professionals can become so attuned to each other's needs within and across units that they make a habit of sensing and meeting those needs instead of offering platitudes like "I'm here if you need me."

This reframing can extend to graduate students and new professionals even if the midcareer professional is not in a supervisory role. By modeling a different approach to work, midcareer professionals can have a positive impact on work culture within the broader unit and act as exemplars for graduate students and new professionals. At their career midpoint, professionals can illustrate that it is possible to perform student affairs work in ways that honor the wellness and whole-person focus of the field's philosophy.

SSAOs

As divisional leaders, SSAOs have a lot of power to reset norms and disrupt ideal worker norms. That said, SSAOs must first model the way and disrupt neoliberal ideologies in their own work lives. We encourage SSAOs to adopt the recommendations given to supervisors to set the tone for the division by mapping the work across functional areas under their purview and reevaluating what look like shortcomings into communal strengths—the long spoon. Alongside this, we recommend that SSAOs consider the needs of the whole division and focus attention in those areas as needed in critical times—the sunflower approach.

Second, we recommend that SSAOs become advocates for abandoning neoliberal ideal worker norms to student affairs' academic partners and external stakeholders. Supporting revisioning the work must come from the top with a clear and distinct message. Doing so could enable SSAOs to lead change efforts in other parts of the university.

Institutional Policy and Practice

Within their own spheres of influence, all professionals should consider how to operationalize us-care at a systems level by developing policy and practice that support the recommendations provided here within their teams. An often-overlooked area that it is important to review at both unit and institutional levels is policies of reward and recognition. From informal awards that single out work well done to additional professional development funding or opportunities portioned out to individuals who go above and beyond, all reinforce organizational norms around what an ideal worker looks like. These recognition structures can be refocused to reward teams who implement us-care approaches to their work. Doing so sends a powerful symbolic message about what is valued within the organization and is a small change that can leverage significant shifts in organizational culture.

At the institutional level we have three key recommendations for transforming policy and practice. First, review all institutional human resources (HR) policies concerning promotion, pay raises, and sharing of duties for ways in which neoliberal ideal worker norms are embedded structurally in the institution. For example, policies should be revised to ensure that workers' career advancement is not penalized by taking time to care for aging parents or other dependents. Second, job sharing and other means of creating systems of long spoons should be reflected in HR policies as valid ways of practicing us-care in the ebb and flow of the academic year. Third, divisional practices must be reviewed for alignment with existing HR policies that may already provide means to support us-care in the workplace. Moreover, inconsistencies in applying existing policies among functional area units must be corrected and brought into alignment with the interest of us-care in mind.

Conclusion

Through each of these scenarios, work–life balance is replaced by strategies that would allow professionals to find the rhythm and flow of work and other life demands. Therefore, we suggest that administrators, faculty, and students engage colleagues and leadership in a dialogue that considers how *rhythm* can take the place of *balance* in conversations about employee wellness. It is important that these conversations center the community, not the individual, as wellness and self-care are community norms and values that reflect the quality of interpersonal relationships. They are not goals for one person to achieve in isolation. Moreover, self-care and us-care represent a continuum, instead of a binary with mutually exclusive options. The more individualized the unit's approach to work is, the more self-care becomes necessary for wellness. However, the more a unit approaches work through a communal ethic, the more self-care recedes, allowing us-care to emerge as an effective strategy for wellness for individuals and the group as a whole.

In the context of community, employee wellness could be met through various modes of work and take into account the identities of employees and the multiple roles they play beyond the office. Finding a rhythm and flow, such that work is integrated into our lives, means seeing ourselves, our coworkers, and our staff as whole people. The ideal worker is a harmful, oppressive construct from which student affairs can be liberated. Indeed, we must if the profession is to truly live into its commitment to serve the holistic needs of postsecondary students.

References

Acker, J. (1990). Hierarchies, jobs, bodies: A theory of gendered organizations. *Gender and Society*, *4*(2), 139–158. https://doi.org/10.1177/089124390004002002

Acker, J. (2006). Inequality regimes: Gender, class, and race in organizations. *Gender & Society*, *20*(4), 441–464. https://doi.org/10.1177/0891243206289499

Aisenberg, N., & Harrington, M. (1988). *Women of academe: Outsider in the sacred grove*. University of Massachusetts Press.

Allan, E. J. (2011). *Women's status in higher education: Equity matters* (ASHE Higher Education Report No. 1). Jossey-Bass.

American Council on Education. (1937). *Student personnel point of view*. Author. http://www.myacpa.org/pub/documents/1937.pdf

American Council on Education. (1949). *Student personnel point of view*. Author. http://www.myacpa.org/pub/documents/1949.pdf

Anderson, M. L., Goodman, J., & Schlossberg, N. K. (2012). *Counseling adults in transition: Linking Schlossberg's theory with practice in a diverse world* (4th ed.). Springer.

Armenti, C. (2004). May babies and posttenure babies: Maternal decisions of women professors. *The Review of Higher Education*, *27*(2), 211–231. https://doi.org/10.1353/rhe.2003.0046

Barnes, C. M., & Van Dyne, L. (2009). "I'm tired": Differential effects of physical and emotional fatigue on workload management strategies. *Human Relations*, *62*(1), 59–92. https://doi.org/10.1177/0018726708099518

Bellas, M. L. (1994). Comparable worth in academia: The effects on faculty salaries of the sex composition and labor-market conditions of academic disciplines. *American Sociological Review, 59*(6), 807–821. https://doi.org/10.2307/2096369

Bender, B. (2009). Job satisfaction in student Affairs. *NASPA Journal, 46*(4), 553–565. https://doi.org/10.1080/00220973.1980.11071773

Boyatzis, R. E., & McKee, A. (2005). *Resonant leadership: Renewing yourself and connecting with others through mindfulness, hope, and compassion.* Harvard Business Review Press.

Brannen, J. (2005). Time and the negotiation of work–family boundaries: Autonomy or illusion. *Time and Society, 14*(1), 113–131. https://doi.org/10.1177/0961463X05050299

Cabellon, E. (2015). *The 2015 student affairs health pledge.* Dr. Ed Cabellon. https://edcabellon.com/2015pledge/

Cannella, G. S., & Koro-Ljungberg, M. (2017). Neoliberalism in higher education: Can we understand? Can we resist and survive? Can we become without neoliberalism? *Cultural Studies, Critical Methodologies, 17*(3), 155–162. https://doi.org/10.1177/1532708617706117

Caproni, P. J. (2004). Work/life balance: You can't get there from here. *The Journal of Applied Behavioral Science, 40*(2), 208–218. https://doi.org/10.1177/0021886304263855

Clouston, T. J. (2014). Whose occupational balance is it anyway? The challenge of neoliberal capitalism and work–life imbalance. *British Journal of Occupational Therapy, 77*(10), 507–515. https://doi.org/10.4276/030802214X14122630932430

Cooper, J. E. (2002). Women faculty overview. In A. M. Martínez-Alemán & K. A. Renn (Eds.), *Women in higher education: An encyclopedia* (pp. 373–380). ABC-CLIO.

Covey, S. R. (2013). *The seven habits of highly effective people: Powerful lessons in personal change.* Simon and Schuster.

Dungy, G., & Gordon, S. A. (2011). The development of student affairs. In J. H. Schuh, S. R. Jones, S. R. Harper, & Associates (Eds.), *Student services: A handbook for the profession* (pp. 61–79). Jossey-Bass.

Feldman, M. (2015). "There's no crying in academia": Acknowledging emotional labour in the academy. *Hook & Eye.* https://hookandeye.ca/2015/10/21/guest-post-theres-no-crying-in-academia-acknowledging-emotional-labour-in-the-academy/

Fish, S. (2009). Neoliberalism and higher education. *The New York Times.* https://opinionator.blogs.nytimes.com/2009/03/08/neoliberalism-and-higher-education/

Fleetwood, S. (2007a). Rethinking work–life balance. *The International Journal of Human Resource Management, 18*(3), 351–359. https://doi.org/10.1080/09585190601167441

Fleetwood, S. (2007b). Why work–life balance now? *The International Journal of Human Resource Management, 18*(3), 387–400. https://doi.org/10.1080/09585190601167441

Ford, K. A. (2011). Race, gender, and bodily (mis)recognitions: Women of color faculty experiences with White students in the college classroom. *Journal of Higher Education, 82*(4), 444–478. https://doi.org/10.1353/jhe.2011.0026

Fried, J. (2002). Ethics and practice. In A. M. Martínez-Alemán & K. A. Renn (Eds.), *Women in higher education: An encyclopedia* (pp. 475–477). ABC-CLIO.

Gildersleeve, R. E., Kuntz, A. M., Pasque, P. A., & Carducci, R. (2010). The role of critical inquiry in (re)constructing the public agenda for higher education: Confronting the conservative modernization of the academy. *The Review of Higher Education, 34*(1), 85–121. https://doi.org/10.1353/rhe.2010.0009

Gill, R. (2009). Breaking the silence: The hidden injuries of neoliberal academia. In R. Flood & R. Gill (Eds.), *Secrecy and silence in the research process: Feminist reflections* (pp. 228–254). Routledge. http://platform-hnu.nl/wp-content/uploads/2015/05/gill-breaking-the-silence-2.pdf

Gill, R., & Donaghue, N. (2016). Resilience, apps, and reluctant individualism: Technologies of self in the neoliberal academy. *Womens Studies International Forum, 54*, 91–99. https://doi.org/10.1016/j.wsif.2015.06.016

Giroux, H. (2002). The corporate war against higher education. *Workplace, 9*, 103–117. https://ices.library.ubc.ca/index.php/workplace/article/view/184051/183878

Guthrie, V. L., Woods, E., Cusker, C., & Gregory, M. (2005). A portrait of balance: Personal and professional balance among student affairs educators. *College Student Affairs Journal, 24*(2), 11–127.

Guy, M. (2013). Emotional labor abroad. *CU Denver Today.* https://www.cudenvertoday.org/mary-guy-emotional-labor/

Harris, A. (2017). A history of self-care: from its radical roots to its yuppie-driven middle age to its election-inspired resurgence. *Slate.* http://www.slate.com/articles/arts/culturebox/2017/04/the_history_of_self_care.html

Howard-Hamilton, M. F., Palmer, C., Johnson, S., & Kicklighter, M. (1998). Burnout and related factors: Differences between women and men. *College Student Affairs Journal, 17*(2), 80–91.

Hughes, M. S. (1989). Feminization and student affairs. *NASPA Journal, 27*(1), 18–27. https://doi.org/10.1080/00220973.1989.11072130

Manning, K. (2001, 23). Infusing soul into student affairs: Organizational theory and models. *New Directions for Student Services, 2001*(95), 27–35. https://doi.org/10.1002/ss.20

Marshall, S. M. (2009). Women higher education administrators with children: Negotiating personal and professional lives. *NASPA Journal About Women in Higher Education, 2*(1), 190–223. https://doi.org/10.2202/1940-7890.1031

Marshall, S. M., Gardner, M. M., Hughes, C., & Lowery, U. (2016). Attrition from student affairs: Perspectives from those who exited the profession. *Journal of Student Affairs Research and Practice, 53*(2), 146–159. https://doi.org/10.1080/19496591.2016.1147359

Martinez-Aleman, A. M., & Renn, K. A. (2002). *Women in higher education: An encyclopedia.* ABC-CLIO.

Ng, R. (1993). "A woman out of control": Deconstructing sexism and racism in the university. *Canadian Journal of Education / Revue canadienne de l'éducation, 18*(3), 189–205. https://doi.org/10.2307/1495382

Ng, R. (1997). A woman out of control: Deconstructing sexism and racism in the university. In J. Glazer-Raymo, B. Townsend, & B. Ropers-Huliman (Eds.), *Women in higher education: A feminist perspective* (pp. 360–370). Pearson Custom Publishing. https://doi.org/10.2307/1495382

Olsen, M., & Peters, M. A. (2005). Neoliberalism, higher education and the knowledge economy: From the free market to knowledge capitalism. *Journal of Education Policy, 20*(3), 313–345. https://doi.org/10.1080/02680930500108718

Perrakis, A., & Martinez, C. (2012). In pursuit of sustainable leadership: How female academic department chairs with children negotiate personal and professional roles. *Advances in Developing Human Resources, 14*(2), 205–220. https://doi.org/10.1177%2F1523422312436417

Philipsen, M. (2008). *Challenges of the faculty career for women: Success and sacrifice.* Jossey-Bass.

Pope, R. L., Reynolds, A. L., & Mueller, J. A. (2019). *Multicultural competence in student affairs: Advancing social justice and inclusion* (2nd ed.). Jossey-Bass.

Shayne, J. (2017). Recognizing emotional labor in academe. *Inside Higher Ed.* https://www.insidehighered.com/advice/2017/09/15/importance-recognizing -faculty-their-emotional-support-students-essay

Silver, B. R., & Jakeman, R. C. (2014). Understanding intent to leave the field: A study of student affairs master's students' career plans. *Journal of Student Affairs Research and Practice, 51*(2), 170–182. https://doi.org/10.1515/jsarp-2014-0017

Sule, V. T. (2011). How race matters: Race as an instrument for institutional transformation: A study of tenured Black female faculty. In P. A. Pasque & S. E. Nicholson (Eds.), *Empowering women in higher education and student affairs: Theory, research, narrative, and practice from feminist perspectives* (pp. 147–162). Stylus Publishing & ACPA.

Tierney, W. G., & Bensimon, E. M. (2000). (En)gender(ing) socialization. In J. Glazer-Raymo, B. K. Townsend, & B. Ropers-Huilman (Eds.), *Women in higher education: A feminist perspective* (ASHE Reader Series, pp. 309–325). Pearson Learning Solutions.

University at Buffalo. (n.d.). *Introduction to self-care: Whether you are a student or a professional working in the field, self-care matters!* https://socialwork.buffalo.edu/ resources/self-care-starter-kit/introduction-to-self-care.html

Walker, M. (2008). *Working with college students & student development theory primer.* https://srs.ucsd.edu/_files/theory/student-development-theory_m-walker.pdf

Wolf-Wendel, L. E., & Ward, K. (2006). Academic life and motherhood: Variations by institutional type. *Higher Education, 52*(3), 487–521. https://doi.org/10 .1007/s10734-005-0364-4

Wolgemuth, J. R., & Harbour, C. P. (2008). A man's academy? The dissertation process as feminist resistance. *NASPA Journal About Women in Higher Education, 1*(1), 183–203.

7

BURNOUT AND COMPASSION FATIGUE IN STUDENT AFFAIRS

Molly A. Mistretta and Alison L. DuBois

E merging student affairs professionals often indicate that they were attracted to the field by the potential of performing personally fulfilling work through directly helping students and providing them with the best possible campus experience. However, as Evans (1983) observed, these young professionals also "often have an unrealistic picture of the profession" (p. 15). Early professional idealism often gives way to the realities of meeting professional ideal worker expectations and the personal toll that student affairs work takes. An ideal worker in student affairs is "always available and working" (Sallee, 2016, p. 53), with no discernable responsibilities outside of the job. In addition, those who work in student affairs are also expected to be emotionless (Acker, 1990), absorbing the emotional burden of their helping role while lacking appropriate professional supports, including effective supervision (Cilente et al., 2006; Tull et al., 2009).

It is important to consider how young workers in the field are socialized to adopt ideal worker norms that they will likely carry with them into future practice. Because of the relentless expectations that student affairs employees work all the time and be emotionless, socialization into these norms all but ensures that the youngest and most inexperienced professionals run the risk of developing burnout, which is the accumulation of chronic stress caused by overwhelming work responsibilities. Many student affairs professionals perceive the need to work more than 50 hours per week (Beeny et al., 2005). The unhealthy expectations of extreme work obligations, such as long hours and stressful conditions, significantly contribute to burnout, which may help explain the estimated 50% to 60% attrition rate for new professionals in student affairs (Tull, 2006).

Student affairs professionals affected by burnout are more susceptible to the development of compassion fatigue, which is the emotional exhaustion felt by staff who have been exposed to trauma and who have struggled to cope with it while in their professional role. Increasingly, student affairs professionals are the first point of contact for students experiencing trauma or crises. The assumption that professionals in student affairs should adhere to ideal worker norms while absorbing chronic stress and student trauma without appropriate professional supports all but makes the development of burnout and compassion fatigue inevitable.

In this chapter, we discuss how the socialization of young student affairs staff may make them more vulnerable to the adoption of ideal worker norms, which increases the potential for burnout and leads to a negative impact on individuals as well as the profession. We also explore how young student affairs staff are more vulnerable to the negative effects of dealing with student trauma, which may lead to compassion fatigue. Finally, we suggest steps for positively socializing young and inexperienced student affairs staff in adopting appropriate professional attitudes and work–life boundaries as well as fostering a healthier work environment benefitting all student affairs professionals.

To illuminate these issues, we include responses generated through a questionnaire filled out by graduate and undergraduate paraprofessional residence life staff at a small, residential liberal arts college as part of an assessment of staff training and supervision. Of a potential 39 participants, 27 responded to the survey, resulting in a response rate of 69%. The purpose of this assessment was to assist departmental leadership in better understanding how their staff coped with a variety of responsibilities associated with their job, particularly the traumatic experiences that students report.

Burnout

A lack of understanding among student affairs professionals regarding the nature and causes of burnout often makes it difficult to proactively address in the workplace. The American psychologist Herbert Freudenberger (1974) coined the term *burnout* to describe the consequences of severe stress in the helping professions. Freudenberger described burnout as a "feeling of exhaustion and fatigue" (p. 160). Later, Maslach and Jackson (1981) defined the phenomenon as "a syndrome of emotional exhaustion and cynicism that occurs in individuals who do 'people work' of some kind" (p. 99). Professional roles that have intense involvement with other people can lead to chronic stress, which is one of the leading causes of burnout (Maslach et al., 2001). The three dimensions of burnout include an overwhelming exhaustion, feelings of cynicism and detachment from the job, and a sense of ineffectiveness and lack of accomplishment. *Exhaustion* refers to feelings of being overextended as well as the depletion of emotional and physical resources (Maslach et al., 2001). *Depersonalization* entails a negative or excessively detached response to a variety of experiences within the job role, while *reduced efficacy* refers to "feelings of incompetence and a lack of achievement and productivity at work" (p. 399).

Burnout can negatively affect student affairs professionals in two distinct contexts: job performance and individual health and wellness (Maslach et al., 2001). With burnout comes disengagement from the job, which may be manifested in absenteeism, a desire to quit, and employee turnover. Of those who choose to stay, workers experiencing burnout generally display lower productivity and declining effectiveness in their roles (Maslach et al., 2001). Individuals with burnout may also negatively influence the local work environment by generating interpersonal conflict, which can disrupt the productivity of others (Maslach et al., 2001). One person's burnout can affect overall morale, perpetuating itself through informal interactions with others in the work environment.

Within individual health and wellness contexts, burnout manifests itself in disproportionately high rates of depression, substance abuse, and suicide (Dyrbye et al., 2008). A growing body of medical research has also discovered that burnout may negatively affect workers' physical health more than previously believed (Melamed et al., 2006). Burnout increases the risk for cardiovascular disease as much as other well-known risk factors such as body mass index, history of smoking, and blood lipid levels (Melamed et al., 2006). Specifically, burnout increases an individual's likelihood of developing myocardial infarction, ischemic heart disease, stroke, and sudden cardiac death. Studies also point to an increased likelihood of type 2 diabetes, male infertility, sleep disorders, and musculoskeletal disorders among those with the extreme physical, mental, and emotional fatigue of burnout (Mayo Clinic Staff, 2018).

Young student affairs staff are especially vulnerable to adopting ideal worker norms as they are socialized into the profession, which makes the development of burnout a rather likely outcome. Magolda et al. (2008) suggested that most young adults struggle with the developmental task of cultivating an internal voice to negotiate external influences that inform their beliefs and behaviors. In this developmental stage, individuals assume authorities have all the answers, identify themselves through external expectations, and defer to others in relationships. Thus, young professionals are vulnerable to burnout as they adopt and internalize ideal worker norms as they are transmitted through formal expectations and informal messages from those in authority.

For paraprofessionals, the socialization process also involves discerning acceptable work behaviors. However, their developmental orientation at this time in their lives means that they will perceive themselves as compared to the external standards of ideal worker norms, which are conveyed through formal and informal messages in the workplace. These expectations put the paraprofessionals in our study at risk for developing beliefs that lead to unhealthy work practices (Everly & Benson, 1989; Maslach et al., 2001; Pines & Aronson, 1988). The inability to separate their own identity from that of their work responsibilities can lead paraprofessionals to perceive that "my job is my life" (James & Gilliland, 2017, p. 551). This attitude is typified by few work–life boundaries, long hours, and limited leisure time.

Responses to our questionnaire indicated that the lack of clear boundaries made it difficult to separate the work role from their personal lives. Paraprofessionals in residence life live alongside the students they serve, and the nature of the job means responding to concerns as they arise. Virtually all respondents cited the lack of clear boundaries as one of the most difficult aspects of the job. One staff member addressed this concern by saying, "It can be hard to separate [your] personal life. Having been in residence life for so long, I think that a lot of my personal life has just melted into residence life. Not many boundaries left." Another commented, "Most of the time I am always accessible, and students frequently knock on my door. It has interrupted my sleep, school, and friendships."

Individuals who are unable to develop a healthy balance between their work life and their professional life often develop a chronic overload in work responsibilities (Maslach et al., 2001). Respondents reported feeling overwhelmed with job tasks that interfered with other aspects of their lives. One respondent reported that the job was "very hard during midterms and [the] time before a break. Bulletin boards, floor programs, and door [decorations] due all at once, plus exams, papers, and assignments. And [staff] meetings!" Another respondent recalled making herself too available for residents, increasing the workload associated with the job. She "always stopped everything [when] they needed something. It was exhausting." Lastly, one respondent described the anger that surfaced in response to the chronic overload associated with their work responsibilities. "I was pissed off because being an RA is too much work."

A second belief that engenders burnout among student affairs staff involves another ideal worker expectation. Some individuals buy into the unrealistic expectation that they must be totally competent, knowledgeable, and able to help everyone (James & Gilliland, 2017). This often involves impractical ideas regarding work performance. Particularly difficult was the perceived expectation that they should always be available to their residents. One respondent stated, "I often feel like I need to keep my door open so that my residents can freely communicate with me. This often causes problems because I can't separate myself from my RA duties while I am in my room."

Respondents also demonstrated they perceived the need to perform all aspects of their job well. One RA shared that she felt she needed to address even the smallest details about community living. She said, "It is hard to remember that I can't freak out about every little thing, like bathroom cleanliness." Lastly, respondents seemed particularly concerned about their ability to respond perfectly to residents in crises. In describing the situations where such action was necessary, one response reflected many of the others who had faced similar situations in that he was "concerned . . . and nervous that I wouldn't be able to handle the situation the way my residents needed me to." Another paraprofessional described these feelings as "stress over wanting to handle it correctly."

Young student affairs workers are also vulnerable to being socialized into a profession with ideal worker norms that always prioritize student needs and wants over their own. Developmentally, they are more likely to defer to others with whom they have relationships (Magolda et al., 2008). Thus, it was not surprising that respondents articulated the belief that in order to accomplish their job and maintain their own sense of self-worth, they needed to be liked and approved of by everyone with whom they worked (James & Gilliland, 2017). In order to maintain the relationship bond, paraprofessionals struggled with asserting themselves, setting limits, saying no, and providing negative feedback to residents. One RA described a situation where he felt he had to prioritize job-related tasks over other legitimate personal concerns:

> One time I was helping a resident setting up a loft kit and I returned back to my room for something, and there I found my girlfriend completely in tears due to a death she had just found out about. I was still in the middle of setting up the loft after this happened.

The RA went on to indicate that it was stressful for him because he felt "I needed to be there for two different people at the same time and I could not. I had to make a compromise between the relationship and my job." Ultimately, the RA felt the correct choice in this situation was to prioritize the resident's needs, although they were less urgent, over those of his girlfriend.

Data from our questionnaire indicate that residence life paraprofessional staff experienced significant frequency and intensity along one of the three dimensions of burnout. Their responses align significantly with the emotional exhaustion subscale in Maslach's burnout inventory (Maslach & Jackson, 1981). Respondents described feeling emotionally drained from their work, frustrated by the time and intensity of the work, and that the expectations require them to work too hard. Additionally, they described feelings of being overwhelmed as they attempted to fulfill the many expectations they perceived they must meet. While burnout can be reversed, it is important to monitor and respond to individuals who may be experiencing burnout. Staff who are experiencing some levels of burnout, and then are subsequently exposed to student trauma, are more likely to develop compassion fatigue (Burnett & Wahl, 2015; Cieslak et al., 2014; Craig & Sprang, 2010).

Compassion Fatigue

Compassion fatigue may arise from frequent and/or intense exposure to trauma. Student affairs personnel can be exposed to trauma in two ways. The first is bearing witness to traumatic events while on the job. Figley (2002) argued that individuals who work directly with others who have experienced trauma can be just as likely to experience traumatic stress. Helping professionals can experience trauma symptoms simply by learning about a traumatic event of another person in their care (Valent, 2002). If secondary traumatic stress is not mitigated early on, compassion fatigue may develop, which is much more challenging to address.

Student affairs professionals experiencing compassion fatigue demonstrate it in a number of dimensions. Behaviorally, an individual may exhibit irritability, impatience, moodiness, and sleep disturbances (Figley, 2002). Cognitively, they may develop decreased levels of concentration and self-esteem, apathy, rigidity of thought processes, or minimization of their problems. Emotionally, individuals may feel powerless, anxious, guilty, angry, numb, fearful, helpless, sad, depressed, emotionally depleted, and hypersensitive. Finally, when the person is questioning their sense of purpose, the spiritual dimension of wellness is affected. Withdrawal from others and demonstrating a lack of intimacy are relational issues that may develop (Figley, 2002). Individuals can experience physical symptoms such as breathing difficulties, aches and pains, and ultimately an impaired immune system. Compassion fatigue also impacts the professional dimension through diminished work performance, low morale and motivation, task avoidance, apathy and negativity toward the work to be done, absenteeism, and exhaustion (Figley, 2002).

Burnout and compassion fatigue have interdependent qualities. As Gentry (2005) found, overworked and emotionally exhausted counselors had less energy to manage compassion stress symptoms, which resulted in greater feelings of helplessness and eventually compassion fatigue. The few studies examining secondary trauma and compassion fatigue in student affairs demonstrate that student affairs professionals feel overworked and emotionally exhausted (Chernoff, 2016; Lynch, 2017; Stoves, 2014). Given the correlation between the heavy workload and students with multiple issues, several student affairs professional roles are particularly ripe for the development of compassion fatigue, including residence life staff, college counseling staff, Greek life staff, disability services coordinators, Title IX coordinators, and behavioral intervention coordinators.

Ideal worker norms that facilitate compassion fatigue pose additional concerns for young paraprofessionals who are experiencing significant shifts in the types of student issues they respond to in the residence hall. Gone are the days when homesick students were an RA's biggest concern. Student death, suicide attempts, sexual assault, domestic violence, and mental health concerns are issues that many paraprofessional residence life staff address with students on a regular basis. The frequency with which these issues occur has increased the "emotional and logistical workload" of their role (Anthony, 2016, p. 10). Increasingly, paraprofessionals in residence life are often the first to engage with students who have experienced trauma, and the resulting emotional toll can have a potentially significant impact on the RA (Paladino et al., 2005). Hochschild (1983) described the difficulty that ideal workers face when they must "suppress feeling in order to sustain the outward countenance that produces the proper state of mind in others" (p. 7) as a form of emotional labor. The assumption that paraprofessionals should be able to manage their own emotions while absorbing chronic stress and student trauma without appropriate professional supports is unrealistic and possibly unethical.

Despite the expectation that ideal workers are emotionless, paraprofessional respondents shared that they often experienced emotional responses to student trauma that they struggle to manage. Eight paraprofessionals in our questionnaire described responses to trauma that aligned with Figley's (2002) emotional dimension of compassion fatigue. When asked to describe their experiences in engaging with residents who report traumatic material, residence life staff frequently cited emotional responses. For some paraprofessionals, the intensity was significant. One RA stated that after spending a great deal of time with different residents coping with a variety of problems, she felt "severe depression, failure, low self-esteem, emptiness, void, tiredness, anger, frustration, loneliness." Another described feeling "stress, guilt, and anxiety." An RA who responded to a resident who reported being sexually assaulted described feelings of "stress, anxiety, exhaustion, and confusion" in the aftermath. A paraprofessional staff member also reported feelings of "guilt and uncertainty" after the death of a resident. She went on to note that counseling assisted her in processing all the feelings associated with responding to this particular incident.

The second way student affairs staff can be exposed to trauma is by possessing a personal traumatic history. Medical researchers have studied the connections between early childhood trauma experiences and long-term health outcomes for decades. Anda et al. (2006) examined the impact of a personal traumatic history on an individual's neurodevelopment and physical health across the lifespan. These traumatic episodes are called *adverse childhood experiences* (ACEs) and include any experience that is stressful or traumatic, such as abuse; neglect; witness to domestic violence; or growing up with alcohol or other substance abuse, mental illness, parental discord, or crime in the home. These ACEs serve as a common pathway to various social, cognitive, and emotional impairments that increase the likelihood of unhealthy behaviors, risk of violence or revictimization, disease, disability, and premature death (Anda et al., 2006). In one study, ACEs were quite common; more than two thirds of the study's participants experienced them, with one in five adults having experienced three or more (Anda et al., 2006).

ACEs are often cooccurring and interrelated, such as an individual experiencing neglect as a child due to a parent abusing an illegal substance. Given Anda et al.'s (2006) estimation of the percentage of individuals who potentially experience ACES, the correlation to student affairs personnel is evident. It is likely that many paraprofessional staff have personally experienced these ACES. Additionally, it is very likely that student affairs personnel are interfacing daily with individuals who themselves have been affected by ACES. While a personal history of trauma does not directly cause compassion fatigue, it does have an impact on how one perceives and responds to the trauma of others. Witnessing the effects of trauma on a student may resurrect a professional's own personal history. In addition, a student affairs professional with ACES may experience an impaired ability to cope with daily stressors, increasing the likelihood of developing compassion fatigue.

Of 27 residence life paraprofessional respondents, 14 identified themselves as having at least one ACE. Two described growing up in a neighborhood that was "high crime." One respondent stated that he lost a family member at a young age, and it was a difficult experience, as he "didn't understand death or what was happening." Several respondents indicated that they grew up in a household where at least one parent was diagnosed with a mental illness. One spoke specifically about a grandmother who "has bipolar depression and I saw her hospitalized twice as a child." Two respondents addressed their own mental health diagnoses as children. Other ACEs reported included alcohol abuse, relationship violence, and sexual abuse. Three respondents indicated that they had experienced two ACEs while growing up, while one more described a childhood with three ACEs.

Respondents also commented on how ACEs might influence their approach to the RA role. One respondent described drug use in the home and identified how it affected him in his role as an RA. "I was very strict about the weed smell in my building. I would get emotional when I smelled it." This created an additional layer of stress and anxiety in dealing with issues related to drug use on his floor.

Alternatively, several students perceived that their ACEs helped them to be more effective in their work with students. One respondent stated that it helps "how [I] would interact or what I would say to a resident when trying to relate to them." Another shared, "I have found myself to be more confident in myself and the work that I do . . . being relatable is also something else I can do." RAs also felt that ACEs enabled them to empathize with their residents. One respondent commented, "I have sympathy and empathy. I am patient." Another said that she believed that "my personal history helps me to be more compassionate toward my residents."

Clearly, responses to our questionnaire indicated that young student affairs paraprofessionals struggled to manage their emotions in response to trauma. In addition, ideal worker norms fuel expectations that student affairs professionals absorb the emotional stress associated with their helping role. Without proactively addressing their own feelings about the trauma their residents are dealing with or the trauma they have experienced themselves, student affairs professionals are more likely to develop and experience the negative effects of compassion fatigue.

Consequences of Ideal Worker Norms

Responses to our questionnaire indicated that the paraprofessional residence life staff on this particular campus had been effectively socialized into ideal worker norms in student affairs. Many articulated the belief they should always be working and available for residential concerns, no matter how minor. They also perceived there was little room for error in their roles and described how that created additional pressure and stress. Ultimately, many paraprofessional staff felt the expectations of the job were too much. While some RAs displayed developmental growth by questioning job expectations that were associated with ideal worker norms, they continued to look to sources of external authority to solve this dilemma. Many RAs said they appreciated the relationship they had with their supervisor. However, they felt they lacked individual agency or supervisory support in setting reasonable work–life boundaries.

While the purpose of the survey was not to diagnose compassion fatigue, it was clear that paraprofessionals also struggled with the negative impact of working with students who have experienced trauma. The most common feelings paraprofessionals reported after dealing with a student's trauma were fear, worry, sadness, anxiety, confusion, and anger. Paraprofessional staff wrestled with these feelings and often turned to outside sources for support. Clearly, they were not emotionless workers but seemed to internalize the message that there was little space for their feelings in the workplace. Paraprofessional staff infrequently identified supervisors or campus counseling staff as potential avenues of support for their trauma-related experiences on the job. When asked who they talk to about stressful situations they experience in their role, common answers included friends, family, and significant others.

With so few supports in place to address the negative effects of ideal worker norms, it is likely that young and inexperienced student affairs staff will adopt attitudes and behaviors that promote the development of burnout and compassion fatigue. Continuing to work in an environment that exacts an emotional and physical toll due to ideal worker norms can increase the chances of a student affairs professional developing burnout. Once someone is experiencing burnout in the workplace, they are more vulnerable to the negative effects of secondary traumatic stress (Figley, 2002). Secondary traumatic stress, coupled with burnout, can create conditions ripe for the development of compassion fatigue. Despite being the subject of extensive research in other helping professions, burnout and compassion fatigue receive little attention in the field of student affairs. Thus, student affairs professionals lack awareness and training in how to identify it or address it. Yet both burnout and compassion fatigue can have negative effects on the social, emotional, and physical well-being of student affairs staff, leading to diminished job satisfaction, poor job performance, and ultimately attrition from the field (Bender, 2009; Guthrie et al., 2005; Howard-Hamilton et al., 1998; Renn & Hodges, 2007).

Recommendations for Practice

Emerging research demonstrates that the effects of burnout and compassion fatigue on student affairs professionals takes its toll both individually and on the profession as a whole. Individually, staff experience negative impacts regarding their personal health. Enthusiasm for working with students diminishes, and promising career trajectories may change or be cut short.

Students and institutions are not well served when staff cannot work to their full capacity. Additionally, the significant attrition rates represent a loss to the profession in terms of valuable skills and potential leaders in the field. The following are a few approaches to assist young professionals in their socialization to the student affairs field. These recommendations challenge the myth of the ideal worker and promote the development of healthy approaches to student affairs work practices.

Graduate Students and New Professionals

Chronic stress for new professionals is associated with heavy workloads, low pay, role ambiguity, and a lack of good supervision and support (Marshall et al., 2016). This leads to job dissatisfaction and disengagement. To retain the approximately 60% of young professionals who leave the field, institutions and graduate programs should focus on helping them develop healthy work practices to avoid burnout.

Several categories of person-centered approaches address burnout (Maslach, 2017). The first category is a focus on health and fitness. This approach is based on the assumption that a healthy person is better able to handle stress. Appropriate amounts of sleep, nutritious meals, and regular exercise should be the essential foundation for all student affairs professionals. The second category focuses on relaxation techniques. The purpose of relaxation techniques is to induce a state of calm to offset the physical and psychological effects of stress. Activities such as yoga and meditation help mitigate stress by decreasing activity in the sympathetic nervous system, otherwise known as the *fight or flight response*, which is typically responsible for constricting blood vessels and raising blood pressure and the heart rate (Tarantola, 2018).

The third category of focus in the prevention of burnout is the development of self-awareness. The more young student affairs professionals are able to recognize their own assumptions about the ideal worker in student affairs and question those norms, the better they will be at developing more realistic expectations of themselves as student affairs professionals. One effective way to challenge ideal worker norms is to discuss them with supervisors and work colleagues. Changing attitudes and work cultures that have been socialized to accept ideal worker norms will require that all stakeholders engage in this work.

A fourth category in the prevention of burnout includes the adoption of mindfulness exercises and seeking counseling with a licensed therapist. Working with a therapist can also help professionals to further question faulty beliefs about themselves as ideal workers and help them to develop coping skills that will effectively help them to better manage stress. Some coping skills are as simple as developing better time-management strategies, conflict-resolution skills, and assertive approaches for improved communication of personal and professional needs. Other coping skills might involve readjusting job expectations, reinterpreting other people's behavior, and imagining new professional goals.

Mitigating burnout might also involve making changes in work patterns. While working less might be the most obvious change to make, it is not always possible. However, staff can find opportunities to incorporate more breaks in their work routine or seek a better balance between work activities they enjoy and the more taxing workplace demands. Burnout can also be addressed by exploring the possibilities of social support through colleagues, supervisors, and mentors at work as well as friends and relatives at home.

One healthy work practice that new professionals should implement early and consistently is the setting of appropriate work–life boundaries. The implementation of healthy boundaries can be critical in allowing the worker to maintain their psychic and physical selves. When working with students in crisis, such boundaries can allow the worker to dissociate from the pain students are experiencing. The successful implementation of boundaries extends through many layers of an individual's professional life. Boundaries ensure that a separation exists between an individual and their work. Maintaining regular work hours, taking periodic breaks throughout the day, and maintaining a manageable workload are just a few examples to promote balance.

New and emerging professionals in student affairs should be intentional in designing self-care routines that will allow them to balance personal health with professional responsibilities. Young student affairs staff members should also take advantage of professional development opportunities to further explore and develop healthy professional practices to prevent burnout and compassion fatigue. In addition, young professionals in the field should seek counseling as an additional support when they find themselves overwhelmed.

Midcareer Professionals

Midcareer professionals are not immune to experiencing burnout and compassion fatigue. The use of self-care plans is particularly important as midcareer professionals may seek to expand their own families at this point in their careers. Self-care plans address specific strategies and behaviors that student affairs personnel can implement while coping with the roles and responsibilities of their job. Self-care plans also address what workers plan to do during times of stress, in addition to crisis planning when traumatic situations occur. In essence, self-care plans help the individual engage in self-reflection by identifying positive aspects of a person's life that can be accessed during times of distress.

These plans can encompass myriad dimensions that include but are not limited to the following domains: physical, psychological, emotional, spiritual, relational, and workplace supports. Examples of physical supports might be incorporating exercise or physical activity into the day, eating healthily, and getting enough sleep at night. Psychological supports could include taking a break from technology, seeking effective supervision, or keeping a reflective journal. Emotional care can include focusing on positive aspects of the day, engaging in a hobby with friends, and having a confidante to whom to vent. Spiritual supports include engaging in mindfulness or meditative practices and attending a religious service. Attending special events and nurturing close relationships can maintain relational supports. Engaging in professional development and maintaining boundaries can serve as workplace supports on a self-care plan.

Access to midlevel career professional development opportunities can provide specific career support, energize and rejuvenate staff, and expand one's social support network. Midcareer professionals may benefit by seeking professional opportunities that will allow them to further develop and expand their professional knowledge and skills. This can provide a sense of professional rejuvenation as well as the means to pursue other professional opportunities within academe.

Supervisors

Burnout and compassion fatigue are both personal and organizational problems, and quality supervision is critical to preventing both. However, they tend to be framed as problems with the person, and solutions overwhelmingly focus on addressing perceived individual inadequacies in dealing with stress. Maslach (2017) noted that most approaches to burnout are preventative, such as teaching resiliency skills to assist staff in coping with or better managing workplace stressors. Other approaches focus on those in the latter stages of burnout, with the goal of reducing the unhealthy deficits acquired under pervasive and chronic stress.

In regard to compassion fatigue, it is the responsibility of supervisors to ensure that staff are not overburdened; work tasks should be distributed appropriately and equitably. Supervisors should conduct audits to determine whether staff are overburdened and in what areas issues can be addressed to relieve worker stress. Supervisors have the primary responsibility of dismantling the unrealistic expectations around the ideal worker in student affairs, helping staff let go of the myths that promote unhealthy behaviors related to establishing appropriate work–life boundaries.

Supervisors should also engage in debriefing with staff encountering traumatic material in the course of their work with students. Debriefing plays an important role in assisting student affairs professionals to develop the skills necessary for working with students who have experienced trauma. Debriefing is a strategy to mitigate the negative effects of secondary trauma. Instead of informal debriefing with friends, family, and colleagues, where the tendency is to share all of the graphic details, Mathieu (2012) recommended *low-impact debriefing*, which involves four key steps to ensure what traumatic material is shared in consultation with a supervisor or fellow colleague does not cause further stress to either party. Supervisors can educate staff regarding best practices in the debriefing process.

Low-impact debriefing suggests staff start from the outside of the story with the least traumatic information, moving gradually toward the core, where the most traumatic material resides. Sometimes sharing graphic details is necessary, but "often it is not" (Mathieu, 2012, p. 45). Supervisors should work with staff to evaluate whether sharing, and how much, of the traumatic material is necessary for a professional discussion focusing on how to best address the needs of the student. Minimizing exposure (and reexposure) to traumatic material is an important strategy for keeping student affairs staff healthy.

Supervisors should also include the development and use of individual self-care plans as part of the supervision experience, revisiting those often to hold staff accountable. This practice also provides administrative personnel with an additional layer of accountability, as they would have tangible behavioral goals that could be activated when the worker is experiencing distress due to the nature of their job. Self-care plans can be adapted to fit the needs of the institution and the nature of the work. Student affairs supervisors should take care to ensure that personnel completing the plans have the access and means with which to carry out the behavioral benchmarks outlined in the plan.

Senior Student Affairs Officers

Senior student affairs officers (SSAOs) should promote burnout and compassion fatigue awareness and training for staff so they can adopt practices that mitigate the effects of chronic stress and secondary trauma. The best way to challenge ideal worker norms and dismantle unhealthy work environments is for the SSAO to lead by example, modeling a healthy professional work–life balance.

Social connection is a critical thread that runs through student affairs work. The opportunity to build and maintain collegial relationships with peers and supervisors can be paramount. Supervisor and peer support are also key factors in job satisfaction and a worker's perceived efficacy. Senior student affairs officers can help in myriad ways: providing support regarding policy, procedures, programmatic guidelines, and paperwork; providing opportunities for workers to process difficult situations, daily stressors and concerns, and toll the responsibilities of the job takes on them; providing access to staff that can support workers' mental health (i.e., college counselors) to help ameliorate the stressors of the experience; and lastly, providing workers with opportunities to connect with others in times of crisis, thereby reducing feelings of isolation (DuBois & Mistretta, 2020). Humor, often seen as a protective factor, can be used as a tool for building social cohesion among staff members. Humor enables individuals to gain perspective, identify the lighter side of a situation, and laugh at themselves. Moran (2002) found that humor can improve immune-system functioning and reduce physiological stress symptoms in individuals at risk for developing compassion fatigue.

A number of components can contribute to cultural change regarding ideal worker norms in student affairs. Workers comply when one person accepts influence from another individual or group with the hope of gaining a favorable reaction or to avoid punishment (Eagly et al., 2004). SSAOs can create opportunities for professional development to raise awareness about burnout and compassion fatigue as another socially binding experience for their workers. Additionally, effective mentoring of inexperienced staff by more-seasoned student affairs officers can ameliorate some of the stressors. A supportive SSAO can assuage anxiety, offer suggestions and alternatives to daily struggles, and provide additional resources when foundational and experiential knowledge is limited and professional development is warranted (DuBois & Mistretta, 2020).

Institutional Policy and Practices

The bottom line for institutions is that attrition of student affairs staff incurs significant costs. Employee turnover creates expenditures associated with recruiting, hiring, and training new staff. Other costs involve the loss of efficiency, lack of consistency and quality in service delivery, and loss of institutional and departmental knowledge (Rosser & Javinar, 2003). Systemic responses to the problems associated with the ideal worker construct that lead to the development of burnout and compassion fatigue are necessary to reduce attrition. While most efforts focus on change at the individual level, as Maslach (2017) suggested, "Organizational intervention can be more productive than individual intervention" (p. 149).

Institutions should evaluate whether the quantitative and qualitative workload in student affairs is supported by current resources and staffing structure. Over time, student affairs professionals have assumed heavier workloads in an environment where most institutions are struggling to manage the challenges of declining financial resources and increased accountability (Anderson et al., 2000). Many additional staff responsibilities are associated with the ever-growing needs of students without commensurate expansion of resources and personnel. Current job roles and responsibilities may need to be reimagined to better distribute work stressors more evenly across the institution.

Institutions of higher education should also promote awareness among their staff regarding burnout and compassion fatigue. Acknowledging that student affairs professionals can develop burnout and compassion fatigue normalizes the experience and combats the perception that staff must adopt ideal worker norms. It would also reduce the stigma for workers who feel there might be negative consequences in admitting they are struggling and perhaps not living up to perceived ideal worker norms. Employee programs addressing burnout and compassion fatigue would also engage the entire institution in examining working conditions that promote its development and prioritize resources to support staff who are struggling with secondary trauma and job stress–related issues. For staff exposed to trauma in the course of their work responsibilities, institutions should provide access to free or affordable counseling services. Institutions should also explore creating policies that provide flextime arrangements or other means of helping workers recover from traumatic or stressful work-related activities. Creation of a culture of healthy professional practice that originates with the institution leads to better outcomes for staff, students, and ultimately the institution.

Conclusion

Confronting ideal worker expectations in student affairs may require a reconceptualization of ideals associated with fit within the profession. Current ideal worker expectations lead to high attrition rates among student affairs staff because many come to see those ideals as unrealistic. In addition, ideal worker expectations reinforce work behaviors that often lead to burnout and compassion fatigue among student affairs professionals. What is needed is the socialization of young workers into the student affairs profession in ways that promote resiliency. The challenge is to design and modify workplaces in ways that will support the satisfaction of core psychological needs through the performance of the job. Perhaps the student affairs profession will then begin to develop new ideal worker expectations that reflect positive engagement with work and personal well-being.

References

Acker, J. (1990). Hierarchies, jobs, bodies: A theory of gendered organizations. *Gender & Society, 4*(2), 139–158. https://doi.org/10.1177/089124390004002002

Anda, R. F., Felitti, V. J., Bremner, J. D., Walker, J. D., Whitfield, C., Perry, B. D., Dube, S. R., & Giles, W. H. (2006). The enduring effects of abuse and related adverse experiences in childhood. A convergence of evidence from neurobiology and epidemiology. *European archives of psychiatry and clinical neuroscience, 256*(3), 174–186. https://doi.org/10.1007/s00406-005-0624-4

Anderson, J. E., Guido-DiBrito, F., & Morrell, J. S. (2000). Factors that influence satisfaction for student affairs administrators. *New Directions for Institutional Research, 27*(1), 99–110. https://doi.org/10.1002/ir.10509

Anthony, C. (2016). Why I left student affairs and how I hope to return. *The Vermont Connection, 37*(1), 2. https://scholarworks.uvm.edu/cgi/viewcontent.cgi?article=1258&context=tvc

Beeny, C., Guthrie, V. L., Rhodes, G. S., & Terrell, P. S. (2005). Personal and professional balance among senior student affairs officers: Gender differences in approaches and expectations. *College Student Affairs Journal, 24*(2), 137–151.

Bender, B. E. (2009). Job satisfaction in student affairs. *NASPA Journal, 46*(4), 553–565. https://doi.org/10.2202/1949-6605.5030

Burnett, H. J., & Wahl, K. (2015). The compassion fatigue and resilience connection: A survey of resilience, compassion fatigue, burnout, and compassion satisfaction among trauma responders. *International Journal of Emergency Mental Health and Human Resilience, 17*(1), 318–326. https://doi.org/10.4172/1522-4821.1000165

Chernoff, C. R. B. (2016). *The crisis of caring: Compassion satisfaction and compassion fatigue among student conduct and behavior intervention professionals* [Unpublished doctoral dissertation]. University of South Florida.

Cieslak, R., Shoji, K., Douglas, A., Melville, E., Luszczynska, A., & Benight, C. C. (2014). A meta-analysis of the relationship between job burnout and secondary traumatic stress among workers with indirect exposure to trauma. *Psychological Services, 11*(1), 75–86. https://doi.org/10.1037/a0033798

Cilente, K., Henning, G., Skinner Jackon, J., Kennedy, D., & Sloan, T. (2006). *Report on the new professional needs study.* American College Personnel Association.

Craig, C. D., & Sprang, G. (2010). Compassion satisfaction, compassion fatigue, and burnout in a national sample of trauma treatment therapists. *Anxiety, Stress & Coping, 23*(3), 319–339. https://doi.org/10.1080/10615800903085818

DuBois, A. L., & Mistretta, M. A. (2020). *Overcoming burnout and compassion fatigue in schools: A guide for counselors, administrators, and educators.* Routledge.

Dyrbye, L. N., Thomas, M. R., Massie, F. S., Power, D. V., Eacker, A., Harper, W., Durning, S., Moutier, C., Szydlo, D. W., Novotny, P. J., Sloan, J. A., & Shanafelt, T. D. (2008). Burnout and suicidal ideation among U.S. medical students. *Annals of Internal Medicine, 149*(5), 334–341. https://doi.org/10.7326/0003-4819-149-5-200809020-00008

Eagly, A. H., Baron, R. M., & Hamilton, V. L. (Eds.). (2004). *The social psychology of group identity and social conflict*. American Psychological Association.

Evans, N. (1983). The status of CSP programs. In N. Evans & R. Bossert (Eds.), *The status of preparation employment opportunities and advancement in the field of student affairs*. Preliminary report for ACPA Commission XII.

Everly, G. S., & Benson, H. (1989). Disorders of arousal and the relaxation response: Speculations on the nature and treatment of stress-related diseases. *International Journal of Psychosomatics, 36*, 15–22.

Figley, C. R. (Ed.). (2002). *Treating compassion fatigue*. Brunner- Routledge.

Freudenberger, H. J. (1974). Staff burnout. *Journal of Social Issues, 30*(1), 159–165. https://doi.org/10.1111/j.1540-4560.1974.tb00706.x

Gentry, J. E. (2005). *Compassion fatigue: Prevention and resiliency*. PESI Healthcare, LLC.

Guthrie, V. L., Woods, E., Cusker, C., & Gregory, M. (2005). A portrait of balance: Personal and professional balance among student affairs educators. *College Student Affairs Journal, 24*(4), 110–127.

Hochschild, A. R. (1983). *The managed heart*. University of California Press.

Howard-Hamilton, M. F., Palmer, C., Johnson, S., & Kicklighter, M. (1998). Burnout and related factors: Differences between women and men in student affairs. *College Student Affairs Journal, 17*(2), 80–91.

James, R. K., & Gilliland, B. E. (2017). *Crisis intervention strategies*. Cengage.

Lynch, R. J. (2017). *Breaking the silence: a phenomenological exploration of secondary traumatic stress in U.S. college student affairs professionals* [Doctoral dissertation, Old Dominion University]. ODU Digital Commons. https://doi.org/10.25777/hyh9-b004

Magolda, M. B., Abes, E., & Torres, V. (2008). Epistemological, intrapersonal, and interpersonal development in the college years and young adulthood. In M. C. Smith & N. DeFrates Densch (Eds.), *Handbook of research on adult learning and development* (pp. 183–219). Lawrence Erlbaum.

Marshall, S. M., Gardner, M. M., Hughes, C., & Lowery, U. (2016). Attrition from student affairs: Perspectives from those who exited the profession. *Journal of Student Affairs Research and Practice, 53*(2), 146–159. https://doi.org/10.1080/19496591.2016.1147359

Maslach, C. (2017). Finding solutions to the problem of burnout. *Consulting Psychology Journal: Practice and Research, 69*(2), 143–152. https://doi.org/10.1037/cpb0000090

Maslach, C., & Jackson, S. E. (1981). The measurement of experienced burnout. *Journal of Occupational Behavior, 2*, 99–113. https://doi.org/10.1002/job.4030020205

Maslach, C., Schaufeli, W. B., & Leiter, M. P. (2001). Job burnout. *Annual Review of Psychology, 52*(1), 397–422. https://doi.org/10.1146/annurev.psych.52.1.397

Mathieu, F. (2012). *The compassion fatigue workbook: Creative tools for transforming compassion fatigue and vicarious traumatization.* Routledge.

Mayo Clinic Staff. (2018, November 21). *Job burnout: How to spot it and take action.* Mayo Clinic. https://www.mayoclinic.org/healthy-lifestyle/adult-health/in-depth/burnout/art-20046642

Melamed, S., Shirom, A., Toker, S., Berliner, S., & Shapira, I. (2006). Burnout and risk of cardiovascular disease: Evidence, possible causal paths, and promising research directions. *Psychological Bulletin, 132*(3), 327–353. https://doi.org/10.1037/0033-2909.132.3.327

Moran, C. C. (2002). Humor as a moderator of compassion fatigue. In C. R. Figley (Ed.), *Treating compassion fatigue* (pp. 147–162). Brunner-Routledge.

Paladino, D. A., Murray, T. L., Newgent, R. A., & Gohn, L. A. (2005). Resident assistant burnout: Factors impacting depersonalization, emotional exhaustion, and personal accomplishment. *Journal of College and University Student Housing, 33*(2), 18–27.

Pines, A., & Aronson, E. (1988). *Career burnout: Causes and cures.* Free Press.

Renn, K. A., & Hodges, J. (2007). The first year on the job: Experiences of new professionals in student affairs. *NASPA Journal, 44*(2), 367–391. https://doi.org/10.2202/0027-6014.1800

Rosser, V. J., & Javinar, J. M. (2003). Midlevel student affairs leaders' intentions to leave: Examining the quality of their professional and institutional work life. *Journal of College Student Development, 44*(6), 813–830. https://doi.org/10.1353/csd.2003.0076

Sallee, M. (2016). Ideal for whom? A cultural analysis of ideal worker norms in higher education and student affairs graduate programs. *New Directions for Higher Education, 2016*(176), 53–67. https://doi.org/10.1002/he.20209

Stoves, D. R. (2014). *Compelled to act: The negotiation of compassion fatigue among student affairs professionals* [Unpublished doctoral dissertation]. Texas A&M University-Corpus Christi.

Tarantola, C. (2018). The proven health benefits of yoga and meditation. *Pharmacy Times.* https://www.pharmacytimes.com/contributor/christina-tarantola/2018/01/the-surprising-ways-a-mindfulness-practice-can-improve-your-quality-of-life

Tull, A. (2006). Synergistic supervision, job satisfaction, and intention to turnover of new professionals in student affairs.. *Journal of College Student Development, 47*(4), 465–480. https://doi.org/10.1353/csd.2006.0053

Tull, A., Hirt, J. B., & Saunders, S. A. (2009). *Becoming socialized in student affairs administration: A guide for new professionals and their supervisors.* Stylus Publishing.

Valent, P. (2002). Diagnosis and treatment of helper stresses, trauma, and illnesses. In C. R. Figley (Ed.), *Treating compassion fatigue* (pp. 17–38). Brunner-Routledge.

8

EMOTIONAL LABOR
AND WELL-BEING

R. Jason Lynch and Kerry L. B. Klima

S tudent affairs work often requires the regular negotiation between felt and displayed emotions. Consider the residential life professional who attends an early morning meeting with only a few hours of sleep after responding to a student crisis. Although they may feel tired, drained, and irritable, they must project an attitude of caring, concern, and responsiveness. Also, consider the career services professional meeting with a senior student who has waited until a month before graduation to start their job search. This may engender feelings of frustration, but the staff member must put aside their frustration to meet organizational perceptions of professionalism. These two hypothetical cases could have been replaced with an endless list of examples of how student affairs professionals engage in *emotional labor*, defined as the management of feeling to create a publicly observable facial and bodily display (Hochschild, 1983), to meet the stated and unstated requirements of their job. But what is the impact of negotiating this type of labor on student affairs professionals?

In this chapter, we explore the emotional labor asked of student affairs professionals and link requirements of emotional labor to ideal worker standards that are reinforced in student affairs work. For the purposes of this chapter, the *ideal worker* may be conceived as an individual who has few personal distractions, such as health, family, and outside interests, that may detract from the work of the organization (Acker, 1990; Williams et al., 2012). To organizational leaders, ideal worker norms assume that professionals and staff are emotionless, unconcerned with personal well-being, and prioritize their job above all else. We argue that the perpetuation of ideal worker standards in student affairs organizations can negatively impact the well-being of professionals. We explore the well-being of professionals through two perspectives: the experiences they bring with them as professionals and the demands placed on them by the student affairs work environment. Finally, we offer recommendations that practitioners, divisional leaders, and the profession at large can use to develop work environments that critically reflect on emotional labor requirements and actively facilitate the well-being of student affairs professionals.

We draw from two qualitative studies that illustrate the intersection of emotional labor and well-being within student affairs work. The first study explored the lived experiences of 30 student affairs practitioners who experienced significant personal impact as a result of supporting students through traumatic life events. Lynch (2017) conducted one-on-one interviews that focused on each participant's personal experience and perceived outcomes as a result of supporting students. Participants were also asked to engage in a visual representation exercise where they used visual art as a mechanism to communicate the emotion and meaning-making involved in their support of students. Participants represented 14 different student affairs functional areas (e.g., housing and residence life, health promotion, academic advising) as well as a broad spectrum of seniority from graduate assistants to senior student affairs administrators. Several practices were employed to ensure trustworthiness within the study, including engaging in triangulation of the data through multiple data collection mechanisms, conducting member checks throughout the data collection and analysis processes, and utilizing a licensed counselor to assist in data analysis as an independent coder.

The second study examined the experiences of eight midlevel student affairs professionals who navigated a mental health condition as a new professional and persisted in the field. Klima (2018) conducted two interviews with nine participants; the first focused on the experiences of professionals navigating their mental health during their first year in the field, and the second explored connections between participant experiences with work–life quality related to their mental health. Interviews were supplemented with a journal exercise where participants were asked to identify five words that described their experience as a new professional who navigated a mental health condition as well as provide a written reflection as to why they chose those five words.

Understanding Emotional Labor

The term *emotional labor* was first coined by Arlie Russell Hochschild in 1983. In her work, she described the commodification of human emotion and defined emotional labor as the management of feeling to create a publicly observable facial and bodily display (Hochschild, 1983). Contemporary scholarship on emotional labor has illustrated that this aspect of work may be performed in a variety of ways, including surface acting, deep acting, and natural expression. *Surface acting* involves adjusting one's outer emotional expressions without altering the internal experience of an emotion (Cheung & Lun, 2015; Hülsheger & Schewe, 2011). This may be exemplified when a student affairs staff member feels internally flustered by an exchange with an angry parent but makes a concerted effort to smile and appear calm despite their internal feelings. *Deep acting* refers to the process of altering one's inner feelings to outwardly display a certain emotion (Brotheridge & Lee, 2002; Grandey, 2000). Using the previous example, this staff member may access a recent happy or comforting memory or engage in deep breathing to conjure an authentically positive expression. Finally, *natural expression* takes place when an individual expresses their genuine emotion—in other words their outward expression matches their internal feeling (Diefendorff et al., 2005).

Although it may be necessary for staff to employ each of these emotional regulation techniques in various contexts for effective job performance, the use of emotional regulation techniques can impact personal well-being. Emotional labor requires individuals to expend energy on the self-control of their emotions (Cheung & Lun, 2015). Studies in both education (Cheung & Lun, 2015; Näring et al., 2006) and service industries (Cheung & Lun, 2015; Muraven & Baumeister, 2000) have demonstrated that surface acting is linked to increased rates of burnout and decreased reports of job satisfaction and psychological well-being. Researchers present mixed results on the impact of deep acting on well-being (Humphrey et al., 2015). Whether engaging in surface or deep acting, both concepts require a certain amount of energy to suppress authentic feelings. Conversely, Cheung and Tang (2010) demonstrated that employees who engage in natural expressions of emotion reported higher rates of job satisfaction and lower levels of psychological distress. However, the link between emotional labor and well-being is more nuanced than the ability to express, or requirement to suppress, what one is feeling.

A number of factors regulate the impact of emotional labor on an individual's well-being. For instance, Hülsheger and Schewe (2011) argued that an employee's desire to be emotionally authentic is directly related to the amount of emotional labor in which the individual engaged. Those wishing to be more authentic may expend more energy in their emotional regulation, thus depleting their emotional and cognitive energy to perform other tasks. However, not all emotions require the same degree of energy expenditure. Experiencing agitation (anger, frustration, anxiousness) had greater ties to reports of burnout and job dissatisfaction. Additionally, the intensity or sustained duration of this feeling contributes to psychological distress (Erickson & Ritter, 2001; Gross, 1998). Interactions with coworkers often require more emotional labor than client or customer interactions (Pugliesi & Schook, 1997). The level of emotional labor involved in these interactions may also be regulated by the length of interactions, the level of familiarity between individuals, and various power dynamics among individuals (Gutek, 1995; Marks, 1994).

Emotional Labor and Higher Education

While much of the literature on emotional labor focuses on service industry professionals, recent research in emotional labor has explored this phenomenon within educational contexts (Constanti & Gibbs, 2004; Sutton, 2004; Yin et al., 2013). In K–12 education, teachers' management of their own emotional expression has been identified as an essential component of effectiveness in the classroom (Constanti & Gibbs, 2004; Näring et al., 2012; Sutton, 2004). In higher education, thought pieces and scholarship have explored the emotional labor performed by faculty members. In one essay, Shayne (2017) argued that faculty of color are often left to shoulder the work involved with providing emotional support of racially minoritized students. She stated,

> Faculty members who perform emotional labor have open-door policies for our hurting students. When students show up clearly in need of support, even if we are buried in course prep, tomorrow's conference presentation, or article deadlines, we take them in, listen, and often offer tissues. (p. 1)

Yet, these faculty are often unrecognized for these efforts, as many consider emotional labor a natural part of supporting their community and not to be considered *work*. Emotional labor is also a gendered experience in the academy. While nontenured faculty report greater demands for emotional labor than tenured peers, woman-identified faculty members continue to report engaging in more emotional labor compared to men regardless of tenure status (Tunguz, 2016).

Although faculty certainly engage in emotional labor in a variety of areas of their work, student affairs professionals are considered to have the most sustained student contact (Lynch, 2017; Reynolds, 2010), and they also expend a great deal of energy on emotional labor. Hochschild (1983) suggested that emotional labor requirements are constructed, in part, by the organization for employees. Since these student affairs professionals have direct and frequent contact with students, there is an assumption from the organization (i.e., university or department) about how they conduct emotionally laborious work. For example, within the context of the ideal worker norm, student affairs professionals should put aside, or turn off, their emotion in order to meet the emotional needs or expectations of students. To date there has been little scholarly discussion of how these acts of emotional labor impact student affairs professionals. In the next section, we highlight the lived experiences of student affairs professionals to illustrate how professionals engage in emotional labor and the subsequent impacts on their well-being.

Negotiating Emotional Labor in Student Affairs

As noted, student affairs staff work within the context of ideal worker norms in college and university settings, particularly in regard to emotional labor demands required when working with students, parents, and colleagues. Within this context, staff are often called to mask their authentic emotions in order to meet explicit or implicit emotional display rules within their organization. Hochschild (1983) described emotional labor acting as managed or situated by the organization and accomplished by the professional and the organization in tandem. As discussed previously, several factors affect how this emotional policing impacts the well-being of staff; yet ideal worker norms assume staff members will sacrifice their well-being for the good of the organization. Drawing on Lynch (2017) and Klima (2018), we illustrate experiences of student affairs professionals who have been negatively impacted by emotional labor through their interactions with students, coworkers, supervisors, institutional leaders, and organizations. Quotes from professionals in this chapter have been masked using pseudonyms in order to protect the anonymity of study participants.

Students

Student support and development is the foundation of the student affairs profession and is often the source of inspiration and purpose for professionals. Yet the participants in our studies reveal that this level of support frequently requires a significant investment of emotional labor and may sometimes come at a cost to the professional. For example, Anna, a residence life staff member in Klima's study, shared how ignoring her mental health to focus on job demands collided with her ability to manage a student staff meeting. She stated

> There were times when I would get super frustrated with little things. You know, leading a staff meeting and having students doing side chatter, and

I would just explode and start yelling at them, and I am a very calm and patient person in general. And so, you know, that is when I realized, "Oh, maybe I need to do something about this," because I was not performing to the best of my abilities.

Given that the ideal worker norm assumes the person is emotionless, Anna's experience of ignoring her internal emotions and well-being demonstrates how continued levels of surface or deep acting can build to the point of eruption: in this case, risking the trust and cohesion of her team, impacting her ability to function in her work, and undermining her sense of self.

In both studies, student affairs professionals described the emotional labor experienced when negotiating professional boundaries with students. They shared how balancing expectations of professionalism and offering authentic student support created a sense of emotional dissonance. Matt, a senior service-learning and leadership professional from Lynch's study, described the emotional labor of supporting students experiencing poverty and not understanding how much of his own personal reaction would be appropriate to share with students. His experience exemplifies the negotiation between surface acting and natural expression when reacting to stories of student trauma. He described his internal struggle, stating,

What I've learned about myself is I don't have a really good perspective on where these boundaries are for me being emotionally available, compassionate, empathetic, and allowing myself to take on too much responsibility or too much contagion from this trauma. . . . I don't know if it's good when I'm hearing a student tell me their life story, and they're doing it in a dispassionate way, [and I] tear up and a tear run[s] down my cheek. I don't know if that's appropriate or inappropriate. I don't know how much time is an appropriate amount of time to help a student solve their own problem. I don't know how much of my family to neglect and my marriage to neglect, or other aspects of my job to neglect to help the student navigate their trauma. So I've learned that I don't have a good bearing on that. . . . They have a very real cost, a very real cost, and I don't know what to do with that I guess.

These experiences demonstrate how student affairs professionals struggle to negotiate surface acting, deep acting, and authentic expression of how they are feeling. While the ideal worker norm views staff as emotionless, Matt's story illuminates how socialization of student affairs professionals may result in the suppression of their own emotional reactions. This can be harmful for both the professional, as they disregard their true feelings, and for students, who may be looking for overt displays of empathy.

Coworkers

As discussed earlier, emotional labor requirements may occur most often when navigating relationships with coworkers (Pugliesi & Schook, 1997). As a highly social profession, student affairs professionals are expected to build relationships with coworkers within and across departments in order to provide seamless support systems for students. Yet, these efforts may often require frequent and sustained amounts of emotional labor. In Lynch's (2017) study, a number of professionals described the emotional labor that coworkers performed in providing support. Jane, a new professional in residential life, exemplified this as she described her reliance on coworkers after a particularly stressful student crisis:

> I just felt like that sometimes the only people I'll go to, to process in the moment, because they can get it, and they can understand what I'm going through, and know why I'm not giving all the details. I think that's another piece. I can't talk to my mom about it, about a lot of this stuff. . . . I'd rather talk to people who can either find out for themselves, because they get sneaky and start looking at reports . . . or looking at duty logs, or they just know. They're like, "Yeah, I know you can't tell me. That's fine. What's coming up for you though?"

Krista, a career services professional, had a different point of view. She pointed out a need for a structured distribution of emotional labor within student affairs departments. She reflected,

> [At my current institution], we are so good at supporting our students and getting our students connected [to resources], but there was never a time for the staff to talk about it. And even, as [resident directors at my old institution], there was never a time for the staff to talk about it, unless we went out for drinks on our own time or went out for coffee or something like that. But there was never a time where we would sit down and actually discuss it and actually really sit there and let people feel, which is such bullshit for a profession that's supposed to be supporting. But who are we supporting? I guess we're supporting the students, right? Okay, yeah, supporting the students at the cost of the staff.

While not a part of most job descriptions, there is some level of expectation that employees are providing emotional support to one another, which can come at a cost. Whether listening to a coworker's struggle to support a student or listening to a coworker's complaint of their peers or supervisors, this emotional labor often goes unacknowledged, despite the energy it consumes.

Leadership and Organizations

Colleges and universities are managed by leaders who adopt policies and practices that intentionally and unintentionally perpetuate ideal worker norms, including stated or implied requirements for emotional labor. For example, an employee may be experiencing a personal hardship at home, but is required to dissociate from their feelings in order to create an amicable work environment for coworkers, students, and other stakeholders. Within the context of college student affairs, these explicit and implicit practices fail to adequately consider the emotionally laborious work of staff or their well-being. One professional in Klima's (2018) study described situations where she negotiated how leave policies would affect her work and her well-being.

> I thought about taking the family medical leave because it was so much turmoil for me. I couldn't concentrate at work. I was constantly agitated. I wanted things to be over quickly. I had no attention span at work. I still struggle with my attention at work. And so that's been really hard.

She continued to question how her decision would be perceived by peers and supervisors, highlighting how merely considering taking time off work induces more mental health concerns.

> But then again that paralyzing fear of what does that look like? What does that mean for my job if I do take that [leave]? What if I need it again, like scared of the unknown like having, nobody talked to us about this.

She struggled to understand how the policies would work, but also knew it may help her with her well-being in the long term.

In Lynch's (2017) study, Luke, a new professional in campus activities, expressed how external norms and expectations within his university conflicted with his own expectations of student support as well as how these norms had a negative impact on him.

> The one thing that I noticed in dealing with those traumatic incidences was I didn't like how much I worried about what the administration was going to do after I handled the situation. That entered into the pattern of feelings that I would feel. I didn't realize how there was something wrong there for me until—I would say until about a year before I left. . . . There seems to be this culture of protecting the university.

Colleges and universities have long valued the holistic well-being of students, as many campuses offer health services, family day care centers, and mental health counseling. Yet this support is rarely extended to the staff of the institutions to the same degree. In Klima's (2018) study, one participant talked about how professionals encourage students to attend counseling appointments for their mental health but may consider keeping their own counseling experiences hidden for fear of judgment or being perceived as taking personal time during the workday. This perceived need to obscure aspects of oneself that contradicts ideal worker standards was also exemplified in Victoria's experience. In Klima's study, Victoria shared,

> When I was going through depression and at the height of my anxiety I wouldn't go [to conference sessions]. I was supposed to attend a conference that was [nearby] and so I would have been able to drive up there and I, I didn't, I didn't want to go. I told my supervisor that, I think I told her like, "Oh I don't think these sessions are going to be helpful for me," when it was really like I didn't want to go there by myself. I'm really overwhelmed. I don't want to have to drive in traffic to get up there, like, I don't want to have to like sit by myself and like be aware of everything that's going on around me. I pretty much removed myself from that realm for about 7 or 8 months.

While obscuring personal appointments or glossing over the truth of their own health are but two examples, many professionals find themselves engaging in emotional labor to be perceived as a strong worker by their supervisors or organizations.

Further complicating matters, student affairs professionals consistently receive mixed messages about managing aspects of their own well-being, such as boundary setting. Although the literature reflects a need for healthy boundaries (Linder, 2011), the lived experiences of professionals exemplifies how departmental and divisional cultures do not allow for this. In Lynch's (2017) study, Rene described the experience of balancing her role as professional helper with a myriad of other responsibilities. During her interview, she exemplified many of the gendered experiences associated with emotional labor, as she consistently found herself providing more than her share of emotional support for an almost constant flow of students in crisis while also balancing the tasks specific to her job. Rene shared,

It just keeps coming. It's a constant deluge. It's never—it will never end, and there's no such thing as a non-busy period for us. I have a list of projects and things that I'm supposed to be doing that I don't even have time to do, and I'm worried that I'm going to be half-assing a lot of it because there's just not time, and I refuse to do this stuff on weekends. I didn't used to be like that, but now that I'm working this full-time job, I am hoarding my personal time because I would probably go insane if I tried to do extra work outside of my job for the job.

Rene actively undermined ideal worker norms and disengaged from the emotional labor of pretending she can continually manage an unreasonable workload. Yet, for many professionals, this act of subversion through self-care may not be an option due to potential job loss or other retaliatory actions.

Our studies illustrate experiences of student affairs professionals who have been negatively impacted by ideal worker standards and the emotional labor required of them by interactions with students, coworkers, and within the organizations. When considering the emotional labor necessitated by ideal worker norms, staff struggled to negotiate what their well-being meant within the organization and as they worked with others.

Recommendations for Practice

Ideal worker standards in student affairs result in staff potentially engaging in high levels of emotional labor, sometimes to the detriment of their personal well-being. Staff can easily find themselves negotiating their authentic emotional responses and the expression of emotions that are deemed acceptable to students, coworkers, and institutional leaders. Drawing on the discussions in this chapter, we provide a series of recommendations for practice to challenge ideal worker norms and emphasize well-being that are tailored to graduate students and new professionals, midcareer professionals, supervisors, senior student affairs officers (SSAOs), organizations, and the greater student affairs profession.

Graduate Students and New Professionals

Through the narratives explored in our research, we recognized how negotiating personal boundaries, self-advocacy, and explicit conversations about wellness and emotional labor were rarely discussed in graduate preparation programs or trainings. Building these skills as a part of early-career development may produce long-term outcomes for building and maintaining wellness for student affairs professionals. Using Guthrie et al.'s (2005) model for professional balance (self-knowledge, intentionality, commitment to self-care, and reflection), new professional and graduate supervisors may provide intentional opportunities, whether in staff meetings or one-on-one settings, to offer space to develop these components of balance and encourage positive well-being. However, if this support is not being provided, new professionals and graduate students may consider building reflective practices, such as journaling or meeting with mentors, to assess their personal values, their own self-knowledge, and their ability to identify and manage their emotions.

Additionally, organizations may consider creating professional development opportunities for graduate students and new professionals in which panels of seasoned professionals share practical examples of caring for their well-being and negotiating emotional labor. Various assessments related to emotional labor and well-being also exist for group or individual use, including the secondary trauma in student affairs professionals (STSAP) scale (Lynch & Glass, 2018) or Diefendorff's et al. (2014) emotional demands–abilities fit assessment. Both measure various outcomes of emotional labor and may be used to provide early intervention for new professionals and graduate students.

Midcareer Professionals and Supervisors

Midcareer professionals and supervisors often work directly with entry-level professionals and graduate students while balancing expectations of senior level officials. These professionals may be required to exercise a greater degree of emotional labor as they engage in interactions with a wider range of stakeholders in student affairs. To that end, it is important that these professionals reflect on boundary setting and practice self-reflection and self-awareness. This may take the form of required regular group meetings where midcareer or middle-management staff can define boundaries through self-reflection and group discussion.

As they manage their own well-being, managers and midcareer professionals can also craft job descriptions and expectations that acknowledge the influence of emotional labor and center the concept of well-being for their employees. For example, a housing and residence life entry-level job description could include a percentage of workload expected for on-call tasks/activities, which does not include more emotional labor work than necessary to continue the organization's functions while considering the professional's labor. Supervisors can also be intentional about processes that encourage holistic development of the professional. For example, in functional areas that commonly engage in late-night and weekend work, providing time off or schedule flexibility for the days following overnight shifts or late and weekend events may help in providing space for the professionals to employ self-care strategies that encourage balance and prevent burnout. By having established policies, staff may be spared the worry of how asking for personal time may be perceived by supervisors or coworkers.

SSAOs

SSAOs are asked to provide vision, communication, and accountability for their divisions. Like midlevel supervisors, SSAOs should understand the emotional labor requirements they ask of their staff as well as establish strategies to center the well-being of staff. This may be done by establishing task forces or ad hoc assessment committees to understand the nature of emotional labor within their organizations as well as how emotional labor factors into cultures of well-being within the organization. SSAOs might also extend a well-being assessment to staff, such as those mentioned earlier, which will provide information to leaders in divisions of student affairs on how to best support staff development in relation to well-being. They may also encourage the formation of division-wide committees where professionals can take ownership of well-being initiatives or implement recommendations for well-being assessments.

Lastly, SSAOs should be transparent in their vision of staff well-being and expectations or organizational norms regarding management of emotional labor. Communicating an explicit vision and organizational norms allows staff within the organization to better balance their own well-being, make more informed decisions about fit, and have firm grounding in which to discuss their needs in regard to balancing wellness. Professionals should always center services on the student experience, learning, growth, and development. However, this can be done without compromising the role and well-being of the staff. SSAOs and supervisors should demonstrate how this negotiation can occur to embody well-being, self-reflection, and care, while keeping the student at the center and a priority.

Recommendations for Organizations

Organizational leaders may adjust practices to ensure that staff well-being is a part of the organizational culture and structure. Human resources along with diversity and inclusion offices should review their institutional policies and practices to identify ways to encourage an acknowledgement of well-being and emotional labor. For example, review job descriptions for functions that may require emotional labor and ensure there are other functions within the position that do not require as much emotional labor. Another example involves the free physical health classes and workout spaces some campuses offer. Campuses could consider offering weekly sessions that support mental and spiritual well-being such as meditation hours, yoga classes, and other reflection activities. However, attention must be given to when employees are encouraged and allowed to participate in activities that attend to the personal self. Some institutions are situated in unionized environments and have strict state laws which regulate time for breaks, lunches, and types of activities that can be performed during the scheduled work time. Human resources can work with external agencies to identify ways to craft policies that are compliant with these organizations and structures but still center the well-being of the employee.

Finally, organizational leaders should seek to actively develop cultures of authenticity in which staff are able to fully share concerns with each other and with leadership. Without constructive avenues for sharing, staff may hold on to emotions over time, resulting in unnecessary emotional labor. Simple check-ins with individual staff members or regular small group debriefs offer opportunities for staff to express emotion in a directed and productive context. These meetings may be focused on dealing with well-being, unpacking recent events that required heavy emotional labor, or offering space to introduce emerging issues within the staff.

Recommendations for the Profession

Although the 2015 joint ACPA & NASPA professional competencies mention personal wellness, these competencies need to be expanded and more explicit. Additionally, the profession needs to provide mechanisms for organizational and personal accountability regarding well-being. This may include a clearer ethics statement on the importance of and processes to encourage self-care and well-being. These may be modeled after other helping profession ethics statements such as the American Counseling Association (2014) code of ethics statement which states,

> Counselors are alert to the signs of impairment from their own physical, mental, or emotional problems and refrain from offering or providing professional services when such impairment is likely to harm a client or others. They seek assistance for problems that reach the level of professional impairment. (p. 9)

The field can draw from their ethics of care and standards to further emphasize the importance of student affairs professionals' well-being, which in turn increases capacity to engage in the emotional labor necessary to support students.

Student affairs practitioners often apply developmental theories to their work with students. For example, fixed and growth mindset work is a strategy to use with students, but can also be applied for the development of staff. Dweck (2008) defined *fixed mindset* as a belief that a person's abilities, intelligence, and talents are fixed and cannot be changed, while a *growth mindset* recognizes a person's ability to develop and grow their abilities, intelligence, and talents. It is important for professionals to reflect on ways they can manage their well-being, because it emphasizes the opportunity for change and growth instead of accepting their status quo. Student affairs national organizations may prioritize professional development that encourages their constituents to think about their well-being from a growth perspective. The emphasis on continuous improvement aligns with the perspective that balance as professionals is a developmental journey.

National organizations frequently offer institutes on assessment and well-being, but these are often primarily focused on students. These events could be expanded to include how to apply similar tenets of support of well-being to staff and professionals. Lastly, professional associations should provide grants for research to better understand professional experiences and interventions regarding well-being and emotional labor. Such funding may encourage and support the examination of professional well-being to provide enhanced understanding of the role of emotional labor in student affairs work.

Conclusion

Emotional labor is often an implicit and undervalued work requirement of human-centered professions such as student affairs. When considered through the lens of ideal worker norms (e.g., emotionless and unconcerned with personal well-being), it becomes clear how emotional labor contributes to attrition rates (Marshall et al., 2016) and reports of professional burnout (Mullen et al., 2018) for staff within student affairs. Using our research to illustrate the impact of the connection between emotional labor and ideal worker norms, we underscored the need for professionals to name emotional labor requirements, create space for emotional authenticity, and further develop policies and practices that allow for balance of student and staff well-being. Collectively, we must encourage all stakeholders within the student affairs profession to critically reflect on the nature and impact of emotional labor within student affairs.

References

Acker, J. (1990). Hierarchies, jobs, bodies: A theory of gendered organizations. *Gender and Society, 4*(2), 139–158. https://doi.org/10.1177/089124390004002002

ACPA & NASPA. (2015). *Professional competency areas for student affairs.* ACPA, College Student Educators International & National Association of Student Personnel Administrators.

American Counseling Association. (2014). 2014 ACA code of ethics. https://www.counseling.org/Resources/aca-code-of-ethics.pdf

Brotheridge, C. M., & Lee, R. T. (2002). Testing a conservation of resources model of the dynamics of emotional labor. *Journal of Occupational Health Psychology, 7*(1), 57–67. https://doi.org/10.1037/1076-8998.7.1.57

Cheung, F., & Lun, V. M. (2015). Emotional labor and occupational well-being: A latent profile analytic approach. *Journal of Individual Differences, 36*(1), 30–37. https://doi.org/10.1027/1614-0001/a000152

Cheung, F., & Tang, C. (2010). Effects of age, gender, and emotional labor strategies on job outcomes: Moderated mediation analyses. *Applied Psychology: Health and Wellbeing, 2*, 323–339. https://doi.org/10.1111/j.1758-0854.2010.01037.x

Constanti, P., & Gibbs, P. (2004). Higher education teachers and emotional labor. *International Journal of Educational Management, 18*, 243–249. https://doi.org/10.1108/09513540410538822

Diefendorff, J. M., Croyle, M. H., & Gosserand, R. H. (2005). The dimensionality and antecedents of emotional labor strategies. *Journal of Vocational Behavior, 66*(2), 339–359. https://doi.org/10.1016/j.jvb.2004.02.001

Diefendorff, J. M., Greguras, G. J., & Fleenor, J. (2014). Perceived emotional demands–abilities fit. *Applied Psychology, 65*(1), 2–37. https://doi.org/10.1111/apps.12034

Dweck, C. S. (2008). *Mindset: The new psychology of success.* Ballantine Books.

Erickson, R. J., & Ritter, C. (2001). Emotional labor, burnout, and inauthenticity: Does gender matter? *Social Psychology Quarterly, 64*(2), 146–163. https://doi.org/10.2307/3090130

Grandey, A. A. (2000). Emotion regulation in the workplace: A new way to conceptualize emotional labor. *Journal of Occupational Health Psychology, 5*(1), 95–110. https://doi.org/10.1037/1076-8998.5.1.95

Gross, J. J. (1998). Antecedent and response-focused emotion regulation: Divergent consequences for experience, expression, and physiology. *Journal of Personality and Social Psychology, 74*(1), 224–237. https://doi.org/10.1037/0022-3514.74.1.224

Gutek, B. A. (1995). *The dynamics of service: Reflections on the changing nature of customer/provider interactions.* Jossey-Bass.

Guthrie, V. L., Woods, E., Cusker, C., & Gregory, M. (2005). A portrait of balance: Personal and professional balance among student affairs educators. *College Student Affairs Journal, 24*(2), 110–127.

Hochschild, A. R. (1983). *The managed heart: Commercialization of human feeling.* University of California Press.

Hülsheger, U. R., & Schewe, A. F. (2011). On the costs and benefits of emotional labor: A meta-analysis of three decades of research. *Journal of Occupational Health Psychology, 16*(3), 361–389. https://doi.org/10.1037/a0022876

Humphrey, R. H., Ashforth, B. E., & Diefendorff, J. M. (2015). The bright side of emotional labor. *Journal of Organizational Behavior, 36*(6), 749–769. https://doi .org/10.1002/job.2019

Klima, K. L. B. (2018). *Hidden, supported, and stressful: A phenomenological study of midlevel student affairs professionals' entry-level experiences with a mental health condition* (Publication No. 10871510) [Doctoral dissertation, Bowling Green State University]. ProQuest Dissertations and Theses Global.

Linder, K. (2011). Why do student affairs educators struggle to set professional boundaries? Establishing and maintaining healthy professional and personal boundaries. In P. Magolda & M. B. Baxter Magolda (Eds.), *Contested issues in student affairs: Diverse perspectives and respectful dialogue* (pp. 434–452). Stylus.

Lynch, R. J. (2017). *Breaking the silence: A phenomenological exploration of secondary traumatic stress in U.S. college student affairs professionals* (Publication No. 9780355348958) [Doctoral dissertation, Old Dominion University]. ProQuest Dissertations and Theses Global.

Lynch, R. J., & Glass, C. R. (2018). The development of the secondary trauma in student affairs professionals scale. *Journal of Student Affairs Research and Practice, 56*(1), 1–18. https://doi.org/10.1080/19496591.2018.1474757

Marks, S. R. (1994). Intimacy in the public realm: The case of co-workers. *Social Forces, 72*(3), 843–858. https://doi.org/10.2307/2579783

Marshall, S. M., Gardner, M. M., Hughes, C., & Lowery, U. (2016). Attrition from student affairs: Perspectives from those who exited the profession. *Journal of Student Affairs Research & Practice, 53*(2), 146–159. https://doi.org/10.1080/ 19496591.2016.1147359

Mullen, P. R., Malone, A., Denney, A., & Dietz, S. S. (2018). Job stress, burnout, job satisfaction, and turnover intention among student affairs professionals. *College Student Affairs Journal, 6*(1), 94–108. https://doi.org/10.1353/csj.2018.0006

Muraven, M., & Baumeister, R. F. (2000). Self-regulation and depletion of limited resources: Does self-control resemble a muscle? *Psychological Bulletin, 126*(2), 247–259. https://doi.org/10.1037/0033-2909.126.2.247

Näring, G., Briët, M., & Brouwers, A. (2006). Beyond demand–control: Emotional labour and symptoms of burnout in teachers. *Work and Stress, 20*(4), 303–315. https://doi.org/10.1080/02678370601065182

Näring, G., Vlerick, P., & Van de Ven, B. (2012). Emotional work and emotional exhaustion in teachers: The job and individual perspective. *Educational Studies, 38*(1), 63–72. https://doi.org/10.1080/03055698.2011.567026

Pugliesi, K., & Schook, S. L. (1997). Gender, jobs, and emotional labor in a complex organization. In R. J. Erikson & B. Cuthbertson-Johnson (Eds.), *Social Perspective on Emotion* (4th ed., 283–316). JAI.

Reynolds, A. L. (2010). Counseling and helping skills. In S. R. Jones & J. H. Schuh (Eds.), *Student services: A handbook for the profession* (pp. 399–412). Jossey-Bass.

Shayne, J. (2017). Recognizing emotional labor in academe. *Inside Higher Ed.* https://www.insidehighered.com/advice/2017/09/15/importance-recognizing -faculty-their-emotional-support-students-essay

Sutton, R. E. (2004). Emotional regulation goals and strategies of teachers. *Social Psychology of Education, 7*(4), 379–398. https://doi.org/10.1007/s11218-004 -4229-y

Tunguz, S. (2016). In the eye of the beholder: Emotional labor in academia varies with tenure and gender. *Studies in Higher Education, 41*(1), 3–20. https://doi.org/ 10.1080/03075079.2014.914919

Williams, C. L., Muller, C., & Kilanski, K. (2012). Gendered organizations in the new economy. *Gender & Society, 26*(4), 549–573. https://doi.org/10.1177/ 0891243212445466

Yin, H., Lee, J., Zhang, Z., & Jin, Y. (2013). Exploring the relationship among teachers' emotional intelligence, emotional labor strategies and teaching satisfaction. *Teaching and Teacher Education, 35*, 137–145. https://doi.org/10 .1016/j.tate.2013.06.006

PART THREE

HOW VARIOUS IDENTITY
GROUPS NAVIGATE STUDENT
AFFAIRS WORK

9

DISCLOSURE, INCLUSION, AND CONSEQUENCES FOR LGBTQ STUDENT AFFAIRS PROFESSIONALS

Carrie A. Kortegast

The field of student affairs is often considered welcoming, affirming, and inclusive for lesbian, gay, bisexual, transgender, and queer (LGBTQ) professionals (Renn, 2003). While individual institutions might be less affirming, the values of the larger field as represented by professional organizations (e.g., American College Personnel Association [ACPA], National Association of Student Personnel Administrators [NASPA], and the Association of College and University Housing Officers – International [ACUHO-I]), standards for professional competency (ACPA & NASPA, 2015), and master's-level professional preparation (i.e., Council for the Advancement of Standards in Higher Education [CAS], 2015) all have statements about diversity, equity, and social justice as a core value and competency. LGBTQ people often choose the field of student affairs because it is a helping field that espouses diversity, equity, and inclusion. These values, in part, drew me to the field of student affairs, first as a practitioner and then as a faculty member.

Writing this chapter has given me pause to reexamine my own experiences navigating the field of student affairs as a White, middle-class, queer, cisgender woman. I have often considered myself "lucky" to have been able to work at both private and public institutions that have been relatively LGBTQ "friendly," or at the very least have nondiscrimination policies that included sexual orientation and gender identity and domestic partner benefits (prior to marriage equality). In retrospect, I knew I could not work just anywhere and structured my career to work at places that were more supportive of LGBTQ student affairs professionals and faculty. I had particular privileges—economic, educational, race, and gender identity—that allowed me to do this. However, my privileged identities could not protect me against experiences of sexism, homophobia, and heterosexism throughout my career. I have received implicit and explicit messages that I should be grateful or was lucky to have particular positions as a queer person. Because I was childfree (not completely by choice) and was unmarried until my mid-30s, I rarely had commitments at home that pulled me away from paid employment. My employers benefited from this as well as the precariousness I often felt as an out professional and faculty member.

In Renn's (2010) article about the state and status of LGBTQ research in the field of higher education, she argued that colleges and universities have "tolerate[d] the generation of queer theory from within but have stalwartly resisted the queering of higher education itself" (p. 132). Thus, queerness has been allowed to exist within institutions but not embraced or changed by these theories or bodies. The same can be said for the field of student affairs. Organizational logics regarding gender, sexuality, and job roles (Acker, 1990) shape how organizations reward particular work and particular bodies. Organizations, including higher education and the field of student affairs, are neither gender-neutral nor asexual (Acker, 1990). To understand an organization as *gendered* means to understand what "advantage and disadvantage, exploitation and control, action and emotion, meaning and identity, are patterned through and in terms of a distinction between male and female, masculine and feminine" (p. 146). These patterns of organizational logics are not only gendered but also heteronormative. Thus, the exploitation of individual bodies vis-à-vis ideal worker norms manifests differently for LGBTQ student affairs professionals.

The purpose of this chapter is to explore how the concept of the ideal worker mediates LGBTQ student affairs professionals' work lives and the consequences for not aligning with organizational logics about the ideal worker. Here, I argue that LGBTQ people in student affairs have simultaneously been exploited and controlled through institutional policies and practices that are embedded in the ideal worker paradigm. While all student affairs professionals are subjected to ideal worker norms, the subjection of LGBTQ individuals is often rooted in institutional and legalized discrimination. Here I will outline the ways in which LGBTQ bodies, identities, and relationships are policed, (de)valued, and regulated within student affairs and higher education. Consequences of ideal worker norms have real and material consequences for LGBTQ individuals.

Interlude About Conflation of Gender and Sexuality

I approach this chapter with some trepidation about representation of a singular understanding of the experience of LGBTQ student affairs professionals. While there are overlapping concerns, experiences, and struggles between these different and distinct identities, presenting them here—together—runs the risk of indicating these identities are just like each other (Halley, 2000). While the acronym LGBTQ often excludes and "normalizes groups of people" (Vaccaro et al., 2015, p. 25), there are overlapping and shared experiences that individuals with minoritized identities of gender and sexuality experience. However, these experiences vary in real and material ways that are often intrinsically interconnected with other social identities (both privileged and minoritized), geographic localities, institutional values, and professional positionality.

Educational research and student affairs practice has an uncomfortable history of the conflation of gender and sexuality in research (Renn, 2010). More recently, professional conferences, both practitioner and higher education researcher, have seen an expansion of programs, sessions, and scholarship about LGBTQ people and topics (Kortegast et al., 2020; Pryor et al., 2017). While there are examples of sessions and papers that attend to a single identity (e.g., transgender, lesbian, gay) or the intersection with other social identities (e.g., class, race, religion), the majority of sessions collapse minoritized identities of sexuality and gender (Vaccaro et al., 2015) under the umbrella of LGB or LGBT(Q) (Kortegast et al., 2020; Pryor et al., 2017). This perpetuates the problem of the conflation of gender and sexuality. Thus, there is still much work to be done to more fully understand how student affairs work values, recognizes, and rewards different bodies and identities within the structure of higher education.

Protecting, Policing, and Regulating LGBTQ Bodies in the Workplace

The recent Supreme Court decision *Obergefell v. Hodges (2015)* expanded the right for same-sex couples to marry in every state. However, the expansion of marriage rights did not eliminate legalized discrimination in other parts of LGBTQ individuals' lives. The notion that someone could be fired or denied public accommodations because they identify as LGBTQ is still an open question. In general, there are no federal protections "with respect to employment, housing, public accommodation, education, and a range of aspects of daily life for LGBTQ Americans" (Fidas & Cooper,

2018, p. 5). On June 15, 2020, the U.S. Supreme Court ruled that firing an LGBTQ person because of their sexuality and/or gender identity was a form of sex discrimination and, thus, illegal. The outcome of this case will have significant consequences for LGBTQ people and employers including those in higher education. Prior to the June 2020 ruling, 22 states prohibited employment discrimination based on sexual orientation and gender identity with an additional 11 states providing protections for just state employees (Human Rights Campaign, 2020). LGBTQ student affairs professionals living in states without employment nondiscrimination policies were often left to rely upon institutional-level policies to provide these workplace protections.

Nondiscrimination policies reflect whose bodies, identities, genders, and relationships are worthy of protection. Increasingly, colleges and universities have added sexual orientation and gender identity/expression into institutional nondiscrimination policies. The exact number of colleges and universities with nondiscrimination policies inclusive of sexual orientation has not been tracked. However, the Trans Policy Clearinghouse indicated that, as of February 2020, 1,055 institutions have nondiscrimination policies that include gender identity and/or expression (Campus Pride, 2020). For states that do not include sexual orientation and gender identity/expression in state statutes, the inclusion of nondiscrimination policies varies state by state and institution by institution. LGBTQ student affairs professionals living in states and working at institutions that do not include sexual orientation and/or gender identity/expression in their nondiscrimination policies "might run the risk of being terminated for being out or because of their LGBTQ advocacy on campus" (Kortegast & van der Toorn, 2018, p. 270).

The choice to not provide protections can be interpreted as the labor or work of LGBTQ people not being as good as the labor of cisgender and straight people—in particular, cisgender straight men. If the ideal worker concept is a "deeply gendered construct" (p. 5, this volume) as Sallee discusses in the introduction to this book, then LGBTQ bodies in and of themselves challenge these gender assumptions both by who they love and how they express themselves. LGBTQ bodies and workers disrupt gendered notions of labor both in and out of the home. The academy, particularly the neoliberal one, prioritizes an individual's value by their ability to provide productive labor (Pitcher, 2018). The enactment of these laws—or not—is tied to whose labor is understood as productive and who is the ideal worker.

The assumption that the ideal worker is cisgender, male, and heterosexual allows for the overt and covert policing of individuals who do not align with this image. This policing and regulation about who does and does not belong within particular workplaces is a consequence of assumptions about the ideal worker. In organizations that are described as "gay friendly," as student affairs is often described (Renn, 2003), LGB employees still report differential treatment and discrimination in their workplace because of their identities (Williams et al., 2009).[1] In a national study of LGBTQ students, faculty, and staff, 20% of staff reported experiencing exclusionary, offensive, hostile, or intimidating conduct because of their identity (Rankin et al., 2010). While 83% of respondents indicated feeling comfortable within their departments/work units, 27% reported feeling uncomfortable with the overall campus climate. Thus, while student affairs professionals may feel accepted within their departments, they still often experience stereotyping, pressure to minimize their openness about their sexuality and gender identity, and incidents of harassment and discrimination.

In efforts to build office cohesion, teamwork, and rapport between colleagues, workplaces often require some level of personal sharing (Fidas & Cooper, 2018). These conversations may focus on children, spouses, relationships, dating, social life, weekend plans, TV shows, movies, and so forth. However, LGBTQ individuals are often held to a double standard in that building team cohesion is based on some degree of sharing of personal information, yet LGBTQ individuals often receive messages "that their sharing is not welcome" (Fidas & Cooper, 2018, p. 14). While the ideal worker construct is predicated on the separation of work and home lives, there are expectations that certain sharing and certain personal life information is important to share for group cohesion. However, LGBTQ workers often have to regulate and police what they share as to not make others uncomfortable or not open themselves up for discrimination.

Perceptions of an individual's work environment impacts an employee's work attitudes, motivation, and performance (Parker et al., 2003). Thus, the psychological climate for LGBTQ student affairs professionals can influence work performance and job satisfaction (Croteau & Lark, 1995; Johnson, 2009). Additionally, perceptions of work environment impact individuals' decisions to stay in or leave a position. LGBTQ workers are more likely to stay in a position if the environment is perceived as very accepting of LGBTQ people (Fidas & Cooper, 2018). Conversely, when work environments are perceived as not very accepting of LGBTQ people, individuals will consider finding new employment. The attrition rates of LGBQ student affairs professionals leaving a position or the field of student affairs because of the campus or departmental environment are unknown. However, Garvey and Rankin's (2018) study of queer and trans-spectrum faculty found a significant relationship between a faculty member's desire to leave and campus climate. Presumably, a similar relationship might exist between campus climate and desire to leave for LGBTQ student affairs professionals.

Employee turnover comes at a cost to all involved. The organization potentially loses a stronger worker and accrues the cost of recruiting, hiring, and training a new employee. For the employee, leaving a position requires time, energy, and a bit of luck in order to find another position that is, at minimum, lateral. The process of voluntarily departing a student affairs position for another position "begins long before official notice to depart is given to a supervisor" (Kortegast & Hamrick, 2009, p. 203). As such, the cumulative effect of a hostile work environment and the policing and regulating of LGBTQ bodies potentially impacts LGBTQ student affairs professionals' ability to be successful, their career trajectories, and their potential for advancement. While student affairs has potentially been a space where queer bodies could exist, the institution of higher education has resisted the queering of itself (Renn, 2010) by maintaining organizational logics that reward and reinforce the ideal worker model.

Disclosure, (Dis)embodiment, and LGBTQ Identity

LGBTQ student affairs professionals' ability to be out and supported in the workplace can shape not only their comfort but also their job performance. Rankin et al.'s (2010) climate study of LGBT individuals in higher education found that 88% of staff and 92% of administrators were out professionally to at least near colleagues.[2] In an earlier study by Croteau and Lark (1995), only 47% of lesbian, gay, and bisexual respondents were out professionally in their work setting. While these studies had different scales and sample sizes, it is fair to say that lesbian, gay, and bisexual student affairs professionals are more likely to be open about their sexuality than in the past. Supportive work environments often allow LGBTQ student affairs professionals to feel more comfortable being out in their workplaces (Kortegast & van der Toorn, 2018). However, there are student affairs professionals who are unable to be open about their sexuality and/or gender identity. This has potential consequences for relationships, job performance, and ability or desire to stay in the position.

Being closeted in the workplace comes at personal costs to the individual and creates a fear of being discovered, which can manifest in lost contributions to communities and workplaces (Maxwell, 2018). Reasons for not being out in the workplace often include not wanting to be stereotyped, not wanting to make other people feel uncomfortable, fear of losing relationships and connections with coworkers, and fear that coworkers might think they are attracted to them (Fidas & Cooper, 2018). A national Human Rights Campaign study about workplace climates for LGBTQ individuals found that 59% of non-LGBTQ respondents believed it was unprofessional to discuss sexuality and gender identity in the workplace

(Fidas & Cooper, 2018). While college and university environments tend to be more progressive than other environments, LGBTQ student affairs workers are not immune to these cultural sentiments about whose relationships are valued and acceptable to talk about. Acker (1990) argued "attempts to banish sexuality from the workplace were part of the wider process that differentiated the home, the location of legitimate sexual activity, from the place of capitalist production" (p. 151). Presumably, Acker was referencing straight women; however, the underlying tenets of the argument can be extended to LGBTQ workers in the idea that sexuality and gender identity have no place in the workplace.

For LGBTQ student affairs professionals who are open about their sexuality, the enactment of outness is often done in careful ways (Kortegast & van der Toorn, 2018). In Barile's (2016) study of 6 gay men and 1 lesbian senior student affairs officers, participants indicated that they "felt uneasy about their disclosures, questioned whether they should disclose their sexualities, and felt others' reactions to the participants' sexualities may have impacted their work" (p. 88). Similarly, in Marshall's (2017) study of 12 LGBTQ student affairs professionals working at LGBTQ centers, participants discussed utilizing their personal LGBTQ identities in their professional roles as LGBTQ educators. These professionals' engagement in queer performatives and aesthetics included "considerations of what participants chose to wear, what personal examples they chose to share in meetings and educational sessions, and how they approached the ability to pass as cisgender and/or heterosexual" (p. 251). Lastly, Kortegast and van der Toorn's (2018) study of 19 gay and lesbian student affairs professionals at small colleges and universities found that while participants were out to at least immediate coworkers, they made statements about not being "in everyone's face," "blatant," or "wearing it like a banner" (p. 273). Seemingly, individuals believed being seen as "too gay" either made others uncomfortable or might be seen as unprofessional. Moreover, across these studies participants minimized their sexuality to ascribe to expectations of the disembodied worker (Acker, 1990).

Understandings of professionalism and how student affairs professionals enact professionalism are deeply gendered. To be professional often requires a "separation of work and sexuality" (Acker, 1990, p. 151), creating a disembodiment of worker from the work. The presence of LGBTQ workers often threatens the illusion of the separation of work from gender and sexuality. Trans*, genderqueer, and gender nonbinary student affairs professionals are often simultaneously hypervisible, invisible, and tokenized (Jourian et al., 2015; Pitcher, 2018) within the field and at institutions. As Jaekel and Nicolazzo (2017) explained,

> Whether we address it or not, our trans* bodies are always already being un/
> made in [higher education and student affairs] classroom spaces. As such,
> we cannot pretend our very materiality is beyond discussion. Regardless of
> how our trans*ness is inscribed on our bodies, we find our very bodily pres-
> ence in classroom spaces to be an important moment of disruption, one in
> which we can "work the weaknesses of the norm" regarding gender (Butler,
> 2011, p. 181). (pp. 168–169)

Queer bodies are often put up for display, examination, and comment. These
bodies are often visual disruptions challenging the disembodiment of the
work from the worker.

In addition, access to appropriate health insurance benefits as well as
benefits that cover gender-affirming and transition-related medical expenses
can be challenging for transgender and gender-nonbinary employees.
Specific health care benefits are linked to the gender markers attached to the
employees' employment files. If an individual indicates "male," then they
receive coverage that aligns with the standards for cisgender men. This can
put transgender employees in precarious positions hampering the health care
they receive and the benefits covered. In an essay about his experience as a
transman in student affairs, Inselman recounted,

> Since I was hired as "male," this meant I would need to change my employee
> file to "female" in order to cover my medical needs [e.g., gynecological
> exam]; at that institution, this would have required revealing my transition
> history to my direct supervisor. To keep stealth, I chose not to amend my
> records. (Venable et al., 2019, p. 175)

Transgender student affairs professionals having to reveal their transition histories potentially reifies false stereotypes of transgender people as
being deceptive; at the same time, it puts them at risk for harassment and
discrimination.

Challenges transgender student affairs professionals face regarding
access to appropriate health care signifies that workplaces and health insurance plans are neither prepared nor ready to meet these employees' health
needs. Consequently, transgender student affairs professionals can exist
within higher education, but institutions are reluctant to meet their health
needs. This legalized and institutionalized discrimination is grounded in
(mis)understandings of gender, gender identity, as well as pathologizing
of transgender individuals. Ultimately, the disembodiment of work from
worker (Acker, 1990) creates the (il)logic that separates health care from
the individual.

Family and LGBTQ Bodies

Comparatively, there are fewer same-sex marriages and couples than heterosexual couples. However, the number of same-sex marriages is increasing (Fisher et al., 2018; Jones, 2017). The exact number of same-sex married couples is unknown, including how many student affairs professionals are in same-sex marriages or couples. Using income tax return information, "same-sex joint filers are generally younger, higher income, less likely to claim dependent children (especially for male couples), and more geographically concentrated than are different-sex filers" (Fisher et al., 2018, p. 1). In some respects, the profile of same-sex married couples aligns with notions of the ideal worker in that they are less likely to have childcare responsibilities and able to dedicate more time to paid employment. And gay men, in particular, have benefited from this through typically higher incomes (Fisher et al., 2018).

Same-sex couples are less likely than their heterosexual counterparts to be raising children: 17% of same-sex households versus 39% of heterosexual households had children under the age of 18 (United States Census Bureau, 2018). However, disproportionally, more same-sex women couples (23%) are raising children than same-sex men couples (10%) according to the United States Census Bureau (2018). Because LGBTQ student affairs professionals are less likely to be married or have children, there might be differential expectations on their time and out-of-work family responsibilities and commitments. In this way, LGBTQ individuals can live up to the norms of the ideal worker as, seemingly, they have reduced time commitments in regard to family and children, thus being able to dedicate more time to paid work (Acker, 1990).

LGBTQ student affairs professionals with partners or spouses continue to face discrimination in the workplace. Both terms, *partner* and *spouse*, are taken up here because prior to 2015 the legal right to marry someone of the same sex was left to the states to decide and not available across the United States. Barile's (2016) study of gay and lesbian SSAOs discussed incidents of discrimination such as being told not to bring their partner to campus events (although heterosexual spouses were in attendance), campuses not providing domestic partner benefits, needing special permission to have a partner live in campus housing, and questioning the need to take time off for a family emergency. Participants in Kortegast and van der Toorn's (2018) study were more positive about how their partners were welcomed and included among colleagues, students, and the institution. However, they discussed how having a partner was a strategy to normalize their relationships and LGBTQ people.

While some LGBTQ student affairs professionals use terms like *partner* and *spouse* to obscure the gender of their significant other, more often this was a strategy to help normalize LGBTQ people and relationships (Barile,

2016; Kortegast & van der Toorn, 2018). The lesbian and gay SSAOs in Barile's (2016) study "perceived that if they were partnered, they were considered less of a danger and more aligned to cultural norms—partnership meant, in other words, 'Look, I'm just like you'" (p. 93). Similarly, Kortegast and van der Toorn (2018) found that lesbian and gay student affairs professionals used relationship status as part of how they enacted outness, often (intentionally or unintentionally) reifying heteronormativity. Having a partner/spouse seemed to serve as a buffer against facing the stereotypes people had of LGBTQ people, particularly gay men.

The legalization of same-sex marriage also shifted institutional policies and practices regarding the recognition of same-sex relationships. In particular, how to provide and offer institutional benefits such as health insurance changed. Prior to the ruling, providing domestic partner benefits was an indication of an LGBTQ-friendly or supportive campus. Domestic partner benefits varied by institution and could have been as minimal as access to the library and recreation center for a domestic partner to as inclusive as providing health insurance benefits (Messinger, 2009). An unanticipated outcome of the legalization of same-sex marriage in the United States was a declining commitment to provide domestic partner benefits, including institutions of higher education (Flaherty, 2014). In order for same-sex couples to maintain health insurance for their partners, they needed to produce a marriage certificate. While some same-sex couples rejoiced in the ability to have their relationship recognized by the state vis-à-vis marriage, other couples, including straight couples, wanted to remain in domestic partnership arrangements (Flaherty, 2014). In order to maintain health care coverage, couples who had no intention of marrying were forced into making choices about either getting married or finding new health insurance options. These policies had the effect of regulating same-sex relationships and recognizing particular types of relationships as valid that were often based on heteronormative relationship standards.

Children and Parenthood

While some LGBTQ student affairs professionals are childless by choice, others might not be, often because of financial constraints. In general, having children for LGBTQ student affairs professionals is a layered, potentially emotional, and complicated decision that goes beyond the question of wanting or not wanting to be parents. The average cost in 2016–2017 for domestic infant adoptions was $40,000, with international adoption being slightly more expensive at $44,000 (Adoptive Families, 2018). Some private colleges and universities offer adoption benefits and some tax deductions are available, but in general, it remains expensive to adopt in the United States. The salary ranges for student affairs professionals, especially early career professionals, are often lower than other industries, making adoption out of reach for many. Adoption out of the foster care system is a potential pathway. However, there are different affordances and constraints in building a family via the foster care system. While more afford-able, the foster care system is designed to reunite children with their biologi-cal parents; thus, individuals often welcome children into their homes with no guarantee that they will be available for adoption. Moreover, not all foster care agencies, public or private, are welcoming to LGBTQ couples (Child Welfare Information Gateway, 2016).

Same-sex couples who want children to whom they are genetically related have few options. Men who are in same-sex relationships are often limited to finding a surrogate, which can be expensive and comes with a variety of risks. Certainly, the ability of women to give birth potentially makes it easier for women in same-sex relationships to have children, but becoming pregnant can be difficult and costly. Assisted reproductive technology, such as IVF, is expensive and requires individuals to take time off from work. The amount of time off depends on number of attempts and distance from a fertility clinic. Moreover, only 13 states require insurance companies to cover infertility treat-ments (National Conference of State Legislators, 2018). Health care plans that do cover infertility treatments contain structural barriers for single women or women in same-sex relationships in accessing these benefits (Liss-Schultz, 2016). The most common barrier is the requirement of having unprotected sex-ual intercourse, which is narrowly defined as sex between a biological man and woman, that does not result in pregnancy for a particular length of time (e.g., 12 months). As single women and lesbian couples are often not able to meet this requirement, they are systematically denied these benefits. Cumulatively, these gendered and heteronormative organizational logics have consequences for LGBTQ student affairs professionals' ability to have children. Subsequently, institutions benefit from individuals not having child-care responsibilities at home, as there is potentially more time to dedicate to their employer.

Family Leave Policies

LGBTQ student affairs professionals have similar concerns as their non-LGBTQ peers regarding taking time off work for medical reasons for self or for a family member. These reasons include financial concerns due to unpaid time off, being sidelined at work, losing their job, and colleagues being upset (Maxwell et al., 2018). However, LGBTQ employees also have additional layers of concerns related to their sexual and gender identities. Concerns include supervisors not seeing LGBTQ relationships and families to be as valid as their non-LGBTQ counterparts, fear of being treated differently by colleagues for taking leave, and concerns of outing themselves as LGBTQ (Maxwell et al., 2018). Generally, colleges and universities have fairly generous vacation and sick-time policies compared to other industries. Depending on departmental practices and culture, using time off might be more complicated and political than whether or not the employee has available vacation and sick time. LGBTQ individuals are not immune from the pressures to live up to ideal worker norms, but their reasons for taking time away from work may be more highly scrutinized. This scrutiny can be deeply embedded in gendered assumptions regarding the distribution of labor regarding child care, as well as who is seen as a "legitimate" family member.

Depending on where LGBTQ student affairs professionals live and the institution they work for, they might be reluctant to take off time if they or a family member is sick (Kates et al., 2018). While marriage benefits have been extended to same-sex couples, until recently that did not preclude them from employment discrimination or termination. For instance, several religiously affiliated colleges and universities have policies prohibiting same-sex marriage and relationships (Gjelten, 2018). In 2019, the president of Baylor University, Linda Livingstone, released a statement affirming the university's stance on "biblical understandings of sexuality" and "marriage between a man and a woman as the biblical norm" (Baylor University, 2019, para. 3). Consequently, marriages between same-sex individuals are not merely not recognized, but also prohibited. Certainly, these policies are out of the norm of the majority of colleges and universities in the United States. However, homophobia, transphobia, and heterosexism still impact how individuals are treated; thus, taking time off can become a risky act for some LGBTQ individuals—it may out them, it may not be approved, and it may result in termination from their workplace.

Consequences of the Ideal Worker Norm for LGBTQ Student Affairs Professionals

The concepts of the ideal worker and gendered organizations have material consequences for LGBTQ student affairs professionals. Despite increased visibility of out LGBTQ student affairs professionals, concerns about a lavender ceiling still exist (Smith, 2013). While cisgender LGB student affairs professionals have experienced more inclusion and visibility, trans*, genderqueer, and gender-nonbinary individuals still experience marginalization within the field of student affairs. What is considered professional within student affairs can be nebulous. How an individual chooses to dress, act, and engage with others is governed by notions of what is or is not professional. Being seen as being "too out" or "too gay" can have an individual's professionalism questioned (Kortegast & van der Toorn, 2018). Moreover, trans*, genderqueer, and gender-nonbinary student affairs professionals' choices around dress are often highly scrutinized. LGBTQ professionals often have to learn how to become "respectably queer" (Marshall, 2017, p. 260) in order to exist within higher education.

LGBTQ individuals' perceptions of the campus environment and their experiences are shaped by their role on campus, social identities, and microclimate (Vaccaro, 2012). *Microclimates* refer to environments that an individual operates within that are relatively small and self-contained (Ackelsberg et al., 2009). For instance, in Vaccaro's (2012) study of LGBT students, faculty, and staff, she found that "all of the participants agreed that heterosexism, homophobia, transphobia, and genderism shaped their campus experiences" (p. 434). However, how it shaped their experiences differed based on their positionalities (e.g., undergraduate student, administrator, faculty), their social identity (e.g., gay, lesbian, bisexual, transgender), and their local environments. Thus, how the ideal worker concept applies to LGBTQ student affairs professionals varies based on social locations, identities, and microclimates.

As discussed in other chapters, depending on the functional area, student affairs work can involve significant night and weekend commitments. It is not uncommon for live-in residence life staff to have to attend to issues in the middle of the night. Similarly, student activities staff often are responsible for nighttime and weekend events that require staffing. These positional needs can put additional strains on individuals with children and partners. LGBTQ individuals are not an exception to this. However, there might be a disproportionate expectation that individuals without partners or children cover evening or weekend events. Often what gets centered is the reason that evening and night commitments might be difficult for some individuals. This can pit single or child-free individuals against people with partners and those with children. As LGBTQ individuals are less likely than their heterosexual counterparts to have children, there might be unfair assumptions about the flexibility of their out-of-work time or judgment on how they spend time not at work. The focus becomes if people have a good enough reason not to be present at evening and weekend events rather than valuing individuals' time away from work.

For new residence life professionals, requirements to live on campus can limit which positions and institutions LGBTQ individuals apply for if they are in a same-sex relationship. Prior to the 2015 Supreme Court's *Obergefell* ruling, colleges and universities in states that did not recognize same-sex marriage could restrict on-campus housing accommodations to only legally married residence life professionals. These rules often required LGBTQ residence life professionals to either decline the position or live apart from their partner. While restrictions on who can reside with a live-in professional remain, most residence life positions with live-in requirements allow same-sex married couples to live together. This practice, however, is murkier at some religiously affiliated colleges and universities as well as institutions that are in very conservative states.

LGBTQ student affairs professionals might also feel pressure to temper their advocacy or radicalism in order to avoid professional consequences. This can manifest in tensions of having to maintain the status quo while trying to make change (Marshall, 2017). Desire to create change on campus, in particular for LGBTQ people, also might come under question. Navigating these political waters can be especially challenging for graduate students and new professionals. Midcareer professionals and senior student affairs professionals still experience pressures to temper radicalism; however, they often have more positional power to enact change on campus. Stalled career advancement, termination, and/or being pushed out are potential consequences for being seen as too radical or challenging organizational logics regarding gender, sexuality, and job roles (Acker, 1990).

Recommendations for Practice

Securing and maintaining employment is fundamental to an individual's livelihood and financial security (Maxwell, 2018). Moreover, many student affairs professionals enter the field with the desire to do personally fulfilling work (Taub & McEwen, 2006). There can be tension between resisting constraints of the ideal worker paradigm and career advancement and security. Opportunities for resistance and promoting more equitable, just, and humane practices change based on positionality, identities, and personal and professional constraints. With that, the following are considerations on how LGBTQ student affairs professionals at various levels can navigate and/or provide support regarding the limitations the ideal worker norm places on LGBTQ bodies.

Graduate Students

Socialization of what it means to be a "good" student affairs professional is often codified in graduate school. LGBTQ individuals often are recruited into the field and into graduate programs with promises that student affairs is a queer-friendly field. The support that students might have experienced as undergraduates often shifts when they are in graduate school, in the sense that the focus is on preparing them to support undergraduate students rather than receiving support themselves. Moreover, graduate school also might be when LGBTQ individuals start experiencing pressure to temper their radicalism, advocacy, or self-expression in the name of professionalism.

LGBTQ graduate students can begin to practice resistance to the ideal worker norm by developing community with other graduate students and finding mentors. Developing a professional network during graduate school can assist master's degree students in navigating genderism and heterosexism they may experience in their assistantship, with peers, in class, and at the institution. Additionally, connecting with LGBTQ professionals through local, state, and/or national organizations can provide paraprofessionals with necessary advice and guidance in navigating institutional cultures as well as the job search process. Different institutions have different campus cultures and will support LGBTQ professionals in different ways. Mentors and faculty members can support LGBTQ graduate students in preparing for the job search process as well as discussing strategies to uncover institutional- and departmental-level supports for LGBTQ student affairs professionals.

New and Midcareer Professionals

Student affairs work can be a transient profession in which people need to leave an institution to move up professionally. This sometimes requires individuals to move away from friends, family, and established support networks. While potentially challenging for many people, this can come with additional challenges for LGBTQ individuals. Challenges can include finding safe and affordable housing, LGBTQ-friendly medical professionals, and connections with local communities. Getting involved with local communities can help LGBTQ student affairs professionals develop outside-of-work hobbies and friendships. This can help with resisting institutional pressure to be ever-available at work, particularly for live-in, residence life professionals.

Midcareer LGBTQ professionals are often caught in the in-between. They have some positional power to help shape policies and practices in their unit, and, as such, they should model equitable practices. They also have more access to senior leadership and can promote institutional equity. However, they are still often subject to institutional pressure to temper their advocacy work in order to achieve career advancement. Thus, developing coalitions and relationships with other LGBTQ individuals as well as allies can help in promoting more equity and inclusion of LGBTQ individuals. While disclosure of LGBTQ identity is a personal choice, being open about identity, relationships, and family may provide possibility around visibility, community, and support for queer individuals on campus including graduate students and new student affairs professionals.

If a department or institutional culture is toxic or unsafe, LGBTQ professionals should consider developing an exit strategy. Individual colleges and universities are often slow to change; thus, waiting for an institution to become more LGBTQ friendly may take a long time and be detrimental to an individual's long-term career. While there is no perfect work environment, there are better places.

Lastly, LGBTQ professionals who are interested in having children might consider developing a family-planning strategy. Becoming parents is often more complicated and costlier for LGBTQ individuals. While this is unfair, having a plan in place and the resources to pursue options allows for more control over a process which, for LGBTQ individuals, is often anything but.

Supervisors

Supervisors play a critical role in LGBTQ student affairs professionals' success and can serve as strong advocates for LGBTQ individuals they supervise. Supervisors can work to understand and use appropriate language and terminology. While language is ever-evolving, using correct pronouns and validating different family configurations through appropriate language matters. They can avoid differentiating between married straight couples and married same-sex couples in reference to spouse (i.e., referring to the straight couples as husband and wife and the same-sex couples as partners). They can also use gender-inclusive language when referring to all couples. Similarly, families, relationships, and identities are complicated and deeply personal. Supervisors should evaluate requests for time off based on institutional and departmental policies and promote practices that are fair and equitable. LGBTQ student affairs professionals will be more likely to stay in a position if they feel cared about and included.

Supervisors can examine and evaluate their own and institutional notions of professionalism. Understandings of professionalism are deeply gendered, raced, classed, and cultural, as Perez discussed in chapter 5. When discussing what is and is not professional, supervisors can evaluate where and what those understandings are based on. For instance, are they based on gendered stereotypes for how particular bodies are "supposed" to act? What implicit and explicit expectations exist regarding dress? Mannerism? Attitude? Upholding professionalism should be based on good, equitable practices and not on reifying particular gender norms.

Supervisors should also be aware of additional labor LGBTQ student affairs professionals are doing outside of their formal job responsibilities to support LGBTQ students and LGBTQ inclusion. Kortegast and van der Toorn (2018) found that gay and lesbian student affairs professionals working at small colleges and universities often assumed informal responsibilities related to LGBTQ support, education, and advocacy. These responsibilities were often assumed because of a vacuum of services and were a benefit to the institution. However, this work and labor often went unrecognized and uncompensated. Supervisors can work to recognize and reward these contributions.

Senior Student Affairs Officers

The cultural landscape which LGBTQ senior student affairs officers (SSAOs) entered as young LGBTQ student affairs professionals 10, 20, or 30 years ago is different than what young LGBTQ professionals are entering today. There can be some generational differences between what is considered professional as well as expectations of recognition, support, and inclusion. Understandings of constructs such as gender and sexuality are more fluid and multidimensional. Moreover, younger LGBTQ professionals, rightly so, have increased expectations of being out, supported, and having their multiple identities validated. However, this might be different and uncomfortable for older professionals who had to adhere to particular expectations of the ideal worker construct in order to maintain and advance their careers. There are opportunities to connect with newer professionals and to offer mentorship. Moreover, SSAOs often have positional power to help shape more equitable practices regarding work expectations and model inclusive practices regarding families and relationships.

Institutional Policies and Practices

Lastly, institutional policies and benefits should be reviewed to see if they align with institutional values but also promote equitable benefits. Many policies disproportionately benefit heterosexual individuals and employees with children (i.e., tuition benefits). Inclusive policies and practices not only attract LGBTQ employees but also will help with retention of these employees. Similarly, administrators might review gendered language, practices, and spaces to evaluate if there are ways to make these practices and spaces more gender inclusive. For instance, practices could include converting single-stall bathrooms to gender-inclusive restrooms and ensuring that both sexual identity /orientation and gender expression/identity are in institutional nondiscrimination policies.

Additionally, job descriptions, benefits, professional development funds, and salaries should be routinely reviewed to assess if there are equity gaps between LGBTQ student affairs professionals and non-LGBTQ individuals. If there are equity gaps, institutions should develop strategies to address them. These routine audits should include reviews of documents, policies, and procedures as well as surveys and feedback from LGBTQ individuals.

Conclusion

Colleges and universities have benefited from the systemic discrimination of LGBTQ people. Historic and current limitations on LGBTQ people's abilities to marry, have children, and secure health insurance coupled with lack of protections against employment and housing discrimination can be powerful environmental presses to not challenge organizational (il)logics and gendered expectations. Fundamentally, the ability to secure and maintain employment is intrinsically linked to an individual's quality of life. As Maxwell (2018) stated:

> Few spaces can have as deep an impact on the everyday lives of LGBTQ people as the workplace. For starters, it is where most of us spend a majority of our waking hours. Jobs account for our livelihood and financial security; we need work to put food on the table for our families and make ends meet. (p. 3)

Given the importance of employment, places of work have a deep impact on LGBTQ individuals' lives, health, and happiness. LGBTQ student affairs professionals, if they have the flexibility, talent, and privilege, can structure their professional careers to work at colleges and universities that are more welcoming, inclusive, and supportive of LGBTQ individuals and rights. However, all LGBTQ student affairs professionals deserve workplace environments that are inclusive, safe, and equitable.

Notes

1. While I have used the broader term *LGBTQ* for this chapter, not all of the literature reviewed included lesbian, gay, bisexual, transgender, *and* queer individuals. Thus, I revised the acronym when appropriate.
2. The study did not clarify who were considered "staff" and who were considered "administrators," nor was there a specific category for student affairs professionals. Presumably, student affairs professionals identified themselves as either staff or administrators rather than the other choices (i.e., faculty, student).

References

Ackelsberg, M., Hart, J., Miller, N. J., Queeny, K., & Van Dyne, S. (2009). Faculty microclimate change at Smith College. In W. Brown-Glaude (Ed.), *Doing diversity in higher education: Faculty leaders share challenges and strategies* (pp. 83–102). Rutgers University Press.

Acker, J. (1990). Hierarchies, jobs, bodies: A theory of gendered organizations. *Gender & Society, 4*(2), 139–158. https://doi.org/10.1177/089124390004002002

Adoptive Families. (2018). *Adoption cost and timing in 2016–2017.* https://www .adoptivefamilies.com/resources/adoption-news/adoption-cost-timing-2016 -2017-survey-results/

American College Personnel Association & National Association of Student Personnel Administrators. (2015). *Professional competency areas for student affairs practitioners.* Author. http://www.naspa.org/images/uploads/main/ACPA_ NASPA_Professional_Competencies_FINAL.pdf

Barile, B. B. (2016). *Queer student affairs officers: The impact of lived experiences and disclosure on professional identity* [Unpublished doctoral dissertation]. Northeastern University

Baylor University. (2019). *Human sexuality at Baylor University.* https://www.baylor .edu/president/news.php?action=story&story=212249

Campus Pride. (2020). *Colleges and universities that cover transition-related medical expenses under student health insurance.* https://www.campuspride.org/tpc/ nondiscrimination/

Child Welfare Information Gateway. (2016). *Frequently asked questions from lesbian, gay, bisexual, transgender, and questioning (LGBTQ) prospective foster and adoptive parents.* U.S. Department of Health and Human Services, Children's Bureau.

Council for the Advancement of Standards in Higher Education [CAS]. (2015). *CAS professional standards for higher education* (9th ed.). Author.

Croteau, J. M., & Lark, J. S. (1995). On being lesbian, gay, or bisexual in student affairs: A national survey of experiences on the job. *NASPA Journal, 32*, 189–197. https://doi.org/10.1080/00220973.1995.11072384

Fidas, D., & Cooper, L. (2018). *A workplace divided: Understanding the climate for LGBTQ workers nationwide.* Human Rights Campaign. https://assets2.hrc .org/files/assets/resources/AWorkplaceDivided-2018.pdf?_ga=2.161474040 .470069434.1541361026-782763098.1541361026

Fisher, R., Gee, G., & Looney, A. (2018). *Same-sex married tax filers after Windsor and Obergefell.* Tax Policy Center: Urban Institute and Brookings Institution. https://doi.org/10.1007/s13524-018-0684-5

Flaherty, C. (2014). New politics of partner benefits. *Inside Higher Ed.* https://www .insidehighered.com/news/2014/07/18/partner-benefits-higher-ed-evolve-more -states-recognize-gay-marriage

Garvey, J. C., & Rankin, S. (2018). The influence of campus climate and urbanization on queer-spectrum and trans-spectrum faculty intent to leave. *Journal of Diversity in Higher Education, 11*(1), 67–81. https://doi.org/10.1037/dhe0000035

Gjelten, T. (2018). Christian colleges are tangled in their own LGBT policies. *National Public Radio*. https://www.npr.org/2018/03/27/591140811/christian -colleges-are-tangled-in-their-own-lgbt-policies

Halley, J. E. (2000). "Like race" arguments. In J. Butler, J. Guillory, & K. Thomas (Eds.), *What's left of theory: New work on the politics of literary theory* (pp. 40–74). Routledge.

Human Rights Campaign. (2020). *State map of laws and policies*. https://www.hrc .org/state-maps/employment

Jaekel, K. S., & Nicolazzo, Z. (2017). Teaching trans*: Strategies and tensions of teaching gender in student affairs preparation programs. *Journal for the Study of Postsecondary and Tertiary Education, 2,* 165–179. https://doi.org/10.28945/ 3859

Johnson, R. B. (2009). *Workplace climate, degree of outness, and job satisfaction of gay and lesbian professional staff in higher education* [Unpublished doctoral dissertation]. University of North Carolina–Greensboro

Jones, J. M. (2017). *In U.S., 10.2% of LGBT adults now married to same-sex spouse*. Gallup. https://news.gallup.com/poll/212702/lgbt-adults-married-sex-spouse .aspx

Jourian, T. J., Symone, S. L., & Devaney, K. C. (2015). "We are not expected": Trans* educators (re)claiming space. *TSQ: Transgender Studies Quarterly, 2*(3), 431–446. https://doi.org/10.1215/23289252-2926410

Kates, J., Ranji, U., Beamesderfer, A., Salganicoff, A., & Dawson, L. (2018). *Health and access to care and coverage for lesbian, gay, bisexual, and transgender individuals in the U.S.* Henry J. Kaiser Family Foundation. https://www.kff.org/disparities -policy/issue-brief/health-and-access-to-care-and-coverage-for-lesbian-gay -bisexual-and-transgender-individuals-in-the-u-s/

Kortegast, C. A., & Hamrick, F. A. (2009). Moving on: Voluntary staff Departures at small colleges and universities. *NASPA Journal, 46,* 183–207. https://doi.org/ 10.2202/1949-6605.6038

Kortegast, C. A., Jaekel, K. S., & Nicolazzo, Z. (2020, Jan). Thirty years of LGBTQ pre-publication knowledge production in higher education research: A critical summative content analysis of ASHE conference sessions. *Journal of Homosexuality,* 1–25. https://doi.org/10.1080/00918369.2019.1702351

Kortegast, C. A., & van der Toorn, M. (2018). Other duties not assigned: Experiences of lesbian and gay student affairs professionals at small colleges and universities. *Journal of Diversity in Higher Education, 11*(3), 268–278. https://doi.org/10 .1037/dhe0000046

Liss-Schultz, N. (2016, August 18). Despicable way that insurance companies screw over lesbians. *Mother Jones*. https://www.motherjones.com/politics/2016/08/ same-sex-couples-infertility-fertility-treatment-discrimination/

Marshall, B. T. (2017). *Bringing ourselves to work: A narrative inquiry of LGBTQ professionals* [Unpublished doctoral dissertation]. Ohio State University

Maxwell, M. B. (2018). Letter from the HRC Foundation's senior VP for programs, research and training. In D. Fidas & L. Cooper (Eds.), *A workplace divided:*

Understanding the climate for LGBTQ workers nationwide (p. 3). Human Rights Campaign. https://assets2.hrc.org/files/assets/resources/AWorkplaceDivided-2018 .pdf?_ga=2.161474040.470069434.1541361026-782763098.1541361026

Maxwell, M. B., Johnson, A., Lee, M., & Miranda, L. (2018). U.S. LGBTQ paid leave survey. Human Rights Campaign Foundation Public Education and Research. https://assets2.hrc.org/files/assets/resources/2018-HRC-LGBTQ -Paid-Leave-Survey.pdf?utm_campaign=Paid%20Leave&utm_source=HRC% 20Website

Messinger, L. (2009). Creating LGBTQ-friendly campuses. *Academe*. https://www .aaup.org/article/creating-lgbtq-friendly-campuses#.W9yPrnpKhQM

National Conference of State Legislators. (2018). *State laws related to insurance coverage for infertility treatment*. http://www.ncsl.org/research/health/insurance -coverage-for-infertility-laws.aspx

Obergefell v. Hodges. (2015). 576 U.S. Page (2015). https://www.supremecourt .gov/opinions/14pdf/14-556_3204.pdf

Parker, C. P., Baltes, B. B., Young, S. A., Huff, J. W., Altmann, R. A., LaCost, H. A., & Roberts, J. E. (2003). Relationship between psychological climate perceptions and work outcomes: A meta-analytic review. *Journal of Organizational Behavior*, *24*(4), 389–416. https://doi.org/10.1002/job.198

Pitcher, E. N. (2018). *Being and becoming professionally other: Identities, voices, and experiences of U.S. trans* academics*. Peter Lang.

Pryor, J. T., Garvey, J. C., & Johnson, S. (2017). Pride and progress? 30 years of AcpA and NASPA LGBTQ presentations. *Journal of Student Affairs Research and Practice*, *54*(2), 123–136. https://doi.org/10.1080/19496591.2016 .1206020

Rankin, S., Blumenfeld, W. J., Weber, G. N., & Frazer, S. J. (2010). *State of higher education for LGBT people: Campus pride 2010 national college climate survey*. Campus Pride.

Renn, K. A. (2003). Out of the closet and into the cabinet: Lesbian, gay, bisexual, and transgender student affairs senior officers. *Leadership Exchange*, *1*, 5–9.

Renn, K. A. (2010). LGBT and queer research in higher education: The state and status of the field. *Educational Researcher*, *39*(2), 132–141. https://doi.org/10 .3102/0013189X10362579

Smith, J. C. (2013). *Cracking the lavender ceiling: Lesbian, gay, and bisexual student affairs professionals and their personal perspectives on career trajectory* [Unpublished doctoral dissertation]. University of California, Los Angeles

Taub, D. J., & McEwen, M. K. (2006). Decision to enter the profession of student affairs. *Journal of College Student Development*, *47*(2), 206–216. https://doi.org/ 10.1353/csd.2006.0027

United States Census Bureau. (2018). *Characteristics of same-sex couple households table package*. https://www.census.gov/newsroom/press-releases/2018/same-sex .html

Vaccaro, A. (2012). Campus microclimates for LGBT faculty, staff, and students: An exploration of the intersections of social identity and campus roles. *Journal of*

Student Affairs Research and Practice, 49(4), 429–446. https://doi.org/10.1515/jsarp-2012-6473

Vaccaro, A., Russell, E. I., & Koob, R. M. (2015). Students with minoritized identities of sexuality and gender in campus contexts: An emergent model. *New Directions for Student Services: Gender and Sexual Diversity in U.S. Higher Education: Contexts and Opportunities, 2015*(152), 25–39. https://doi.org/10.1002/ss.20143

Venable, C. J., Inselman, K., & Thuot, N. (2019). Negotiating fit while "misfit": Three ways trans professionals navigate student affairs. In B. J. Reece, V. T. Tran, E. N. DeVore, & G. Porcaro (Eds.), *Debunking the myth of job fit in higher education and student affairs* (pp. 167–194). Stylus.

Williams, C. L., Giuffre, P. A., & Dellinger, K. (2009). The gay-friendly closet. *Sexuality Research & Social Policy, 6*(1), 29–45. https://doi.org/10.1525/srsp.2009.6.1.29

IO

(EN)COUNTERSPACES

An Analysis of Working Conditions for Student Affairs Professionals of Color in an Un-Ideal World

Ginny Jones Boss and Nicole Bravo

L ittle is known about how student affairs professionals manage work–life balance, and even less is known about how student affairs professionals of Color experience it. The limited literature on this group signals they navigate similar issues as their White counterparts regarding low retention of new professionals, lack of advancement opportunities, and problems with poor compensation (Gardner et al., 2014; Jackson & O'Callaghan, 2009). To exacerbate these issues, student affairs professionals of Color navigate racialized environments that take a toll on their physical, emotional, and social well-being. Amid these added challenges, they may feel pressure to capitulate to ideal worker norms.

Ideal worker norms are predicated on the idea that a worker can be solely devoted to their work without external concerns, such as taking care of family, and consequently are raced, gendered, and classed (Acker, 1990, 2006, 2009). Ideal worker norms tend to skew in favor of White men who are unencumbered with such concerns. Yet, as Acker (2006) argued in later work, an ideal worker could also be one less likely to disrupt the status quo and accept low wages. Previous literature has explored the gendered nature of ideal worker norms, but much remains unknown about how inequality regimes, those policies and practices that maintain inequality (Acker, 2006) within organizations, are raced.

In this chapter, we use critical race theory (CRT) (Ladson-Billings, 1998) and the concept of hegemonic Whiteness (Bonilla-Silva, 2006; Cabrera, 2018a) to explicate the ways inequality regimes create pressure for student affairs professionals of Color to disappear through assimilation to White culture while simultaneously being forced into hypervisibility against a Whitewashed backdrop. The pressure to disappear is rooted in implicit and explicit messages to maintain the status quo. At the same time, student affairs professionals of Color are pressured to perform uncompensated physical, mental, and emotional labor to support themselves, colleagues, and students through racism and discrimination in addition to their daily work. The pressure to conform to ideal worker norms and not disrupt the status quo, amid racialized environments that offer low pay and lack support, may account for poor working conditions and departure from the field. The purpose of this chapter is to interrogate the demands ideal worker norms place on student affairs professionals of Color through a combination of Acker's (2006, 2009) writings with tenets of CRT and hegemonic Whiteness. Hegemonic Whiteness and CRT shine a spotlight on the racialized aspects of maintaining the status quo, which involve upholding and ascribing to Whiteness. As a result of this interrogation, we offer the concept of (en)counterspaces as opportunities for healing, building community, and learning and strategizing ways to improve working conditions for professionals of Color.

CRT and Hegemonic Whiteness

CRT is a valuable framework for examining race and racism in educational institutions (Ladson-Billings & Tate, 2006; López, 2003) and has been suggested as a tool for exploring racist institutional norms (Harper, 2012). CRT posits that American society is founded in institutional racism, and therefore racism is present in the everyday experiences of people of Color. Despite the fact that all facets of society operate on and perpetuate racism, the presence of racism in society is systematically normalized and denied (Bonilla-Silva, 2006), allowing racism to exist both visibly and invisibly. This paradox describes hegemonic Whiteness (Cabrera, 2018a), the process by which Whiteness is constructed as the standard and preferable way of being (Cabrera, 2018b; López, 2003). Whiteness is embedded in the status quo, and failing to assimilate carries significant consequences. Yet, embodying and espousing Whiteness comes with tangible privileges.

Whiteness is a social and economic resource that allows those who embody it, White and White-passing people, to dominate workspaces. White employees on average are paid more and hold more positions of power. They are also more likely to be recognized for their individual accomplishments rather than lumped into a larger ethnic group (Elliott &

Smith, 2004; Nkomo & Al Ariss, 2014). Those who espouse Whiteness also receive certain privileges. The hegemony of Whiteness creates conditions where many White people remain oblivious to the privileges they receive from it. While people of Color can also embody and espouse Whiteness, they usually do so as a survival mechanism. Whiteness is the professional standard against which all employees are evaluated (DiAngelo, 2011; McCoy & Rodricks, 2015); therefore, success in the workplace is determined by how well people of Color assimilate to White culture (Green, 2008). When people of Color perform Whiteness, they can increase the privileges they are afforded and may elevate themselves over colleagues of Color who do not (or cannot) assimilate in similar ways. Employees of Color who fail to conform face sanctions such as social stigmatization, poor performance evaluations, and job actions such as probation or termination (Green, 2008).

To combat how racism functions both visibly and invisibly in all aspects of society, CRT encourages the use of counterstorytelling (Delgado & Stefancic, 2001), or the act of people of Color telling the stories of their experiences to raise consciousness about racism (Bell, 2003; Matsuda, 1991). Reitman (2006) asserted that naming and reflecting upon how White supremacy operates has the power to subvert "embedded systems of dominance and oppression" (p. 267) within organizations. This concept holds considerable potential for employees of Color, many of whom are acutely aware of the racism and discrimination they experience (Cabrera, 2018a) but are unlikely to speak out about their experiences for fear of the social, financial, and professional consequences they will face (Reitman, 2006). Counterstorytelling can serve as a "cure for silencing" (Delgado & Stefancic, 2001, p. 43) by providing spaces for people of Color to recognize, name, and share their experiences.

Ideas of intersectionality and anti-essentialism suggest that people's identities are multifaceted and a simple understanding of race alone is not enough to convey a person or group of people's experiences (Crenshaw, 1991; Delgado & Stefancic, 2001). Intersectionality names the points at which oppressive structures and multiple marginalized identities overlap (Crenshaw, 1991). Although CRT starts with the premise that society and organizations are racist, it also illuminates other structures of oppression, such as sexism and classism. Anti-essentialism recognizes that when the intersectionality of people's identities is recognized, one person's or group's story should not necessarily represent the experience of the whole (Grillo, 1995). In this chapter, we focus primarily on the raced nature of the work of student affairs professionals of Color. However, we also acknowledge that the working experiences of student affairs professionals of Color are often more complex at the intersections of their identities.

Relatedly, we promote an anti-essentialist reading of our analysis, asking readers to not hold the examples presented here as representative of the whole of the experiences of professionals of Color. Instead, use them as a launch pad for further exploration of the inequality regimes impacting student affairs work.

Working Experiences of Student Affairs Professionals of Color

In many ways, university campuses serve as microcosms of society. On campus, student affairs professionals of Color are confronted with the same or similar stressors they deal with in their lives outside of work, including experiences of racism, discrimination, and isolation (Gonzalez & Kemp-DeLisser, 2010; Husband, 2016; Jackson & O'Callaghan, 2009; Lozano, 2017). External social issues (e.g., the #BlackLivesMatter movement, news, politics) are addressed on college campuses in ways that are emotionally exhausting and mentally taxing for student affairs professionals of Color. Amid their own coping processes, they often support students of Color who are also wrestling with these racialized campus and societal issues (Alvarez & Liu, 2002; Gonzalez & Kemp-DeLisser, 2010; Jackson & O'Callaghan, 2009; Maramba, 2011). The added labor of supporting students outside the parameters of their direct job responsibilities, tokenization by their colleagues and supervisors, and experiences of marginalization often lead student affairs professionals of Color to experience compassion fatigue (Davis, 2019) and racial battle fatigue (RBF) (Bhattar, 2013; Garcia, 2016; Gardner et al., 2014; Gonzalez & Kemp-DeLisser, 2010; Husband, 2016; Jackson & O'Callaghan, 2009; Lithgow et al., 2018; Smith, 2004). RBF is the result of a collection of "social-psychological stress responses (e.g., frustration, anger, exhaustion, physical avoidance, psychological or emotional withdrawal, escapism, acceptance of racist attributions)"experienced by people of Color who are constantly exposed to systemic and structural oppression (Smith et al., 2007, p. 552). The experiences of many student affairs professionals of Color are paradoxical. Professionals of Color are simultaneously hypervisible due to their racialized existence in a Whitewashed environment and how they are expected to help advance institutional diversity efforts and invisible due to systemic ignorance of the racism they experience and the hidden labor they perform in support of students and colleagues of Color (Lithgow et al., 2018). This paradox is directly linked to hegemonic Whiteness; professionals of Color are tokenized for their marginalized identities while being pressured to assimilate to White organizational norms.

Invisibility and the Ideal Worker

Lithgow et al., (2018) used the phrase "out of body experience" (p. 78) to describe how professionals of Color are forced to dissociate from their racial identities in order to align with Whiteness. As a result of ideal worker norms, professionals of Color are expected to be compliant and maintain the status quo (Green, 2008), but they are also expected to perform additional labor related to their racial identities. For example, professionals of Color are often pressured to take on diversity work that is not directly related to their job requirements (Gardner et al., 2014; Husband, 2016; Maramba, 2011). Yet they are still expected to perform as well as their White colleagues who do not have to take on additional work. New professionals must teach themselves to manage these additional burdens of systemic racism while receiving little if any recognition for doing so (Boss et al., 2018). Many professionals of Color report feeling unseen and unsupported in relation to their experiences with racism and subsequent RBF (Lithgow et al., 2018; Smith, 2004). When professionals of Color speak out about their struggles with racism, they are often met with disbelief and inaction from White colleagues. For example, Bhattar (2013) shared, "It is exhausting to constantly explain myself to people and have them question whether or not I am telling the truth" (p. 32).

These experiences highlight how institutions of higher education utilize hegemonic Whiteness and the concept of the ideal worker to exert dominance over professionals of Color. Reitman (2006) named this process "whitewashing" and explained that "whitewashing denies racial politics through choices about racialized language and invisibility and the promotion of a repressive type of multiculturalism" (p. 268). Furthermore, the concept of disembodiment that Acker (1990) mentioned in her analysis of the ideal worker demonstrates how invisibility exacerbated RBF for professionals of Color. Employees are forced to hide and minimize their identities in the name of being professional (Acker, 1990; Green, 2008). Hiding, minimizing, or not being aware of one's identities is a privilege experienced by people with dominant identities. In contrast, many professionals of Color do not have the luxury of hiding their identities and can suffer professional consequences for not minimizing those aspects of their identity that disrupt ideal worker norms. Many professionals of Color also suffer personal consequences, such as a decline in their emotional well-being, when they attempt to minimize their racial identities in order to align with Whiteness (Green, 2008; Smith, 2004). Ideal worker norms influence a culture in which professionals of Color are expected to endure oppression without challenging the systems that create it. Thus, professionals of Color often work in institutions that exploit their labor and disregard their personhood (Davis, 2019; Husband, 2016).

Labor and Hypervisibility

Paradoxically, professionals of Color also experience hypervisibility based on their embodied racial characteristics. The constant work required of ideal worker norms is compounded for student affairs professionals of Color by the additional labor they engage in to support students of Color (Maramba, 2011). Hypervisibility occurs when professionals of Color are underrepresented on their campus and thus stand out or are singled out as a result of their minoritized status (Bhattar, 2013; Garcia, 2016; Lithgow et al., 2018; Maramba, 2011). In her study of Asian American and Pacific Islander women professionals in student affairs, Maramba (2011) described hypervisibility as the result of "feelings of tokenization and feeling used as a 'diversity' representative" (p. 345). Participants in her study described being called upon to serve diversity initiatives at their institutions. Bhattar (2013) described his experience of tokenization on campus, being called on to serve on multiple committees at his university. In his description of his experience serving on a search committee, he shared, "I found myself having to be the 'diversity voice,' asking questions that address social justice issues and consistently bringing awareness to issues of inclusion in the search process" (p. 31). While other scholars have detailed the ways universities tokenize professionals of Color (Bhattar, 2013; Cabrera, 2018a; Jackson & O'Callaghan, 2009; Lithgow et al., 2018; Maramba, 2011), some scholars note that hypervisibility also presents internalized labor obligations among this group. Garcia (2016) shared the accounts of professionals who felt the need to support students of Color, because the professional was the only person of Color in their department or campus. In these examples, the ideal worker norm of tireless work comes as a direct result of the hypervisibility of professionals' racial and ethnic identities.

The Ideal Worker and Inequality Regimes

Literature on the experiences of student affairs professionals of Color and the ideal worker begin to converge at a call for intersectionality. Both bodies of scholarship suggest that notions of the ideal worker and the experience of professionals of Color are raced, gendered, and classed. Acker (2006) argued that the practices and processes of organizations can produce inequalities at any or all of the intersections of race, gender, and class. She offered that the picture of the ideal worker may shift depending upon the job. When jobs require workers who will be compliant and work for low wages, the ideal workers are often women of Color (Acker, 2006). As Sallee argues in the introduction of this book, new professionals are expected to work tirelessly for low wages. In addition to their daily work, professionals of Color also engage in added labor connected to their intersected identities (Bhattar, 2013; Garcia, 2016; Husband, 2016; Lithgow et al., 2018; Maramba, 2011). Acker's (2006) assertion that hiring practices reveal an organization's processes for identifying an ideal worker illuminates the invisibility/hypervisibility paradox described previously. Acker suggested that both the use of social networks and assumptions of competence, where competence is attributed to White men more than any other group, are a cause for inequalities in the workplace. Within this regime of inequality, professionals of Color may be hired on the assumption that any competence is tied to their racial identity or merely to fulfill antidiscriminatory hiring practice requirements. Under these assumptions, professionals of Color become attractive hires in satisfying a need or mandate, but they are expected to uphold Whiteness within the organization.

Many professionals express frustration with the field's supposed dedication to racial justice, despite professionals of Color being financially and socially disenfranchised (Bender, 2009; Lithgow et al., 2018; Nkomo & Al Ariss, 2014; Roediger, 2005). People of Color are expected to perform labor that White people are not, and for far less compensation, if compensated at all. This phenomenon can be observed in the differentiated pay received by faculty and administrators of Color, particularly when the focus of their work is identity-based (Boss et al., 2019). Acker (1990) argued that men might enjoy the privilege of having women in their lives who will take up the labor of caring for their home and children so the men can focus primarily on their jobs. In this way men are ideal for the working environment, because they are unencumbered by external obligations. Similarly, and exacerbated by colonization and colonial logics, people of Color have served similar functions for both White men and women, freeing time for White men and women to focus on other matters and have access to economic gain. In higher education, those who are rewarded, financially and otherwise, for the retention, progression, and graduation of students of Color are rarely the student affairs professionals of Color who have supported them. Instead, high-level administrators, the majority of whom are White, receive accolades for the labor of entry-level and midcareer professionals.

Many of the issues named in this chapter have deep structural and systemic roots within U.S. society in general, and higher education specifically. It is necessary to understand inequality regimes in higher education to better understand how ideal worker norms impact the workload of professionals of Color. As Acker (2009) suggested, inequality regimes include:

> systematic disparities between participants in power and control over goals, resources, and outcomes; workplace decisions such as how to organize work; opportunities for promotion and interesting work; security in employment and benefits; pay and other monetary rewards; respect; and pleasures in work and work relations. (p. 443)

While their raced embodiments and willingness to support students of Color may make professionals of Color ideal workers for student affairs, their experiences demonstrate the inequality regimes present in higher education. Full understanding of inequality regimes impacting professionals of Color necessitates an intersectional understanding of higher education, though a helpful starting place may be understanding how race impacts valuations of student affairs work.

A shift in focus in the field to a lens that includes interrogating the embeddedness of racism in the academy (Harper, 2012) is necessary for illuminating inequality regimes. As Nkomo and Al Ariss (2014) and Harper (2012) suggested, we must begin to address Whiteness itself rather than focusing most of our attention on the "diversity" of non-White racial/ethnic groups. It is only when we understand the structural foundations that uphold systems of oppression that we can begin to dismantle them. Acker (2009) argued that practices that perpetuate inequality are challenging to document because they are "often subtle and unspoken" (p. 210). Both Acker (2009) and Cabrera (2018a) suggested those who are marginalized are best able to name and tell the stories of their experiences. Student affairs professionals of Color have also expressed the importance of sharing their stories to make visible much of the work they perform that has been rendered invisible and thus devalued by their institutions (Alvarez & Liu, 2002; Bhattar, 2013; Gonzalez & Kemp-DeLisser, 2010; Jackson & O'Callaghan, 2009; Lozano, 2017; Maramba, 2011). Despite the value of telling their stories, some student affairs professionals of Color may be hesitant to do so, given the risk associated with highlighting their identities in their work (Bhattar, 2013; Gonzalez & Kemp-DeLisser, 2010; Lozano, 2017). The need to be seen and yet the fear of the response to being seen reflect the internalized impacts of the hypervisibility/invisibility paradox mentioned earlier. Ideal worker norms are pervasive in higher education, and pressure to conform occurs as early as at the graduate program level and persists through upper-level administration (Wolf-Wendel et al., 2016). As such, we believe it is important for constituent groups interested in improving working conditions for professionals of Color to give focus to building (en)counterspaces.

Recommendations for Practice

Student affairs professionals of Color experience compassion fatigue and RBF at all levels of the field, and those working with them may be at various stages of understanding how to develop strategies for addressing the raced aspects on ideal worker norms. As such, we present recommendations in the following three areas: gaining awareness, increasing knowledge, and revising policy and practice. We believe much of this work may occur in (en)counterspaces, which involve constituent groups creating opportunities for student affairs professionals of Color to share their counterstories and engage in community healing practices.

An (en)counterspace is the call for White professionals and administrators to actively seek out ways to encounter the experiences, knowledge, aspirations, and needs of professionals of Color. Rather than reinforcing spaces in which professionals of Color are exploited as voices of diversity or pressured to conform to institutional standards of Whiteness and disembodiment, (en)counterspaces provide opportunities for professionals of Color to fully embody their racial/ethnic identities without fear or consequences. The specific methods for building community and engaging in healing will be different in each context; they will differ for not only each space but also each individual participating in the space. These practices may include naming and confronting the racism and other forms of oppression professionals of Color experience; sharing strategies for navigating hostile institutional environments; sharing personal stories and anecdotes to form connections and share counterhistories; and collaborating to create further opportunities for community support and healing. Regardless of the specific methods each (en)counterspace uses to serve its participants, (en)counterspaces center healing for student affairs professional of Color and collective work for dismantling racism.

(En)counterspaces are not predicated on the assumption that countering racism should be the responsibility of those being oppressed. For professionals of Color, (en)counterspaces are focused on healing and building community, not on solving institutional oppression through the labor of these professionals. When White professionals are invited to (en)counterspaces for the purposes of hearing the counterstories of professionals of Color, they are better positioned to dismantle oppressive structures from an informed place. As such, student affairs professionals of Color should not be solely responsible for organizing time and physical spaces for (en)counterspaces.

Faculty, professionals, and administrators across identities and at all levels should actively acknowledge the need for such spaces and advocate for their creation. There is a delicate balance to be attended to; White professionals and administrators should not dictate or preside over such spaces. Instead (en)counterspaces should be participatory in nature and should include localized, insider knowledge for locally tailored solutions. White professionals and administrators should play an active role in recognizing opportunities for (en)counterspaces, help normalize the need for such spaces, and allocate resources such as physical meeting spaces and financial support for these opportunities and the resulting policy and practice efforts. In the following sections we describe ways each constituent group may begin constructing (en)counterspaces.

Graduate Preparation Faculty

Graduate preparation faculty in higher education and student affairs programs have the potential to be powerful influencers in how graduate students and new professionals understand and engage with the field. As such, there is great responsibility in helping emerging professionals understand how ideal worker norms may impact emerging professionals' future work.

Graduate preparation faculty should represent the diversity of ideas and experiences necessary for transformative student affairs practice. It is important that hiring practices for preparation faculty are intersectional through the recruiting and vetting process. While faculty of Color may be able to provide support and mentorship for emerging professionals of Color, it should not be assumed they have the capacity to do so. Even when faculty of Color focus on race in their work, they should not be expected to take up full responsibility for supporting emerging professionals of Color. All preparation faculty should gain awareness of the raced aspects of ideal worker norms professionals of Color may experience. These faculty members may begin by gaining greater awareness of the experiences of student affairs professionals of Color including by reading literature that details the experiences of professionals of Color, particularly literature written by these professionals, or connecting with alumni of Color and soliciting narratives of their experiences. Of course, this is not an inclusive list of activities. Similarly, faculty looking to move from awareness to knowledge can gather data, including narratives and artifacts from alums and other professionals of Color.

In an effort to challenge ideal worker norms, specifically raced aspects of these norms, faculty may benefit from learning about critical and race theories as well as critical, antiracist pedagogical approaches in the classroom. A revision of practice for some faculty would involve taking up critical pedagogies. Taking up critical pedagogies is not simply urging faculty to address the needs of graduate students of Color. Indeed, if faculty want to improve conditions for professionals of Color, they must acknowledge their complicity in reinforcing ideal worker norms and the raced nature of those norms. In addition to listening to the narratives of professionals of Color, they must challenge White students to recognize and respond to racism in the academy. In this way, White faculty have a particular opportunity to model the way for White students and the program's constituent partners.

In further acknowledging their complicity in perpetuating ideal worker norms, faculty can examine the ways they encourage students to engage in their preparation work. Whether through classroom assignments, cohort dynamics, or practical experiences, faculty should learn to name ideal worker expectations and the inequality regimes that result. Given this chapter's explicit focus on professionals of Color, it is important for faculty to address and have students work through not only macrolevel instances of racism but also microlevel instances of racism that are more subtle and difficult to challenge. Policies for addressing racialized incidents should be included in graduate student handbooks. The recommendations mentioned here extend to the partnerships many higher education and student affairs programs engage in with practical experience providers. Faculty have great opportunity to work with those providers to ensure students learn about ideal worker norms and racial dynamics in the academy and how to contextualize the labor professionals of Color often take up in support of students.

Graduate Students and New Professionals

Graduate students and new professionals of Color may have particular need for (en)counterspaces, as many have not yet built professional networks. Graduate students of Color may be in programs in which they are the only or one of a few racially minoritized students. Relatedly, new professionals may not have enough professional experience or context to prepare themselves for the realities they will face once they enter the field full time. Graduate students and new professionals of Color can gain awareness of what to expect by seeking meaningful connections with other professionals of Color. With a greater understanding of what awaits them after graduation, emerging professionals of Color will be better prepared to recognize and challenge ideal worker norms. Support can be established within graduate programs, institutions, regional and national student affairs associations, and even through social media. The joining of and formation of these communities can create opportunities for self-care and community support, which can be protective factors against the mental and emotional traumas graduate students and new professionals can experience as a result of ideal worker norms.

Graduate students and new professionals of all races and ethnicities should have a thorough knowledge of how structural racism operates in the academy. Graduate students should read relevant literature to increase their knowledge in this area; the literature presented and cited in this chapter is a good place to start but must be supplemented by other readings as well. Being aware of how racism pervades institutions of higher education may help mitigate feelings of imposter syndrome, because individuals may be better able to identify how White supremacy and harmful ideal worker norms contribute to feelings of burnout, inadequacy, and insecurity in professionals of Color.

Last, in order to subvert the invisibility and disembodiment professionals of Color so often experience, graduate students and new professionals should actively build coalitions within and across identity groups. Establishing communities and collaborating with trusted advocates can help graduate students and new professionals of Color create spaces of activism and resistance. Building coalitions and identifying advocates surpasses simply networking with others of shared identities and moves into executing tangible efforts to work with and for each other to promote racial justice and social justice. Student affairs professionals of Color and graduate students can form bonds not only with their peers but also with professors, supervisors, and mid- and upper-level administrators, in order to establish networks of affinity and shared purpose. Coalitions provide opportunities to collaborate on social justice and identity work together, which can take the burden off of someone who previously felt as if they must shoulder the work themselves. Mentorship should also play a role in this endeavor. Established professionals should make concerted efforts to reach out to and include newer professionals in their efforts to increase equity and provide identity support.

Midcareer Professionals

Given the field's attrition rates, midcareer student affairs professionals can offer much from their experiences and institutional knowledge. Midcareer professionals of Color may be in the precarious position of needing to advocate for themselves and on behalf of their supervisees, while finding fewer colleagues of Color at their career level in the field. Similar to the recommendations we have put forth for graduate students and new professionals, midcareer professionals of Color could benefit from coalition building and allyship to mitigate compassion fatigue and RBF. Both White professionals and professionals of Color need to gain awareness of how hegemonic Whiteness presents added stress and labor for student affairs professionals of Color. These professionals can begin by listening to the stories of student affairs professionals of Color. They can read the literature cited here and engage in conversation with their peers and supervisees of Color. These professionals increase their knowledge by learning and understanding critical and race theories. Such an understanding can illuminate the need of student affairs professionals of Color to tell their stories and to have spaces in which their identities are affirmed. Relatedly, increasing knowledge can aid midcareer professionals in managing feelings of defensiveness and fragility (their own or others) that can occur when confronted with concerns about racism and Whiteness. Midcareer professionals can disrupt hegemonic Whiteness and the notion of the ideal worker by (a) challenging policies and practices that do not account for the intersected nature of professionals' identities and the labor taken up by student affairs professionals of Color, (b) examining themselves for tendencies toward placing student affairs professionals of Color in the bind of invisibility and hypervisibility, and (c) unpacking their conceptions of what constitutes professionalism or an ideal worker and making efforts toward a supervisory style that is more racially inclusive and antihegemonic. While all midcareer professionals can benefit from the awareness, knowledge, and policy and practice recommendations offered here, considerations of workload can be a double-edged sword for midcareer professionals of Color who are navigating positions of power while themselves feeling disempowered. In such cases, midcareer professionals of Color may also benefit from participating in affinity groups, building coalitions, and identifying advocates within regional and national professional development venues.

Senior Student Affairs Officers

As leaders of their divisions on campuses, senior student affairs officers (SSAOs) have the opportunity to set the tone for everyday practices. Given the complexity and intersectional nature of identity, both White SSAOs and SSAOs of Color should be proactive about raising awareness about issues impacting student affairs professionals of Color. Attending professional development sessions in which student affairs professionals of Color discuss their experiences and soliciting stories from the midcareer and entry-level professionals on their campus can provide a foundational understanding of how student affairs professionals of Color experience the field and their work on campus. While local, insider knowledge will be helpful for crafting local solutions for professionals of Color, awareness of the broader experiences of professionals of Color may aid in effective recruitment and retention of talented professionals. In seeking out this information, SSAOs must also recognize that their positions of power may make professionals reticent to share their experiences. One such way would be to conduct a climate study that focuses on data shared by professionals of Color. Professionals of Color should be invited to take an active role in the meaning-making process of the data produced, and they should be compensated for the time and labor they contribute. Another way would be to seek out writing and research from and about professionals of Color in student affairs. Moving into action, SSAOs can identify practices that uphold Whiteness within their institutions and actively develop new practices that support and center professionals of Color. This would include a critical examination of their campus's workload requirements for student affairs professionals and accounting for the invisible labor often taken up by student affairs professionals of Color. The SSAO's role in bringing attention to systemic and structural inequities is rife with complexity and necessitates an intersectional approach and engagement of critical leadership.

Conclusion

When it comes to ideal worker norms, the experiences and expectations of student affairs professionals of Color are made more complex by the racialized nature of their work and evaluations of their work. Inequality regimes in higher education are felt by professionals of Color when they feel the need and are pressured to be disembodied workers who work tirelessly and unemotionally to maintain the status quo. Due to inequality regimes, professionals of Color may be seen as ideal workers, based upon assumptions of compliance and acceptance of low wages without regard to either's impact on working conditions. We need to better understand the ways in which ideal worker norms are communicated to and internalized by student affairs professionals of Color. We must continue to explore the disjuncture in policy and practice that perpetuates ideal worker norms for professionals of Color. Most importantly, we must take an intersectional approach that recognizes the embeddedness of not only racism but also other oppressive ideologies, such as sexism and classism. In doing so, ideal worker norms can be challenged on the varied ways they impact those with subordinated identities, and antiracist efforts can be better actualized in student affairs work..

References

Acker, J. (1990). Hierarchies, jobs, bodies: A theory of gendered organizations. *Gender and Society, 4*(2), 139–158. https://doi.org/10.1177/089124390004002002

Acker, J. (2006). Inequality regimes: Gender, class, and race in organizations. *Gender & Society, 20*(4), 441–464. https://doi.org/10.1177/0891243206289499

Acker, J. (2009). From glass ceiling to inequality regimes. *Sociologie du Travail, 51*(2), 199–217. https://doi.org/10.4000/sdt.16407

Alvarez, A. N., & Liu, W. M. (2002). Student affairs and Asian American studies: An integrative perspective. *New Directions for Student Services, 2002*(97), 73–80. https://doi.org/10.1002/ss.40

Bell, L. A. (2003). Telling tales: What stories can teach us about racism. *Race Ethnicity and Education, 6*(1), 3–28. https://doi.org/10.1080/1361332032000044567

Bender, D. (2009). *American abyss: Savagery and civilization in the age of industry.* Cornell University Press.

Bhattar, R. G. (2013). Crossroads and complexities: Experiences of a Queer, Desi, Hindu man in student affairs. In L. W. Watson & J. M. Johnson (Eds.), *Authentic leadership: Discussion of LGBTQ work as culturally relevant and engaged authentic leadership* (pp. 29–37). Information Age.

Bonilla-Silva, E. (2006). *Racism without racists: Color-blind racism and the persistence of racial inequality in the United States* (2nd ed.). Rowman & Littlefield.

Boss, G. J., Davis, T. J., Porter, C. J., & Moore, C. M. (2019). Second to none: Contingent women of Color faculty in the classroom. In R. Jeffries (Ed.), *Diversity, equity, and inclusivity in contemporary higher education* (pp. 211–225). IGI Global.

Boss, G. J., Linder, C., Martin, J. A., Dean, S. R., & Fitzer, J. R. (2018). Conscientious practice: Post-master's student affairs professionals' perspectives on engaging social justice. *Journal of Student Affairs Research and Practice, 55*(4), 373–385. https://doi.org/10.1080/19496591.2018.1470004

Cabrera, N. L. (2018a). Where is the racial theory in critical race theory?: A constructive criticism of the crits. *The Review of Higher Education, 42*(1), 209–233. https://doi.org/10.1353/rhe.2018.0038

Cabrera, N. L. (2018b). *White guys on campus: Racism, White immunity, and the myth of 'post-racial' higher education.* Rutgers University Press.

Crenshaw, K. (1991). Mapping the margins: Intersectionality, identity politics, and violence against women of color. *Stanford Law Review, 43*(6), 1241–1299. https://doi.org/10.2307/1229039

Davis, T. J. (2019). What does it mean for student affairs educators to maintain self-care in turbulent times? Practicing self-care in student affairs is a radical notion and it shouldn't be. In P. Magolda, M. Baxter Magolda, & R. Carducci (Eds.), *Contested issues in troubled times: Student affairs dialogues about equity, civility, and safety* (pp. 433–445). Stylus.

Delgado, R., & Stefancic, J. (2001). *Critical race theory: An introduction.* New York University Press.

DiAngelo, R. (2011). White fragility. *International Journal of Critical Pedagogy, 3*(3), 54–70. https://libjournal.uncg.edu/ijcp/article/view/249

Elliott, J. R., & Smith, R. A. (2004). Race, gender, and workplace power. *American Sociological Review, 69*(3), 365–386. https://doi.org/10.1177/000312240406900303

Garcia, G. A. (2016). Exploring student affairs professionals' experiences with the campus racial climate at a Hispanic Serving Institution (HSI). *Journal of Diversity in Higher Education, 9*(1), 20–33. https://doi.org/10.1037/a0039199

Gardner, L., Barrett, T. G., & Pearson, L. C. (2014). African American administrators at PWIs: Enablers of and barriers to career success. *Journal of Diversity in Higher Education, 7*(4), 235–251. https://doi.org/10.1037/a0038317

Gonzalez, J., & Kemp-DeLisser, K. (2010). Two student affairs professionals' journeys to (un)cover. *The Vermont Connection, 31*, 118–127. https://www.uvm.edu/~vtconn/v31/Gonzalez_Kemp-DeLisser.pdf

Green, T. K. (2008). Discomfort at work: Workplace assimilation demands and the contact hypothesis. *North Carolina Law Review, 86*(2), 378–440. https://scholarship.law.unc.edu/nclr/vol86/iss2/5

Grillo, T. (1995). Anti-essentialism and intersectionality: Tools to dismantle the master's house. *Berkeley Womens Law Journal, 10*(1), 16–30. https://lawcat.berkeley.edu/record/1115249/files/fulltext.pdf

Harper, S. R. (2012). Race without racism: How higher education researchers minimize racist institutional norms. *The Review of Higher Education, 36*(1), 9–29. https://doi.org/10.1353/rhe.2012.0047

Husband, M. (2016). Racial battle fatigue and the Black student affairs professional in the era of #BlackLivesMatter. *The Vermont Connection, 37*, 91–98. https://scholarworks.uvm.edu/tvc/vol37/iss1/10

Jackson, J. F., & O'Callaghan, E. M. (2009). *Ethnic and racial administrative diversity: Understanding work life realities and experiences in higher education.* Wiley.

Ladson-Billings, G. (1998). Just what is critical race theory and what's it doing in a nice field like education? *International Journal of Qualitative Studies in Education, 11*(1), 7–24. https://doi.org/10.1080/095183998236863

Ladson-Billings, G., & Tate, W. F. (2006). Toward a critical race theory of education. In A. D. Dixson & C. K. Rousseau (Eds.), *Critical race theory in education: All Gods children got a song* (pp. 11–30). Taylor & Francis.

Lithgow, I., Roundtree, C. V., Scypion, W. -S. H., & Williams, M. (2018). Welcome to the sunken place. *The Vermont Connection, 39*, 77–86. https://scholarworks.uvm.edu/tvc/vol39/iss1/13

López, G. R. (2003). The (racially neutral) politics of education: A critical race theory perspective. *Educational Administration Quarterly, 39*(1), 68–94. https://doi.org/10.1177/0013161X02239761

Lozano, A. (2017). Breaking the Black/White binary in higher education leadership. *About Campus, 21*(6), 27–31. https://doi.org/10.1002/abc.21276

Maramba, D. C. (2011). Few and far between: Exploring the experiences of Asian American and Pacific Islander women in student affairs administration. In G. Jean-Marie & B. Lloyd-Jones (Eds.), *Women of Color in higher education:*

Turbulent past, promising future diversity in higher education (Diversity in Higher Education, 9, pp. 337–359). Emerald Group Publishing.

Matsuda, M. J. (1991). Voices of America: Accent, antidiscrimination law, and a jurisprudence for the last reconstruction. *Yale Law Journal, 100*(5), 1329–1407. https://doi.org/10.2307/796694

McCoy, D. L., & Rodricks, D. J. (2015). Critical race theory in higher education: 20 years of theoretical and research innovations. *ASHE Higher Education Report, 41*(3), 1–117. https://doi.org/10.1002/aehe.20021

Nkomo, S. M., & Al Ariss, A. (2014). The historical origins of ethnic (white) privilege in US organizations. *Journal of Managerial Psychology, 29*(4), 389–404. https://doi.org/10.1108/JMP-06-2012-0178

Reitman, M. (2006). Uncovering the white place: Whitewashing at work. *Social & Cultural Geography, 7*(2), 267–282. https://doi.org/10.1080/14649360600600692

Roediger, D. R. (2005). *Working towards Whiteness: How America's immigrants became White: The strange journey from Ellis Island to the suburbs.* Basic Books.

Smith, W. A. (2004). Black faculty coping with racial battle fatigue: The campus racial climate in a post-civil rights era. In D. Cleveland (Ed.), *A long way to go: Conversations about race by African American faculty and graduate students* (pp. 171–190). Peter Lang.

Smith, W. A., Allen, W. R., & Danley, L. (2007). "Assume the position. . . you fit the description": Psychological experiences and racial battle fatigue among African American male college students. *The American behavioral scientist, 51,* 551–578. https://doi.org/10.1177/0002764207307742

Wolf-Wendel, L., Ward, K., & Kulp, A. M. (Eds.). (2016). *How ideal worker norms shape work-life for different constituent groups in higher education (New Directions for Higher Education No. 176).* Jossey-Bass.

II

THE CLASSED CONSTRUCT
OF STUDENT AFFAIRS WORK

Sonja Ardoin

When individuals from poor and working-class backgrounds have the opportunity to attend college and pursue what is deemed "professional" employment—such as serving as a student affairs educator—they are thought to have "made it" and others assume that they will navigate the workplace environment with ease (Stephens & Townsend, 2017). However, that is not often the reality because workplaces, including the academy, are classed spaces, which typically expect all employees to abide by middle- or upper-class ways of being. Although those from poor and working-class backgrounds may have the credentials and qualifications to be excellent student affairs educators, they may not feel welcome in the field or in the academy based on social class differences and experiences with classism.

Additionally, the ideal worker schema, or the belief that a person "exists only for the work" (Acker, 1990, p. 149) assumes that individuals will devote their entire being to their work. While the ideal worker construct is most often related to gender dynamics in the workplace, particularly in higher education, this concept can also be transferred to race, social class, sexuality, and ability and highlight other -isms that show up in the academy. Lester, 2016 invited scholars to dig into the ideal worker schema through multiple dimensions of identity to "reveal new areas of understanding of work–life in higher education" (p. 98).

This chapter attempts to respond to Lester's (2016) suggestion by exploring the holistic nature of social class identity, how class(ism) shows up in the workplace and in student affairs work, why the ideal worker concept is challenging for individuals from the poor and working classes, and what can be done to begin rethinking and reframing expectations around social class in student affairs.

The Comprehensiveness and Influence of Social Class Identity

Social class is defined as "a relative social ranking based on income, wealth, education, status, and power" (Leondar-Wright & Yeskel, 2007, p. 314). While it is common to reduce social class to one of its components—particularly socioeconomic status (SES), occupation, or education level—with the aim of getting to a singular definition or comparable statistic, social class is more than any one of these or even the combination of all three (Garrison & Liu, 2018). The terms *social class* and *SES* should not be viewed as interchangeable (Liu, 2011); rather, social class identity should be recognized as fluid, performative, and difficult to define (Martin et al., 2018). This is highlighted by the frame of each person possessing three forms of class identity, including class of origin; current, felt class; and attributed class—which are, correspondingly, "where we came from, what we think about ourselves, and what others think of us" (Barratt, 2011, p. 7).

The student affairs field needs to distinguish *SES* or *financial capital* from *social class identity*. The terms are often conflated, which reduces comprehension of what social class identity is and how it shows up in the workplace. SES or financial capital are the money and wealth-based resources that people possess. These are considered the more objective markers of social class because they can (generally) be quantified (Adams et al., 2018; Soria, 2018). Scholars and administrators tend to lean toward this narrow understanding of social class because it is easier to measure. Yet, societal messages that it is taboo to talk about money or wealth often cause people to refrain from discussing even this narrow frame of social class (Martin et al., 2018); this is known as "the class-avoidance phenomenon" (Mantsios, 2018, p. 173), and such avoidance limits understanding of social class identity while also silencing the conversation about it. Both are damaging to workplaces and those who are employed within them.

To expand perspectives, social class identity needs to be acknowledged in its comprehensive form, including a variety of kinds of capitals (e.g., knowledge, resources, and opportunities), such as the following:

- financial capital, or money and other forms of wealth;
- cultural capital, or specific knowledge and material markers of class (e.g., preferences for food, clothing; access to and understanding of health care);
- social capital, or the people in one's community or network;

- linguistic capital, or language acquisition, word choice, and accent;
- navigational capital, or familiarity with and understanding of systems;
- aspirational capital, or the chance to cultivate dreams and goals;
- academic capital, or the access to formal educational institutions; and
- resistant capital, or the ability to recognize inequity and desire to change (Barratt, 2011; Bourdieu, 1986; Liu, 2011; Yosso, 2005).

These capitals can show up in student affairs roles from the interview process through one's time at the institution. For example, some search committees feel compelled to bring candidates to "nice" restaurants for interview meals, aligning with the cultural capital of the middle or upper classes, while candidates from poor and working-class backgrounds may prefer and perform better in restaurant environments that are more casual. This difference in cultural capitals might create negative perceptions about the candidate's "fit" at the institution. Navigational capital can also show up in the interview process—understanding when to follow up and with whom and how to negotiate an offer—and throughout one's time on campus because of institutional politics, human resources policies, or evaluation processes. Individuals with middle- or upper-class forms of navigational capital generally have more familiarity with navigating higher education systems, thus giving them advantage as student affairs educators, bolstering their perceived alignment with the ideal worker construct, and increasing their likelihood of hire, success, and promotion.

Every person possesses these varying forms of capital in different ways; however, forms of capital held by those in the middle and upper classes are generally privileged in workspaces and society (Adams et al., 2018; Barratt, 2011; Bourdieu, 1986; Yosso, 2005), resulting in classism. Leondar-Wright and Yeskel (2007) defined *classism* as "the institutional, cultural, and individual set of practices and beliefs that assign differential value to people according to their [social class]" (p. 314). Four forms of classism, offered by Liu (2011), are (a) downward, or against those from perceived lower classes; (b) upward, or against those from perceived higher classes; and (c) lateral, or in comparison to those perceived to be in a similar social class. Engaging in any of these three forms of classism can result in the fourth form of classism: (d) internalized classism, which is when people accept stereotypes about their social class that influence their feelings about themselves (Liu, 2011).

Downward, upward, and internalized classism can be readily observed in student affairs. Returning to the example of candidate meals during interviews, downward classism might occur if an interviewer from a middle- or upper-class background judges the candidate's manners in a "nice" restaurant because the candidate does not seem to know how to function within that environment. Similarly, upward classism might simultaneously arise if the candidate assumes they will not be able to connect with campus colleagues because of the proclivity for "fancy" meals and, thus, assumes that colleagues at the institution are not like them. The candidate may then engage in internalized classism by assuming that they are not "classy" enough to work at this institution or perhaps in the student affairs field because of the expectations to perform certain forms of middle- and upper-class capitals that may not be inherent to or valued by the candidate.

Additionally, social class can influence an individual's values. People from poor and working-class backgrounds are often taught collective values such as humility, loyalty, and communal orientations while those from middle- and upper-class backgrounds are typically engrained with more individualistic values like self-expression, self-confidence, and success (Stephens & Townsend, 2017). This may create confusion and tension between student affairs colleagues from different social class backgrounds, between supervisors and supervisees with different social class value systems, or between educators and students from varying social classes. For example, a student affairs supervisor from an affluent background may believe that taking credit for the work of their employees or teams is typical, harmless behavior, while their supervisees from poor or working-class backgrounds may view the behavior as deceitful and lose trust in their supervisor.

Class and Classism in the Workplace

Social class influences career development through access to resources and perceptions that shape career aspirations, development, and attainment (Swanson & Fouad, 2015). In fact, in the United States, employers associate social class with employee appeal, viewing those from middle- and upper-class backgrounds as more desirable workers (Rivera & Tilcsik, 2016). Acker (2006) emphasized that "class inequalities are simultaneously created in the fundamental construction of the working day and of work obligations" (p. 448). Social class differences and classism permeate the workspace in two ways. First, individuals bring their personal social class worldviews into the work environment. This includes their perspectives on money and wealth, including its importance and how it should be used (or not); how and in what ways they prefer to connect to colleagues; and their tastes and preferences for clothing, food, and how they use time. Second, colleagues judge one another's forms of capital to develop "social rankings" at work (Gray & Kish-Gephart, 2013, p. 671). Tied to the first form, people assess one another based on social class worldviews and then use these critiques to determine where individuals should be placed in the informal colleague hierarchy (e.g., social rankings). This contributes to why work-based social gatherings are often hosted at the affluent colleague's home or the restaurant owned by a colleague's family member— a combination of an individual's social class worldview with their social rank at work and an instance of downward classism.

These concepts build on Bourdieu's (1985, 1991) work on individual and organizational *habitus*—or dispositions, expectations and behaviors— that inform individual and collective assumptions and behaviors. Conflicting habitus between an individual and the organization or between individuals within the organization create two kinds of "class salient encounters" (Gray & Kish-Gephart, 2013, p. 671) in the environment: (a) within-class encounters, where individuals are deviating from their own social class– appropriate norms, and (b) cross-class encounters, where individuals are challenging each other's habitus. For example, when someone purposefully changes their accent or dialect, a colleague who shares their social class and habitus may notice this shift and question the person's authenticity, accuse them of "class passing," or perceive them as disloyal. This is lateral classism. Cross-class encounters could be typified by someone from the working class experiencing air travel for the first time with their middle- or upper-class colleague; there would be significant differences in their navigational capital and cultural capital around the process and its customs. Instances of upward or downward classism can occur in these situations. Cross-class encounters are known to increase social class and classism consciousness (Liu, 2011) by emphasizing the unearned advantage given to individuals from a privileged social class and creating barriers for individuals from the poor or working class (Gray & Kish-Gephart, 2013).

The resulting implications of these salient encounters are deemed *class work*—"interpretive processes and interaction rituals" used to manage these encounters and the subsequent "existential anxiety" deriving from them (Gray & Kish-Gephart, 2013, p, 671). Class work typically necessitates that employees cope with classism by conforming to preexisting class rules and justifying and preserving class distinctions. Student affairs educators should be aware of both the micro and macro perspectives on social class in workspaces, noting that "microlevel behavior reflects and reinforces institutional structures of domination" (p. 671) and "inequities become institutionalized and maintained over time" (Gray & Kish-Gephart, 2013, p. 672). For example, although a student affairs educator from the poor or working class may possess the same academic and financial capital as their colleague, they may misstep around the academy's expectations of finesse, refined manners, and particular style and tastes by using profanity to make a point, wearing the "wrong" type of clothing, or not revering people for their titles (McNamee & Miller, 2009). Social class challenges and classism are ever present in organizations, including the field of student affairs (Gray & Kish-Gephart, 2013).

Some of the class salient encounters, class work, and classism that occur in workplaces are fueled by the myth of meritocracy, or the belief that success is based on merit and people all have the chance to succeed if they have the "right stuff," including attitude, skills, and hard work (Gray & Kish-Gephart, 2013; McNamee & Miller, 2009). This myth is undoubtedly an illusion when considering the ways that a person's multiple identities, including social class, limit access to opportunities, create barriers, and incite stereotypes and discrimination. However, when the myth of meritocracy is perpetuated in higher education, those realities are often ignored and set people up to internalize classism, with those from upper classes believing they are deserving and those from poor and working classes believing they are not (Adams et al., 2018).

The Ideal Worker Construct as a Classed Concept

Rather than a person with a rich, complex life and multiple obligations, the ideal worker construct frames employees as people who "exist only for the work" (Wolf-Wendel et al., 2016), and their job descriptions are written as such, assuming that individuals devote their entire selves to their work (Acker, 1990). Two main notions anchor ideal worker norms: (a) ever-present availability and (b) lack of caregiver responsibilities (Hochschild, 1995; Sallee, 2016; Williams et al., 2013; Wolf-Wendel et al., 2016). This concept favors those who can subscribe to this standard, because they align with the ideal and do not threaten the archetype, and compromises opportunity for those who need—for multiple reasons—to give energy and attention to both professional and personal responsibilities.

Social class becomes a consideration in the ideal worker construct because to be an ideal worker, one would need to be single, partnered with another individual who primarily serves as a caregiver, and only employed in one job in order to meet the expectation of total devotion to work (Acker, 1990). Many student affairs educators, particularly those from poor and working-class backgrounds, have multiple roles and responsibilities in their lives and some work multiple jobs in order to meet financial obligations (e.g., supporting family, student loan repayment).

Ideal worker norms compel employees to be constantly available and without other job or life responsibilities (Acker, 1990; Hochschild, 1995; Sallee, 2016; Williams et al., 2013; Wolf-Wendel et al., 2016), and employees are also expected to understand and conform to middle- or upper-class standards—a "professional" way of knowing, being, and doing—regardless of their class of origin or background (Wolf-Wendel et al., 2016). Adams et al. (2018) described

> norms of "professionalism" as one mechanism by which intersectional class inequalities are reproduced because they are culturally specific in terms of class as well as ethnic and linguistic cultures, and are gendered, so that anyone who is not both gender-conforming and at home in dominant White, middle-class culture may be seen as unprofessional and lose status as a result. (p. 168)

This demonstrates how professionalism can be a form of classism and class work (Gray & Kish-Gephart, 2013); student affairs educators are expected to conform to the preexisting social class rules of higher education environments, which favor the norms, behaviors, and values of White middle- and upper-class men.

The Social Class Ideal in Student Affairs Work

Professions are considered the "learned occupations" of the "upper class" who engage in work that includes "expertise, collective organization and collegial control, ethical standards, and work [of] 'public service'" (Brint, 1993, p. 270; Carpenter & Stimpson, 2007). In short, working in a profession, like student affairs, and engaging in professionalism are ways of communicating "cultural labeling" (Brint, 1993, p. 264) to the world. It is a marker, or indicator, of social class, informing others that this type of work is important and generally reserved for individuals in the middle and upper classes. This is why people often ask new acquaintances what they do for work; they are attempting to discern culture—or social class—based on employment.

The field of student affairs has an implicit assumption that "professionalism pervades all activities in the field" (Carpenter & Stimpson, 2007, p. 265) and is "expected on campus and by peers" (Carpenter & Stimpson, 2007, p. 269), yet many of these concepts are not taught in graduate preparation programs or university onboarding processes. Rather, it is just assumed and expected that people will embody professionalism; this is classism in action and requires poor and working-class student affairs professionals to engage in class work in order to learn and conform to these expectations and manage downward, lateral, and internalized classism. Two of the many ways social class, class work, and classism show up in professionalism—dress and social connection—can also be framed, respectively, as forms of cultural capital and social capital (Barratt, 2011; Bourdieu, 1986; Yosso, 2005).

Professional Dress: A Form of Cultural Capital

Knowing what to wear and when to wear it can be confusing because professional dress is "rarely written and largely unspoken" (p. 173) yet "the quality most associated with being unprofessional is appearance or dress" (Thornton, 2015, p. 174). This confusion is heightened when individuals come from a poor or working-class background where family members wore uniforms or casual clothing to work. Discerning business from business casual or "dressing for the day" can result in self-consciousness if the guess seems wrong based on what peers are wearing, comments are made about one's attire, or one experiences feelings of discomfort in that type of clothing. Additionally, professional dress requires owning the items necessary to meet that definition. In writing about office dress codes, Thornton (2015) explained that "learning to fit the mold can have deleterious effects . . . [can] harm self-esteem" (p.174) and can "mask unconscious bias developed by a select group of insiders, intended to keep outsiders out" (p 175). This is another way internalized and downward or lateral classism, respectively, can permeate student affairs.

Dress falls in the realm of cultural capital (Bourdieu, 1986; Liu, 2011; Yosso, 2005) and people's association with materialism (Liu, 2011). Cultural capital influences socialization about what types of clothes people may prefer to wear, how individuals perceive the process of shopping, and the definition of *work clothes*. For many individuals from poor and working-class backgrounds, work clothes are often understood as items that are comfortable, breathable, and okay to be ruined. However, the field of higher education and student affairs offers opposing messages, instilling that work clothes should be "professional," which often means more confining, refined, and pricier. Add materialism to this—whether or not people care about clothing as a possession and how much they are willing to spend on it—and a wide array of lenses around professional dress or so-called work clothes can be concocted.

Additionally, some institutions also highly encourage—in reality, require—student affairs educators to dress in school colors or collegiately licensed logo attire on certain days of the week or for specific events. Yet, frequently the institution does not supply the clothing, leaving employees to contend with hefty bookstore prices (Ardoin & martinez, 2018). There are also expectations that individuals know what to wear to university events, conferences, or peer social gatherings. As Lubrano (2004) recognized, "Clothes become vital for the proper office portrait" (p. 130). All of this concern over dress exists despite the facts that student affairs work is rarely impacted by clothing choice and people's work should "speak much more loudly than how [they] look" (Rios, 2015, para. 12).

Professional dress illustrates classism, class work, and ideal worker norms. Student affairs educators are expected to know what to wear, possess it, and feel—or at least portray—comfort wearing it, all of which speak to class work of conforming to the preexisting rules of dress and, thus, justify and preserve class distinctions around professionalism (Gray & Kish-Gephart, 2013). Also, appearance and dress are used as "a kind of rhetorical device promoting credibility to project an image of competence that matches [one's] skills" (Thornton, 2015, p. 173); this highlights how dress can often be a component required for career advancement. So, if someone does not dress professionally, they are essentially not doing what is required for normal career advancement, which is something the ideal worker construct demands (Williams, 2000).

Social Connection: A Form of Social Capital

Social class can influence how people engage with others, form connections, and develop collegial relationships. Stephens and Townsend (2017) compared the tendency of individuals from poor and working-class backgrounds to seek interdependence and connection with the inclination of individuals from the middle and upper classes toward independence and separation. They credit this to poor and working-class families impressing upon children that "it's not all about [them]" (Stephens & Townsend, 2017, para. 3) and instilling values of "solidarity, humility, and loyalty" (Stephens & Townsend, 2017, para. 3) while more affluent families tell their children "the world is your oyster" (Stephens & Townsend, 2017, para. 4) and encourage values of "uniqueness, self-expression, and influence" (Stephens & Townsend, 2017, para. 4). Should these variances take root in children from different social classes, it sets them up with challenges in cross-class understanding and in interpreting workplace expectations that prioritize independence and autonomy as ideal worker norms. For example, employees from working-class backgrounds may be more focused on work as a collaborative process and a pathway to help their families or give back to their communities, while the higher education environment, which is rooted in middle- and upper-class capitals, stresses the celebration of individual accomplishments and often provides accolades to supervisors rather than teams. This can create disconnects between colleagues as well as between poor and working-class individuals and their work environment.

Essentially, social class inequity is maintained in the workplace because of these behavior distinctions (Aydin et al., 2018). Haney (2016) reported that those from working-class backgrounds continue to feel "out of place" (p. 144) in higher education, regardless of how long they have worked in the academy, because of the ways language (e.g., linguistic capital) and networking (e.g., social and navigational capital) create challenges to social connection and sense of belonging. Poor and working-class people "report that the tone of speech and word choice they are forced to use in academic settings contrasts sharply with the language and tone they learned at home, forcing them to be extremely deliberate in choosing their speech" (Haney, 2016, p. 144)in conversations at work or with colleagues. Thus, it is not surprising that employees from poor and working-class backgrounds—including student affairs educators—report having issues of fit in their workspaces because of social class differences (Ardoin & martinez, 2018; Stephens & Townsend, 2017). If people are obliged to change their communication patterns, or *code-switch*, just to make small talk, they will likely limit those social encounters. People from poor and working classes sometimes prefer to sacrifice the social connection instead of trying to fill "the impossible gap between themselves and their colleagues" (Lubrano, 2004, p. 85).

In addition to how people interact, where they interact socially can also fall along social class lines. In student affairs work, building connection circles or networks often occurs through campus events and professional meetings. These spaces are inherently classed and sometimes require an invitation, funding, or a combination thereof. For example, in the president's box or a similar space at major athletic events, significant connections, fund-raising leads, and decisions can be made, but people may not be invited to those events or feel comfortable attending them because of class work and classism (upward, downward, lateral, or internalized) that may arise (Gray & Kish-Gephart, 2013). Similar challenges are present with professional meetings. Often, those require registration fees, travel costs, time away, and navigation of the professional association environment itself. Poor and working-class individuals may find themselves disoriented when entering a new professional association or a particular meeting for the first time. It is awkward to not know the "rules" of the environment or how different forms of capital will be received there. It can heighten social class distinctions and classism consciousness and causes individuals to question their behaviors and engage in more internalized classism (see Liu, 2011).

Professional dress and social connection—or cultural and social capital (Barratt, 2011; Bourdieu, 1986; Yosso, 2005)—are only two instances of the many ways social class, class work, and classism show up in professionalism. For a robust analysis of how professional socialization and professionalism can privilege those with majority identities and further marginalize employees with minoritized identities, such as being from a poor or working-class background, see chapter 5 by Perez in this volume.

Class and Ideal Worker Passing: Obvious Forms of Class Work

Concepts of *passing* and *revealing*, or ways that people shape others' beliefs about them (Goffman, 1963), are used to describe how people manage some underserved social identities, such as being a member of the poor or working class (Reid, 2015).

> People may either misrepresent themselves as members of the favored group—thus, passing—or disclose that they are nonmembers—thus revealing. Passing can be intentional, as when a person lies about his or her identity, or accidental, as when others make incorrect assumptions; revealing also occurs across a continuum of intentionality. (Reid, 2015, p. 999)

When student affairs educators from the poor or working classes experience dissonance between their own habitus or social class worldview and the expectations of the professional paradigm, they may engage in *class passing*, or the practice of hiding their class background by conforming to the professional status quo (e.g., the ideal worker construct) and letting others believe they too are from the middle or upper classes and are primarily devoted to work (Acker, 1990; Gray & Kish-Gephart, 2013). When people's personal and professional identity are at odds with the ideal worker construct, people have the choice of "passing as having embraced it or revealing their deviance" (Reid, 2015, p. 997); however, the taboo nature of discussing social class and the potential to conceal that aspect of identity may mask how someone rejects ideal worker norms because their colleagues may not be aware of their social class identity or the individual may be class passing (Goffman, 1963; Reid, 2015). Engaging in class or ideal worker passing can be considered elements of class work because the "behavior reflects and reinforces institutional structures of domination" (Gray & Kish-Gephart, 2013, pp. 671–672).

hooks (2000) cautioned that passing behavior is "allying [one]self with the class interest of the upper classes and colluding in [one's] own exploitation" (p. 77). This practice of class passing also means that student affairs educators are neither addressing the classism present in the academy nor allowing students to see educators who may represent their social class identity, thus weakening the diversity and inclusion of the overall institution. However, it should be noted and respected that some individuals engage in class passing as a form of self-preservation and health and safety based on their environmental circumstances and the professional paradigm.

The Culture of Busy: A Misconstrued Form of Aspiration Capital

Beginning with graduate preparation, student affairs educators are taught that they should work for more hours than they are paid. Graduate assistantships and internships of 20 hours per week stretch to more than 30-hour weeks; 100 hour to 300 hour practica are required and not often compensated. The culture of the field and socialization into it inform people that they should generally be working more than the 40 hours stated in most job descriptions (Nelko, 2015), often on nights and weekends and sometimes to the detriment of personal care and needs (Sallee, 2016). These practices misconstrue busyness or devotion to work as a form of aspirational capital, or the focus on pursuing dreams and goals (Yosso, 2005).

Then, when individuals become full-time employees, there are veiled (for obvious reasons) practices of asking those who are hourly not to document overtime, and those who are salaried are informed that 40 hours is the baseline, with the rationalization that additional time and effort should be contributed because of individuals' passion for the work and the intrinsic value they should find in it. This comes from the ideal worker devotion schema that drives "the cognitive belief, moral commitment, and emotional salience of making work [our] central focus of life" (Williams et al., 2013, p. 211). It is considered a "class act"—or "way of signaling elite status" to work "long hours of high intensity work" as opposed to just "punching the clock" when the hours are up (Williams et al., 2013, p. 213). This is classist and creates complexity for student affairs educators from poor and working-class backgrounds because, perhaps unlike their family members who have firm hours or use literal time cards, there is no concrete way to measure when student affairs work is done. Thus, confusion arises about when it is deemed okay to stop for the day or even use vacation time.

This work devotion schema then fuels individuals to operate in a culture of busy as a competition, with the assumption that whoever has the calendar with no free blocks and never takes vacation days is the most valuable (Dickinson, 2016). People convince themselves that they should serve on the committee, attend the event, or pick up the shift in order to prove their aspirations and status with the ideal worker construct, which is deemed an asset to the organization. The seductive nature of the work devotion schema gives us evidence of our "strong work ethic, [which] helps form [our] sense of self and self-worth" (Williams et al., 2013, p. 211). While this aligns with ideal worker norms, it is inequitable and discouraging for those who do not want to, or cannot, engage in the competition; those with other jobs, people, pets, and duties which they have or want to attend; or those who define their self and self-worth in other ways.

Class divides show up here as well; research (e.g., Heymann, 2005) shows that those from poor and working-class families frequently rely on family for childcare, which can be less reliable, and serve as caregivers for family members, which requires significant time and energy depending on their access to health care, while those from more affluent backgrounds can outsource such duties to daycares, nursing homes, and other such venues. These personal obligations and how class influences available time can conflict with ideal worker norms because it interrupts people's ability to be always available for work (Acker, 1990). The dynamics can also compel poor and working-class people to engage in class work because availability expectations are "inequities [that] become institutionalized and maintained over time" (Gray & Kish-Gephart, 2013, pp. 671–672).

Recommendations for Practice: Rethinking and Reframing Expectations Around Ideal Worker Norms as a Classed Construct in Student Affairs

Knowing that the ideal worker construct creates challenges around social class identity and encourages some forms of classism, it is our responsibility to rebuke the use of the ideal worker frame within student affairs and rethink and reframe social class expectations in the field.

Strategies are offered for student affairs educators at various points in their careers to showcase that change can ignite from any level within the organization and will likely have to happen at multiple levels to truly incite a cultural shift.

Graduate Students and New Professionals

Because the ideal worker construct permeates U.S. employment and the culture of busy persists, graduate students and new professionals would benefit from discussing expectations with their supervisors. Examining expectations—those both spoken and unspoken (e.g., professional dress)—in the field through a critical lens that interrogates both one's own social class worldview and the classist practices of their institution of employment could be helpful in deciding ways to engage in the profession and discerning what could and should be challenged around social class and ideal worker norms. Setting up specific conversations with faculty members, supervisors, and colleagues can be valuable time to inquire about both the micro and macro perspectives on social class in workspaces (Gray & Kish-Gephart, 2013). Reading social class literature and institutional policies or listening to podcasts on social class in the workplace might also prove illuminating.

Talking through what time and scheduling look like for student affairs educators on the campus could provide framing as well, because it can be common for student affairs educators who strive to embody the ideal worker construct to "impose evening and weekend hours on themselves" without having clarity around "how many evening and weekend hours they needed to work in order to be successful in their jobs or to appear as ideal workers" (Wilk, 2016, p. 41). This can be especially useful for graduate students and new professionals who may need to pursue secondary jobs or "side hustles" for financial reasons, which pushes against the ideal worker schema. New professionals in student affairs should (try to) attain clear expectations and control their calendars in an attempt to respect their own needs, values, and worldviews.

Midcareer Professionals

Midcareer professionals might consider serving as "professionalism guides" for graduate students and new professionals, helping them navigate the assumptions, expectations, and unwritten social class rules of the higher education and student affairs environments. Reid (2015) suggested that colleagues who have spent more time in the workplace should discuss the conflicts they have faced between expected professional identities (e.g., the ideal worker construct) and experienced professional identities (e.g. their individual professional identity, in combination with their social class identities). These conversations and reality checks can help newer employees understand how to negotiate variances between ideal worker norms and social class, including misalignments between poor and working-class worldviews and values and the academy's middle and upper class milieu.

Supervisors

Those who have the responsibility of guiding colleagues as supervisors need to recognize that supervision is a "class practice" (Acker, 2006, p. 450) and supervisors in student affairs can send "mixed messages to [supervisees] about the ideal worker" (Wilk, 2016, p. 42). They need to consider how their own social class identity will be similar to or different from their supervisees, how class work could arise, and why clarity is critical. For example, Acker (2006) shared that supervisors "may expect a certain class deference or respect for authority. . . . [Supervisees] may assume that their positions require deference and respect but also find these demands demeaning or oppressive" (p. 451).

Practicing synergistic supervision and assessing evaluation processes might be helpful in addressing social class identity, class work, and the ideal worker construct. Practicing synergistic supervision helps to "achieve organizational goals and also attend to the personal and professional welfare of [employees]" (Winston & Creamer, 1997, p. 197). This process of engagement between the supervisor and supervisee creates a trusting dynamic that establishes clear expectations and allows for challenges—such as social class dynamics—to be recognized, named, and addressed. As Ardoin and martinez (2018) pointed out, it is helpful for supervisees and supervisors to talk about their social classes, particularly their backgrounds, to understand how some of their differences in opinion, communication, or behavior may be based in class. It also allows the supervisee to show up as their whole self (e.g., person and professional) rather than solely as a worker, thus challenging the ideal worker construct. And when student affairs educators can show up in their whole identity, supervisors can support supervisees with managing their lives holistically through letting go of the work devotion schema and adopting flexible options that exist in the environment (Lester, 2016).

Supervisors can take this style of supervision a step further by assessing employee evaluation processes to determine how they might be portraying the ideal worker construct and favoring particular social class worldviews. With an understanding that student affairs educators from poor or working classes may thrive through interdependence or practice humility to a detriment in an evaluation process, supervisors can rethink and rebuild the evaluation document and process to recognize individuals' interdependent strengths and draw out their accomplishments in ways that do not compromise their values, such as humility.

Senior Student Affairs Officers

Individuals who serve as senior student affairs officers (SSAOs) have the unique opportunity to focus on broader shifts with wider impact. Two ways that SSAOs may challenge ideal worker norms and classism in their divisions are (a) creating a culture of collaboration and (b) considering how work is rewarded. As Stephens and Townsend (2017) noted, interdependency and connection are important to people from poor and working-class backgrounds. SSAOs might revisit the focus of collaboration in their divisions, reconsider siloed structures, encourage sharing of financial and human resources, and brainstorm ways to cross-train people across functional areas. These efforts can increase employees' cultural and social capital and elevate their level of connection and interdependency. As Carpenter and Stimpson (2007) offered, "Competition within [divisions and] institutions for resources or influence is cancerous and wrong. . . . There is no place in our practice for pettiness, competition, or greed in whatever forms" (pp.

280–281). Similarly, SSAOs might also consider how work in their division is rewarded. When divisions of student affairs allot recognition or awards to only those who subscribe to the ideal worker construct or navigate the class dynamics of the institution with ease because they identify as middle or upper class, it furthers classism and class work in the division (Bailyn, 2006; Gray & Kish-Gephart, 2013).

Suggestions for Practice and Policy

While change of any kind in higher education and student affairs can take more time than people might prefer and cultural transformations often happen glacially, if the goal is more equitable workspaces and educational environments, change must be relentlessly sought. Four suggestions on how to begin shifting practices and policies related to social class and the ideal worker schema are offered: (a) talking about social class and our worldviews (Barratt, 2011; Bourdieu, 1986; Liu, 2011; Yosso, 2005); (b) recognizing the value-add that student affairs educators from poor and working-class backgrounds bring to their offices, institutions, and the field at large; (c) reducing class work (Gray & Kish-Gephart, 2013) in student affairs specifically and higher education more broadly; and (d) shifting institutional policies and practices.

Engage in Social Class Identity Conversation

While this may sound simple, social class identity conversations can be quite a challenge. Social class is often a taboo topic (Martin et al., 2018); pushing past that taboo to engage in social class conversation is demanding work. Student affairs educators should begin by engaging in some self-work around their three forms of class—class of origin; current, felt class; and attributed class—which, as described earlier, are "where we came from, what we think about ourselves, and what others think of us" (Barratt, 2011, p. 7). Exploring how student affairs educators individually define each of these forms of class for themselves and whether there is consistency or fluidity in their class identities could be helpful in raising consciousness of social class. Then, it may be beneficial to have student affairs educators consider how social class identity shows up within the office, institutional, and broader student affairs environments. This follows Gray and Kish-Gephart (2013) suggestion to pay attention to both the micro and macro class dynamics at play in workspaces. Once people have had time to reflect and process, perhaps over a few hours, days, or even months, then they could be invited to begin sharing their own social class stories and experiences of salient class encounters, class work, and classism in student affairs and higher education (Gray & Kish-Gephart, 2013; Liu, 2011).

It is only when student affairs educators have done their own self-work around class identity that they should begin considering how to engage students in the conversation. Familiarizing themselves with the concepts and methods first will help them process their own tough spots as learners before facilitating social class conversations as educators. At that point they can use their own learning and areas of growth as tools of instruction and examples for others to begin their own social class work. But the most critical part of this is to try to talk about social class, even when it is messy and uncomfortable and resisted.

Recognize Individuals' Value-Add

Rather than succumbing to class stereotypes about the deficits of individuals from poor and working-class backgrounds, differences can be reframed as value-adds. Sometimes this is attempted and even successful in working with students, but efforts in accomplishing this with colleagues often fall short, likely because of the myth of meritocracy, the culture of busy, and other socialization messages received from society (Liu, 2011; McNamee & Miller, 2009). It would be helpful to consider how having people with varying kinds of capital—financial, cultural, and social, among others—can breathe new perspective and understanding into workplace environments and the field of student affairs. This has helped in the development of campus jargon dictionaries, food pantries, career center clothing closets, childcare centers, and many other initiatives that are beginning to represent varying social classes on campus. Having individuals from poor and working-class backgrounds in higher education allows new perceptions about programs, policies, and practices to emerge and provides representation for students to potentially "see themselves" in the campus offerings and within the institutional administration.

Reduce Classism and Class Work

While there are certain to be class salient encounters between colleagues in student affairs and between educators and their institutions for a long time, the four forms of classism (upward, downward, lateral, and internalized) and class work—or conforming to preexisting class rules and preserving class distinctions (Gray & Kish-Gephart, 2013)—associated with these encounters can be reduced. Rather than using class work as a defensive strategy for those from middle and upper classes and moments of internalized classism for those from the poor and working classes, we can rethink and reframe these encounters as opportunities for healthy cross-class conversation and learning, which emphasizes the importance of the first suggestion in this section of cultivating class conversations in student affairs and across campus. In addition, when "class work" is reduced, incidents of downward, upward, and lateral classism (Liu, 2011) are also lessened in higher education workplaces. As Ardoin and martinez (2018) suggested, "Let us intentionally take time to get to know our colleagues and their valuable forms of class capital—and share our own—in order to recognize additional ways of functioning across class identity as colleagues [and] educators" (p. 115).

Shift Policies and Practices on Hiring and Flexibility of Hours
Finally, any student affairs educator, regardless of years in the field or place on the organization chart, can strive to shift institutional policies and practices around the ideal worker construct and social class identity. Two methods of attempting this are adding social class background as a form of diversity representation in hiring and promotion practices and pushing for flexibility programs that invite different work time and type arrangements for employees.

Often when diversity and inclusion are discussed on campuses, only the big three—race/ethnicity, gender, and sexuality—receive attention. While these are critical to consider, so is social class, and it is often missing from the conversation and efforts to increase representation. When people are serving on a search committee or as hiring managers, they might consider suggesting, within legal bounds, that social class background be considered a value-add for candidates who offer new social class worldviews or lobby to move forward a candidate who showcased an understanding of social class and classism consciousness (Liu, 2011) in their student affairs work.

Also, consider pushing for flexibility programs that allow for formal or informal creativity with availability such as flextime, part-time schedules, compressed workweeks, telecommuting, and job shares (Williams et al., 2013). It may mean baby steps with supervisors and longer conversations with an SSAO or a human resources director, but keep exploring possibilities to name and contest the ideal worker construct and classism. Then, if and when flexibility programs begin to take shape, divisions can do some culture shifting to highlight these programs and assure employees that utilizing them will not result in reputational, evaluation, promotion, or monetary risks (Williams et al., 2013).

Conclusion

While this chapter may create more questions than answers, a starting point for forward movement is to ruminate on how social class worldviews (Barratt, 2011; Bourdieu, 1986; Liu, 2011; Yosso, 2005) interact with ideal worker norms (Acker, 1990) and begin considering how the student affairs field can begin to rethink and reframe workspaces to be more inclusive of colleagues from poor and working-class backgrounds. Create space for reflection and conversations about social class. Identify how class work may be happening in an office or department. Scrutinize the culture of conformity to preexisting class rules and the way classism has been institutionalized. The ideal worker construct and classism will continue to permeate the higher education workplace until student affairs educators from across social classes work together to deconstruct the concepts and diminish their influence.

References

Acker, J. (1990). Hierarchies, jobs, bodies: A theory of gendered organizations. *Gender and Society*, *4*(2), 139–158. https://doi.org/10.1177/089124390004002002

Acker, J. (2006). Inequality regimes: Gender, class, and race in organizations. *Gender and Society*, *20*(4), 441–464. https://doi.org/10.1177/0891243206289499

Adams, M., Hopkins, L. E., & Shlasko, D. (2018). Classism: Introduction. In M. Adams, W. J. Blumenfeld, D. C. J. Catalano, K. S. DeJong, H. W. Hackman, L. E. Hopkins, B. J. Love, M. K. Peters, D. Shlasko, & X. Zuniga (Eds.), *Readings for diversity and social justice* (pp. 164–172). Routledge.

Ardoin, S., & martinez, b. (2018). No, I can't meet you for an $8 coffee: How class shows up in workspaces. In B. Reece, V. Tran, E. DeVore, & G. Porcaro (Eds.), *Debunking the myth of job fit in student affairs* (pp. 97–118). Stylus.

Aydin, A. L., Ullrich, J., Siem, B., Locke, K. D., & Shnabel, N. (2018). The effect of social class on agency and communion: Reconciling identity-based and rank-based perspectives. *Social psychological and personality science*, *1*(11), 735–745. https://doi.org/10.1177/1948550618785162

Bailyn, L. (2006). *Breaking the mold: Redesigning work for productive and satisfying lives*. Cornell University Press.

Barratt, W. (2011). *Social class on campuses: Theories and manifestations*. Stylus.

Bourdieu, P. (1985). The market of symbolic goods. *Poetics*, *14*(1-2), 13–44. https://doi.org/10.1016/0304-422X(85)90003-8

Bourdieu, P. (1986). The forms of capital. In J. G. Richardson (Ed.), *Handbook of theory and research for the sociology of education* (pp. 241–258). Greenwood.

Bourdieu, P. (1991). *Language and symbolic power*. Harvard University Press.

Brint, S. (1993). Eliot Friedson's contribution to the sociology of professionals. *Work & Occupations*, *20*(3), 259–279. https://doi.org/10.1177/0730888493020003001

Carpenter, S., & Stimpson, M. T. (2007). Professionalism, scholarly practice, and professional development in student affairs. *NASPA Journal*, *44*(2), 265–284. https://doi.org/10.2202/0027-6014.1795

Dickinson, E. E. (2016). The cult of busy. *John Hopkins Health Review*, *3*(1), 26–37.

Garrison, Y. L., & Liu, W. M. (2018). Using the social class worldview model in student affairs. *New Directions for Student Services, 162*(2018), 19–33. https://doi .org/10.1002/ss.20259

Goffman, E. (1963). *Stigma: Notes on the management of spoiled identity.* Simon & Schuster.

Gray, B., & Kish-Gephart, J. J. (2013). Encountering social class differences at work: How "class work" perpetuates inequality. *Academy of Management Review, 38*(4), 670–699. https://doi.org/10.5465/amr.2012.0143

Haney, T. J. (2016). "We're all middle-class here": Privilege and the denial of class inequality in the Canadian professoriate. In A. L. Hurst & S. K. Nenga (Eds.), *Working in class: Recognizing how social class shapes our academic work* (pp. 141– 156). Rowman and Littlefield.

Heymann, J. (2005). Inequalities at work and at home: Social class and gender divides. In J. Heymann & C. Beem (Eds.), *Unfinished work: Building equality and democracy in an era of working families* (pp. 89–121). The New Press.

Hochschild, A. R. (1995). The culture of politics: Traditional, postmodern, cold- modern, and warm-modern ideals of care. *Social Politics, 2*(3), 331–346. https:// doi.org/10.1093/sp/2.3.331

hooks, b. (2000). *Where we stand: Class matters.* Routledge.

Leondar-Wright, B., & Yeskel, F. (2007). Classism curriculum design. In M. Adams, L. A. Bell, & P. Griffin (Eds.), *Teaching for diversity and social justice* (2nd ed., pp. 308–333). Routledge.

Lester, J. (2016). Complexity of work–life identities and policy development: Implications for work–life in higher education. *New Directions for Higher Education, 2016*(176), 53–67.

Liu, W. M. (2011). *Social class and classism in the helping professions: Research, theory, and practice.* SAGE.

Lubrano, A. (2004). *Limbo: Blue-collar roots, white-collar dreams.* Wiley.

Mantsios, G. (2018). Classism in America. In M. Adams, W. J. Blumenfeld, D. C. J. Catalano, K. S. DeJong, H. W. Hackman, L. E. Hopkins, B. J. Love, M. K. Peters, D. Shlasko, & X. Zuniga (Eds.), *Readings for diversity and social justice* (pp. 173–182). Routledge.

Martin, G. L., Williams, B., & Young, C. R. (2018). Understanding social class as identity. *New Directions for Student Services, 2018*(162), 9–18. https://doi.org/10 .1002/ss.20258

McNamee, S. J., & Miller, R. K. Jr. (2009). *The meritocracy myth* (2nd ed.). Rowman & Littlefield.

Nelko, J. (2015). *Making your job a 40-hour commitment.* Student Affairs Collective. https://studentaffairscollective.org/making-your-job-a-40-hour-commitment -sacareer/

Reid, E. (2015). Embracing, passing, revealing, and the ideal worker image: How people navigate expected and experienced professional identities. *Organizational Science, 26*(4), 997–1017. https://doi.org/10.1287/orsc.2015 .0975

Rios, C. (2015). *You call it professionalism; I call it oppression in a three-piece suit.* Everyday Feminism. http://everydayfeminism.com/2015/02/professionalism-and-oppression/

Rivera, L. A., & Tilcsik, A. (2016). Class advantage, commitment penalty: The gendered effect of social class signals in an elite labor market. *American sociological review, 81*(6), 1097–1131. https://doi.org/10.1177/0003122416668154

Sallee, M. (2016). Ideal for whom? A cultural analysis of ideal worker norms in higher education and student affairs programs. *New Directions for Higher Education, 2016*(176), 53–67. https://doi.org/10.1002/he.20209

Soria, K. (2018). Counting class: Assessing social class identity using quantitative measures. *New Directions for Student Services, 2018*(162), 49–61. https://doi.org/10.1002/ss.20261

Stephens, N., & Townsend, S. (2017). Research: How you feel about individualism is influenced by your social class. *Harvard Business Review Digital Articles,* 2–5. Harvard Business School Publishing Corporation. https://hbr.org/2017/05/research-how-you-feel-about-individualism-is-influenced-by-your-social-class

Swanson, J. L., & Fouad, N. A. (2015). *Career theory and practice: Learning through case studies* (3rd ed.). SAGE.

Thornton, K. (2015). Parsing the visual rhetoric of office dress codes: A two-step process to increase inclusivity and professionalism in legal-workplace fashion. *Legal Communication & Rhetoric: JALWD, 12,* 173–193. https://ssrn.com/abstract=2679721

Wilk, K. (2016). Work–life balance and ideal worker expectations for administrators. *New Directions for Higher Education, 2016*(176), 37–51. https://doi.org/10.1002/he.20208

Williams, J. (2000). *Unbending gender: Why family and work conflict and what to do about it.* Oxford University Press.

Williams, J. C., Blair-Loy, M., & Berdahl, J. L. (2013). Cultural schemas, social class, & the flexibility stigma. *Journal of Social Issues, 69*(2), 209–234. https://doi.org/10.1111/josi.12012

Winston, R. B., Jr., & Creamer, D. G. (1997). *Improving staffing practices in student affairs.* Jossey-Bass.

Wolf-Wendel, L., Ward, K., & Kulp, A. (2016). Editors' notes. *New Directions for Higher Education, 2016*(176), 5–9. https://doi.org/10.1002/he.20205

Yosso, T. (2005). Whose culture has capital? A critical race theory discussion of community cultural wealth. *Race Ethnicity and Education, 8*(1), 69–91. https://doi.org/10.1080/1361332052000341006

12

INTERROGATING THE "IDEAL" NEW PROFESSIONAL IN STUDENT AFFAIRS

Melanie Lee and Megan Karbley

Research indicates that 50% to 60% of new professionals leave student affairs within the first 5 years of full-time work (Harned & Murphy, 1998; Lorden, 1998; Saunders et al., 2000; Tull, 2006). Eager and armed with student development theory and often several semesters' worth of practical experience, new professionals enter the full-time student affairs workforce ready to put theory into practice. In their new roles, new professionals in student affairs are often called upon to take on responsibilities outside regular work hours (Casey, 1995; Komives & Woodard, 2003). Such duties might include attending student meetings and events into the late evening, responding to on-call emergencies into the early morning, and spending weekends at staff trainings and retreats. These off-hour requests likely do not include any additional compensation and, depending on the institution, may or may not include additional paid time off or compensatory time. This rigorous schedule blurs boundaries between work and personal life (Boehman, 2007). Such schedules and blurred boundaries may influence professionals' desire to stay in the student affairs field, particularly new professionals learning to navigate expectations of their respective roles.

This chapter seeks to uncover what factors influence new professionals' desire to remain in, or leave, student affairs. To learn more about new professionals' experiences in student affairs, we undertook a study to expand on previous inquiries related to the first years of employment for new professionals (Clinte et al., 2006; Renn & Hodges, 2007). The study was designed to explore not only job satisfaction but also aspects of ideal worker norms (Acker, 1990) in a new professional's first 5 years of employment. This chapter also explores how aspects of the new professional's experience may align with ideal worker norms and how the student affairs environment maintains or challenges notions of the ideal worker. In short, we found that new professionals' experiences aligned with ideal worker norms while simultaneously illuminating the importance of a sense of belonging for new professionals in their first 5 years of employment to increase persistence toward a lifelong career in the field of student affairs.

What the field has learned about new professionals in the past 20 years largely comes from two foundational studies (Renn & Hodges, 2007; Renn & Jessup-Anger, 2008), which established that new professionals greatly value relationships with colleagues, peers, and students; fit with an institution or organization; and a sense of preparedness for their roles. Factors such as fit and readiness to engage in the work of the field inform satisfaction with a role and a sense of purpose in the work. In contrast, studies on intent to leave and attrition find satisfaction, burnout, feeling valued (personally and as a professional), and work/family conflicts influence new and seasoned professionals alike (Marshall et al., 2016; Silver & Jakeman, 2014). Lorden (1998) highlighted dissatisfaction, disillusionment, and frustration as significant contributors to attrition in student affairs in the late 20th century. While not a staff-based theory of retention, affirmations of key tenets of Strayhorn's (2012, 2019) theory of sense of belonging can be traced through these previous studies; feeling valued and affective commitment to the institutions where professionals worked was important in determining whether they stayed in the field of student affairs or departed. More recently, Boehman (2007) found that overall job satisfaction and affective commitment—a person's emotional commitment to an organization— positively contributed to the commitment of student affairs professionals to remain in the field. Applying these factors alongside new professionals' sense of belonging (Strayhorn, 2019) can help to elucidate professionals' intentions to remain in the field. Strayhorn (2019) defined *sense of belonging* for college students as:

> a perceived social support on campus, a feeling or sensation of connectedness, and the experience of mattering or feeling cared about, accepted, respected, valued by, and important to the campus community or others on campus such as faculty, staff, and peers. (p. 4)

Sense of belonging, as mentioned, was intended to better understand college students' experiences, yet can assist in understanding how new professionals experience job satisfaction, a sense of connectedness or belonging, and support from the institution.

While studies have rarely focused on factors that influence intent to leave the field, prior to a professional's departure from the field, the findings in this chapter still confirm past studies' focus on the importance of support for growth and advancement as a way to mitigate attrition from student affairs. Through the lens of the ideal worker (Acker, 1990), and using data that focuses on new professionals' reported intention to stay in student affairs, this chapter explores factors that contribute to the attrition of new professionals in student affairs. This chapter posits that a lack of support for growth, support for advancement, or a strong sense of belonging for new professionals aligns with the notion that the ideal worker is simply a cog in the machine: replaceable and without dimension or emotion. When left unsupported, feeling out of place, and facing burnout, the new student affairs professional embodies the expectations of the ideal worker as an emotionless steward of the organization.

Methodology

Previous studies related to new professionals in student affairs have primarily utilized qualitative methods (Evans, 1988; Marshall et al., 2016; Renn & Hodges, 2007; Renn & Jessup-Anger, 2008). Few quantitative studies have explored the experiences of new professionals, those who exit the field, or long-term commitment to the field (Boehman, 2007; Ward, 1995). As such, we chose to conduct a quantitative study with a few open-ended questions to identify relationships between factors that influence new professionals' intention to stay in student affairs. Additionally, the open-ended questions we posed provided participants the opportunity to suggest ways to bolster support of new professionals and a sense of belonging.

The survey was distributed through a national listserv comprising faculty and program coordinators for higher education or student affairs master's degree programs. To gather as many participants as possible, without collecting identifying information about each participant, we purposefully recruited participants in multiple ways (Wiersma & Jurs, 2009). Social media was another outlet of distribution and recruitment. Lastly, NASPA, a major student affairs professional organization, was utilized to distribute the survey specifically to the new professional constituency group.

Overall, 221 respondents began the electronic survey. Then, data from respondents who did not meet criteria for participation were removed, such as those who stated they had worked full time in higher education or student affairs for 5 or more years. After those who were missing data and respondents who did not fit the criteria as new professionals were removed, usable data from 191 respondents remained for new professionals who completed the survey instrument in its entirety (see Table 12.1). Similar to Marshall et al.'s (2016) study, it was not possible to run robust statistical tests that might indicate strength of correlation to explain relationships for identity groups as originally reported by participants. Therefore, STATA, a statistical software, was used to conduct descriptive statistical analysis as well as chi-square tests to identify any significant relationships between a new professional's reported years to stay in the field and various factors of influence. To ensure validity of the data, deductive analysis of the open-ended responses from participants was conducted to triangulate the quantitative findings.

Of the 191 respondents, 29 identified as men and 158 identified as women. There were 2 respondents who identified as transgender and 2 as genderqueer. Nearly 84% of respondents identified as White, 6% as Black or African American, less than 1% as Native American or Alaska Native, 2% as Asian or Asian American, 2% as multiracial, 2% preferred not to respond, and 3% of respondents provided an open response. Within the open responses, participants identified as "Middle Eastern" and "Latina/o/x." The majority of respondents identified in the age range of 26 years to 30 years of age, with the second most frequent age range of 21 years of age to 25 years of age. Only 12 respondents indicated that they were 31 or older. Additionally, 181 of the 191 study participants reported they were not a caregiver for a child.

Of primary interest to this study are rates of self-reported intention to stay in the field. Respondents provided a wide range of answers, with 11.5% of respondents indicating they intend to stay in the field for 0 to 5 years, 24% plan to stay 6 to 10 years, 10% plan to stay 11 to 15 years, and more than half of respondents (54.5%) plan to stay in the field 16 or more years (see Table 12.2). Although past studies indicated approximately half of new professionals exit the field of student affairs within 5 years of beginning their tenures, this chapter's survey findings suggest that only 11% of new professionals actually intend to leave the field in the first 5 years (Harned & Murphy, 1998; Lorden, 1998; Saunders et al., 2000; Tull, 2006). This discrepancy suggests that something happens in the intervening 5 years to influence employee departure.

Our study sample did not represent diverse voices or experience. For example, while gender identity influenced intent to stay in the field or leave, the study was not designed to examine the intersections of how identities inform experiences. Thus, without regression modeling or robust statistical analysis, this study is unable to offer recommendations for practices centering multiple identities or make claims of intersecting logics of oppression

TABLE 12.1
Demographics of Study Participants

Demographic	Response	Number of Respondents	Percentage of Respondents
Gender	Man	29	15.18
	Woman	158	82.72
	Transgender	2	1.05
	Open Response[a]	2	1.05
Race	White	160	83.77
	Black or African American	12	6.28
	Native American or Alaska Native	1	0.52
	Asian or Asian American	4	2.09
	Multiracial	4	2.09
	Open Response[b]	6	3.14
	Prefer Not to Respond	4	2.09
Age	21–25 years old	61	31.94
	26–30 years old	118	61.78
	31–35 years old	9	4.71
	36–40 years old	0	0
	41–45 years old	1	0.52
	46–50 years old	2	1.05
	50+ years old	0	0
Child Caregiver	Yes	10	5.24
	No	181	94.76

a. Open response in gender yielded two responses of "genderqueer."
b. Open response in race yielded both "Middle Eastern" and "Latino/a/x."

TABLE 12.2
Years to Stay

Participants by Reported Years to Stay in the Field	Frequency	Percent of Participants
0–5 years	22	11.52
6–10 years	46	24.08
11–15 years	19	9.95
16+ years	104	54.45

such as gender-, race- and class-based discriminations that could influence the experiences of new professionals in student affairs.

Findings

Study results revealed significant relationships between a participant's reported intended years to stay in student affairs and the following variables: the influence of hours worked, support in the workplace, and satisfaction with time and energy input into respective jobs. The next sections discuss factors related to the new professional experience of survey respondents and the influence on new professionals' intended years to stay in student affairs.

Hours Worked

One study participant, a White woman who planned to leave the student affairs field within the next 5 years, put it succinctly: "We need more balance to be able to support a family life." As Acker (1990) argued, the ideal worker is one whose "life centers on his full-time, life-long job, while his wife or another woman takes care of his personal needs and children" (p. 149). The participant's quote illustrates the importance of time, through hours worked in a given week, in balancing an identity outside that of an employee. The findings indicate that new professionals in student affairs are considering how time and hours worked influence their intention to remain in the field. Of all study respondents, 84% agreed that hours worked had an influence on their reported years to stay in student affairs. One participant reiterated the notion of time as it related to the ideal worker construct by saying, "I think there is a higher likelihood of [new professionals'] time being taken advantage of because of the perception they do not have a family/kids to go home to."

Other participants commented on the demand of the field by concluding, "I couldn't imagine having children," and "I don't see myself having a family if I stay in higher ed." Those participants offer the insights that to belong to their student affairs organizations, they would need to reconsider how they fit within the larger field of student affairs. If they did not anticipate fitting in, their only choice would be to depart the field entirely. Further, while some study participants only alluded to the lengthy hours and grueling work demands as possible reasons for intent to leave the field, other participants clearly stated notions such as,

> There is also a highly competitive stream of advancement, and this often pushes those wishing to have families out of the field so they can have more flexible schedules and care for the child at home since paychecks in student affairs often do not cover the cost of childcare.

Within the open-ended responses, we found participants directly stating intentions to leave alongside reasons why they intended to leave or why they believed others would depart the field. Some participants noted the extended hours expected of new professionals, while other participants noted pay for hours worked as a primary reason for departure. As one participant stated, "We have to stop the 'busy culture' that says 50 to 70 hours are expected for a salaried employee. It's exhausting and it makes people leave, pushing even more work on those of us who are left." Here, this participant brings to light the importance of feeling valued, an aspect of a sense of belonging, alongside the ideal worker construct. By picking up extra tasks and work, this participant outlined a perceived lack of value by being "exhausted" and that the extra "busy culture" contributes to "making people leave." This study confirmed findings from previous studies that indicate roughly half of new professionals depart the field at some point (Harned & Murphy, 1998; Lorden, 1998; Saunders et al., 2000; Tull, 2006). It has also begun to build some understanding around the reasons why so many new professionals intend to leave student affairs before they actually depart.

Workplace Support

The second grouping of significant findings from our study relates to workplace support. Specifically, we inquired about workplace support related to growth of the individual, established work hours, and individual advancement in the field. All three subcategories of support in the workplace held significant relationships with intended years to stay in student affairs. Participants were asked to indicate the degree to which they felt opportunities for advancement influenced their reported years they intended to stay in the field. The majority of respondents noted support for advancement strongly influenced or somewhat influenced their intention to stay in the field. For participants, support for growth, established work hours, and advancement mattered in whether participants reported an intent to stay or leave the field. Each of the three categories of support equated to a sense of belonging and feeling valued and cared about (Strayhorn, 2012) as members of the workplace community.

Support for Growth

Support for growth within student affairs contributes to attrition or the desire to leave the field. For all participants, a feeling of support to grow in the workplace was statistically significant with their reported years to stay in student affairs. The salience of support for growth was further evidenced in the open-ended participant responses. Many participants noted the importance of mentorship as an expression of support for growth. One participant wrote that support for new professionals should happen by "pay[ing] special attention to working collaboratively with new professionals, offer[ing] encouragement, and also mentorship." Support for growth as a mechanism of feeling cared for is evident in these findings. While participants were not asked if this influence was positively or negatively associated with their reported years to stay in student affairs, this significant relationship could align with previous findings. As such, this may be an area where further interrogation around these relationships should be considered for future inquiry.

Support for Advancement

Research from the turn of the century suggested that lack of advancement opportunities and ambiguity in how roles situated into organizations contributed to the larger canon of why professionals exited the field (Blackhurst et al., 1998; Rosser & Javinar, 2003). The study participants also noted some degree of pessimism in relation to the factor of advancement in the field. One participant commented that "it still feels like a *huge* mountain to climb to make it to the next level." While another participant outlined the impact of a bottleneck effect for those hoping to advance, they said, "There are a lot of new professionals and not near as many midlevel positions." Identifying pathways to success at each institution for new professionals could be a crucial factor in choosing to stay in the field or leave (Hurtado & Carter, 1997; Strayhorn, 2012). Not identifying such pathways decreases a sense of belonging and a sense that a new professional fits in the organization. Consider, for example, if the purpose of student affairs professionals was only to work within an organization and not advance, as in the spirit of the ideal worker. New professionals could very well embody the ideal worker in student affairs. However, it is generally understood that graduate programs seek to provide preparation beyond the ideal worker construct so that a career in student affairs is fulfilling and rewarding and includes all identities and experiences of new professionals.

The most significant finding related to support for growth was rooted in encouragement for participants to advance in the field. We posed this question for participants to designate the extent to which they agree that their workplace is supportive of their advancement in the field. The reported years to stay in the field and the extent to which participants felt their workplace was supportive of their advancement in the field held a strong statistical relationship ($p<0.000$). One study participant echoed the statistical findings by noting the importance of support for advancement in the life of a new professional. They stated a need to "create direct pathways to promotion," by "giving new professionals supervisory experience, or don't require the next level up to have professional staff supervision." Although organizational structure could have an influence on intent to stay in the field, responsibilities and personal support might also serve as contributing factors to the salience of support for advancement.

The relationship between planned years in the field and workplace support to advance could mean that new professionals seeing student affairs professionals who look like them, have similar experiences, or possess similar skill sets throughout the ranks of divisions of student affairs is positively associated with this statistical relationship. One study participant reiterated the importance of "seeing yourself in a pathway to advance" when they commented that "new professionals are an incredibly diverse group, but the diversity of professionals in the field is not at all reflected in senior leadership. This has a painfully adverse effect, and it is critical that it is rectified." Here, the tenets of a sense of belonging come to fruition. The perceived support, connectedness, and value (Strayhorn, 2019) of a new professional's place in the role are of the utmost importance to stay in the field.

Job Satisfaction

The final significant relationship among variables in this study relates to a new professional's reported intent to stay in the field and current job satisfaction.

We asked participants to indicate their current levels of satisfaction by responding to which statement most closely aligned with their current role: "If I put more time and energy into my role, I would be more satisfied with my current role," "if my colleagues or supervisor put more time and energy into my development, I would be more satisfied with my role," or "I am satisfied with the investment in my role by myself and my colleagues or supervisor." Just over half (53%) of study participants noted they were currently satisfied with the time and energy they and colleagues invested into their role while just under half (47%) indicated if they or colleagues put more time or energy into their personal development, they would be more satisfied with their jobs. The "reality of the work" illustrated a powerful reflection point for new professionals. One participant noted:

> I love this work, but I don't think I was prepared for the reality of it. . . . Just be aware that no matter how prepared you think you are/how much you love the work and so on, actually being in the field can still kick you in the butt and make you question this. Your institution (and its struggles/ triumphs), responsibilities, job area, and so on, all play into this.

As the participant outlined, reflection and preparation related to the work, the systems new professionals are part of, and the passion with which new professionals approach their work might not be "enough" to combat ideal worker norms. In fact, one study participant captured our significant findings by noting,

> I hear people wonder occasionally why someone would leave the student affairs world. From what I feel and what I have heard, it largely goes back to not feeling supported or valued in the field. I don't have all the answers as to how to have people feel supported or valued, but I think the first step is remembering that we are human, that we want our time to be valued either monetarily or in achieving/impacting something, and our past experiences [are] valued and utilized.

Sense of belonging (Strayhorn, 2019) is articulated by this new professional as a key component in their experiences. The survey respondent shared concerns about the value of their humanity being considered in their day-to-day experiences in the field. Years worked, hours worked, support for growth and advancement, and the investment of time and energy all propel the notion that new professionals in student affairs are valued for more than just the labor they provide to the organization.

Recommendations for Practice

The ideal worker construct exists in contrast to the richness of multiple and intersecting identities of professionals in student affairs. New professionals who feel supported, feel a sense of belonging in the workplace, and feel supported to advance are more likely to persist toward a life-long career in student affairs. In the following section, we offer recommendations for various stakeholders in student affairs. In an effort to model sense of belonging, challenge ideal worker norms, and respect the voices of those who responded to the study survey, we included survey participants' quotes and feedback related to suggestions to improve support for new professionals.

Recommendations are proposed for specific behaviors that could address, in part, attrition of new professionals from the field. As such, the recommendations will explore methods for retaining new professionals: The survey conducted for this chapter showed that only 11% of new professionals intend to leave the field within the first 5 years (compared to the approximately 50% that do leave the field). To this end, the subsequent suggestions intend to address the gap between intention to stay and actual departure. Additionally, new professionals should consider exploring, through self-reflexivity, how they occupy space within their institution.

Graduate Students and New Professionals

Participants noted the importance for new professionals to "get involved on campus" and "use networks in and out of [the] institution" to support their work as new professionals. Without explicitly naming the concept, some participants described involvement and connection with networks similar to Strayhorn's (2012) definition of *sense of belonging* for college students. Thus, one recommendation for new professionals to increase their sense of belonging might be to not only join in-campus networks and off-campus professional organizations but also establish non-student affairs avenues to connect with local community members and supports outside of the division.

Further, a clearer understanding of how time and energy are valued for both new professionals and employers could improve communication about boundaries related to work–life integration and dismantling ideal worker construct norms. This recommendation echoes previous calls to assist in the transition process for all new professionals or recent graduates (Frank, 2013; Renn & Hodges, 2007; Renn & Jessup-Anger, 2008; Silver & Jakeman, 2014) and may alleviate the feelings of isolation or possibly ease the burden of adjusting to a new reality. Multiple participants provided recommendations for new professionals to build cohorts of other new professionals to share experiences and develop understandings around what might be commonplace in the field. Again, participants noted the importance of connectedness and feeling valued as tenets akin to the foundations of a sense of belonging. One participant commented, "Shared experiences could help us quantify what is 'normal' within our field, and what indicates an actual problem." In short, graduate students and new professionals could benefit from more intentional reflective practices and support strategy development prior to and during the transition from graduate school to the first professional role postdegree. An example of this may be creating a division-wide committee focused on professional development, support, and networking for new professionals. The committee may include seasoned and new professionals invested in building a sense of community within the student affairs division while supporting a new professional's development and growth within the field through meetings, in-house professional development opportunities, and opportunities to network outside their offices or departments. The investment and connection with and on behalf of new professionals could illustrate that the division-wide community is a place where new professionals belong.

Midcareer Professionals

Midcareer professionals could challenge the notion of the ideal worker as always available and emotionless through modeling these behaviors in order to support a sense of value to the organization. Some participants noted that the sense of value they brought to the organization came through how midcareer professionals shared information or the levels to which they were transparent about organizational changes, thus increasing their sense of feeling valued by the institution, and in turn increasing their sense of belonging. Intentional coaching and transparency were specific recommendations for midcareer professionals. To offer transparency illustrates to new professionals that they are part of the organization and their contributions and involvement are valued, accepted, and important. This intentional coaching might come in the form of training around time-management techniques, then living that same practice in the workplace, discussing family or caregiving responsibilities outside of work (pets, children, parents), and tactfully sharing emotions related to work. One study participant articulated this delicate balance by noting a need to

> help new professionals see that there are times where we have to work above and beyond the normal number of hours, but balance that out with time

off or further flextime so new professionals are not overworked, abused, and fleeing from our profession.

In essence, modeling the version of themselves as colleagues to new professionals could support the concept that new professionals are not just disembodied workers. This might be accomplished through supervisors encouraging new professionals to take time away from the office after busy-season work and leave at the end of the business day.

Supervisors

To help address new professionals' satisfaction with input in their own experiences, supervisors should invite new professionals to share their thoughts and feelings and encourage them to identify solution-oriented feedback. Such a move would align with placing value on a new professional to increase their sense of belonging to the organization. Through seeking input, supervisors defy the disembodied ideas of new professionals as part of the ideal worker construct. To increase input, supervisors could also consider avenues through which new professionals might be invited to participate in upper-administration planning and/or meetings as a means to support their voice and offer professional development and leadership opportunities. Simultaneously, supervisors should learn how new professionals hope to be supported, how new professionals define advancement, their goals for the time they are in the field, and how they actively incorporate their growth plans when delegating tasks and developing new programs.

Recommendations for supervisors to support growth, advancement, and the challenge to the disembodied worker might include similar strategies of modeling made for midcareer professionals but could also be enhanced to increase a sense of belonging for new professionals with intentional planning. One participant commented that supervisors should focus on support at the very beginning of a new professional's tenure through "proper onboarding." One suggestion for intentionally designed onboarding is for supervisors to support a new professional's clarity of purpose, connection to institutional goals, and time and space for reflection. A series of questions to consider might include the following: "What do we believe in around here? What are my strengths? What is my role? Who are my partners? What does my future look like here?" (Harter, 2019). Supervisors could incorporate that reflection throughout the academic year during one-on-one meetings and as part of growth plans. The explicit exploration of how a new professional fits into the organization provides an opportunity for a sense of belonging to increase while at the same time working to dismantle the notion that new professionals should adhere to ideal worker norms.

In addition to support for growth, some study participants reflected on the importance of supervisors modeling expectations regarding hours worked. Survey participants provided multiple examples of supervisors communicating beyond traditional business hours. Clarifying and communicating expectations around when and how time and energy are to be invested is one definitive mechanism supervisors can employ to challenge the ideal worker's boundaries within the power structure of supervisor and supervisee. In short, student affairs educators should challenge themselves to model behavior with intentionality so new professionals understand they are not simply an extension of their offices and departments. Student affairs leaders should also challenge themselves and colleagues to foster spaces and initiate processes for new professionals to engage in dialogue without fear of retribution so they may honor their shared commitments and expectations.

Senior Student Affairs Officers

Given their responsibility for the entirety of divisions of student affairs, senior student affairs officers (SSAOs) are responsible for all recommendations mentioned to this point: modeling behavior, fostering spaces of candor and constructive feedback, and encouraging whole-person development of new professionals. Where SSAOs' responsibilities differ, however, is the degree to which hiring practices, departmental climate, and professional development are valued and emphasized. One study participant said SSAOs should "practice and support application of ethics as individuals and as a department to build a good culture." For example, departments might encourage and support new professionals' participation in institutional search committees and other committee work to provide new staff members opportunities to connect to the larger institutional goals. As the leaders of divisions of student affairs, SSAOs hold the responsibility to chart the course of their organizations (Komives & Woodard, 2003). Another study participant noted that SSAOs can model supportive behavior by occasionally volunteering their time in the same manner that is expected of new professionals. The example set forth by SSAOs could illustrate that new professionals are indeed cared for, valued, and part of the same organization as SSAOs.

These supports from SSAOs signal that new professionals are valued, heard, and worth investing in, all benchmarks of a strong sense of belonging (Strayhorn, 2019) and in contrast to the ideal worker construct (Acker, 1990). Additionally, given the importance participants placed on opportunities for growth, SSAOs should prioritize professional development, even when additional funds are unavailable for new professionals to travel or attend conferences and workshops. Commitment in the way of granting time away from the office or from work is one way that SSAOs can immediately support growth and development of new professionals. In doing so, SSAOs could illustrate to new professionals the value of hours worked while also fostering a culture for new professionals to feel like they belong. Further, SSAOs might partner with human resource units at their institution to deliver workshops and programming geared toward professional development of staff. Often, an institution will house conflict management, budget, and supervision workshops and certificates for employees across the institution. SSAOs possess the capital to chart a commitment of support, growth, and advancement for new professionals in the field.

Recommendations for Policy and Practice

As suggested by the findings related to support for growth and advancement in the field, treating the new professional as a "disembodied" worker (Acker, 1990, p. 144) remains an influence on attrition. In order to counter such attrition, two specific recommendations for policy adjustments in divisions of student affairs are offered. First, based on some respondents' reporting feeling devalued because they were not able to share their voice or that their personal time was impacted by unrealistic after-hours expectations, policies related to employee review processes might undergo revision. Employee review processes could include more intentionality in regard to professional development. For example, the language in performance reviews might be framed as growth and progression toward professional goals and utilize scales to chart growth or progress from evaluation to evaluation (Boggs, 2014). Second, developing policies and mechanisms to incorporate more frequent evaluation or professional development plan assessments, rather than utilizing only an annual evaluation, is recommended by CUPA-HR as a best practice (Travis, 2017). Such intentionality to build, visit, and revisit a development plan could signal to new professionals and seasoned professionals alike that the organization is a partner in their professional journey, instead of a mechanical environment where employees input time and energy.

To facilitate such professional development feedback loops, divisions of student affairs might hire professionals who will supervise or oversee evaluative processes that value growth and development of colleagues. Job descriptions should contain explicit duties framed with developmental language and demonstrate how the organization is committed to its staff. Instead of only stating that organizations value diverse hires (Ahmed, 2012), job postings and interview processes that embed specific tasks and duties related to the whole person in regard to supervision are recommended.

Conclusion

As the field continues to grow and increasingly reflect its students, student affairs professionals must be thoughtful and consider how the field perpetuates the notion of the ideal worker or creates its own version of the ideal worker. Acker's (2006) later work provides a frame through which student affairs professionals should consider how "work organizations are critical locations for the investigation of the continuous creation of complex inequalities because much societal inequality originates in such organizations" (p. 1). All members of student affairs, new professionals and seasoned professionals alike, are encouraged to find and foster moments and spaces where their humanity can illuminate the richness that the field embodies.

References

Acker, J. (1990). Hierarchies, jobs, bodies: A theory of gendered organizations. *Gender and Society, 4*(2), 139–158. https://doi.org/10.1177/089124390004002002

Acker, J. (2006). Inequality regimes: Gender, race, and class in organizations. *Gender and Society, 20*(4), 441–464. https://doi.org/10.1177/0891243206289499

Ahmed, S. (2012). *On being included: Racism and diversity in institutional life.* Duke University Press.

Blackhurst, A., Brandt, J., & Kalinowski, J. (1998). Effects of personal and work-related attributes on the organizational commitment and life satisfaction of women student affairs administrators. *NASPA Journal, 35*(2), 86–99. https://doi.org/10.2202/1949-6605.1067

Boehman, J. (2007). Affective commitment among student affairs professionals. *NASPA Journal, 44*(2), 307–328. https://doi.org/10.2202/1949-6605.1797

Boggs, J. (2014). *5 simple steps to improve performance reviews.* CUPA-HR. https://www.cupahr.org/5-simple-steps-improve-performance-reviews/

Casey, C. (1995). *Work, self, and society: After industrialism.* Routledge.

Clinte, K., Henning, G., Skinner, J. J., Kennedy, D., & Sloan, T. (2006). *Report on the new professional needs study*. American College Personnel Association. http://www.myacpa.org/docs/npsfinalsurveyreportpdf

Evans, N. J. (1988). Attrition of student affairs professionals: A review of the literature. *Journal of College Student Development, 29*(1), 27–36.

Frank, T. E. (2013). *Why do they leave? Departure from the student affairs profession* [Unpublished dissertation]. Virginia Polytechnic Institute and State University.

Harned, P. J., & Murphy, M. C. (1998). Creating a culture of development for the new professionals. *New Directions for Student Services, 1998*(84), 43–53. https://doi.org/10.1002/ss.8404

Harter, J. (2019). *5 questions every onboarding program must answer*. Gallup Workplace. https://www.gallup.com/workplace/247598/questions-every-onboarding-program -answer.aspx

Hurtado, S., & Carter, D. F. (1997). Effects of college transition and perceptions of the campus racial climate on Latino college students' sense of belonging. *Sociology of Education, 70*(4), 324–345. https://doi.org/10.2307/2673270

Komives, S. R., & Woodard, D. B. (2003). *Student services: A handbook for the profession*. Wiley.

Lorden, L. P. (1998). Attrition in the student affairs profession. *NASPA Journal, 35*(3), 207–216. https://doi.org/10.2202/1949-6605.1049

Marshall, S. M., Gardner, M. M., Hughes, C., & Lowery, U. (2016). Attrition from student affairs: Perspectives from those who exited the profession. *Journal of Student Affairs Research and Practice, 53*(2), 146–159. https://doi.org/10.1080/19496591.2016.1147359

Renn, K. A., & Hodges, J. (2007). The first year on the job: Experiences of new professionals in student affairs. *NASPA Journal, 44*(2), 367–391. https://doi.org/10.2202/1949-6605.1800

Renn, K. A., & Jessup-Anger, E. R. (2008). Preparing new professionals: Lessons for graduate preparation programs from the national study of new professionals in student affairs. *Journal of College Student Development, 49*(4), 319–335. https://doi.org/10.1353/csd.0.0022

Rosser, V. J., & Javinar, J. M. (2003). Midlevel student affairs leaders intentions to leave: Examining the quality of their professional and institutional work life. *Journal of College Student Development, 44*(6), 813–830. https://doi.org/10.1353/csd.2003.0076

Saunders, S. A., Cooper, D. L., Winston, R. B., & Chernow, E. (2000). Supervising staff in student affairs: Exploration of the synergistic approach. *Journal of College Student Development, 41*(2), 181–192.

Silver, B. R., & Jakeman, R. C. (2014). Understanding intent to leave the field: A study of student affairs master's students' career plans. *Journal of Student Affairs Research and Practice, 51*(2), 170–182. https://doi.org/10.1515/jsarp-2014 -0017

Strayhorn, T. (2012). *College students' sense of belonging: A key to educational success for all students*. Routledge.

Strayhorn, T. (2019). *College students' sense of belonging: A key to educational success for all students* (2nd ed.). Routledge.

Travis, A. (2017). Performance reviews on trial: Practical lessons for HR teams. *The Higher Education Workplace.* https://www.cupahr.org/hew/files/HEWorkplace-Vol9No2-Performance-Reviews-on-Trial.pdf

Tull, A. (2006). Synergistic supervision, job satisfaction, and intention to turnover of new professionals in student affairs. *Journal of College Student Development, 47*(4), 465–480. https://doi.org/10.1353/csd.2006.0053

Ward, L. (1995). Role stress and propensity to leave among new student affairs professionals. *NASPA Journal, 33*(1), 35–44.

Wiersma, W., & Jurs, S. G. (2009). *Research methods in education: An introduction* (9th ed.). Pearson.

13

FATHERS IN STUDENT AFFAIRS

Navigating a Gendered Organization

Margaret W. Sallee, Alyssa Stefanese Yates, and Michael Venturiello

For more than half of its existence, student affairs has been a field dominated by women (Ford, 2014). The profession was born in the early 20th century when staff members were hired to provide guidance and discipline to college students, fulfilling *in loco parentis* responsibilities previously expected of faculty members (Long, 2012). Although initially staffed by men, women quickly found a role for themselves in student affairs, first as deans of women (Hoffman, 2011) and soon populating all positions. Over the past half-century, women have come to represent a majority of student affairs professionals (Ford, 2014). For example, in 1990, women constituted a majority of members in two major student affairs professional associations, accounting for 64% in one and 57.6% in another (McEwen et al., 1990). Recent data obtained from NASPA (2018) suggest that this gender imbalance remains ever present in student affairs, particularly at lower levels, where nearly 70% of new and midlevel student affairs professionals are women. Women and men have achieved near gender parity at the top levels of student affairs; of association members who reported a gender, women and men represent 52% and 48% respectively of all vice presidents and associate vice presidents for student affairs. These numbers are striking in comparison to other higher education leadership positions. For example, 70% of college presidents are men (American Council on Education, 2017), which suggests that women are more likely to attain leadership positions in student affairs than in other domains.

Perhaps because it is dominated by women, student affairs is often referred to as a feminized field (Stimpson & Filer, 2011; Yakaboski & Donahoo,

2011). Additionally, student affairs professionals are often expected to provide guidance and help develop students' "soft skills," to identify their values and interests, and to help them transition out of college. These expectations are associated with qualities that are typically labeled as feminine, such as caring and nurturing (Hughes, 1989). As a result, the profession suffers from the same issues as other low-status, feminized fields like teaching and nursing, including low pay and low prestige. Although men in women-dominated professions may face challenges, they also accrue advantages by being tokens in their field, including riding the "glass escalator" to better pay and promotion, unlike their women colleagues and women counterparts in men-dominated fields (Budig, 2002; Snyder & Green, 2008; Williams, 1992). In part, as Christine Williams (1992) suggested, men are pushed into such positions out of a belief that they are better suited for leadership. The advantages that men accrue highlight the ways in which women-dominated professions remain deeply gendered. Student affairs is no exception.

Despite the feminization of the field, student affairs, like nearly all professions, is guided by ideal worker norms, which are themselves a masculine construct and assume that employees are available to work at all hours with no responsibilities in the home (Acker, 1990). The profession relies on employees constantly working, often with little consideration of outside responsibilities. Such norms have particular consequences for parents and play out differently for men and women.

In this chapter, we focus on how fathers working in student affairs are affected by ideal worker norms. In particular, we argue the ways that fathers experience ideal worker constraints are compounded by their gender; they are expected to work tirelessly and often not expected to make time for family. Those who do make time for family receive mixed signals; although they may be praised through interactions with some individual actors, the overarching messages they receive from the field imply that their behaviors diverge from the norm. As we suggest, these divergent reactions stem from the status of student affairs as a gendered organization (Acker, 1990). We draw on Acker's (1990) work on gendered organizations to make sense of the challenges that fathers face working in the field. Although Acker's work is typically used to examine the gendering of an individual organization, such as a department, university, or church (e.g., Erickson, 2012; Gardner, 2013; Manville, 1997), we argue that the entire student affairs profession, with its shared norms and values, can be analyzed from the same lens.

Developed at the same time as her expansion on the ideal worker, Acker (1990) argued that organizations are gendered in five ways. First, organizations are gendered based on divisions along lines of gender. In typical organizations, men are more likely to be leaders while women are more likely to be administrative assistants.[1] Second, organizations are gendered based upon symbols and images deployed to support those divisions. Men are frequently portrayed as strong while women are not. Third, organizations are gendered based on interactions between and across genders. Traditional gender norms call for men to hold doors for women and to pay on dates. Acker (1990) suggested that these three processes—divisions along lines of gender, symbols and images, and interactions—contribute to the fourth process, creating differences in individual identity. By repeatedly seeing that men are more likely to be leaders and should hold the door and pay for women, both men and women internalize these identities as part of their own. Fifth, these differences in individual identity inform the gendered nature of organizations. We use Acker's five processes to explore the ways in which men both challenge and are challenged by ideal worker norms and the role that student affairs as a profession plays in reproducing gendered ideal worker norms. Ideal worker norms and gendered organizations assume that White, cisgender, heterosexual identities represent the default; our analysis primarily interrogates the gender divide and the ways in which heteronormative assumptions inform expectations about appropriate professional and paternal behaviors. (For more on differences in ideal worker norms by gender/sexuality and race/ethnicity, see chapters 9 and 10.)

We draw on data generated from a case study (Merriam & Tisdell, 2016) of 24 fathers working in student affairs. All participants were required to have at least one child under the age of 18 living at home. Participants came from across the United States and worked in a variety of institutional types but were predominantly concentrated at research institutions. Participants worked in a range of functional areas, including residence life and student activities, and in leadership positions, including vice chancellors and deans of students. The majority of participants (21) were White, 2 were African American, and 1 was multiracial. We achieved greater diversity in the sexuality of the sample: 16 fathers identified as straight and 8 identified as gay or queer.

The first and third authors conducted face-to-face, phone, or Skype interviews with each participant, which constituted the primary method of data collection. Interviews typically lasted between 45 minutes and an hour and were recorded and later transcribed. Data analysis was a multistep process, in which the first and third authors agreed on codes and then jointly coded transcripts to ensure agreement, before dividing up subsequent transcripts. Trustworthiness was ensured through investigator triangulation—as two authors collected and analyzed data—and peer review. (For a more thorough description of the methodology, see Sallee, 2019.)

In what follows, we use Acker's (1990) five processes to explore how student affairs is a gendered organization that perpetuates ideal worker norms, which has implications for the ways in which fathers working in student affairs navigate parenthood and their careers. Despite its status as a feminized field, student affairs is still guided by traditional gender norms, assuming that men can leave all of their personal responsibilities to their (women) partners. We conclude by offering suggestions for ways that student affairs professionals can push back against ideal worker norms that have particular consequences for fathers working in the field.

Student Affairs: A Gendered Organization

Similar to other professions, student affairs is both affected by and perpetuates gender norms, namely the ideal worker construct that is rooted in women managing the domestic sphere and men dominating the professional one (Kerber, 1988; Yakaboski & Donahoo, 2011). We utilize Acker's (1990) five processes to investigate the field's gendered nature and its effect on fathers working in student affairs.

Divisions Along Gender Lines

Acker (1990) found that organizations initially become gendered when men and women are positionally, physically, or influentially separated and distinguished within the workplace. Although student affairs is considered a feminized field (Hamrick & Carlisle, 1990; Hughes, 1989; McEwen et al., 1990; Yakaboski & Donahoo, 2011), it perpetuates divisions between genders by horizontally and vertically separating men and women within the organizational structure.

As mentioned earlier in this chapter, student affairs parallels other feminized professions, such as nursing and teaching, in elevating a disproportionate number of men to leadership positions, which subsequently relegates women to entry and midlevel, support-based positions (Wilson, 2008; Yakaboski & Donahoo, 2011; Zorn, 2007). As one participant described, "What I've witnessed and experienced is men at more senior level positions. . . . It feels like it's more female populated at entry-level and midmanagement. The minute it goes to the top, it seems to be more male centric." Another participant explained:

> When I started out, I felt as though I was one of the few men in a field dominated by women. And the farther on that I went in my career, . . . I realized that, "Well gosh! The leaders are a bunch of White guys!"

Although national data suggest that men and women equally fulfill senior student affairs roles, men remain overrepresented in these positions when compared to their presence in entry-level positions, thus illustrating that men in student affairs tend to be promoted over women, much like in other professions (Budig, 2002; Snyder & Green, 2008; Williams, 1992). Student affairs divides genders vertically along organizational structure as well as horizontally by specialization or functional area, echoing previous research on feminized fields (Snyder & Green, 2008). For instance, one participant noticed more men fulfilling roles in student affairs that involved little direct student contact: "I think the typical man in student affairs is gonna be . . . working kind of in not support roles, but your assessment, IT, people who work in student affairs on the business side of things." Other participants echoed this sentiment of men and women being separated by functional area:

> A lot of [men in student affairs] are on the business end of things. So, doing facilities or operations or campus rec just got moved out of our department, or, out of our division. But before that, they were the only department that was predominantly male, outside of the housing operations staff.

By separating the genders between levels and functional areas, student affairs creates a power differential between the genders and promotes traditional gender norms.

Deployment of Symbols and Images

Acker (1990) found organizations are also gendered through their utilization of symbols and their reproduction of cultural images, such as the archetypal student affairs professional as always working and fathers as solely breadwinners. As discussed earlier in this volume and well documented in research (i.e., Anthony, 2016; Long, 2012; Marshall et al., 2016), student affairs is a demanding field that levies high expectations on its employees, which can include fulfilling on-call responsibilities, irregular work hours, and "other duties as assigned." These unique expectations cultivate a lofty image of the ideal student affairs professional who should be working all the time. One participant shared:

> If you're going to do student affairs right, in my opinion, it is not a 9 to 5 job. And so, you gotta be here at night, you gotta be here on the weekend . . . And so, you're not home at 6 o'clock, you know? To be with your kids for the evening.

Other participants articulated that they feel pressured to not only put work before outside responsibilities, including family, but also continually contribute to the organization in order to be considered a good student affairs professional: "I feel it['s] just being part of the field that, you know there's this pressure to always be doing more." Participants described the ideal student affairs professional as one who is often expected to prioritize work before children and remain either physically or mentally tethered to campus at all times.

The pressure participants felt to embody the ideal worker image, as a function of their gender identity, is rooted in cultural images of men as workers and breadwinners (Emslie & Hunt, 2009; Marsiglio et al., 2000); in comparison, women are seen as caregivers whose careers are secondary to their domestic responsibilities (Bear & Glick, 2017). As one participant expressed:

> This concept of the male as the provider or whatever, that's still very much, that persona is very much alive and thriving in our world today, at least in the United States, I guess. And that's a hard, that's a hard script to break out of, and there's a lot of pressure I think that comes along with that script. Because nowhere in that script does it say that you should be nurturing, that you should be caring, that you should, focus on the [softer] characteristics of fatherhood.

The image of acceptable fatherhood in student affairs aligns with these long-standing, cultural images surrounding fatherhood, namely fathers as providers; for example, as we discuss later in the chapter, participants felt pressured to return to work immediately after the birth of their children and were not given the same attention or concern as expecting mother colleagues. These examples highlight the field's espoused image of fathers as uninterested in spending quality time with their children or unnecessary in the hands-on aspects of childrearing. Instead, the field supports this narrow imagery of fathers and communicates that fatherhood should have no detrimental effect on men's ability to fulfill ideal worker norms.

Fathers in student affairs appear to feel pressured to conform to ideal worker norms because of the messages implicit in gender-related symbols and images. Student affairs continues to perpetuate a somewhat antiquated image of fatherhood, which equates fathers with breadwinners and minimizes their ability to resist established gender norms in order to be engaged fathers. These symbols are promulgated through the behaviors of institutional actors, which is captured within Acker's (1990) third process: interactions between and within genders.

Interactions Between Genders

Acker's (1990) third process suggests that organizations are gendered through interactions between and across genders, which reinforce differences in gender identity. Student affairs fathers received many messages that suggested that parenting belongs in women's domain while work belongs to men, or those who embody the ideal worker. However, the field sends mixed messages, condemning men for taking paternity leave but praising them for occasionally bringing their children into the workplace. Fathers feel isolated from one another and tend to build communities with working mothers, thus reinforcing the notion that parenting is a gendered responsibility.

Fathers in this study reported that both women and men colleagues seemed to suggest that women were expected to take parental leave while men were not. One father shared the story of a colleague who hired four women and one man who all welcomed children into the home in a short period, yet balked when the father took paternity leave, saying "that freaked her out. She wasn't counting on that at all." Another father shared his interactions with his colleagues who seemed to suggest that both women and men should get back to the workplace as soon as possible, but that women received more latitude:

> I think in the work there's an espoused value of work–life balance that is, I think, applauded to all the women who really disconnect from work when they are on maternity leave. . . . Most of my coworkers have given me that but a lot of them . . . have been like "well you know you're still gonna be there for when the students come back right?" I cannot imagine having that conversation with a mother on maternity leave. That would be a lot different. So, I think that there's that sort of like feeling of it being a luxury versus a right for me to be on leave right now.

While this father was allowed to take paternity leave, he was still expected to be available to the organization in ways that mothers were not. However, not all participants encountered such strong reactions to taking paternity leave. One father described how some of his women colleagues in their late 20s and early 30s supported his decision to take leave: "For them I think having a kid and going on paternity leave, [they] never really saw it as any different from maternity leave or being a mother." Such differences might be due to shifts in generational attitudes, though they were not widely reported by the fathers in this study.

Although women were given more latitude to take parental leave, fathers reported that women encountered harsher penalties when trying to combine family and work while men tended to be praised. One father neatly summed up the different ways that society approaches mothers and fathers:

> I think a lot of times guys get the rap of [they're] supposed to be like the dad, the parent that doesn't know anything and then if they do "oh they're so good." And then moms are supposed to be the experts and know everything and then oh on top of that have a career and . . . be able to [deal with] all of the challenges that women have in the workplace in general. . . . I'm certain that it's harder for women than it is for men.

Many of the participants provided examples to illustrate the different responses that women and men received. For example, one participant shared how his wife was constantly asked when she would "slow down and be a mom" while he was never faced with that question. Another father felt that he was allowed to bring his children to campus for events in ways that his wife and women coworkers might not be. He explained:

> If I [brought] my boys into work . . . I got a lot of attention. And it was the overall perception, I think, was sort of, "Oh, look at that. How cool is that? What a great dad! He brings his kids in and how much fun. . . ." My wife does that, and the perception is, "Boy, she just can't handle the work–life balance. She doesn't know how to take care of her kids." You know? So, there's definitely some inequality there.

As his children were growing up, this father found that he had a lot of freedom to bring his children to campus and even received praise for doing so, while his wife received opposite messages. Another father reinforced popular sentiments that praise fathers for being involved and penalized mothers.

> It may be, culturally not valued for [women] . . . to do that. I don't know why, but that seems to be the case. . . . But with men it's like, "Oh yeah you should go take time to do this . . . with your kids" whereas I don't see the women doing that.

As one father pointed out, men may feel like they have more agency to make such choices, perhaps from their position of privilege.

> [I] still have the privilege of being male so the perception still is that even though I'm still a dad managing multiple things and as the primary parent, the world treats me differently. You know I probably feel more empowered to say, "Nope I'm not going to attend that event 'cause I got to do

something with my kid" and experience less guilt or feel like it has less repercussions than some of my female colleagues.

In short, fathers in student affairs explained that in their interactions with colleagues they both had more agency to be involved fathers and received more praise for doing so than colleagues who were mothers. When parenting occasionally intruded into the workplace, they were allowed to make space for it while mothers were more likely to be punished.

Perhaps participants perceived that this praise stemmed from the fact that many felt that they were one of the only fathers in their divisions of student affairs. Many of the participants felt isolated and reported that they did not discuss parenting with other fathers. One father shared, "I think that because I have not found a lot of other dads in student affairs, if you will, that it's been harder to relate to people." Other fathers shared that while they had colleagues who were fathers, these identities did not come up in conversation: "I didn't hear very often that my male counterparts were talking about parenting. That they were putting more of the parenting on their spouses." He later went on to add, "With my male peers . . . it was seen as sort of odd that I was doing things like picking up my child or going to a parent/teacher day." Despite this lack of fatherhood community, many of the student affairs fathers reported talking to mothers in the office about parenting. One father described how his woman supervisor frequently checked in with him and his husband about parenthood. Another father described how he frequently discussed parenting with women in the office, but did not have similar conversations with men, even those who were fathers.

> If I think about some of the guys I work with . . . they don't necessarily talk about their kids as much or their involvement in the role of parenting, they're much more business-focused. Whereas some of the women I work with, they're always talking about their kids and what's going on and more forthcoming or sharing with that part of their life. But the men just don't, in my experience, don't seem to be sharing that as much.

In short, interactions between and across these genders suggested that parenting was an activity that generally resided in women's domain. Although some men reported that they wanted to be involved fathers, they did not always get the support to do so. Men navigated conflicting assumptions that expected them to adhere to ideal worker norms by minimizing parental leave and being constantly available to the campus, although they reported occasional praise for violating gender norms by bringing in their children. These conflicting experiences of and expectations placed on fathers working in student affairs highlight the mixed responses of organizational actors to the gendered nature of student affairs. Some student affairs professionals perpetuate the long-standing gendered expectations in the field, such as supervisors who expected fathers to immediately return to work after the birth of a child, while others actively resist it, such as the fathers who chose to be more engaged fathers and their colleagues who praised and/or allowed for that behavior.

Individual Identity

Acker's (1990) fourth process involves individuals' internalizing the organization's gendered messages, namely its gendered divisions, symbols and images, and interactions, as part of their identity. Due to the nature of student affairs as a profession, fathers in the field may adopt an identity that aligns with traditional gender roles and behaviors that the organization communicates, such as defining fathers as solely breadwinners and ideal workers. However, some participants also adopted identities that pushed against these stereotypical norms promoted by the gendered organization. Building on the examples provided in these processes, some participants identified in expectedly gendered ways that highlighted their adoption of the field's ideals surrounding parenthood and professionalism. As one participant explained, "We appear to have these traditional roles. She's the stay-at-home mom and I'm the guy that goes out and works." This dualistic perspective of parenthood, namely the father as the provider and the mother as the primary caregiver, was echoed by another participant, a senior student affairs officer (SSAO), who described the division of labor in his household and his participation in traditional gender roles:

> [My wife] does a lot of the pretty traditional maintaining the home front. . . . She runs the errands, and does the cooking, cleaning, and things like that. . . . My kids know that [if] they want any like lifesaving provisions, they go to my wife 'cause she'll do it and she'll never ask questions . . . so I'm trying to somehow contextualize these very traditional gender norms that are in my family.

Another participant presented himself in a similar way:

> I don't claim to be the best dad in the world. I'm not [the] most patient person and . . . I think that my wife's the one that knows, and I don't remember who my kids' teachers were, and I don't remember, I didn't pull teeth, you know, my wife's the one that did all the dental care and the medical care, and I think a lot of fathers would find that way.

Instead, this participant described his wife as fulfilling the primary caregiver role, which he believed is reflective of the majority of fathers in the field.

Although some participants presented this stereotypical gendered identity, the majority of participants vocalized resistance to the gendered nature of student affairs by either identifying as engaged fathers or seeking to prioritize their parental identity over their professional one. As one participant shared:

> I certainly enjoy my work, but I don't live and die by my work. And I think that makes me stick out a bit in the field. At least as someone who wants to do his best work, but also not live and die by it.

This quotation simultaneously emphasizes the participant's recognition of the dominant ideal worker construct and gendered expectations within student affairs and his rejection of it by refusing to "live and die by it." In other words, he expressed that there is more to his identity than his work. Similarly, other participants prioritized their personal identities, those of father and husband, above their professional capacity, with comments such as "as long as I can be a really good dad and husband, that's all that really matters to me right now," and

> I always say my favorite job is being a husband and a father but then it makes it sound like it's employment and it's not. In terms of my priorities being a husband and a father are the things I enjoy most.

Participants also frequently expressed their identity shifting from solely their professional title, status, and prestige to their parental role:

> My identity, it's kind of, it's a funny thing, because as you're going up into your career, especially when you're younger, you wanted your identity to be the dean or the vice president or the provost or whatever it is, but as, as I've gotten older, that doesn't carry the weight anymore. If I'm known the rest of my life as dad, that's fine with me. . . . That carries much more weight now.

Fathers illustrated both examples and counterexamples of Acker's (1990) fourth process. Some exemplified the internalization of gendered messages by limiting themselves to the identities of worker and breadwinner; however, other participants resisted traditional gender norms by identifying as engaged fathers. Those fathers who resisted gendered messages and the ideal worker construct by articulating personal identities and commitments outside of student affairs work foreshadow professionals' ability to push back against the field's gendered nature.

Organizational and Social Structures

Finally, Acker (1990) argued that gender is implicated in the creation and re-creation of social structures, including organizations and professional fields. Although organizations and their practices may be portrayed as gender-neutral, gender is implicit in the way organizations function and the messages that employees receive. As we have discussed throughout, gender is implicated in the ways in which student affairs professionals interact with one another, both about work-related and family-related matters.

Many participants discussed the messages they received about the time commitment required to work in student affairs, which often means parents miss out on time with their families. One participant described how he worked with colleagues who had "24-hour expectations," which frustrated the father, who said that he "felt like I could still do my work well without having to feel like I was on call at 10:00 p.m." Another participant echoed the similar demands placed on those in the field:

> It's not a typical 9 to 5 job. So, it's not like I'm gonna be leaving at 5 o'clock every day and be home in time. There's often things that take place, not to mention if it's on a weekend, I'm expected to be there. Often my trainings are at nighttime, when students can be available.

This father was not the only one who noted that students' availability drove their schedules. Another participant discussed the toll that late-night programming takes: "You don't get paid for that time, so sometimes you can work . . . 60 to 70 hours a week, but only get paid for 40, but you know, you do it for the students." These participants' comments reveal the ways in which ideal worker norms are implicit in student affairs; participants were expected to work beyond the typical workday, often to support their students at the expense of their children.

Several fathers discussed the toll that these work expectations take on their families. While many lamented these expectations, some reported that this was simply one of the expectations of working in the field. Said one father, "My approach to this work is 'We work 'til the work is done' and I miss dinners and different things over the course of the busy academic semester." Although this father seemed to accept this as standard operating procedure, other participants complained about how such expectations had consequences for their families:

> It's been stressful because, like I said, my goal has been to be the best dad that I can be, and at least it feels sometimes like it's in conflict with what it takes to do this job well. You know, in terms of being accessible to people

at all times, and whenever there's a campus emergency or whenever there's an issue, or being able to, to stick around for a lot of hours. So those two things are sort of in conflict. . . . Even though I have the support of my supervisor, I'm still trying to adjust with that being okay.

As this father pointed out, there are no easy solutions to resolving this conflict; student affairs seems to require constant availability, which interferes with family obligations. These requirements also depend on employees having someone else available to tend to their children. Although this is framed in a gender-neutral manner (and is expected to have an impact on employees of all genders), as we outlined earlier, in reality women bear the brunt of childrearing. By not readily acknowledging the gendered assumptions that undergird student affairs work, the field leaves gender roles intact.

And, in fact, the field continues to promote traditional gender roles, both on individual campuses and across the profession. Several participants discussed seeing presentations at different national conferences with panels about motherhood in student affairs, thus excluding fathers. One father described a session at a student activities conference:

One of the educational sessions' topics that . . . [was] getting the most buzz was kind of a practical experience on being a mom and working in student activities office[s]. But yeah, now that I think about it, it could have been being a parent working in student activities offices.

Another father was even stronger in his critique of the exclusion of fatherhood from similar sessions:

One of the things that gets me frustrated sometimes, you go to conferences and I'll still see sessions or articles about women balancing being mothers . . . with a student affairs career and I think what that misses is that, as a field we've talked so much about equity and you know balancing things and [promoting] feminism. What that approach misses is there are fathers that want to have that same balance as well and be involved, have the career as well that are also trying to figure out how to do this.

This father felt that the field in general missed the opportunity to include men in the conversation, thus replicating the assumption that parenting remained a concern solely for women and reinforcing traditional gender roles. Another father chimed in with similar concerns:

You don't ever see about balancing [work and family] as a male, as a father. It's kind of just expected that the fathers are going to be the ones pushing things forward in the field, you know pushing their career, and the family takes the back seat. That's something that I think as a field we don't really do well and doesn't match up with our reported values as a field.

Even conversations at national conferences continued to promote a separation of parents' responsibilities, thus excluding fathers from the conversation, leaving the burden on mothers, and sending the message to institutional leaders to concentrate their resources on supporting mothers alone, potentially at the expense of men. Such action is detrimental to both genders, excluding men from the conversation and placing greater burden on women to balance parenthood and their careers, ultimately leaving oppressive structures in place.

As we have illustrated in this chapter, student affairs reifies traditional gender norms through its separation of genders in both position and functional area as well as the deployment of symbols that paint the ideal father working in student affairs as one who financially provides for his children, but may not spend time with them. Interactions between genders reinforce these messages as many fathers reported not being expected to spend much time with their children, though they occasionally received praise when they did. As a result, fathers reported a struggle in identity—many pushing back against ideal worker norms to be engaged fathers. Yet, they were pushing against a system and a field that promulgates such norms. Student affairs professionals need not accept these norms without question. We end this chapter by offering strategies that various stakeholders might use to push back against a gendered system and to move the field toward more gender equitable practices and expectations.

Recommendations for Practice

The experiences of participants suggest a number of ways in which fathers at various career stages might benefit from particular interventions. Ultimately, it cannot be left up to the individual to change the system; as our analysis has made clear, the entire field of student affairs is complicit in perpetuating gendered norms. We begin by offering suggestions of tools that individuals can use to navigate the gendered system and conclude by focusing on initiatives that those in power can put into place to challenge and, ideally, eradicate these norms.

Graduate Students and New Professionals

Many participants discussed the seemingly nonstop expectations of work in the field. Regardless of whether one has children, such overwork is not healthy and may lead to burnout (Lorden, 1998). Institutions might implement a series of workshops for graduate students and new professionals that focus on self-care and creating boundaries between their personal and professional lives. Additional workshops might focus on the challenges that parents, and fathers in particular, face in navigating work and family concerns. Establishing healthy patterns early in their careers will pay dividends for newer professionals down the road.

Additionally, graduate students and new professionals who are parents are more likely to have younger children. As a result, programs or workshops that are targeted toward these populations should take into account their familial demands and schedule programs at times that do not conflict with family responsibilities. Institutions might also consider offering free childcare to facilitate attendance. However, providing childcare should not be used as a way to facilitate employees to work more. The ultimate goal is to ensure that employees engage actively in both roles: professional and parent.

Finally, given the perceived dearth of fathers in the field, graduate students and new professional fathers could benefit from being matched with a senior mentor in the field. Newer professionals might benefit from conversations with senior mentors who have also navigated the challenges of work and family. Such a program would help to lay bare the realities of fathering in student affairs while also building a community of fathers in the field.

Midcareer Professionals

Midcareer professionals, particularly men, may have children of any age, given men's ability to father children throughout their lifespan. As a result, some of the suggestions provided for early career professionals with young children are relevant here. Additionally, fathers with older children have unique needs, such as helping them navigate the teenage years and college application process. This group of employees might benefit from a series of workshops, scheduled during typical work hours, that focuses on such issues. Additional workshops might also focus on helping this group of professionals unlearn unhealthy work habits. The type of workshop provided is less important than the institution simply acknowledging and supporting their employees' lives outside of work.

Supervisors

Given the important role that supervisors play in setting the tone for office culture, they can provide a positive example for their subordinates by adopting healthy work–life behaviors. This might take the form of limiting the number of late nights that they work, not sending unnecessary work emails outside of standard work hours, and encouraging their employees to do the same. Given that many student affairs units require night and week-end hours, supervisors should also encourage employees to take time off to compensate for extra hours worked; for example, an employee might come in late Friday morning after working into the night on Thursday. Further, those supervisors who have children might bring their children to events and into the office from time to time. Seeing supervisors engage in such behaviors will signal to employees of all genders that work/family integration is valued in the unit.

Supervisors can also encourage—rather than discourage—working fathers to take advantage of institutional policies and services that are targeted toward parents. For example, all employees are eligible under federal law to take leave under the Family and Medical Leave Act due to the birth or adoption of a child. Additionally, some states offer paid family leave, and at most institutions employees can access sick and vacation time to care for new children. Supervisors can equally encourage fathers and mothers to use such policies to allow them time to bond with their children.

SSAOs

SSAOs play an important role in establishing the tone for the entire division. As such, SSAOs can role model healthy work/family behaviors. For example, they might keep reasonable office hours so staff members do not see them working until late in the evening. Similarly, those with families might frequently discuss their children and even bring them to campus on occasion, so employees can see that combining parenting and professional responsibilities is supported at the highest levels.

Additionally, SSAOs are critical in establishing reasonable expectations for their employees. This role includes encouraging their employees to establish healthy boundaries between work and family, such as not letting work encroach on defined family time. SSAOs can show that even the most senior and critical of employees can establish and commit to work–life boundaries by being forthcoming and clear about their own with employees and developing a thorough plan for coverage of all matters during any planned absence. For example, SSAOs can role model that it is acceptable to disconnect from campus and take uninterrupted vacation time by scheduling annual family vacations and preparing employees for their absence through training on procedures and organizational structures to be followed in their stead.

Institutional Policies and Practices

To help dismantle the gendered organization, institutions might take a number of steps, beginning with dismantling artificial gender divisions. In student affairs, this initiative might take the form of actively recruiting more men into the profession while also mentoring more women to advance to senior levels, thus leading to greater parity between genders. Additionally, men and women might be encouraged to consider all functional areas, rather than continuing the concentration of men in particular areas, such as recreation. Such divisions lay the foundation for suggesting that men and women are different and thus deserve different treatment. Institutions might also mandate search committee trainings to address bias in the search process and ensure that there is gender diversity in hiring pools for leadership positions. Furthermore, institutions could benefit from developing training and onboarding sessions that acknowledge the often-demanding expectations of student affairs work and convey the institution's commitment to professionals' work–life balance, self-care, and holistic well-being.

As participants' experiences suggest, parenting is a concern for men and women alike. Policies should be offered on a gender-neutral basis, addressing the needs of parents, rather than mothers and fathers. Doing so will also acknowledge the concerns of parents who do not identify on the gender binary. Of course, there are instances where policies are gender-specific— such as childbearing leave or breastfeeding. However, by adopting gender-neutral language and policies when possible, institutions will send the message that parenthood is a concern for employees of any gender.

At the same time, however, given that many fathers feel isolated in navigating their parenting responsibilities, institutions might create a fathering support group for interested staff, faculty, and students. Such a group could meet regularly to allow fathers an opportunity to discuss unique concerns about navigating work and parenting. Additionally, the group might sponsor child-friendly outings to allow fathers across campus to connect in different settings.

Parenthood should also be made visible on campus. Institutions might sponsor a Take Your Child To Work Day and encourage all employees to participate. Additionally, institutions could sponsor family-friendly events, such as movie nights or carnivals, designed to appeal to all on campus with children. Activities need not be targeted simply to mothers or fathers. Rather, by making parenthood visible, institutions can challenge the value placed in the ideal worker construct's separation of work and family.

As participants' experiences made clear, the contemporary student affairs field is one that is rife with contradictions. On the one hand, it is mired in a separation between genders, both in employment and in norms related to parenting. On the other hand, many participants noted that they saw themselves as different from the stereotypical norms of fatherhood, yet they felt pressured to go against dominant gender and ideal worker norms in order to enact an engaged father identity. By adopting some of these suggestions, student affairs divisions and those who populate them can take steps to break down gender barriers and allow all people to thrive in both the workplace and the home.

Note

1. Although Acker's (1990) treatment of gendered organizations only considered their impact on men and women, trans* individuals and those outside the gender binary are also affected. However, we leave such analysis for other work.

References

Acker, J. (1990). Hierarchies, jobs, bodies: A theory of gendered organizations. *Gender Society, 4*(2), 139–158. https://doi.org/10.1177/089124390004002002

American Council on Education. (2017). *American College President Study: 2017.* Author.

Anthony, C. (2016). Why I left student affairs and how I hope to return. *The Vermont Connection, 37*(2), 8–15. https://scholarworks.uvm.edu/cgi/viewcontent.cgi?article=1258&context=tvc

Bear, J. B., & Glick, P. (2017). Breadwinner bonus and caregiver penalty in workplace rewards for men and women. *Social Psychological and Personality Science, 8*(7), 780–788. https://doi.org/10.1177/1948550616683016

Budig, M. J. (2002). Male advantage and the gender composition of jobs: Who rides the glass escalator? *Social Problems, 49*(2), 258–277. https://doi.org/10.1525/sp.2002.49.2.258

Emslie, C., & Hunt, K. (2009). "Live to work" or "work to live"? A qualitative study of gender and work–life balance among men and women in midlife. *Gender, Work and Organization, 16*(1), 151–172. https://doi.org/10.1111/j.1468-0432.2008.00434.x

Erickson, S. K. (2012). Women Ph.D. students in engineering and a nuanced terrain: Avoiding and revealing gender. *The Review of Higher Education, 35*(3), 355–374. https://doi.org/10.1353/rhe.2012.0019

Ford, D. (2014). *Rising to the top: Career progression of women senior-level student affairs administrators* (Publication No. ED568556) [Doctoral dissertation, University of Arkansas, Fayetteville]. ProQuest LLC

Gardner, S. K. (2013). Women faculty departures from a striving institution: Between a rock and a hard place. *The Review of Higher Education, 36*(3), 349–370. https://doi.org/10.1353/rhe.2013.0025

Hamrick, F., & Carlisle, W. (1990). Gender diversity in student affairs: Administrative perceptions and recommendations. *NASPA Journal, 27*, 306–311.

Hoffman, J. (2011). Each generation of women had to start anew. In P. A. Pasque & S. E. Nicholson (Eds.), *Empowering women in higher education and student affairs* (pp. 32–46). Stylus.

Hughes, M. S. (1989). Feminization and student affairs. *NASPA Journal, 27*(1), 18–27.

Kerber, L. K. (1988). Separate spheres, female worlds, woman's place: The rhetoric of women's history. *The Journal of American History, 75*(1), 9–39. https://doi.org/10.2307/1889653

Long, D. (2012). The foundations of student affairs: A guide to the profession. In L. J. Hinchliffe & M. A. Wong (Eds.), *Environments for student growth and development: Librarians and student affairs on collaboration* (pp. 1–39). Association of College & Research Libraries.

Lorden, L. P. (1998). Attrition in the student affairs profession. *NASPA Journal, 35*(3), 207–216. https://doi.org/10.2202/1949-6605.1049

Manville, J. (1997). The gendered organization of an Australian Anglican parish. *Sociology of Religion, 58*(1), 25–38. https://doi.org/10.2307/3712104

Marshall, S. M., Gardner, M. M., Hughes, C., & Lowery, U. (2016). Attrition from student affairs: Perspectives from those who exited the profession. *Journal of Student Affairs Research and Practice, 53*(2), 146–159. https://doi.org/10.1080/19496591.2016.1147359

Marsiglio, W., Amato, P., Day, R. D., & Lamb, M. E. (2000). Scholarship on fatherhood in the 1990s and beyond. *Journal of Marriage and the Family, 62*(4), 1173–1191. https://doi.org/10.1111/j.1741-3737.2000.01173.x

McEwen, M. K., Engstrom, C. H., & Williams, T. E. (1990). Gender diversity within the student affairs profession. *Journal of College Student Development, 31*(1), 47–53.

Merriam, S. B., & Tisdell, E. J. (2016). *Qualitative research: A guide to design and implementation* (4th ed.). Jossey-Bass.

NASPA. (2018). *Data on NASPA members, disaggregated by gender and professional level.* Author.

Sallee, M. W. (2019). Complicating gender norms: Straight versus gay and queer fathers in student affairs. *The Review of Higher Education, 42*(3), 1233–1256. https://doi.org/10.1353/rhe.2019.0035

Snyder, K. A., & Green, A. I. (2008). Revisiting the glass escalator: The case of gender segregation in a female dominated occupation. *Social Problems, 55*(2), 271–299. https://doi.org/10.1525/sp.2008.55.2.271

Stimpson, R. L., & Filer, K. L. (2011). Female graduate students' work–life balance and the student affairs professional. In P. A. Pasque & S. E. Nicholson (Eds.), *Empowering women in higher education and student affairs* (pp. 69–84). Stylus.

Williams, C. L. (1992). The glass escalator: Hidden advantages for men in the "female" professions. *Social Problems, 39*(3), 253–267. https://doi.org/10.2307/3096961

Wilson, R. (2008). Two colleges, two presidents, one marriage. *The Chronicle of higher education, 54*(24), A1. https://www.chronicle.com/article/2-colleges-2-presidents-one-marriage/

Yakaboski, T., & Donahoo, S. (2011). In (Re)search of women in student affairs administration. In P. A. Pasque & S. Errington-Nicholson (Eds.), *Empowering women in higher education and student affairs: Theory, research, narratives, and practice from feminist perspectives* (pp. 270–286). Stylus.

Zorn, J. (2007). It's women's work. *Yearbook of the Association of Pacific Coast Geographers, 69*, 14–30. https://www.jstor.org/stable/24043264

14

WORK–LIFE INTEGRATION

Women Administrators in Student Affairs and Higher Education Managing Work and Family

Sarah Marshall

W ork–life balance is an elusive and unrealistic goal. Managing a professional career with a meaningful personal life is not about balance; it is about rhythm, management, and the integrated natures of our lives. Seeking this mysterious work–life balance, I dedicated years of research to how women college and university administrators, primarily in student affairs, manage work and family. Through this research, I discovered work–life management is a complex problem that implicates the individual, institution, and profession. While the resolution of this systemic issue involves change at all levels, this chapter highlights individual strategies senior-level leaders utilized to survive and excel within the current system. The intent of this chapter is to combat ideal worker norms by sharing participants' strategies for successfully incorporating both meaningful personal and professional lives along with their recommendations for systemic change. While the majority of this book focuses on the systemic nature of this problem, this chapter intentionally focuses on how individuals navigate the academy while advocating for change. Fully acknowledging the institutional challenges, a focus on how individual women navigated the academy offers insight and hope for others who intend to do the same. This chapter provides the wisdom from 25 cisgender females who advanced to senior ranks of university administration while raising children.

Within this chapter, I offer a portrait of gendered higher education and how ideal worker norms manifest for women. Next, I introduce the challenges associated with work–life management in student affairs followed by participant strategies for managing both. The chapter concludes with recommendations for women in student affairs, their institutions, and the profession. By better understanding work–life issues, challenges, and possible solutions that challenge ideal worker norms, professionals can strategically change the work culture, redesign work, implement training programs, and tailor career programs or assistance strategies enabling employees to be more engaged, productive, and fulfilled.

Gendered Higher Education and Student Affairs

The use of the gendered organizations framework provides a guideline for analyzing the role of gender in the structure of student affairs. While the gender divide within leadership in student affairs is slowly decreasing, existing challenges continue to prevent women from assuming leadership roles (Airini et al., 2011; Johnson, 2017). Barriers at the societal and institutional level often influence women's personal decision-making in relation to career and leadership aspirations (Airini et al., 2011; Moodly & Toni, 2015; Shepherd, 2017). Additionally, their ambitions are often swayed by probable work–family conflict as well as plans for a future partner and family (Coyle et al., 2015; Ganginis Del Pino et al., 2013).

Regardless of the increase in women's career experiences and educational credentialing, women continue to fall behind men in achieving high-level leadership roles within higher education (Johnson, 2017). While the increase in women deans and senior-level administrators may signal genuine improvement, according to Biddix (2013), women are still underrepresented in these positions. Employment patterns in the academy reflect the pattern in the larger professional world. Positions with higher status, power, and remuneration are generally dominated by men (Monroe et al., 2008). The function of patriarchy within higher education means there are some women who ascend to the ranks of president, provost, or senior officer; however, to gain these opportunities, women must operate by the rules often established by men (Bierema, 2003). Failure to adhere to these expectations may result in lack of advancement for women or prohibit those who do advance from leading authentically.

While some women professionally advance to senior leadership positions, as Johnson, 2017 stated, "It is easier to allow a few women to occupy positions of authority and dominance than to question whether social life should be organized around principles of hierarchy, control, and dominance at all" (p. 17). Despite apparent increases of women in positions of authority, discrimination continues to manifest through gender devaluation and tokenism, processes whereby the status and power of an authoritative position is downplayed when that position is held by a woman (Monroe et al., 2008).

With gender devaluation, women take on service tasks and other unattractive responsibilities despite knowing the disadvantages of spending time for which they will not be rewarded.

A companion to gendered organizations are the gendered norms associated with the ideal worker, which serves as a barrier to successful work–life management in higher education and student affairs (Acker, 1990; Wilk, 2016). Specifically, ideal worker norms offer insights into student affairs workplace culture, as the nature of these positions lend themselves to someone who is expected to put work before all other responsibilities. In a world of do more with less, extreme job expectations and 24/7 obligations exacerbate the conflict between responsibilities for family and success at work. Related consequences may include women leaving the profession due to higher levels of stress and burnout.

Student affairs workplace culture and norms align with the ideal worker concept (Nobbe & Manning, 1997; Wilk, 2016). In one study, almost half of the senior student affairs officers surveyed reported working 60 hours per week, and only half rated their level of balance as better than average (Beeny et al., 2005). The expectation of working excessive hours coupled with a self-sacrificing mentality leads to the attrition of talented individuals, including mothers, from the profession(Marshall et al., 2016).

The work–family balance experiences of student affairs professionals are especially influenced by ideal worker norms (Wilk, 2016). It can be difficult to find successful integration when a myriad of professional and personal responsibilities conflict. Within student affairs, the very nature of administrative work includes long hours and weekend obligations, which may pose a challenge for women university administrators who have children. Although the reality of working while raising a family is a challenge in any profession, in student affairs there seems to be an elevated sense of the importance of attempting to model healthy living while helping others create a balance in their academic, personal, and professional lives (Joyce-Brady, 2004; Marshall, 2009; Renn & Hodges, 2007; Renn & Hughes, 2004). Possibly due to socialized professional standards, some women in student affairs believe the realities of combining a family and a career may be incompatible with the current values of the profession (Marshall, 2009), thus forcing them to choose between career and family or to exit the profession all together (Marshall et al., 2016).

Traditional gender roles reinforce men as the primary economic providers while women provide care for the home and children. As reinforced in chapter 13 about fathers in student affairs, within gendered organizations, organizational structures exclude participation from those with significant responsibilities in the home (Sallee, 2012), thus creating disproportionate challenges for women. The gendered nature of organizations assumes employees can work extended hours without outside obligations. Although the desire to successfully manage work and family is not limited to one gender, women are affected differently than men because women still assume the majority of childcare and household responsibilities, even when working full-time (Jones, 2012). Additionally, women are also burdened with the third shift (Hochschild, 2012), which includes the mental strain of constantly cycling through the needs of the family. Gendered norms disadvantage women and limit their advancement. Monroe et al. (2008) expanded on the impact of gendered organizations, arguing that gender does not impose limits on women's professional success; rather, children, family, and domestic responsibilities do.

In my investigation, participants represented 25 different higher education institutions and assumed multiple roles within the university: 13 worked in student affairs/student services, four in academic affairs, three in development, three were university presidents (two of whom came from student affairs), and two in business operations. While some participant expertise expanded beyond student affairs, given that participants were all part of the higher education landscape, their collective wisdom resonated within student affairs and academe as a whole. Given the complexity and diverse scope of student affairs, divisional alignment varies from campus to campus and may include some of the departments represented in this study. At the time of the interview, all participants had school-aged children or younger, while 16 were married to a man and 9 were divorced and sharing custody with their ex-partners.

Primary data originated from personal interviews lasting between 90 and 120 minutes. Participants also shared their curriculum vitae, organizational charts, and job descriptions. Data were analyzed via open and axial coding (Creswell, 2013). Once themes were identified, the constant comparative method was employed to identify themes that cut across interviews (Boeije, 2002). In the presentation of data, pseudonyms were used to protect participant anonymity. The most striking finding from the interviews was the ongoing tension between professional success and family duties, but participants also offered insights into the successful integration of work and family as well as strategies for successful navigation. The value of learning from individual strategies benefits working mothers in the profession as well as informs institutional perspectives and practices.

Work–Life Realities and Strategies

Consistent with work–life literature, every participant shared the incompatible tension between career and family. All told stories of exhaustion, stress, and constant anxiety. When describing work–life management, participants recounted an environment they survived, rather than thrived in—especially when their children were smaller and their careers advancing. Many respondents told of the pain felt as they were torn between children and the job. Similar to academic mothers, they felt exhaustion and the sense of despair as they chose between what felt like irreconcilable conflicts, often leaving women drained emotionally and unsatisfied with whatever solutions were created (Monroe et al., 2008).

Participants held themselves to high standards and attributed their failures less to gender discrimination and more to their own inadequacies. Unexpectedly, the women saw child-related demands as less relevant for the university. Several respondents suggested that the tension between children and professional life was simply a fact to be accepted, a tension prevalent to professional women, not simply those in higher education. Not one woman in the study said gender limited her potential. That said, they recognized they had to work harder to achieve the same success as their men counterparts. In this case, they recognized the gender disparities. Nonetheless, participant strategies for successful management proved antithetical to ideal worker norms. Participants found strategic ways to advance their careers and raise children. Based on the example of the women in this study, if women find similar pathways to successful work–life integration, collaboratively they may shift the culture of the organization and profession. Collectively, working mothers can effect change for themselves, for other working parents, and for future student affairs professionals.

In navigating the tension between career and family, participants started to recognize the tension between institutional accountability and individual responsibility but offered more insights into individual responsibility. Administrative mothers shared how being a mother and a senior-level administrator was complicated, challenging, and exhausting. On a more positive note, these women led gratifying, rewarding, meaningful lives that they loved and would not change. They embraced their multifaceted lives filled with both routine and unforeseen challenges. While recognizing the challenges, they provided their strategies and wisdom, which were antithetical to ideal worker norms, to help other women who sought similar personal and professional successes. They shared their strategies as ways to help other women, and men, navigate the higher education landscape, fully believing that additional representation would help dismantle the gendered organization. Consciously or unconsciously, they effected change on a much broader scale than they imagined. They did so by demonstrating effective management of dual roles, which aided in the erosion of the ideal worker construct.

In this study, women managed their complexities through an intricate array of coping strategies and support systems. Specifically, their self-constructed strategies centered around key themes that resonated with each participant: developing personal insight, building support systems, and letting go. While application of these strategies may resonate with working professionals in general, the added complexity of managing a career and family warrants focus for women in student affairs. As discussed in the recommendations section, while individual strategies are shared, managing work–life issues is not an individual problem, but rather a structural and an institutional problem. These women successfully navigated a patriarchal system and their strategies may prove insightful especially in combating ideal worker norms. That said, the system needs to be reshaped to ensure that all capable, driven women who want to succeed holistically in all areas of their lives are able to do so, without feeling like they are doing something wrong or feeling like they are doing many things and none of them well.

Developing Personal Insight

Through the process of regular self-reflection, women prioritized their needs and created their own definitions of success, especially in relation to their physical and emotional well-being. For some, the need for reflection came after an awareness of a loss of personal identity that resulted from constantly putting their needs last. As Karen reflected:

> One of the things I realized about 5 years after my daughter was born is that I lost touch with myself. I woke up one day wondering where I went. I remember asking myself, "Where did I go?" My life was all about my work and my family. I had no personal hobbies, many acquaintances but few friends. When asked by a therapist, "What makes you happy? What brings you joy other than your family?" I had no response. I had to do a lot of soul searching to find that answer. Once I had it, I knew I had to make time to allow joy back into my life. I also had to learn to embrace quality "me" time and do the things that fueled my soul.

Aligning with the ideal worker norm, participants conveyed an initial denial of self-care leading to a loss of self. Without a strong understanding of themselves and their personal and professional needs, women felt inadequate both at work and at home. Suggestions for staying in touch with themselves centered on regular reflection and prioritization. Some participants meditated daily. They used this dedicated time to clear their minds, focus their attention, and center themselves. Some commented on how meditation increased their concentration, decreased anxiety, and improved their overall feelings of happiness. Others allocated time at the beginning and end of each day to prioritize and plan how they would focus their energies. With regular focus, participants frequently revisited their priorities in an effort to align them with their allocation of time. This constant reflection and planning kept them centered and focused, especially during their busiest times. Rather than give into self-sacrifice, participants recognized the significance of self-care and self-reflection to center themselves and affirm their worth and competence. This shift in thinking dismantles the ideal worker construct and collectively has the potential to dismantle the current student affairs workaholic culture.

Developing personal insight also related to knowing limits, stressors, and motivators. The more the women were aware of their needs, the more they recognized when they deviated too far from their priorities and needed to realign. As one participant reflected:

> I had to think hard about my needs and myself. I needed to determine what made me happy. What stressed me out? Being more in touch with my feelings allowed me to foresee or expect potential problems. I considered my most productive times—morning or evening? I learned to work when I was most efficient and that as an introvert, I needed downtime to reinvigorate. I needed to learn how to identify when I was out of sorts and how to realign when necessary.

Taking time to reflect allowed participants to clearly understand themselves in an effort to be productive and to know when they needed to readjust. Women in this study acknowledged that they lived complicated lives with often-competing demands. Knowing themselves and their limits, they could effectively communicate them to their support systems and seek help when necessary. By role modeling their time allocation and articulating their priorities, they pave the way for others to follow.

Defining Success

A workplace constructed around ideal worker norms presumes employees separate home from work and place their work duties before all personal responsibilities (Davies & Frink, 2014; Isdell, 2016). Student affairs mothers do not fit this framework due to the integrated nature of their lives. As such, their definitions for professional success deviate from ideal worker norms. Women often define *professional success* as individual achievement, having passion for their work, receiving respect, and making a difference. Men often list financial achievement as part of their professional success as they see themselves as working for their family (Groysberg & Abrahams, 2014). Similarly, defining her own successes helped Gwen alleviate the guilt she felt about not giving enough at home or at work:

> I often revisit how I define work–life wins. Is it that I am home 4 nights per week for dinner, knowing what is going on in my family's lives, having emotional energy at home, reading to my kids each night? Once you have defined success or your work–life win—the guilt will be manageable. Guilt is powerful. With guilt comes regret. I intentionally manage my expectations and celebrate my successes rather than feel guilty about where I think I fell short.

By self-defining success, participants were able to challenge the ideal worker norm by redefining professional satisfaction and dispelling the social workplace norms. Participants learned to navigate work and home priorities by defining success for themselves and focusing on their accomplishments rather than unfinished tasks. By establishing reasonable expectations for themselves, they reduced the guilt about not giving enough to either area of their lives. Understanding their limitations and recognizing their self-worth aided participants in combating institutional norms that favored the unrealistic gendered ideal worker norms. If others in student affairs adopted similar commitments, our current "work above all else" norm could be eradicated.

Care for Self

Antithetical to ideal worker norms, women in this study learned to put their physical and emotional needs first. They recognized that when their lives were out of sync and the demands were extreme, they sacrificed their health. Unlike many working mothers who rearranged their schedules, gave up sleep, and sacrificed their health to achieve their goals (Allen et al., 1995), participants learned that self-care was critical. As Diane pointed out:

> [Not prioritizing your health] is ironic because people often neglect their health in the name of "working harder." If your body isn't healthy, the harder you work, the less productive you will be. The key is to determine how to get work done and remain healthy at the same time.

Participants recognized the costs of not taking care of their physical or mental health. As Ebony commented, "If you are not taking care of yourself, it will catch up with you. You may be haggard or tired at a meeting, oversleep, or let down your child." For the most part, participants regularly exercised, tried to eat healthy, and took small steps to ensure their well-being. As Maria reminded:

> Exercise doesn't need to be intensive or long. Short spurts is completely acceptable. I take frequent breaks and walk for 10 minutes. This boosts my energy and sharpens my focus. Sometimes if someone wants to meet with me, we will walk and talk. Also, it goes without saying, you need to get enough sleep. Stay hydrated and have healthy snacks on hand.

Darleen commented on how early in her career she compromised her health. When she realized that she needed to make changes in her life, she made small changes first:

> I started with taking a multivitamin every day. I made that initial change and felt good about it. Rather than beat myself up about what I wasn't doing, I focused on what I was doing right. Next, I vowed to drink eight glasses of water a day. That was the next change. After I mastered those, I added a 10-minute walk to my lunch. Next, I stopped eating after 7:00 [p.m.]. I knew I needed to make changes regarding my health. Focusing on one small change at a time worked for me.

The student affairs administrator role naturally aligns itself with individuals who can separate their work and personal responsibilities and always prioritize work commitments when overlap occurs (Isdell, 2016). As a result, student affairs professionals often compromise their own basic needs. As the women in this study discovered, compromising their own well-being was not an option. They found ways to address their personal needs without compromising their professional priorities, thus proving that ideal worker expectations can be thwarted. If more student affairs professionals adopted similar self-care strategies, the norm would shift from constantly sacrificing self to making self a priority to be more effective at work.

Building Support Networks

Having a partner at home to assume caregiving and other personal tasks allows an employee to fully focus on their responsibilities at work and may lend itself to professional advancement (Isdell, 2016). Contrary to the ideal worker norm (Davies & Frink, 2014), the women in this study did not have at-home partners to assume the tasks related to maintaining the family and home and, consequently, often had to seek outside assistance. The most frequently mentioned strategy women used to manage their multiple roles was to have diverse and expansive support systems, including strong, behind-the-scenes supporters such as family, friends, employers, mentors, and role models. By relying on these support systems, they shifted from feeling individually inadequate to embracing collective action. In accordance with the literature, women who were able to maintain successful work and family lives did so when support mechanisms were in place (Cheung & Halpern, 2010; Ezzedeen & Ritchey, 2008). In addition to the aforementioned, support also included paid and unpaid assistance. They used outsourcing to help them do the less-important tasks, such as housekeeping, lawn care, grocery shopping, and meal preparation (Cheung & Halpern, 2010). While recognizing that outsourcing is not financially viable for many, it did allow the women in this study to focus on their higher priority of spending time with their families.

Dependable Childcare

When asked about their strategies for managing the complexity of their lives as mothers and full-time professionals, most interviewees emphasized the importance of quality, trusted, loving childcare for their children, both during the business day as well as after hours. None had access to campus childcare facilities, so they used in-home care, daycare centers, after-school programs, and summer camps. Regardless of daycare type, the women all agreed that having quality daycare allowed them to lessen their guilt and concentrate more fully on their work. As Yolanda explained:

> I spent a lot of time trying to find quality care for these kids. I went through various configurations over the years. I had people coming into my home. I took them to a daycare center at one point. I really intended to try to find care where [my children] were treated kindly and compassionately. I wanted them to be in a warm, loving environment. Once they had this, I could concentrate on my job.

The mothers were responsible for obtaining their own childcare and admitted their work–life balance would not be possible without this critical support. Imagine if higher education institutions provided quality, trusted, loving childcare, both during the business day as well as after hours. The shift in responsibility from the individual to the organization would mean a major step forward toward supporting working parents in the academy.

Flexible Supervisors and Trusted Mentors

In addition to finding guidance from previously mentioned sources, a few participants underscored the support they received from other professionals. In most cases, participants sought out colleagues, supervisors, and mentors who served as advisers, career advancers, and emotional supporters regarding both personal and professional matters. Donna spoke appreciatively of how her mentor guided her career by offering advice and training. In her case, she sought out this mentor and cultivated the relationship:

> We hired a new dean. I was a faculty member and approached her, [saying,] "I like how you work. I like how you work with people, and I like your style." She sat me down and spent an hour telling me who she was and how she got there. I said, "I know this is another really dumb question but, would you mentor me to get there?" She just smiled and said, "I would be honored to." The dean started meeting with me on a weekly basis and helped me work through my career options and personal challenges. She happened to be a single mother, divorced, so she really understood.

Several other interviewees mentioned the support they received from their supervisors. Participants indicated how they valued candid and trusted conversations regarding their personal and professional lives. Yolanda saw her supervisor as a mentor. A mother herself, Yolanda's supervisor encouraged her to put her family needs first:

> My boss will say, "Your families come first." I think that's one thing I've learned. Family comes first, but you shouldn't abuse that philosophy. If you tell them that their families do come first, they'll attend their son's ball game, but they'll also get the work done. I think [my supervisor] sets that tone and it works.

To successfully integrate work and family, flexible supervisors were essential. Due to the unique nature of student affairs work, participants embraced the overlap between the two and recognized the spillover of their professional responsibilities into their personal hours. Understanding this spillover, supervisors allowed for flexible work hours, which allowed administrative mothers the freedom to navigate their personal needs during normal business hours. While participants sought out mentors and articulated their needs to supervisors, the current culture of student affairs dictates that the individual seek out support and personally advocate for accommodations that may or may not align with workplace culture. While individual activism leads to change, our current professional norms place too much pressure on working mothers to elicit the support that should be availed to all student affairs professionals to maintain healthier work–life integration.

Letting Go

Finally, participants had an awareness of their personal and professional limitations. Knowing that they could not adequately service all of their responsibilities at home and at work, participants prioritized their obligations, forced themselves to remove the unnecessary, and learned to say "no." As Samantha reinforced, "Remember, you can do anything once you stop trying to do everything."

Women prioritized the obligations in their lives. This coping strategy helped them organize their days and allocate their time. They understood that there were not enough hours in the day to accomplish everything; therefore, they relinquished some of the dispensable aspects of their professional lives. Gwen candidly talked about how she did not attend unimportant events:

> [Being a mother and a vice president] is a great thing but I'm not 100% in either role. That is not a statement of guilt. I just got back from this monthly meeting. It's one of these meetings that I go to, and they want to meet the day before about what they are going to meet about the next day, and then they want to have a follow-up luncheon. No. I am not coming to the early meeting and I'm not going to stay for lunch. I am probably going to go home over my lunch hour. You cut away every nonessential thing.

Letting go also pertained to women releasing some other personal obligations. Participants recognized they simply could not do all of what was expected, especially to their level of perfection. These administrative mothers admitted learning to becoming somewhat comfortable with letting less-important things go. This included unkempt homes, unwashed laundry, or eating out.

The next theme associated with letting go was somewhat uncharacteristic of these women and in direct conflict with ideal worker norms. Participants learned to say "no." Most agreed that a career in higher education required working many late nights and weekends, and the amount of work was never-ending. With their personal interests in mind, women found ways to decline additional responsibilities despite guilt they felt. Women turned down professional opportunities and limited the number of student events they attended in order to have more time with their families. Madeline described the strategy she used to limit her attendance at student events. She informed students why she could not attend and discussed the importance of role modeling priorities for her students. She wanted them to understand that although she supported them and their endeavors, she also had personal commitments. This strategy seemed successful, as the students apparently understood her dilemma:

> I feel that I model for other young women who work at the institution and also for our students. From my example they know that your life is made up of many different parts. I might tell students that, "I may not be able to be at X event of yours, I'd love to be there, but my daughter has whatever." I think it is important to just acknowledge my personal commitments and there is no apology. I think students understand that and it is one thing that we need to model and show.

Finally, while women had personal and professional goals, they also understood that they were unable to have everything they wanted all at the same time. Most admitted that having a family and a career was complex yet rewarding. They also knew that at various stages of their lives, they made certain trade-offs. Rather than give up their goals or interests, participants let some things go until a later point in their lives, when they could act on them more successfully. To this end, participants limited their involvement in professional organizations, turned down international speaking engagements, and delayed advanced degrees. While these opportunities were still attractive, participants intentionally delayed their participation until a time when their work–life interface allowed for these additional commitments. They did not lose sight of these, just simply delayed them until a more convenient time.

Although motherhood may have shifted professional and personal priorities, it did not shift participants' professional ambitions. Women used multiple strategies to increase their successful navigation of work and home. They maximized their time, set priorities that aligned with their values, learned to say "no" to less important obligations, and let go of their need to be perfect. These strategies, which are anti-ideal worker strategies, allowed them to be more present at work and at home and lessened the guilt associated with managing both roles effectively.

Recommendations for Practice

The intent of this chapter was to deconstruct ideal worker norms by sharing participants' strategies for successful work–life integration along with their recommendations for systemic change. Fully acknowledging the institutional challenges, this chapter intentionally deviated from the others by focusing on how individual women navigated the academy. The attention given to work–life balance in current literature reinforces that there are no easy solutions to administrative motherhood. In all actuality, integration of work and family is highly personalized and further complicated by institutional and professional factors. Divergent from other chapters in this book, shared recommendations focus on the individual and the organization. Although this study focused on the strategies senior-level administrators used to manage their work and family lives, more investigation is needed to determine how institutional practices may meet the needs of working parents. Institutions and employers are tasked with supporting working parents by assisting and providing resources as well as for setting reasonable expectations apart from the ideal worker norm. The interviews revealed both a cautious optimism and diminished expectations for change. Most openly advocated for change but preferred nonthreatening collective actions. Not surprising given the gendered socialization into the profession which reinforces parenthood as a deviation from the norm, many participants identified the burdens they carry as the result of their own choices, and few women asked for institutional intervention toward a more just reconciliation between the commitment to family and the commitment to career. This idea that the sole responsibility rests on the individual is alarming and only further demonstrates the entrenchment of ideal worker norms within the academy. To that end, this chapter concludes with recommendations for women in student affairs, institutional leaders, and the profession. Each offers perspective informing the complexities of gender bias in professional academic life.

Institutional and Professional Action

Having more women in positions of power helps but is not a complete solution. Redefinition of professional success beyond simply the traditional, linear male model in which the professional focuses fully on a career with few family obligations is necessary. Worthy of mentioning, participants recognized that family versus career is a human problem, not just one with which women wrestle. Male norms also trap men into stereotypes, making it difficult for men to break out of traditional roles, if they so desire. We need to respond to this challenge by developing more flexible work models so both men and women can excel at home and at work. Flexible work models may lead to lesser attrition and higher rates of job satisfaction.

Workplace flexibility, whether formalized via human resources or negotiated between employee and supervisor, is essential to promoting a feeling of trust and institutional loyalty. In exchange for their commitment to their work and its extended work hours, institutions can provide student affairs administrators flexibility to tend to personal responsibilities during traditional working hours. Institutional loyalty also increases when women perceive they have the freedom, flexibility, and control over how they manage their family and work roles (Isdell, 2016). In addition to promoting flexible work schedules, flexibility to work from alternative locations and accommodation for hours worked during evenings and weekends should also be considered.

Perhaps an even better solution would be to redistribute the large amount of work that already exists. Considering workweeks of 50 to 60 hours are common among student affairs professionals, working less is imperative. Even though budgets are tight and institutions are trying to do more with less, reducing work hours would be a solid investment because collectively and intentionally reducing the work week would allow those within the academy to enjoy their professional endeavors and carry out meaningful personal lives.

Next, institutions and professional organizations should refine and promote mentoring programs. Mentoring should be multifaceted and comprehensive so that all new professionals, not just women, are mentored. As professional growth is ongoing, mentoring also should extend beyond new professionals. As a result, mentorship is vital as individuals advance professionally.

Lessons learned from the participants suggest that it is vital that women continue to learn from and support each other. Via formal mentoring programs or informal collegial relationships, student affairs mothers can find solace in learning from the experiences of other working professionals. Identifying other working mothers at their institution or within the field may provide women a network to exchange strategies and solutions related to work–family issues and help them feel connected to other women who are similarly committed to their careers and families. Fellow mothers can help each other navigate work–life policies such as the Family and Medical Leave Act (FMLA), institutional resources such as lactation locations, or childcare options. Fostering an environment where women at all levels, and across the university, can discuss their experiences regarding work–life management can create a culture of sharing and support. Mentoring programs should continue to be offered and accessed through professional associations such as NASPA or ACPA. Ongoing mentoring can provide an objective sounding board and help women develop external networks of support. While these programs are already offered to some degree, the associations should partner with universities to align their efforts to help ensure role models for women in the administrative pipeline.

Most importantly, institutionally and professionally, improved practices are needed to facilitate work–life management and create a culture that supports women's advancement to leadership. One way to do this is by providing ongoing professional development at every level. Professional development targeting career advancement for women in the student affairs pipeline is essential to their career trajectories. Training via professional associations or at the institutional level can include skill-building on how to make strategic career decisions, leadership training programs, stress management, and opportunities for job promotion. These training opportunities will allow women to determine a plan for career advancement. Also, to recruit and retain professionals to the academy, an investment must be made to provide quality, affordable childcare. Knowing that their children are well cared for is critical to any working parents' productivity and professional success.

Employees' physical and emotional wellness must be a priority. Given the stressors related to managing work and family, wellness policies enacted by human resources or at the department level are imperative. Setting, and regularly revisiting, work–life goals for the office is one way to enact a culture that supports all employees. Promoting wellness and self-care may include allowing employees time to exercise during the workday, encouraging lunch and other small breaks during the day, promoting the use of vacation time, and leaving work at reasonable times.

Knowledgeable and supportive supervisors are critical to the success of administrative mothers. The supervisor–employee relationship is critical to job satisfaction, employee morale, and retention (Marshall et al., 2016). Supervisors must understand how to apply work–life-related policies in a manner that supports both the individual and institution. To further affect practice, supervisor training should be implemented including employer/employee relations, conflict mediation, and work–life challenges.

Women in Student Affairs

My study captured the experiences of the few who achieved professional success while raising a family, despite the gendered organizations they encountered. For some women, challenges faced by administrative mothers were not insurmountable, particularly with the infusion of a comprehensive support network, adequate finances, and the development of strategies for success. For others, no amount of bootstrapping would have made success or advancement in student affairs a reality for them. If women lack adequate support or cannot afford access to quality childcare, then trying harder is not an option. Although this chapter provided individual strategies for combating engrained workplace norms, the primary problem remains organizational.

While women in this study role-modeled effective strategies for managing work and family, they also recognized that the culture of student affairs remains unsupportive of working parents. They argued that some of this was due to the professional culture of academe and some to the perceptions of society in general. To reverse these perceptions, we need to increase awareness within the profession, educate younger women that having a career and raising a family is possible, unite working mothers on campus, include men in the work/family conversation, and educate employers that working mothers are a valuable investment in the future success of colleges and universities.

To mothers in student affairs: *You are enough*. Do not allow unrealistic ideal worker expectations lead you to doubt your self-worth, competence, or ability to effectively parent. To create a greater sense of centeredness, a greater sense of work–life integration, all women in student affairs must begin to recognize the ideal worker notions to which they consciously or unconsciously ascribe. They need to set boundaries and push toward excellence, not perfection. Until a systemic kind of recognition about the impossibility of the ideal worker norm takes hold, women are left to orchestrate the change they most need in their own lives and their own careers. Work–life integration is not just another *do it yourself* project for women in student affairs. The fight is not over until institutions begin to challenge and change, through meaningful dialogue and policies, these deeply seated notions and barriers that push women toward the superwoman ideal.

References

Acker, J. (1990). Hierarchies, jobs, bodies: A theory of gendered organizations. *Gender & Society, 4*(2), 139–158. https://doi.org/10.1177/089124390004002002

Airini, C. S., Collings, S., Conner, L., McPherson, K., Midson, B., & Wilson, C. (2011). Learning to be leaders in higher education: What helps or hinders women's advancement as leaders in universities. *Educational Management Administration & Leadership, 39*(1), 44–62. https://doi.org/10.1177/1741143210383896

Allen, K., Jacobson, S., & Lomotey, K. (1995). African American women in educational administration: The importance of mentors and sponsors. *The Journal of Negro Education, 64*(4), 409–422. https://doi.org/10.2307/2967264

Beeny, C., Guthrie, V. L., Rhodes, G. S., & Terrell, P. S. (2005). Personal and professional balance among senior student affairs officers: Gender differences in approaches and expectations. *College Student Affairs Journal, 24*(2), 137–151.

Biddix, J. P. (2013). Directors, deans, doctors, divergers: The four career paths of SSAOs. *Journal of College Student Development, 54*(3), 315–321. https://doi.org/10.1353/csd.2013.0056

Bierema, L. (2003). The role of gender consciousness in challenging patriarchy. *International Journal of Lifelong Education, 22*(1), 3–12. https://doi.org/10.1080/02601370304825

Boeije, H. (2002). A purposeful approach to the constant comparative method in the analysis of qualitative interviews. *Quality and Quantity, 36*(4), 391–409. https://doi.org/10.1023/A:1020909529486

Cheung, F. M., & Halpern, D. F. (2010). Women at the top: Powerful leaders define success as work + family in a culture of gender. *American Psychologist, 65*(3), 182–193. https://doi.org/10.1037/a0017309

Coyle, E. F., Van Leer, E., Schroeder, K. M., & Fulcher, M. (2015). Planning to have it all: Emerging adults' expectations of future work–family conflict. *Sex Roles, 72*(11–12), 547–557. https://doi.org/10.1007/s11199-015-0492-y

Creswell, J. W. (2013). *Qualitative inquiry & research design: Choosing among five approaches* (3rd ed.). SAGE.

Davies, A. R., & Frink, B. D. (2014). The origins of the ideal worker: The separation of work and home in the United States from the market revolution to 1950. *Work and Occupations, 41*(1), 18–39. https://doi.org/10.1177/0730888413515893

Ezzedeen, S. R., & Ritchey, K. G. (2008). The man behind the woman: A qualitative study of the spousal support received and valued by executive women. *Journal of Family Issues, 29*(9), 1107–1135.

Ganginis Del Pino, H. V., O'Brien, K. M., Mereish, E., & Miller, M. J. (2013). "Leaving before she leaves": Considering future family when making career plans. *Journal of Counseling Psychology, 60*(3), 462–470. https://doi.org/10.1037/a0032651

Groysberg, B., & Abrahams, R. (2014). Manage your work, manage your life. *Harvard business review*, 1–10. https://hbr.org/2014/03/manage-your-work-manage-your-life

Hochschild, A. R. (2012). *The second shift: Working families and the revolution at home.* Penguin.

Isdell, L. (2016). *Work–family balance among mothers who are mid-career student affairs administrators at institutions recognized for work–life policies* [Doctoral dissertation, University of Kansas]. ProQuest No. 10130103.

Johnson, H. L. (2017). *Pipelines, pathways, and institutional leadership: An update on the status of women in higher education.* American Council on Education.

Jones, B. D. (2012). *Women who opt out: The debate over working mothers and work–family balance.* New York University Press.

Joyce-Brady, J. (2004). How did I arrive here? A journey with family and student affairs. In K. A. Renn & C. Hughes (Eds.), *Roads taken: Women in student affairs at mid-career* (pp. 113–122). Stylus.

Marshall, S. M. (2009). Women higher education administrators with children: Negotiating personal and professional lives. *NASPA Journal About Women in Higher Education, 11*(1), 188–221. https://doi.org/10.2202/1940-7890.1031

Marshall, S. M., Gardner, M. M., Hughes, C., & Lowery, U. (2016). Attrition from student affairs: Perspectives from those who exited the profession. *Journal of Student Affairs Research and Practice, 53*(2), 146–159. https://doi.org/10.1080/19496591.2016.1147359

Monroe, K., Ozyurt, S., Wrigley, T., & Alexander, A. (2008). Gender equality in academia: Bad news from the trenches, and some possible solutions. *Perspectives on Politics*, *6*(2), 215–233. https://doi.org/10.1017/S1537592708080572

Moodly, A. L., & Toni, N. (2015). Women's access to higher education leadership: Where are the role models? *Journal of Social Sciences*, *45*(1), 45–52. https://doi .org/10.1080/09718923.2015.11893486

Nobbe, J., & Manning, S. (1997). Issues for women in student affairs with children. *NASPA Journal*, *34*(2), 101–111. https://doi.org/10.2202/1949-6605.1014

Renn, K. A., & Hodges, C. (2007). The first year on the job: Experiences of new professionals in student affairs. *NASPA Journal*, *44*(2), 367–391. https://doi.org/ 10.2202/1949-6605.1800

Renn, K. A., & Hughes, C. (2004). *Roads taken: Women in student affairs at mid-career*. Stylus.

Sallee, M. W. (2012). The ideal worker or the ideal father: Organizational structures and culture in the gendered university. *Research in Higher Education*, *53*(7), 782–802. https://doi.org/10.1007/s11162-012-9256-5

Shepherd, S. (2017). Why are there so few female leaders in higher education: A case of structure or agency? *Management in Education*, *31*(2), 82–87. https://doi.org/ 10.1177/0892020617696631

Wilk, K. E. (2016). Work–life balance and ideal worker expectations for administrators. *New Directions for Higher Education*, *2016*(176), 37–51.

CONCLUSION

Reimagining Student Affairs

Margaret W. Sallee

L inked by a common interrogation of ideal worker norms, the chapters in this volume grappled with how the nature of student affairs work impacts student affairs professionals. Across chapters, contributors described the never-ending demands of the field and the resulting toll on professionals' personal lives and selves. However, as Acker (1990) pointed out, organizations that depend on ideal worker norms do not care about the impact on the individual. Instead, the employee simply exists to meet the needs of the organization. Such a perspective is problematic as it is likely to lead to burnout and attrition from the field. In this concluding chapter, I return to ideal worker norms and consider how contributors across the volume provided evidence of its existence and promulgation in student affairs. I then discuss additional similarities across chapters before concluding with recommendations for practice and future areas of inquiry.

The Hegemony of Ideal Worker Norms

The ideal worker is one who is able to fully devote themselves to the needs of the organization while leaving any personal obligations, including childrearing, to their spouses (Acker, 1990; Williams, 1989). In short, the ideal worker subordinates their needs to those of the organization. As Acker (1990) explained, the ideal worker is "a disembodied worker who exists only for the work" (p. 149); as a result, this worker is also assumed to be emotionless. The contributors in this volume explored the ways in which ideal worker norms are reflected in current student affairs work.

As the contributors in this book made clear, ideal worker norms are flourishing in student affairs. However, the chapters also underscored the importance of context in how ideal worker norms play out. For example, Pamela Graglia, Karla Pérez-Vélez, and D-L Stewart's chapter took on how the current turn toward neoliberalism creates heightened pressures for efficiency and production that allows ideal worker norms to thrive, much to the detriment of employees' well-being. Carrie A. Kortegast examined how national legislation shapes LGBTQ employees' worklives. For example, before same-sex marriage was codified into law through the Supreme Court decision in *Obergefell vs. Hodges*, many residence life professionals were not able to live with their partners due to dated campus policies restricting cohabitation benefits to married, and therefore opposite-sex, couples. These employees were asked to be ideal workers by literally separating their work and personal lives.

Context need not take such a macro perspective, however. As C. Casey Ozaki and Anne M. Hornak argued, institutional context also influences how ideal worker norms unfold. Student affairs professionals at community colleges, for example, spend much of their time working with high-needs students, which creates different demands than those placed upon professionals at liberal arts colleges and other institutional types. Their chapter underscores that ideal worker norms do not—indeed, cannot—look the same in all environments. Rather, the skills that each organization demands of its employees differ. What remains common, however, is the expectation that employees give tirelessly of themselves for the organization.

Differences abound even across the same campus. Benjamin B. Stubbs illustrated the demands placed on those working in campus life. He further interrogated the role that individual supervisors play in perpetuating ideal worker norms, both explicitly and implicitly. Melanie Lee and Megan Karbley also found that supervisors play a critical role in shaping new professionals' intention to leave the field, in part because of perceived investment in the employee. In short, ideal worker norms are not monolithic. However, their specter looms large over student affairs and its employees.

As has been written elsewhere (Marshall et al., 2016) and as many of the contributors in this book discussed, student affairs is a field that expects tireless devotion from its employees. Benjamin B. Stubbs highlighted the demands placed on employees in campus life to work all hours, well beyond a 40-hour work week. As he explained, professionals in those areas receive the message that such schedules are simply the way the field must operate. Similarly, as Amy S. Hirschy and Shannon D. Staten discussed, residence life places similar demands on its employees, who are expected to respond to the needs of students, regardless of the hour. Such intense work expectations may lead employees to experience burnout and other consequences.

If ideal workers are simply "disembodied worker[s]" (Acker, 1990, p. 149), this suggests that one employee is interchangeable for the next, which means that organizations do not need to consider the unique skills, values, or needs that each employee brings. It also suggests that organizations bear no obligation in providing development or advancement opportunities for employees. Yet, as Melanie Lee and Megan Karbley found in their study of new professionals, those employees who perceived opportunities for advancement and support for their growth were those who were most likely to report a commitment to a career in student affairs. Supervisors and organizations who do not support their employees' growth are short-sighted, as the employee may leave and a new employee will need to be trained. Of course, from the ideal worker perspective, such an outcome is not problematic, as the new worker will be trained to meet the organization's needs. This approach to employee development is ironic, given the focus in student affairs on students' holistic development and attention to individual self-worth. The field cannot expect its employees to promote one set of values when working with students while being governed by a different set of norms in their professional lives. The norms of the field need to shift.

Although the ideal worker is expected to be emotionless, the contributors in this volume underscored how student affairs work requires intense emotional labor. The paraprofessionals in Molly A. Mistretta and Alison L. DuBois's chapter contended with both burnout and compassion fatigue in their work with those living in residence halls. Similarly, R. Jason Lynch and Kerry L. B. Klima highlighted how student affairs professionals can experience secondary trauma through the process of working with students who are contending with personal issues. The majority of student affairs professionals have not been trained as counselors. Some may have taken a counseling class in their graduate programs, but most student affairs graduate preparation programs do not devote a significant part of their curriculum to counseling issues. Nonetheless, student affairs professionals may find themselves counseling students on a regular basis and not know how to process the information their students share. Ideal worker norms assume that an employee would simply take in that information and move on, but in reality, student affairs professionals may be deeply affected by such disclosures. Absent significantly increasing counseling centers on each campus, the organization needs to find ways to help employees navigate this burden.

In addition to internalizing their students' emotional burdens, many student affairs professionals contend with additional demands as they navigate the field as a member of a minoritized group. As Acker (1990) suggested, the ideal worker is a gendered construct and is clearly based on a (cisgender) male worker. However, the construct is also deeply raced and classed. In short, the ideal worker, as originally conceived, is a White, cisgender, heterosexual, middle-class man. This creates problems for those who fall outside this group, as many chapter contributors highlighted. Rosemary J. Perez explored how those from minoritized groups, including racial and ethnic minorities as well as those with children, could not live up to ideal worker norms in graduate programs. Other chapter contributors argued that those from minoritized groups had extra labor placed upon them, simply to navigate an organization and society not designed for them. Ginny Jones Boss and Nicole Bravo underscored how the academy promotes hegemonic Whiteness, thus creating challenges for professionals of color, while Sonja Ardoin explored how poor and working-class professionals engage in "class work" (Gray & Kish-Gephart, 2013) to navigate the middle-class values of universities. Carrie A. Kortegast explored how LGBTQ professionals might be challenged in their lives and work by processes that others take for granted, such as marriage and childbearing. She further pointed out how transgender employees challenge the notion of the disembodied worker through their very existence. All of these groups have to abide by norms of the majority that may actively be working against their needs. Further, these groups—along with those of other minoritized identities—may spend a significant amount of time providing assistance to students of the same background, thus carrying their additional emotional burdens. These demands are not acknowledged as part of the ideal worker construct, which expects that all employees will perform the same work and respond to the organization in the same way.

Finally, the ideal worker is expected to be childless, or at the very least, have a spouse to take care of their children. However, as Sarah Marshall as well as Margaret W. Sallee, Alyssa Stefanese Yates, and Michael Venturiello wrote in their chapters, many student affairs professionals successfully combine the demands of work and family. However, employees are often left on their own to navigate the demands of childrearing. Yet, as the parents profiled in these chapters illustrated, student affairs can be a space that embraces parenting; those who thrive are those who have strong support networks, both on and off campus.

Student affairs professionals are socialized to fulfill the role of the ideal worker, as both C. Casey Ozaki and Anne M. Hornak as well as Rosemary J. Perez discussed in their chapters. For many, this socialization occurs in graduate programs, while others are socialized through on-the-job training. Implicit (and often explicit) in this socialization are notions of professionalism, which, as Perez discussed, are a set of undefined values about how to exist in the field. The ideal worker is expected to exhibit professionalism, yet may not know exactly what professionalism entails. And, as discussed earlier, these norms and values are often problematic for those from minoritized groups, again underscoring that few can live up to the norms of the ideal worker.

Using a variety of frameworks that brought different aspects of ideal worker norms into analytical focus, the contributors to this volume illustrated how these norms are pervasive in student affairs practice—and simultaneously do great harm to those in the field. Working long hours leads employees to exhaustion. Contending with students' heavy emotional demands places similar burdens on employees. Student affairs professionals are not emotionless automatons designed to meet the needs of the organization. They are, however, people with great passion for helping the students whom they serve. It is time for organizations to shift their practices to support student affairs professionals in leading healthy professional and personal lives.

Recommendations for Practice

Although each of the chapters in this book offers recommendations for practice for a variety of constituency groups, additional recommendations arise out of examining the similarities across the chapters. In what follows, I offer a brief consideration of recommendations for practice based on the previous discussion. Unlike the other chapters in the book, I offer recommendations for all on a campus, rather than disaggregated by particular groups.

Dismantle Context-Specific Ideal Worker Norms

As the contributors made clear, context makes a difference for how ideal worker norms play out. The expectations associated with student affairs work at a community college are different than those at a research university. Similarly, the requirements of a job in student activities are different than those in residence life. However, across settings, employees—and particularly those with power—need to challenge and dismantle ideal worker norms. Student affairs has long thrived on the notion that effective and valued professionals work long hours, potentially sacrificing themselves and their families for the sake of students. However, as the chapters in the book make clear, such expectations have serious consequences for employees. Student affairs professionals can take steps to push back against these norms, but the actions needed will differ by context. For example, in some settings, this might include limiting night and weekend hours. In others, it might include an understanding that when staff regularly attend late-night events, they be given flexibility to take other parts of the day off in an effort to avoid burnout. Student affairs professionals should identify how ideal worker norms shape their workplace and take concrete steps to dismantle them.

Reembody the Disembodied Worker

Some of the chapters illustrated how organizations might treat student affairs professionals as disembodied workers, viewing one employee as interchangeable for the next. Yet, each employee brings their own skills, values, and interests to their positions. Colleges and universities should honor and develop the strengths each individual brings by investing in their employees. This might take the form of providing professional development opportunities, both on campus and at regional and national conferences. It might also involve tailoring the position to fit each employee's strengths and interests. Doing so will prove mutually beneficial to the employee, who is able to perform personally fulfilling work, and to the organization, which capitalizes on the employee's skills and is more likely to retain a satisfied worker.

Organizations might also consider how to support employees' progression through the field. As the literature and chapters in this volume suggest, some employees leave the field out of a perceived (or real) lack of opportunity for advancement. Institutions might engage in succession planning, training midcareer professionals to eventually assume senior-level positions. Other possibilities include promoting employees to new positions designed to fit the needs of the organization and the individual. Creative solutions are necessary in order to retain qualified staff; doing so will also benefit the organization.

Support Professionals' Emotional Needs

Student affairs professionals are clearly not emotionless ideal workers. In fact, as the chapters made clear, many are shouldering significant emotional burdens as they provide support to students in crisis as well as navigate their own concerns. Just as institutions show concern for students' mental health, so too must they show concern for the mental and emotional health of their employees. Although many institutions offer Employee Assistance Program (EAP) benefits that typically give staff access to at least a handful of counseling sessions, more needs to be done. Campus counseling centers might offer weekly group sessions for student affairs professionals to process the interactions that they have with students. Such sessions could also equip professionals with the coping skills to better be able to emotionally handle students' demands.

Additionally, institutions might also offer a semester-long professional development seminar on counseling skills. Such training might be helpful to provide professionals the foundation to respond to student needs. Finally, institutions should also find ways to increase students' access to mental health services as a way to alleviate the burdens placed on student affairs professionals. Most university campuses have understaffed counseling centers (Mowbray et al., 2006), thus turning student affairs professionals into de facto counselors. Institutions should invest additional resources in hiring more counselors. Doing so would meet the needs of students while also reducing pressure on noncounseling student affairs staff.

Acknowledge the Labor Performed by Minoritized Professionals

Student affairs professionals from minoritized groups perform labor that their counterparts do not, both in providing assistance to others from their background and shouldering greater burdens in navigating an organization not designed to meet their needs. Although the ultimate aim should be to transform institutions and society to be just and equitable, other interventions are needed in the meantime. First, institutions might seek to hire more diverse staffs. Given that the majority of student affairs professionals are White women, the field could benefit from training and hiring more professionals of color. As institutions' student bodies are becoming more diverse, it is imperative that staff reflect that diversity. Doing so will also help to shift the burden across many, and not just the handful of people of color who might be on a campus. Such recommendations extend to members of other minoritized groups as well.

Second, institutions should acknowledge the types of labor that those from minoritized groups perform, including additional advising for students or providing outreach to various communities. Such labor should be incorporated into official job responsibilities and therefore free employees up from other parts of their jobs. Supporting students is important work, but not at the expense of professionals' own well-being. Institutions should take steps to support their employees so that they do not feel the pressure to work at all hours of the day in order to accomplish the tasks associated with their job descriptions as well as the extra labor they are compelled to perform.

Support Professionals' Off-Campus Lives

Although the ideal worker might not have any responsibilities outside the workplace, most people do. Institutions should recognize that work cannot and should not be all-consuming, thus taking away time for employees' personal lives. Institutions can support student affairs professionals who are parents through a number of avenues, including providing appropriate parental leave for childbirth or adoption, ensuring adequate on-campus childcare, supporting flexible schedules to allow employees to accommodate their competing demands, and providing camps and programs during school breaks. However, parenting is just one obligation that employees might have. Some might be caring for aging parents. Still others might have an array of personal interests that give them joy. All employees should be supported in having healthy boundaries between work and home to allow them to live their personal lives to the fullest.

Make Expectations Explicit

Ideal worker norms shape student affairs work, yet may never be explicitly articulated. This parallels concerns identified in several chapters about norms of professionalism, which are similarly undefined. Graduate students and new professionals need to be explicitly informed what is expected of them. Notions of professionalism should be spelled out so that those from minoritized backgrounds do not have to guess how to navigate an unfamiliar environment. This could take the form of a professional seminar in graduate school where students are instructed in the norms of the field, including standards of dress, expectations about workplace comportment, and so forth. Institutions might also offer a mentoring program, matching new professionals with more senior professionals who could provide such guidance one-on-one. Institutions should demystify what professionalism entails while simultaneously working to broaden the definition so that those from a variety of backgrounds do not feel that they need to change their behavior in order to fit the student affairs mold.

Looking Toward the Future

The field is ripe for action. In addition to suggesting the need to transform student affairs work, the chapters in this volume suggest a number of avenues for future research. Although there is significant literature on the experiences of minoritized student groups, there is significantly less literature on how student affairs staff from minoritized backgrounds navigate their positions. Additional research on the experiences of those discussed in the book—LGBTQ+ professionals, professionals of color, and professionals from poor and working-class backgrounds—is needed to understand how these groups are differentially impacted by ideal worker norms and other demands placed upon them by the field. There is also a dearth of research on the experiences of student affairs professionals with disabilities; this absence needs to be rectified. Understanding the multifaceted experiences of all professionals is an important step in transforming practice.

As the contributors in Part Two of this volume explored, student affairs professionals engage in significant emotional labor and may experience burnout and compassion fatigue due to the requirements of their positions, ultimately impacting their well-being. Although this line of inquiry is well established in other fields (Maslach & Jackson, 1981), the topic has received limited attention in the higher education literature, beyond a handful of dissertations. Future areas of inquiry might further investigate how student affairs professionals are affected by burnout and explore which coping strategies best serve professionals' needs. Other studies might explore differences in these phenomena by position level, institutional type, and functional area. This is an understudied area and one that is ready to be expanded.

Finally, future scholarship might directly interrogate the impact of ideal worker norms on student affairs professionals. Many of the contributors in this volume offered a thoughtful consideration of how the norms impact particular populations. Future empirical inquiries might directly investigate how various populations—further delineated by demographic group and employee level—are impacted by ideal worker norms. Explicitly understanding how these norms operate will help dismantle them. We owe it to student affairs professionals to offer the same attention to their holistic selves as we do to the students they serve. The future of the field depends on it.

References

Acker, J. (1990). Hierarchies, jobs, bodies: A theory of gendered organizations. *Gender & Society, 4*(2), 139–158. https://doi.org/10.1177/089124390004002002

Gray, B., & Kish-Gephart, J. J. (2013). Encountering social class differences at work: How "class work" perpetuates inequality. *Academy of Management Review, 38*(4), 670–699. https://doi.org/10.5465/amr.2012.0143

Marshall, S. M., Gardner, M. M., Hughes, C., & Lowery, U. (2016). Attrition from student affairs: Perspectives from those who exited the profession. *Journal of Student Affairs Research and Practice, 53*(2), 146–159. https://doi.org/10.1080/19496591.2016.1147359

Maslach, C., & Jackson, S. E. (1981). The measurement of experienced burnout. *Journal of Occupational Behavior, 2*, 99–113. https://doi.org/10.1002/job.4030020205

Mowbray, C. T., Mandiberg, J. M., Stein, C. H., Kopels, S., Curlin, C., Megivern, D., Strauss, S., Collins, K., & Lett, R. (2006). Campus mental health services: Recommendations for change. *American Journal of Orthopsychiatry, 76*(2), 226. https://doi.org/10.1037/0002-9432.76.2.226

Williams, J. C. (1989). Deconstructing gender. *Michigan Law Review, 87*(4), 797–845. https://doi.org/10.2307/1289293

ABOUT THE CONTRIBUTORS

Sonja Ardoin (she/her/hers) is a learner, an educator, a facilitator, and an author. Proud of her hometown of Vidrine, Louisiana; her working class, Cajun roots; and her first-generation college student to PhD journey, Ardoin holds degrees from Louisiana State University, Florida State University, and North Carolina State University. She considers herself a scholar-practitioner of higher education, serving as an administrator for 10 years before shifting to the faculty in 2015. She is currently an assistant professor of student affairs administration at Appalachian State University. Ardoin studies social class identity, college access and success for first-generation college students and students from rural areas, student and women's leadership, and career preparation and pathways in higher education and student affairs. She stays engaged in the field by presenting, facilitating, and volunteering with a variety of professional associations and nonprofit organizations.

Ginny Jones Boss (she/her/hers) is an assistant professor of leadership studies at the University of Georgia. At the heart of her research and practice as a faculty member is a commitment to support those whose aim is to better the profession of higher education and student affairs (HESA), giving particular focus to women of Color and students of Color. As such, her research looks at HESA graduate preparation and professional outcomes, teaching and learning, and faculty development and support. These strands weave together in support of a robust learning environment in which faculty and HESA administrators can best engage the work of supporting learning and development and understand the complex role of identity in those processes.

Nicole Bravo (she/her/hers) is an accommodations counselor and alternative testing coordinator at San Jose State University, where she works to challenge ableism and increase accessibility in higher education. She earned her MA in student affairs administration at Michigan State University. She has worked in various functional areas, including multicultural affairs and LGBTQ+ affairs, to serve marginalized students and work toward systemic change.

Alison L. DuBois (she/her/hers) has worked with children and adolescents across a number of environments ranging from therapeutic to educational for the past 22 years. Her pre-K–12 professional background with children includes working as a teacher, an administrator, and a clinical therapist. Since entering academia, DuBois has taught a number of classes ranging from testing and assessment to educational psychology in the undergraduate school and counseling classes in the graduate school. Her research interests include the effects of trauma on a child's psychopathological development, the effects of burnout and compassion fatigue in education, and the effective treatment of challenging behaviors in the classroom. DuBois has been researching and presenting on this topic to sizeable audiences regionally and nationally for the past 8 years and is currently an associate professor and director of the graduate program at Westminster College in Pennsylvania.

Pamela Graglia (she/her/hers) is an affiliate faculty member in the student affairs in higher education master's program and also serves as the interim assistant director for apartment communities in university housing at Colorado State University. Her research interests include transformative learning, transformational change, and postmodern representations that disrupt dominant ways of knowing and challenge what it means to produce and disseminate "knowledge."

Amy S. Hirschy (she/her/hers) is an associate professor in the College of Education and Human Development at the University of Louisville. She holds degrees from Vanderbilt University, the University of South Carolina, and Stetson University. Experiences at private liberal arts colleges and larger state institutions inform both her research and teaching. Hirschy's research interests include socialization to the student affairs profession, normative structures in student affairs, and college student persistence and retention theories.

Anne M. Hornak (she/her/hers) is a professor in higher education at Central Michigan University (CMU). She earned her PhD in higher, adult, and lifelong education from Michigan State University. She joined the faculty at CMU in 2009 and during her tenure she has served as a program coordinator, as well as the department chair from 2012 to 2017. Hornak's research focus is community college student affairs and leadership, ethical decision-making, and intercultural development.

Laura Isdell (she/her/hers) is an executive director of admissions and prospective students in the Office of Student Success and Completion at Lone

Star College in Texas. She earned her EdD in higher education administration from the University of Kansas. Her dissertation focused on mothers in midlevel student affairs who were navigating work and family commitments while working at an institution consistently recognized for work–life balance by the *Chronicle of Higher Education*'s Great Colleges to Work For annual survey. She has held positions in admissions, enrollment management, orientation, student housing, student leadership, and academic advising at 2- and 4-year institutions.

Megan Karbley (she/her/hers) is an assistant dean of students at the University of North Carolina at Greensboro and a PhD student in the educational leadership and cultural foundations program. Her research interests include restorative practices in response to sexual violence and bias incidents, the intersections of White privilege and access in education, and LGBTQ community building in educational institutions.

Kerry L. B. Klima (she/her/hers) is associate director of assessment and evaluation in the division of student affairs at California State University, Long Beach. She earned her PhD in higher education administration from Bowling Green State University. For her dissertation, she interviewed midlevel professionals who were asked to recall and describe their experiences as entry-level professionals negotiating a mental health condition (depression and/or anxiety). Her work experiences in student affairs include academic support services, academic advising, student leadership, and student activities at a variety of institutional types and in both academic affairs and student affairs.

Carrie A. Kortegast (she/her/hers) is an associate professor of higher education at Northern Illinois University. She has authored several publications on the experience of LGBTQ students and student affairs administrators and the use of visual methods in research, pedagogy, and practice. She has presented on the experiences of LGBTQ students and student affairs professionals at national conferences including the Association for the Study of Higher Education, ACPA: American College Educators International, and NASPA: Student Affairs Administrators in Higher Education. Prior to teaching, she served as a student affairs administrator for 9 years. She has also been active in the NASPA Gender and Sexuality (formerly GLBT) Knowledge Community serving as the national cochair from 2006 to 2008.

Melanie Lee (she/her/hers) is a student in the educational leadership and policy PhD program at the University of Utah. Her research agenda includes the experiences of college students with disabilities and their engagement with student leadership programs, as well as equitable design of leadership programs. Lee is also coeditor (with Annemarie Vaccaro and Ryan Miller) of a special issue of the *Journal of Postsecondary Education and Disability* (2020) titled *Challenges and Opportunities for Assessing, Evaluating, and Researching Disability in Higher Education.* Additionally, she serves as the associate director for education, support, and assessment within the Office of Student Success and Empowerment and is an adjunct instructor in the leadership studies minor at the University of Utah.

R. Jason Lynch (he/him/his) serves as an assistant professor of higher education at Appalachian State University. His dissertation and published works explore how traumatic life events impact the well-being of campus stakeholders. As a pilot to his dissertation exploring the lived experience of secondary trauma in student affairs professionals, he developed the secondary trauma in student affairs professionals scale to measure symptoms associated with secondary trauma. His scholarship and practice are grounded in a variety of professional experiences within housing and residential life, fraternity and sorority life, multicultural affairs, assessment and evaluation, and statewide system-level policy and administration.

Sarah Marshall (she/her/hers) is a professor of educational leadership with an emphasis in higher education administration at Central Michigan University. She also directs the graduate certificate in college teaching program. Prior to joining the professoriate in 2001, she was a university administrator primarily in the area of student services/student affairs administration. She earned her PhD in higher education administration and MEd in college student personnel from Loyola University Chicago and her BA in Spanish and economics at Albion College. Her research interests include teaching techniques to enhance student learning, work–life management, university leadership, and the profession of student affairs.

Molly A. Mistretta (she/her/hers) is an assistant professor in the Department of Counseling and Development at Slippery Rock University in Pennsylvania. She teaches courses across the curriculum in the student affairs and higher education and clinical mental health counseling programs. Previously, Mistretta served as an associate dean for a small residential liberal arts college, overseeing residential programs, first-year transition programs, and support services for at-risk students. Her research interests include effects of compassion fatigue and burnout among paraprofessional staff in higher education, and the scholarship of teaching and learning for emerging professionals in K–16 settings.

C. Casey Ozaki (she/her/hers) is an associate professor in the Department of Education, Health, and Behavior Studies at the University of North Dakota (UND). Her research focuses on community college student persistence, community college student affairs, and the assessment of learning in the creative arts. She is also serving as a faculty fellow for inclusive excellence at UND, focusing on diversity, equity, and inclusion work with faculty and academic programs.

Rosemary J. Perez (she/her/hers) is an associate professor in the Center for the Study of Higher and Postseconday Education at the University of Michigan. Her research leverages the strengths of student development and organizational theories to explore individual and organizational learning and development in collegiate contexts. She primarily uses qualitative methods to explore how people cultivate their voices as they make meaning of their experiences; the nature of intercultural learning and development; and the professional learning and development of graduate students and new practitioners. Across her program of research, Perez's work explores the tensions between structure and agency and how power, privilege, and oppression affect individuals and groups within higher education. Her teaching, research, and praxis reflect her commitment to empowering individuals and communities as we work toward creating a more equitable and just society.

Karla Pérez-Vélez (she/her/hers) serves as an associate director in the center for academic services and advising at the Colorado School of Mines. She has worked in advising and housing throughout her career in addition to having served as faculty member. Her research interests include social justice as competency; women in higher education; international issues in higher education; Latina/o/x college completion and academic support; assessment and evaluation in higher education; and intersections of race, ethnicity, and gender in academia.

Margaret W. Sallee (she/her/hers) is an associate professor and the higher education program coordinator in the Department of Educational Leadership and Policy at the University at Buffalo. Her research focuses on two broad areas: faculty work and the graduate student experience. She uses a critical lens to examine the intersection of individual experiences and organizational culture to interrogate the ways in which gender and other social identities operate on college campuses. She has spent much of the past decade focusing on work–life balance and the ways in which institutional norms and culture shape parents' experiences on and off-campus. She also is deeply interested in how gender affects individuals' experiences and is particularly interested in the role that gender and masculinities play in men's lives.

Shannon D. Staten (she/her/hers) is the executive director of university housing at Florida State University. She holds degrees from Marshall University, the University of North Texas, and the University of Louisville. She has worked in student housing throughout her career creating physical and learning environments that help students succeed. Her research interests focus on factors that contribute to student success and higher education management practices.

D-L Stewart (he/they/his/their) is a professor in the School of Education and cocoordinates the student affairs in higher education master's program and teaches in the higher education leadership doctoral program at Colorado State University. Stewart's scholarship and teaching are motivated by an ethic of love grounded in justice and informed by an intersectional framework that recognizes both the lived experiences of individuals with multiple marginalities, as well as the material effects of interlocking systems of oppression. Over the course of their faculty career, he has focused most intently on issues of race and ethnicity, sexuality, and gender, as well as religion, faith, and spirituality in their research, teaching, and service to professional organizations and institutions across the nation.

Benjamin B. Stubbs (he/him/his) works in the division of academic engagement and student affairs at the University of West Florida. His areas of responsibilities have included campus recreation and leadership development at the University of Tennessee, and student activities, campus involvement, fraternity and sorority life, leadership development, community service, the student union, and assessment at the University of West Florida. He holds a BA in English literature from the University of West Florida, and an MS in college student personnel and a PhD in higher education administration from the University of Tennessee. He is an affiliate faculty member in the education research and administration department at UWF and is currently studying trends in higher education governance and policy that relate to the student experience.

Michael Venturiello (he/him/his) is assistant director of student engagement at the Robert F. Wagner Graduate School of Program Service at New York University. He earned his EdM in higher education administration from the University at Buffalo and his BA in English literature with a minor in anthropology from the State University of New York at Geneseo. He is a recipient of the Gleason Ambassadorship in Student Affairs, and his work focuses on diversity and inclusion, first-generation students, and LGBTQ-identified students. Research topics include queer studies and the intersections of gender, sexuality, and professional identity.

Lisa Wolf-Wendel (she/her/hers) is a professor of higher education in the Department of Educational Leadership and Policy Studies at the University of Kansas. She is also the associate dean for research and graduate studies in the School of Education. Wolf-Wendel earned her undergraduate degree in psychology and communications from Stanford University in 1987 and her doctorate in higher education from the Claremont Graduate University in 1995. Wolf-Wendel is the author of numerous books and refereed journal articles on topics related to equity issues in higher education. Her research focuses on faculty issues including studies of the academic labor market, the needs of international faculty and faculty from historically underrepresented groups, and several recent research projects pertaining to the policy response of academic institutions in the wake of demands for dual career couple accommodations and work/family balance.

Alyssa Stefanese Yates (she/her/hers) is a doctoral student and graduate research assistant in the higher, adult, and lifelong education (HALE) program at Michigan State University. She earned her EdM in higher education administration with a concentration in student affairs administration from the University at Buffalo and her BA in English literature with minors in women and gender studies and philosophy from the State University of New York (SUNY) at Geneseo. In 2014, she was the first SUNY Geneseo student to receive Campus Compact's Newman Civic Fellowship for her social justice work surrounding natural disaster relief efforts and equitable social services. Her research interests include the historic and current experiences of cis-gender women in higher education, and the effects of gender identity and expression on student and leadership development.

episodic power, 44

Fair Labor Standards Act, 46–47, 52
fathers
    as breadwinner/provider, 261–
        262, 266–267, 274
    expectations of, 262–268, 270
    in student affairs, 258, 260–270
    stereotypical images of, 259,
        266–267, 274
Freudenberger, Herbert, 141

graduate students in student
    affairs preparation programs,
    3, 21–22, 57, 86, 97–108,
    210–211, 304
Greek life. *See* campus life

habitus, 222, 228
hegemonic Whiteness, 10, 201–206
    and tokenization of marginalized
        student affairs educators, 204,
        206
    definition of, 202
Hochschild, Arlie Russell, 160
Housing. *See* housing and residence
    life
housing and residence life, 3, 56,
    58–68, 87, 143, 146, 160,
    191–192, 259, 298

ideal worker norms
    adoption by new student affairs
        educators, 22–23, 34, 76,
        84, 103–104, 133, 140–141,
        142–143, 201, 205, 211–212,
        240–249
ideal worker norms
    and disembodiment of LGBTQ
        professionals, 185–186

and disembodiment of
    professionals of color, 205,
    209
and dominance of professionals
    of color, 205
and effect of intersecting
    identities, 206, 249
and emotional labor, 107, 126,
    129–130, 146, 159–160,
    163–168
and gender identity, 182–186,
    262, 263
and LGBTQ student affairs
    educators, 180, 182–184,
    187–192
and neoliberalism, 9, 120,
    124–131, 297–298
and socialization, 75–89
as inequality regimes, 6, 201–
    202, 203–209, 211
as classed, 223–230
as gendered construct, 5–6, 16,
    182, 299
as racialized construct, 201–202,
    204, 206–207, 214, 299
at baccalaureate undergraduate
    institutions, 82–85
at community colleges, 77–82
at research/doctoral institutions,
    85–89
definition of, 1, 4–7
hegemony of, 297–301
in opposition to self–care, 120,
    126—127
institutional costs, 20–21
perpetuation by colleagues, 22,
    25, 42–43, 83, 103–104, 265,
    268
perpetuation by peers, 21–22,
    42–43, 101–102

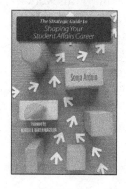
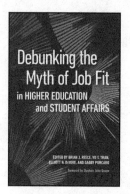